Asian/Oceanian Historical Dictionaries
Edited by Jon Woronoff

Historical Dictionary of the Gulf Arab States

Malcolm C. Peck

Asian Historical Dictionaries, No. 21

The Scarecrow Press, Inc.
Lanham, Md., & London
1997

SCARECROW PRESS, INC.

Published in the United States of America
by Scarecrow Press, Inc.
4720 Boston Way
Lanham, Maryland 20706

4 Pleydell Gardens, Folkestone
Kent CT20 2DN, England

British Cataloguing-in-Publication Information Available

Library of Congress Cataloging-in-Publication Data

Peck, Malcolm C.
    Historical dictionary of the Gulf Arab States / Malcolm C. Peck.
        p.   cm. — (Asian historical dictionaries ; no. 21)
    Includes bibliographical references (p.   ).
    ISBN 0–8108–3203–8 (alk. paper)
    1. Persian Gulf states—History—Dictionaries. I. Title. II. Series.
DS247.A15P43 1997
956.7044'03—dc20   96–33632

ISBN 0–8108–3203–8 (cloth : alk.paper)

This dictionary is dedicated to the memory of my father, Wilfred Peck, to my mother, Ruth Murdoch Peck, and to my wife, Aida, and son, John.

Contents

Editor's Foreword

Although small in area and in population, the Gulf states are extremely significant in certain ways. They are major sources of crude oil, which has generated remarkable economic growth and allowed uncommon levels of affluence. They are strategically located in the Middle East, close to the dominant regional powers Saudi Arabia, Iran, and Iraq– too close for comfort at times. But they have nonetheless managed to achieve and sustain statehood and to gradually modernize their societies.

For such reasons, there is little doubt that readers will find this volume particularly useful. It is all the more welcome coming at this time, after the war with Iraq and liberation of Kuwait. This is one of the few books that can describe that sad chapter and hopeful turning of a new page. Yet, while focusing on the present period, the author reaches far back into history and covers not only political events but important economic, social, cultural, and religious aspects as well. For those who want to know more, there is a substantial bibliography.

Dr. Malcolm C. Peck has been closely involved in Middle East affairs for thirty years, with a special interest in the Gulf states. Director of Programs at the Middle East Institute for over a decade, then Arabian Peninsula affairs analyst with the Department of State, he is presently a program officer at Meridian International Center in Washington, D.C. He has written numerous articles and contributed to books on the Middle East as well as authoring *The United Arab Emirates: A Venture in Unity.*

Jon Woronoff
Series Editor

Preface

Since Jon Woronoff invited me to prepare a historical dictionary covering the five small Gulf Arab states, the Gulf crisis of 1990/91 has drawn special attention to that part of the world. It has therefore seemed appropriate to include considerable information on recent and current developments, despite the emphasis on the past, which is implicit in the title. As five countries are covered, and one of them is a federation of seven distinct and autonomous entities, he and I agreed that separate, substantial entries should be devoted to each Gulf Arab state, rather than simply use the introduction to provide sketches of them.

The information provided is intended to be useful for academic and other researchers, and in a form that is convenient for diplomats and business people, as well as individuals who are merely curious to know something more about an important and interesting part of the world.

In transliterations from the Arabic I have generally omitted the diacritical marks. Initial and final *hamzas* and *ayns*, the weak and strong glottal stops in Arabic, are not indicated. Where deemed helpful, medial hamzas and ayns are represented by apostrophes (' and ' respectively). Members of ruling families are alphabetized by first names, and the Arabic definite article *al* is disregarded in alphabetization of entries, as is the *Al* denoting important families. Spellings are intended to be consistent with general American usage.

Acknowledgments

I would like to acknowledge the kindness of Dr. Emile Nakhleh and Dr. John Duke Anthony, past presidents of the Society for Gulf Arab Studies, in conveying information on Gulf developments from their personal observations. Discussions of Gulf Arab state affairs with them and other friends and colleagues who are specialists on the history, politics, economics, and culture of these countries have been stimulating and helpful. The staff of the Middle East Institute library was kind and responsive in facilitating my research there.

My wife, Aida, deserves acknowledgment for not holding me to a previous, solemn promise never to undertake another book project in my "spare" time. I am grateful to two Meridian International Center colleagues for their help. Ms. Beth Wood kindly read through the manuscript and considerably reduced the number of glitches in the text. Ms. Debra Forbes-Gray provided crucial assistance in the final formatting of the text for publication. I owe a particular debt of gratitude to Mr. Frank M. Graves and Mr. Robert A. Pease, whose ruthless editorial eyes have spared me numerous embarrassments. Special thanks are also due my son, John, whose computer expertise was critical in the preparation of this book. He was an active and valued partner in the enterprise.

Abbreviations and Acronyms

ABC	Arab Banking Corporation
ABEGS	Arab Bureau of Education for the Gulf States
ADCO	Abu Dhabi Company for Onshore Oil Operations
ADDF	Abu Dhabi Defense Force
ADFAED	Abu Dhabi Fund for Arab Economic Development
ADMA-OPCO	Abu Dhabi Marine Areas Operating Company
ADNOC	Abu Dhabi National Oil Company
AGCC	*See* **GCC**
AGU	Arab Gulf University
AIOC	Anglo-Iranian Oil Company
AISCO	Arab Iron and Steel Company
ALBA	Aluminum Bahrain
AMIO	Arab Military Industries Organization
ANM	Arab Nationalists' Movement
APOC	Anglo-Persian Oil Company
Aramco	Arabian American Oil Company
ASRY	Arab Shipbuilding and Repair Yard
AWACS	Airborne Warning and Control System
BANOCO	Bahrain National Oil Company
BAPCO	Bahrain Petroleum Company
BBME	British Bank of the Middle East
BCCI	Bank of Credit and Commerce International
BDF	Bahrain Defense Force
BP	British Petroleum

BPD (bpd)	Barrels per day (usually lower case)
BSOAS	*Bulletin of the School of Oriental and African Studies*
CAT	Contracting and Trading Company
CFP	Compagnie Française des Pétroles
CNU	Council of National Unity (Bahrain)
DLF	Dhofar Liberation Front
DUBAL	Dubai Aluminum Company
DUCAL	Dubai Cables
DUGAS	Dubai Gas Company
EA	Economic Agreement
EU	European Union (formerly European Community)
FAO	Food and Agriculture Organization
FNC	Federal National Council (UAE)
GCC	Gulf Cooperation Council
GDP	Gross Domestic Product
GIC	Gulf Investment Corporation
GOIC	Gulf Organization for Industrial Consultancy
ICO	Islamic Conference Organization
IJMES	*International Journal of Middle East Studies*
IJIA	*Iranian Journal of International Affairs*
IOPEC	Independent Oil Producing and Exporting Countries
IPC	Iraq Petroleum Company
JGAPS	*Journal of Gulf and Arabian Peninsula Affairs* (in Arabic)
JIME	Japanese Institute of Middle East Economics
JSAMES	*Journal of South Asian and Middle Eastern Studies*
KAF	Kuwait Air Force
KFAED	Kuwait Fund for Arab Economic Development
KIA	Kuwait Investment Authority
KIO	Kuwait Investment Organization
KNPC	Kuwait National Petroleum Company
KOC	Kuwait Oil Company
KPC	Kuwait Petroleum Company
LNG	Liquefied Natural Gas
MIDEASTFOR	Middle East Force

NDFLOAG	National Democratic Front for the Liberation of Oman and the Arab Gulf
OAPEC	Organization of Arab Petroleum Exporting Countries
OBU	Offshore banking unit
OIC	*See* **ICO**
OPEC	Organization of Petroleum Exporting Countries
PDO	Petroleum Development Oman
PDRY	People's Democratic Republic of Yemen (former)
PFLO	Popular Front for the Liberation of Oman
PFLOAG	Popular Front for the Liberation of Oman and the Arab Gulf. *Also refers to* the Popular Front for the Liberation of the Occupied Arab Gulf
PLO	Palestine Liberation Organization
PRC	People's Republic of China
RAF	Royal Air Force
RDF	Rapid Deployment Force
RDJTF	Rapid Deployment Joint Task Force
SAF	Sultan's Armed Forces
SCC	State Consultative Council
SFC	Supreme Federal Council
SOAF	Sultan of Oman's Air Force
SoCal	Standard Oil of California (now Chevron)
SOLF	Sultan of Oman's Land Forces
SON	Sultan of Oman's Navy
TOL	Trucial Oman Levies
TOS	Trucial Oman Scouts
UAE	United Arab Emirates
UDF	Union Defense Force
U.K.	United Kingdom
UN	United Nations
U.S.	United States
USCENTCOM	U.S. Central Command
USNIP	U.S. Naval Institute Proceedings
USSR	Union of Soviet Socialist Republics (former)
YAR	Yemen Arab Republic (former)

Introduction

In 1990–91 the Persian/Arab Gulf came dramatically to American and world attention with the Iraqi invasion of Kuwait on August 2, 1990, and the seven months of tension and violence that followed. Until it was briefly eclipsed by the extraordinary events in Eastern Europe and the Soviet Union in 1989–90, the Gulf region had already been at or near the forefront of Western, particularly American, security concerns for a decade, from the Iranian hostage crisis of 1979–81 to the U.S. "reflagging" of Kuwaiti tankers in 1987–88. Indeed, by the 1980s the Gulf region had become in terms of security interests the third most important area to the United States after its own territory and that of Western Europe. The assumption of this status is, however, recent. It is only in the past quarter of a century that the Gulf has progressed from being a relative backwater to being an area of leading international importance and concern. This is the result obviously of its vast oil reserves and strategically located territory. Of the roughly one trillion barrels of proven oil reserves in the world, about two-thirds are to be found under or around the Gulf. The small states covered in this volume, Bahrain, Kuwait, Oman, Qatar, and the United Arab Emirates (UAE), possess about 20 percent of the world's total. Although the ending of the cold war lessens the level of possible conflict in the Gulf area, because it is no longer a potential arena for superpower conflict, the Gulf crisis of 1990–91 and the tensions that remain there suggest

that it will continue to be a region of great strategic interest and concern. This seems likely to be the case for so long as the West, Japan,
and other advanced industrialized countries remain extensively dependent on its oil and while the Arab states of the Gulf themselves continue
to be weak and require outside support to survive threats from their
large and dangerous neighbors.

Beyond the strategic and economic importance conferred upon them
by their vast oil reserves, the Gulf Arab states are worthy of attention

Persian/Arab Gulf Region

Source: *The World Factbook 1994*
(Central Intelligence Agency)

for the inherent interest of their history and culture. No area of the
world has yielded more revealing and exciting archaeological finds in
the past few decades than in these states. Investigations have brought to
light extensive evidence of an important culture as old as Egypt of the
Pharaohs or ancient Babylon, which was virtually unknown previously
except through rare references in the records of other civilizations.
Frequent and dramatic finds continue to be made on this archaeological
frontier. In February and April 1992 the press reported discoveries of
very old ruins at two sites in western Oman, the remains of Ubar and
Saffara, centers of trade in frankincense and spices that made South

Arabia wealthy. The story of civilization along what is now the Arab littoral of the Gulf and into the Omani hinterland has been taken back to the late fourth or early third millennium B.C., when a trading culture arose which interacted with Sumer to the north and Mohenjo-Daro to the south and east. The inhabitants of this area were among the great mariners of the ancient world, who by the early Islamic era had turned the Indian Ocean into an Arab lake, carrying articles of commerce and the Islamic faith as far as the coast of China. In the recent past the Gulf Arab states formed a fascinating laboratory of accelerated physical, economic, and social change in a culturally conservative setting.

These states are not artifacts of British imperial policy, as many instant experts tried to suggest in television interviews during the 1990–91 Gulf crisis. It is certainly true that their borders were in large measure drawn by the British and that treaty relationships with Britain served to freeze political power relations as they had existed in the 19th century. Nevertheless, the antecedents of the modern Gulf Arab states are long-established, most dating back more than two centuries. The continued existence of these states into the last decade of the 20th century, in defiance of the confident predictions of many political scientists who, decades ago, viewed them as anachronisms soon to be swept away by the tides of history, suggests a rather remarkable inherent strength. This in large measure reflects the power of traditional legitimating factors in the face of extraordinarily rapid and far-reaching change.

Perhaps most obviously, the Gulf Arab states share geographic and demographic similarities. Except for Oman, all are very small, several being little more than city-states. Each is extremely arid, most of the territory consisting of desert or semidesert land, and all experience extreme summer heat and, along the coast, high humidity, with temperate winters. All are oil-producers that, despite efforts to diversify, remain essentially "one-crop economies," either wealthy or super-wealthy. Oil incomes have brought rapid economic development to the Gulf Arab states, which have become social welfare states. Rapid development has, in turn, made all of them considerably dependent on imported labor and skills. In extreme cases like the UAE and Qatar, more than four-fifths of the total population and over 90 percent of the labor force is now foreign. Oil wealth has also ended a rather comfortable obscurity for these states, thrusting them into the international spotlight and exposing them to new threats and dangers.

Several basic, shared cultural values serve to bind the Gulf Arab states together. They are, of course, all Arabic-speaking, with only minor dialectal variations in the spoken language. All are conservatively Islamic, with Islam declared to be the official religion and virtually 100 percent of the indigenous population Muslim. In each state Islam is the single most significant cultural influence, shaping in very large measure the social and political life of each. Tribal values also remain of crucial importance in establishing and affirming identity and loyalty in societies that lack complex hierarchical or class structures. Also shared is an essentially uniform political culture reflecting the simple organization of Gulf Arab society and the small size of the communities that make up the states. Thus rulers have exercised authority through the *majlis* system, linking them with their subjects through the mechanism of direct, face-to-face meetings. With the growth of their populations, the increasing complexity of suddenly wealthy societies, and the introduction of Western concepts of more open political systems, the Gulf Arab states have all begun to move from what one Gulf Arab wit has dubbed "shuocracy" (from the Arabic word *shura*, meaning "consultation") to modern democracy. That process was confirmed and advanced in Kuwait with the parliamentary election of October 5, 1992. In the other Gulf Arab states there has been some progress toward expanding the role of the existing consultative councils, though none is yet close to becoming an elected legislative body.

Iraq's invasion of Kuwait reminded the Gulf Arab states of an uncomfortable, shared feature, their inability to defend themselves against external security threats. It was this sense of threat that was primarily responsible for the establishment of the Gulf Cooperation Council (GCC) in 1981, linking the five small Gulf Arab states together with Saudi Arabia. In the wake of the Gulf crisis all have been forced to reevaluate their security situation, and all have confirmed and extended their security ties to the United States. They have indicated that they will not normalize relations with Iraq so long as Saddam Hussein is in power, although the strength of this commitment varies among the states other than Kuwait, and they remain deeply concerned about the potential threat from Iran and the unpredictability of political events there. Finally, shaken by the hostilities and suspicions aroused by the Gulf crisis, they have taken steps to reduce their dependence on the skills of Palestinian expatriate labor, and their relations with Arab states, including Jordan, Sudan, and Yemen, which exhibited sympathy for Iraq in the crisis, remain generally strained.

At the same time, together with their numerous and fundamental similarities, the Gulf Arab states display a number of noteworthy differences. All are wealthy, but Kuwait, Qatar, and the UAE are distinguished by their superwealth, having the highest per capita incomes in the world, while the more modest oil income of Bahrain and Oman sets them apart. Bahrain, with slight oil wealth discovered early, has experienced a long and, by Gulf standards, gradual development. Comparatively, it has a large and diversified labor force in a more varied and complex economy, with less dependence on expatriate skills than is the case with its neighbors. Oman is similarly less dependent on imported labor than the three other states, with much of its labor force still involved in traditional economic pursuits. In other ways, too, Oman is distinctive. It is a Persian/Arab Gulf state only by virtue of the few miles of coast along the western side of its Ras Musandam exclave at the Strait of Hormuz. Through much of its modern history it has been oriented more toward the Indian subcontinent and East Africa than the Gulf. It has a large hinterland, with more area than all of the other Gulf Arab states combined, and a significantly varied topography, which makes a rather extensive agriculture possible. The other Gulf Arab states have overwhelmingly urban populations, while that of Oman is largely rural. Since ancient times, Oman served as a refuge for persecuted groups of various kinds, including the Ibadis, a branch of Islam separate from both Sunnis and Shias, who form the majority of the Omani population. Oman's geography has helped to orient its commercial and political ambitions toward the Indian Ocean and its Asian and African littorals and has helped to insulate it from the Arab-Israeli conflict and inter-Arab contentions.

Among and between the Gulf Arab states there are also noteworthy cultural differences. While Gulf Arabs are predominantly Sunni, with significant Shia minorities, Bahrain is 65 percent–70 percent Shia. It is more heterogeneous than the other states, with a Sunni minority and a Shia majority community that is divided between Arab or *Baharna* Shia and those of Iranian origin, as well as a highly diverse expatriate popu-lation. Bahrain is also marked by its well-developed state administrative apparatus, its experience with trade unions and radical politics, and its substantial indigenous, professional middle class. Like Kuwait, it is socially and intellectually more liberal, open, and sophisticated than the other Gulf Arab states. Dubai shares their commercial astuteness and sophistication, and Sharjah boasts a vigorous life of the arts, literary and other.

Moreover, there are differences in their political culture. Kuwait and Bahrain have both experimented with elected national assemblies, Bahrain only briefly. Kuwait remains the only Gulf Arab state with such an institution, which was suspended in 1986 but restored through elections held on October 5, 1992. On October 7, 1996 elections returned a somewhat more pro-government parliament than the one elected four years previously. The crown prince, Shaikh Sabah Ahmad Al Sabah, remained foreign minister and first deputy prime minister and the ruling family kept control of the ministries of defense, interior, finance, and information. While it remains to be seen how far the assembly can expand its political authority, it seems certain that parliamentary rule is permanently established in Kuwait. The Kuwaiti Parliament has begun serious action on significant issues, including expansion of the electoral franchise. Oman's new consultative council has moved a step closer to being a real legislative body, while the other states have progressed more cautiously toward political systems that are participatory in a meaningful way.

Political and other differences among the Gulf Arab states are significant. However, their shared cultural heritage, elements of common history, and similar concerns over current threats to their well-being and survival are far more pronounced and fundamental. This was illustrated in the unfolding of unsettling events in the latter half of 1995 and the first months of 1996 and in the Gulf Arab states' reactions to them.

In the months that followed Shaikh Hamad bin Khalifa Al Thani's overthrow of his father, Shaikh Khalifa, as ruler of Qatar, in June 1995, his activist foreign policy, which included a meeting with then Israeli prime minister Shimon Peres and overtures to Iran and Iraq, all seeking to establish normal relations with those countries, was a source of concern to the other Gulf Arab rulers. When, in December 1995, the other GCC rulers supported a Saudi candidate, Jamil al-Hejailan, to be the council's new secretary-general instead of the Qatari candidate whom Hamad had proposed, he left the summit meeting before the vote was held, an unprecedented action. Subsequently Bahrain received the ousted Qatari ruler as a head of state and Hamad retaliated by permitting a Bahraini opposition leader to be interviewed on television.

Shaikh Zayid bin Sultan Al Nuhayyan, president of the UAE, offered headquarters to Shaikh Khalifa. Shaikh Hamad then accused his GCC neighbors of sending armed men into Qatar to attempt his assassination. By late spring of 1996, however, he had warmly received the new GCC secretary-general, and Saudi Arabia had affirmed that its now mutually agreed border with Qatar would be clearly demarcated to avoid disputes such as the one that had rankled since 1992. Further, Shaikh Zayid appeared to be offering permanent residence in Abu Dhabi to the ex-ruler. The Gulf Arab states, in typical fashion, had submerged or at least put aside for the moment their fraternal squabbles at a time of general dangers and uncertainties.

At the same time, other developments continued to cause concern. In mid-1996 the Shia antigovernment protests, some violent, which had begun in late 1994, continued in Bahrain. Whether the Islamic Republic of Iran was significantly involved, as Bahrain charged, the protests represented a real challenge to the government at a time of economic downturn that caused high rates of Shia unemployment. There was no doubt about Iranian actions on the island of Abu Musa, whose ownership is disputed with the UAE, where the Islamic Republic has built fortifications and is now constructing a port. Perhaps most troubling was the June 25, 1996, truck bombing, apparently by Islamic militants, which killed 19 American servicemen in Dhahran in Saudi Arabia's Eastern Province. This event, apparently related to the November 1995 bombing of the U.S. Military Training Mission in Riyadh, developed from circumstances peculiar to Saudi Arabia but reflected the potential danger for the small Gulf Arab states in hosting significant numbers of U.S. military personnel in a conservative Sunni Muslim environment.

The election of a Likud-led government in Israel in late May 1996 under Prime Minister Binyamin Netanyahu, who had already indicated his intention of curtailing if not rejecting basic elements of the Oslo agreement between the government of his predecessor, Shimon Peres, and Palestine Authority President Yasser Arafat, was another troubling development for the Gulf Arab states. Like the U.S., they had anti-cipated a Labor victory, assuring continuation of the peace process and the advancement of incipient economic and other cooperative ties between them and Israel. As the statements issued at the Arab summit of late June, called to consider Arab responses to the new situation, suggested, this was now in considerable doubt. With President Clinton, seen in the Arab world as one-sidedly pro-Israel, now well launched in his campaign for reelection, scant serious American pressure on Israel to fulfill its previously agreed Oslo commitment was anticipated.

Thus the Gulf Arab states faced in mid-1996 a number of dangers and uncertainties. With the possible exception of Bahrain, however, none of them appeared to face imminent threats to their basic stability.

The Dictionary

A

ABBASIDS. The Abbasid dynasty, established A.D. 750, succeeded the Umayyads, rulers of the first Arab-Islamic empire. The imperial capital was moved from Damascus to Baghdad, located strategically with reference to land and sea communications and commanding the newly captured territories to the east. The early phase of Abbasid rule is commonly referred to as the Golden Age, because of the intellectual and artistic efflorescence made possible by political stability and the fruitful interaction of representatives of the several major cultural traditions embraced by this cosmopolitan state. Unity and stability also made possible the great age of commerce in the Gulf. Beginning in the eighth century A.D. Arab trading vessels ventured as far as the China coast and came to dominate the Indian Ocean trade routes. Within a century of its establishment the Abbasid Empire entered a period of decline. Effective power passed to a praetorian guard of Turkish soldiers, and the empire fragmented as independent states emerged. The Gulf area enjoyed continuing prosperity for another two centuries until the Fatimid caliphate, with its capital in Cairo, rerouted much of the trade through the Red Sea.

ABU DHABI.
Land and people. Abu Dhabi is the largest of the seven emirates

that constitute the United Arab Emirates. The city of the same name, capital both of the emirate and (provisionally) of the federation, occupies an island whose shape resembles that of the Arabian gazelle, hence the name means literally "father of the gazelle." In area, population, and wealth Abu Dhabi dominates the UAE. Its hereditary ruler, Shaikh Zayid bin Sultan Al Nuhayyan, is also president of the federation.

The emirate of Abu Dhabi accounts for some seven-eighths of the UAE's total land area of roughly 32,000 sq mi (82,902 sq km). It is largely desert, with a 260-mile Gulf coastline made up of sandy beaches and salt flats called *sabkhas.* Significant oases, where fairly extensive agriculture is possible, are found at al-Liwa and al-Ain. The population of the emirate of Abu Dhabi is 798,000 (official 1991 estimate) 42 percent of the UAE's total of 1.9 million, with more than 500,000 in Abu Dhabi City and over 100,000 in al-Ain. Fewer than a fifth of the emirate's inhabitants are indigenous, reflecting its enormous dependence on the physical, technical, and managerial skills of other Arabs as well as Asians, Europeans, and Americans. South Asians constitute by far the largest expatriate community. Indeed, the largest national community in Abu Dhabi is its Indians, with Pakistanis also outnumbering Abu Dhabi natives.

Economy. The wealth that has triggered the economic boom, in turn requiring importation of expatriate skills, derives from oil. Of the UAE's 92.9 billion barrels of proven reserves, some 90 percent are in Abu Dhabi, and the emirate also possesses three-fifths of the UAE's considerable gas reserves. Abu Dhabi alone has more than three times the oil reserves and about half the natural gas reserves of the United States. Abu Dhabi's oil wealth has made possible not only its dramatic rise from poverty, before oil production began in 1962, to extraordinary affluence, but has made the UAE's population overall among the world's wealthiest, with an estimated per capita income of $24,000 in 1993. It was the determination of Abu Dhabi's ruler, Zayid bin Sultan Al Nuhayyan, to share the wealth of his emirate with the poorer members of the UAE that made the federation viable. On a wider stage he has used largesse as politically astute economic development aid to Arab and other Third World countries.

Abu Dhabi has tried to promote economic diversification both to counter the potential vulnerability inherent in a "one crop" economy, as illustrated by the downturn in oil prices and consumption in the mid-1980s, and to prepare for the day (however far off) when oil and gas reserves are exhausted. The paucity of other natural resources has limited progress toward this goal, and most diversification has taken the form of industries based on hydrocarbons as either feedstocks or a source of cheap energy. Examples are the manufacturing of refined oil products as well as ammonia, sulfur, fertilizer, and cement. Beyond the hydrocarbon sector, major efforts have been devoted to agriculture, using capital-intensive approaches to produce as much as possible in a harshly arid environment.

The 1991 collapse of the Bank of Credit and Commerce International (BCCI), in which Abu Dhabi was a 77 percent share-holder, raised concerns for both the economic and political health of the emirate. Shaikh Zayid was reported to have spent up to $6 billion in a vain effort to avert the bank's collapse. By January 1994 it was apparent that Abu Dhabi had weathered the fallout from the BCCI scandal when it reached an agreement with U.S. government officials that permitted U.S. arrest of Saleh Naqvi, a prime suspect in the affair who was being held in Abu Dhabi.

History. The history of Abu Dhabi is largely the story of the Bani Yas, a tribal confederation of central Arabian origin, and their leaders, a clan called the Al Nuhayyan. In the 17th and 18th centuries the Bani Yas emerged as the dominant power in the general area now occupied by Abu Dhabi. The discovery of drinkable water on Abu Dhabi Island in 1761 led to permanent settlement there, and by the 1790s it had become the seat of the ruling shaikh. Thus the Bani Yas, a seminomadic population whose power had been confined to the land, gained an outlet to the Gulf and became a maritime power as well. When the British established themselves as the arbiters of Gulf affairs in the early and mid-19th century, the prevailing power relationships were in effect frozen. This favored the largely land-based Bani Yas and Abu Dhabi over their Qawasim rivals of Sharjah and Ras al-Khaimah, whose maritime preeminence had been undercut by the British. Strong leadership, notably by Zayid the Great in the late 19th and early 20th century, and by his namesake, the present ruler, reinforced by the oil wealth of recent years, has maintained the emirate's dominant position in the Trucial States and later in the independent federation of the United Arab Emirates.

Political dynamics. Despite the creation of modern institutions of governance and administration, the nature of political authority in Abu Dhabi has remained essentially traditional and patriarchal. The Al Nuhayyan hold an effective monopoly of political power, maintaining ties to traditionally important commoner families and paying due regard to the expectations of tribal factions and the religious establishment. The distinguishing feature of Shaikh Zayid, Abu Dhabi's ruler for the past 30 years, is his capacity to embody and project the traditional values, which confer legitimacy upon a hereditary leader in Gulf Arab society, while understanding and dealing astutely with contemporary political and economic realities. Thus Abu Dhabi has not only been the dominant factor in the UAE but has played a significant role in inter-Arab affairs. *See also* AL NUHAYYAN, BANI YAS, UNITED ARAB EMIRATES, *and* ZAYID BIN SULTAN.

ABU DHABI DEFENSE FORCE (ADDF). *See* ARMED FORCES.

ABU DHABI FUND FOR ARAB ECONOMIC DEVELOPMENT (ADFAED). Chartered in 1971 and operational in 1974, ADFAED was inspired by the Kuwait Fund for Arab Economic Development and has served as Abu Dhabi's principal means for providing economic assistance beyond the borders of the UAE. Like the Kuwait fund, its *raison d'être* is both philanthropic and pragmatic. It reflects both the sense of obligation that Abu Dhabi feels toward less economically favored brothers as well as the realization that its wealth is an asset of great political and diplomatic utility if adroitly managed. ADFAED provides most aid in the form of concessional, long-term loans to carefully evaluated projects largely in the Arab world, but in a number of non-Arab Asian and African countries as well. Abu Dhabi's program has been one of the most generous in the world in per capita terms and, despite a diminution in aid grants and loans following the decline in oil revenues in 1983, ADFAED has continued to provide generous assistance from funds replenished by loan repayments. Following the Gulf crisis of 1990-91, political considerations have entered into aid decisions, with assistance withheld from countries that were perceived to have supported Iraq.

ABU MUSA. The island of Abu Musa is located in the lower Gulf almost midway between Iran and the UAE, about 45 mi (72 km) from either shore. Approximately 3 mi (5 km) long and almost as wide 'at one end, the island has long been used by fishermen and contains red oxide, formerly mined by European concessionaires for use in paint manufacture. The shah of Iran challenged Sharjah's well-established historical claim, for strategic and political reasons, just as Great Britain was preparing to relinquish its protective status in Sharjah. A compromise was reached at the end of November 1971, recognizing Sharjah's sovereignty, except for an area occupied by Iranian military forces. It was agreed that any oil production, which subsequently began from a modest offshore field, would be shared equally. The compromise averted bloodshed, which occurred in Iran's seizure of the nearby Tunbs from Ras al-Khaimah. However, Shaikh Khalid of Sharjah lost his life in January 1972, at least in part because of his agreement with the Iranians, when his cousin, Saqr bin Sultan, a former ruler whom the British had deposed, attempted a coup with the aid of popular discontent over Sharjah's concession to Iranian pressure. In April 1992 Iran extended the scope of its control over the island, increasing Gulf Arab fears of their large neighbor. *See also* TUNBS.

ACHAEMENID EMPIRE. The Persian empire established in the sixth century B.C. was the most extensive created to that time anywhere in the world. It embraced the great littoral areas on both sides of the Arabian Peninsula and brought a degree of unity to the Gulf, where order was maintained by a fleet under the Achaemenids' Phoenician vassals. Notable were the conquests of Cyrus the Great and the development of cuneiform writing.

ADNAN. In pre-Islamic times the tribes of Arabia were perceived as belonging to one of two groups, that of the southern or "old" Arabs or that of Arabs of northern origin who had migrated to the south. Each group had a mythic, eponymous ancestor, Adnan being the father of the northern Arabs and Qahtan of the southerners. These identities have been important historically in determining tribal loyalties. The roughly correspondent division between Ghafiri and Hinawi in Oman and the lower Gulf has remained significant to the present time. *See also* GHAFIRI, HINAWI, *and* QAHTAN.

AFGHANISTAN, ISLAMIC STATE OF. The Gulf Arab states were disturbed by the advent of a Marxist government in Kabul in 1978 and more so by the Soviet invasion of Afghanistan in December of the following year and the puppet regime that was then installed under General Najibullah. Private religious groups in the Gulf Arab states supported fighting groups in what then became war in Afghanistan. Fears of Soviet designs and of increased superpower intrusion in the Gulf region abated with the Soviet troop withdrawal in 1989.

Subsequently, the Gulf Arab states continued their support of the Mujahedin opposition to the Najibullah government, which collapsed in April, 1992.

AFLAJ. *See* FALAJ.

AGRICULTURE. Despite the extreme aridity of the Arab Gulf region, agriculture formerly employed most of the labor force and produced much, if not most, of the wealth. With the advent of oil-based economies the agricultural sector has shrunk to relative insignificance as a contributor to national income. All these states, however, have made considerable efforts to promote agriculture for strategic, political, and social as well as economic reasons. Increased production of vegetables, fruits, and livestock has helped to check rapidly rising food import costs, keep rural population on the land, and reduce dependence on foreign sources. All the Gulf states face the problems of scanty fertile land and, in an extreme way, scarce water resources. Each has applied the latest technology available for increasing agricultural yields in arid lands. While agricultural problems and developments are similar throughout the Gulf area, each country exhibits peculiarities worth noting.

Oman has more land under cultivation (about 100,000 acres, 156 sq mi or 404 sq km) than the other Gulf states, though this represents about 0.2 percent of its 82,000-sq mi (212,435 sq km) total area. By contrast with the more urbanized states of the Gulf, half or more of the Omani labor force is engaged in agriculture. Nevertheless, agriculture currently accounts for about 2 percent of GDP compared with a preoil contribution of roughly a third. With fairly modest oil reserves and production, Oman from the late 1970s has devoted considerable effort to increasing agricultural production to reduce foreign exchange spent on food imports and improve prospects for food self-sufficiency or modest exports in the postoil era. Dates and limes are exported, while bananas, citrus fruits, and coconuts (in the southern province of Dhofar) are also grown in significant quantity. Important vegetables include alfafa grown for fodder. Livestock, including experimental breeds of cattle, is significant, and egg and poultry production now satisfies a large part of local consumption. Virtually all crops depend on irrigation, and available water resources would permit some expansion of Omani agriculture.

In the UAE roughly 65,000 acres are under cultivation and produce about 1 percent of GDP. The most extensive agricultural area is in the emirate of Ras al-Khaimah. There, as elsewhere, agriculture requires irrigation. This has severely taxed UAE groundwater supplies and led to considerable effort to develop more efficient use of scarce water. Despite these constraints, the UAE has increased agricultural production more than twofold since independence. Around half the nation's total fruit and vegetable needs are met, with some vegetables exported in modest quantities, while a considerable part of its dairy product requirements is domestically produced, and the country is virtually self-sufficient in eggs and poultry. The emirate of Abu Dhabi leads the way in afforestation in the Gulf area with several million trees planted, irrigated by groundwater or by treated waste water.

With only 3,000 to 4,000 acres under cultivation, Kuwait still manages to produce about half its fresh vegetable consumption and somewhat smaller percentages of milk and poultry. Added to the scarcity of its water for irrigation is its salinity, a problem faced still more urgently in Bahrain and Qatar, where overuse of aquifers has permitted seepage of seawater. Although neither state has achieved its aim of self-sufficiency, each has improved agricultural production to satisfy a large part of the demand for fruits, vegetables, poultry, eggs, and milk.

AHL. *Ahl* means "family" or "kinfolk," usually in the extended sense. The term, as used in traditional tribal societies such as those covered in this volume, can have a fairly broad frame of reference, for example, to a clan or division of a tribe.

AHL AL-BALAD. This is a broad and rather fluid concept, meaning literally "people of the country." It serves to distinguish groups in various areas from outsiders, whether foreigners or members of the wider society.

A'ILAH. *A'ilah* refers to a family or household as defined by patrilineal descent. It may be used to denote the nuclear family of parents and children or the more extended family that has typically lived under one roof in the societies of the Gulf Arab states. The word has a powerful resonating force in traditional Arab society because it identifies the social unit of greatest strength and cohesion, to which unquestioning loyalty is still given.

AL-AIN. Meaning "the spring" in Arabic, *al-Ain* is a cluster of towns and villages around oases in the emirate of Abu Dhabi, about 100 mi (161 km) east of the city of Abu Dhabi. Ownership of the area was long contested among Abu Dhabi (or Great Britain as its protector), Oman, and Saudi Arabia, with the dispute finally resolved only in 1977. The cluster of oases is shared with Oman, whose part is called al-Buraimi, and is a significant agricultural area. In al-Ain the separate settlements have fused into a major urban area with a population of more than 100,000, home to the UAE National University.

AIRLINES. *See* GULF AIR *and* EMIRATES AIR.

AJMAN. The name refers both to one of the seven emirates that compose the United Arab Emirates and to the town in which most of its inhabitants live. With an area of 150 sq mi (387 sq km) it is the smallest emirate, while its population of about 65,000 ranks it sixth. Most of Ajman is in an enclave within Sharjah, with two small, detached parcels of land further inland. The town occupies a sand spit that is separated from the mainland by a shallow lagoon. Like the other oil-less emirates, Ajman is economically dependent on the federal treasury. Reflecting its long orientation toward the Gulf, its shipbuilding yards still produce the traditional dhows. The dominant tribe is the Nu'aim, from which Ajman's rulers have traditionally been drawn. The emirate's government has remained patriarchal and uncomplicated, with its administration carried out mainly by Al Nu'aimi family members.

AKHDAR, JEBEL. *See* JEBEL AKHDAR.

AL. The term denotes an extended family or clan and is generally used to refer to a ruling family, for example, the Al Nuhayyan of Abu Dhabi. (The word is transliterated with a capital "A" to distinguish it from the definite article "al.")

ALBA (ALUMINUM BAHRAIN). ALBA was formed in 1971 to help diversify Bahrain's economy in the face of declining oil production. It was one of the first jointly funded ventures in the Gulf, with 20 percent of the capital provided by the Saudi Public Investment Fund, 60 percent from the Bahraini government, and 20 percent from two private investors. It burns local natural gas in boilers to furnish steam to turbine electric generators for the electrolytic separation of aluminum metal from imported alumina pellets. ALBA has proved a success, undergoing a $1.5 billion expansion program in the early 1990s, which boosted its annual production to 460,000 tons for export to Middle Eastern and other Third World countries, while spinning off several subsidiary firms that manufacture aluminum products.

ALBUQUERQUE, GENERAL ALFONSO DE (1453–1515). A brilliant military strategist, Albuquerque led the Portuguese effort to dominate the trade between Europe and the East Indies in the early 16th century by seizing strong points commanding access to the Indian Ocean. The ruthless nature of the Portuguese conquest negatively colored Gulf Arabs' early views of all Europeans.

ALEXANDER THE GREAT (356–323 B.C.). The world conqueror turned his attention to Arabia and the Gulf following his expedition to India. He intended to make Babylon his imperial capital and a great maritime center whose ships would dominate the Gulf and the Indian Ocean. At the time of his death he was about to launch a naval expedition to conquer and colonize the coastal areas of the Arabian Peninsula.

ALGERIA. Relations between Algeria and the Gulf states have been generally friendly, especially as that country's policies continued to move away from its earlier radical stances. Like the Gulf states, Algeria sought to play a mediatory role in the Iran-Iraq war. While the Algerians have tended to be more hawkish in OPEC councils, pushing for higher prices than the Gulf Arab states generally desire, these interests have been fairly well harmonized. In Abu Dhabi an Algerian team has played a key role in helping to run that emirate's national oil company. The Gulf Arab states have been concerned about the crisis in Algeria following the military's cancellation of the elections, scheduled for January 1992, that would have given victory to the Islamic Salvation Front, a party committed to establishing a government based upon Islam. The assassination of President Boudiaf, in June, 1992, and the state of near civil war that has followed have intensified that concern.

AL ALI. The Al Ali (also referred to as the Al Mualla) constitute the main tribe of the emirate of Umm al-Qaiwain. The ruling family bears the same name. A considerable number of the tribe's members are also found in Ras al-Khaimah.

AMIR. *See* EMIR.

AMIRATE. *See* EMIRATE.

AMIRI DIWAN. *See* EMIRI DIWAN.

ARAB BANKING CORPORATION (ABC). In 1980 the governments of Kuwait, the UAE, and Libya created the Arab Banking Corporation as a joint venture with an authorized capital of $1 billion. ABC has a special commitment to the Gulf Arab area, helping to put to productive use the area's oil-generated wealth. It has become a major factor in Gulf area and international merchant banking.

ARAB BUREAU OF EDUCATION FOR THE GULF STATES (ABEGS). Established in 1975, ABEGS is the first Gulf Arab regional organization established to accomplish a specific functional purpose. It includes Iraq as well as Saudi Arabia and the five Gulf states covered in this volume. ABEGS is an informational clearing house and coordinating mechanism for all educational matters relating to the Gulf region. It promotes research as well as exchanges and contacts involving both faculty and students in Gulf area universities.

ARAB FUND FOR ECONOMIC AND SOCIAL DEVELOPMENT. The fund is based in Kuwait and has been an important means for disbursing foreign aid to both Arab and non-Arab developing countries. Saudi Arabia and Libya have also contributed to the fund. *See also* KUWAIT FUND FOR ARAB ECONOMIC DEVELOPMENT.

ARAB GULF COOPERATION COUNCIL (AGCC). *See* GULF CO-OPERATION COUNCIL.

ARAB IRON AND STEEL COMPANY. Supported by investment from Kuwait and Iraq as well as Bahrain, where it is located, the company is one of several Gulf Arab efforts to promote industrial activities that can extend their economic base beyond the oil and gas sector.

ARAB-ISRAELI CONFLICT. Until 1971 (1961 in the case of Kuwait) British responsibility for the Gulf Arab states' foreign affairs insulated them from the full impact of the conflict, although demonstrations of support for the Palestinians date back to the 1930s in the time of the British Palestine mandate. Since gaining their independence they have supported the Palestinians and the Arab confrontation states diplomatically and financially. Their support has been motivated in part by genuine sympathy for brother Arabs to whom they believe a great injustice has been done. It has also reflected political and security concerns that grew out of a large Palestinian presence in each of these states, especially Kuwait, as well as the general instability that continuation of the Arab-Israeli conflict created throughout the Arab world. When Iraq invaded Kuwait and the Palestine Liberation Organization (PLO) supported that move, virtually all governmental financial aid to the Palestinians was cut off by all of the Gulf Arab states. However, the Gulf states have supported the Israel-PLO agreement of September 13, 1993, which led to Palestinian self-rule in Gaza and Jericho under the title Palestinian Authority as a step toward self-rule in all of the occupied territories. With the exception of Kuwait they have pledged financial support to help promote Palestinian economic development. *See also* ISRAEL *and* PALESTINIANS.

ARAB LEAGUE. *Also* LEAGUE OF ARAB STATES. The Arab League was established in Alexandria, Egypt, at a 1944 meeting of representatives of Egypt, Iraq, Syria, Lebanon, Saudi Arabia, Transjordan, and Yemen, the Arab states that had then achieved nominal independence, with observers from the British Palestine Mandate and from French-ruled North Africa also attending. The league came into formal existence the following year when the 1944 protocol was ratified. It was intended to be the vehicle through which effective unity of the Arab world would be achieved. While that dream has not been realized, the league has remained an important mechanism for dealing with inter-Arab concerns, although it remains to be seen how well the league can overcome the damage caused by the 1990-91 Gulf crisis. The record of recent years suggests that the prospects for meaningful economic, political, and military integration or at least cooperation are much greater among smaller groupings such as the Gulf Cooperation Council (GCC), comprising the six Gulf Arab states with their broadly similar economies, polities, and security concerns. All the states covered in this dictionary became members of the Arab League upon achieving independence.

ARAB MILITARY INDUSTRIES ORGANIZATION (AMIO). Established in 1975, the AMIO sought to create joint military production capacity involving Egypt and the Gulf Arab states largely by combining the industrial capacity of the former with the wealth of the latter. It was also intended to promote military planning among those countries. These efforts were suspended in 1978 because of Egypt's adherence to the Camp David agreements with Israel, but resumed with Egypt's readmission to Arab councils a decade later. The AMIO has shown little ability to achieve its principal goal of significantly reducing its members' dependence on outside weapons sources. In 1993 the Gulf Arab states announced plans to invest significant funds in the AMIO.

ARAB NATIONALISTS' MOVEMENT (ANM). Established by Palestinian students at the American University of Beirut in the 1950s, the ANM aimed at unification of the Arab world, seeing in that the solution to its problems. The ANM gained a foothold in Kuwait in the 1960s, where it was directed by Ahmad al-Khatib, a radical member of that country's national assembly. From Kuwait the movement sought to spread its influence throughout the Gulf but, apart from its impact in Bahrain, where several representatives to that country's short-lived national assembly in the mid-1970s were members of or sympathizers with the ANM, its role was not great. In later years the ANM has spent most of its force, although one of its progeny, the Popular Democratic Front for the Liberation of Palestine, continues as an extremist splinter group.

ARAB SHIP REPAIR YARD (ASRY). The creation of ASRY in 1977 was a major part of the continuing effort to broaden the industrial base of the Gulf Arab countries beyond the oil and gas sector. Owned and funded by the seven members of the Organization of Arab Petroleum Exporting Countries (OAPEC), Bahrain, Iraq, Kuwait, Libya, Qatar, Saudi Arabia, and the UAE (the Libyan and Iraqi shares are essentially symbolic), ASRY has succeeded commercially by providing a conveniently located facility for repair of ships, many in the supertanker class. Of equal or greater significance is its success as a means of transferring key elements of industrial technology, in promoting technical and managerial training for Gulf Arabs, and in spinning off new business ventures in the Gulf.

ARABIAN GULF STATES FOLK HERITAGE CENTER. Established in 1981 and located in Doha, the capital of Qatar, the center reflects a concern increasingly felt in the Gulf Arab states for preserving aspects of traditional culture in the face of rapid material and social change. Efforts have been undertaken to collect such elements of the cultural heritage as poetry and stories, as well as objects representing folk crafts.

ARABIAN GULF UNIVERSITY (AGU). Created by the six GCC states and Iraq in 1980, the AGU's handsome, modern campus is located in Bahrain and has been in use since 1988. Including a college of medicine, it was intended to reduce duplication of higher education facilities in the Gulf. However, by mid-1992 the university was experiencing difficulties in gaining funding from the Gulf states and its future was in doubt. The University of Bahrain has taken over the AGU campus while its eventual fate is being determined.

ARABIAN MISSION OF THE DUTCH REFORMED CHURCH OF AMERICA. The Arabian Mission brought modern education and, most notably, modern medicine to the Gulf area, starting in the 1890s. Missions and hospitals were established in Oman, Bahrain, Kuwait, and Iraq, and by the early years of the 20th century were providing treatment for thousands of patients each year. In Bahrain the American Mission Hospital, established in 1902, still exists, providing a wide range of medical care. In March 1988 the American Mission Hospital Society-Bahrain was formed to take over the hospital's management from the Reformed Church. The representatives of the Arabian Mission constituted the most significant American presence in the Gulf before the involvement of American oil companies commenced in the 1930s. Their dedicated work generated much goodwill and helped to create a positive image of America and Americans.

ARABIAN PENINSULA. One of the world's largest peninsulas, the Arabian Peninsula is a vast, roughly trapezoidal land mass of more than a million sq mi (2.6 million sq km), aligned on a northwest to southeast axis. Its length is about 1,500 mi (2,414 km) with the width varying from 600 mi (965 km) in its narrow northern portion to 1,300 mi (2,092 km) in its southern extremity. The Red Sea defines the peninsula's western border, the Gulf of Aden and the Arabian Sea mark the southern boundary, while the Persian/Arab Gulf and Gulf of Oman form the eastern boundary. There is no clear northern delineation where the peninsula merges with the Syrian Desert. Saudi Arabia occupies the great bulk of the peninsula, while the countries covered in this volume (excepting the island state of Bahrain) account for 10 percent-11 percent of its territory.

Geologically, the western third of the Arabian Peninsula is referred to as the Arabian Shield, an igneous-metamorphic complex among whose major features are a mountain range paralleling the Red Sea and extensive lava beds and gravel plains. The eastern portion of the peninsula rests upon sedimentary strata in which the greatest part of its oil wealth is found. On the western edge of this Arabian Shield, limestone ridges form dramatic escarpments, while to the east the land slopes gently into the Persian/Arab Gulf. Most of the Arabian Peninsula is extremely arid, although parts of the southwest quadrant receive monsoon rains, making rain-fed agriculture possible. It contains the world's largest continuous body of sand, the *Rub al-Khali*, or "Empty Quarter," which is larger than France.

Through most of its history the peninsula has been relatively isolated from the mainstream, as reflected in its Arabic name *Jazirat al-Arab* or "island of the Arabs." The obvious and profoundly important exception to this was the birth of Islam in the sixth century A.D. and its subsequent rapid spread throughout the Middle East and beyond. Characteristically, the area soon reverted to its accustomed backwater status, largely left to its own little-noted affairs until the discovery and exploitation of its vast oil reserves thrust it once again into international prominence.

ARABIAN SEA. An arm of the Indian Ocean, the Arabian Sea is bordered on the northwest by the Arabian Peninsula and on the north by Iran and Pakistan. The Gulf of Aden, the Gulf of Oman and, at one remove, the Red Sea and Persian/Arab Gulf are extensions of the Arabian Sea.

ARABS. All the indigenous inhabitants of the countries covered in this volume are part of the Arab people. Definitions vary as to the elements of Arab identity, but it is generally accepted that an Arab is one whose mother tongue is Arabic and who cherishes the culture to which it has given expression. Arabs of the Arabian Peninsula add to this a sense of ethnic or even racial self-identity as the descendants of the original "Arabs," in contrast to the "Arabized" population outside Arabia.

ARCHAEOLOGY. Significant archaeological work began in the Gulf Arab states with a Danish expedition to Bahrain in 1953, where remains of an advanced maritime civilization dating back to the early third millennium B.C. were found. Believed by its discoverers to be the site of the fabled ancient Dilmun and perhaps the Biblical Garden of Eden, the Bahrain find proved to be part of a civilization that had been present throughout the Gulf. Exciting discoveries relating to this and later periods in Gulf history continue to be made, especially in the United Arab Emirates and in 1992 in Oman, where the remains of Ubar and Saffara Metropolis, ancient emporia of key importance to the frankincense trade, were discovered.

ARMED FORCES. The armed forces of all five countries covered in this volume are small and weak, incapable of presenting credible deterrence against attack from larger neighbors, let alone any of the great powers outside of the Gulf region. Until 1961 in Kuwait and 1971 in the other states the British were responsible for external security. Thus the development of modern armed forces began only very recently. Their small populations preclude the creation of large land forces, and they have generally concentrated investment in naval assets and air power. Their wealth permits acquisition of modern weapons systems which are not manpower-intensive and which hold greatest promise of blunting if not deterring the kinds of threats posed and on several occasions carried out by Iran during the Iran-Iraq war and, of course, by Iraq against Kuwait in August 1990. A brief description of the armed forces of the Gulf Arab states and their incipient attempts at military cooperation follows.

Oman. The military forces of Oman, numbering 35,700 (including 6,000 royal household personnel), are among the most professional and best trained in the Gulf. Their quality reflects the long involvement of seconded and contract military personnel from Great Britain, up to the highest levels, and the experience of combat in two operations against domestic military threats in the Jebel Akhdar campaign of the 1950s and the Dhofar Rebellion of the 1960s and 1970s. The ruler, Sultan Qabus bin Said, is a graduate of Sandhurst and, as supreme commander, takes a very close interest in the armed forces. The Sultan of Oman's Land Forces (SOLF), or army, accounts for 20,000 of the personnel of the Sultan's Armed Forces (SAF). The SAF dates from 1958 when, with British advice and assistance, it was formed from separate security forces. Despite an Omanization program in recent years, many British,

Jordanian, and Pakistani advisers have continued to be needed, and considerable numbers of non-Omani troops, particularly Baluchi recruits from Pakistan, are still required to fill manpower needs. The SOLF, armed mainly with British and U.S. weapons, is essentially a light infantry force designed to be sufficient to counter the threat of an immediate neighbor or to fight a delaying action against a major invasion.

The Sultan of Oman's Navy (SON), created in 1975, is a light but effective patrol force that faced the threat of the Iranian navy in the Strait of Hormuz during the Iran-Iraq war. Its personnel has been expanding in recent years, currently numbering close to 3,000, and its craft include two minesweepers and several patrol boats armed with surface-to-surface missiles as well as guns.

The Sultan of Oman's Air Force (SOAF) was formed in 1959 and numbers about 3,500 men. It has had jet fighter aircraft and helicopters in its inventory since 1969 and currently disposes two fighter/ ground attack squadrons plus a limited surface-air missile defense. The air force has, in recent years, received the lion's share of new weaponry, such as the Tornado interdictor/strike aircraft produced by a British-German-Italian consortium, reflecting the primary importance given by all the Gulf Arab states to airpower as their principal line of defense.

Prior to the Iraqi invasion of Kuwait in August 1990, Oman had shown a greater willingness than the other Gulf Arab states to cooperate openly with the West in the military sphere. In the late 1970s and early 1980s agreements were reached with the U.S. to provide for American access to Omani facilities, especially in emergency situations. Supplies were prepositioned at military facilities, several of which the U.S. undertook to upgrade, most importantly the air base on Masirah Island. By the mid-1980s the Omani government had grown noticeably less enthusiastic toward overt military cooperation with the U.S., as was evident in the strained 1985 negotiations extending U.S. access rights.

This reflected in part Oman's establishment in 1985 of diplomatic relations with the Soviet Union, which had come to appear less menacing under Mikhail Gorbachev, as well as the normalization of relations with the Soviets' Arabian Peninsula protégé, South Yemen. It was also presumably occasioned by a more neutral stance vis-à-vis Iran, as Oman attempted to move away from confrontation to a kind of *modus vivendi*. Nevertheless, together with the other Gulf Arab states, Oman made available its facilities, especially military airfields, to assist Desert

Shield/Desert Storm operations following Iraq's invasion of Kuwait. The principal U.S. defense agreement, made in June 1980, was renegotiated in December 1990.

Kuwait. Of all the Gulf Arab states Kuwait has been in the most vulnerable military position, in immediate proximity to two threatening and overwhelmingly more powerful neighbors. Iran menaced Kuwait throughout the Iran-Iraq war of 1980/88, taking direct action against its territory on more than one occasion. Iraq, since Kuwait's independence in 1961, has several times bluffed military invasions either to redraw disputed borders or to enforce claims to all of Kuwait's territory, and in August 1990, invaded and occupied its neighbor.

Against the wholly disproportionate forces of either of these two neighbors, Kuwait's armed forces, totalling 12,000 men, could expect to do little more than inflict a maximum cost on the invader and delay his progress, while awaiting the aid of other GCC states and over-the-horizon U.S. forces. In the event of Iraq's invasion on August 2, 1990, it did less than that. Despite the massing of Iraqi troops on the border, previous false alarms had persuaded the Kuwaiti leadership that they faced only another bluff. The defense minister downgraded the armed state of alert just before the invasion, and a large part of the Kuwaiti officer corps was permitted to remain on leave. As a result, virtually no organized resistance was offered, with the defense minister joining most of the rest of the ruling family in quickly fleeing to Saudi Arabia. (Fahd al-Ahmad, a brother of the ruler, gave his life leading troops against the Iraqi onslaught.)

The army is the largest of the three branches of the armed forces, with three brigades (one armored), and suffers from a severe manpower shortage. Most of its weapons are of U.S. and British manufacture, although for largely political reasons, its past attempt to steer a neutralist course between the superpowers, it purchased quantities of Soviet weapons, including surface-to-air missiles. The National Guard, a semi-autonomous force, is assigned guard duties on the border and in the oil fields.

A small, 1,200-man navy has, until recently, been little more than a purely coastal defense force. As in Oman, it is the air force whose development has been emphasized in the past few years. The Kuwaiti Air Force (KAF) has a strength of about 2,500 men and some 72 combat aircraft. It is tied into the Saudi Arabian air defense network so as to be able to utilize information provided by the Saudi Air Warning and Control System (AWACS). In 1988 the Reagan administration concluded a deal with Kuwait for the sale of 40 F-18 fighter-bombers and about 600 Maverick missiles for a reported $1.9 billion. The aircraft replaced U.S.-manufactured A-4s that were in Kuwait's inventory, with deliveries of the F-18s completed in 1994. Kuwaiti pilots acquitted themselves well during Desert Storm, flying missions from Saudi airfields in the aging A-4s that they had flown out of Kuwait as the Iraqis invaded.

As with the other Gulf Arab states a major weakness of the Kuwaiti armed forces has been their extensive dependence on foreign advisers for daily management and operation. The country's large arms inventory suffers from its mix of U.S., British, French, and Soviet weaponry with limited interoperability as well as simply the inability to absorb effectively the sheer amount of sophisticated weaponry.

In the aftermath of the Iraqi invasion and occupation, a certain ambivalence has marked Kuwaiti thinking on how best to provide for the state's future security. Some were persuaded that Kuwait must look in large part to enhanced military power of its own to counter future aggressors, and in 1991 Kuwait earmarked some $5 billion to strengthen its armed forces. However, the prevailing view was that, whatever improvement might be effected in its own military capabilities, Kuwait would be obliged to depend on powerful friends for its essential security. After having previously seen the U.S. as, at most, a distant over-the-horizon presence, Kuwait had initialed a Defense Cooperation Agreement with the U.S. in September 1991 to stockpile U.S. military equipment and engage in joint training and exercises. In subsequent months several exercises were carried out with the U.S. Marines as well as with the British Royal Marines. In early 1993 Kuwait signed a defense memorandum with the Russian Federation.

Bahrain. The Bahrain Defense Force (BDF) numbers just over 6,000, with most of that number in the army, which is in effect a small, light infantry force. Until 1979 the navy was only a coast guard force; its purchase of attack gunboats and missile boats starting in that year led to the creation of a small combat force. The air force began modestly with two small helicopters in 1977. A 1985 purchase of Northrop F-5s from the U.S. was Bahrain's first acquisition of fixed-wing military aircraft. In 1987 12 F-16s were added to the dozen F-5s already in service. Despite this upgrading of naval and air forces, the BDF remains a largely token military force. Its air force is effectively integrated into the air defense system of Saudi Arabia, its immediate neighbor and close ally, to which Bahrain looks for protection.

Bahrain inherited good military facilities from the British, for whom the island had been a significant military asset in the Gulf. These included an airfield and naval base. Following the British military withdrawal in 1971, the U.S. Navy's Middle East Force, which had maintained a small flotilla at Jufair since 1949, was permitted to retain home-porting privileges. Since 1977 a new agreement permitting U.S. warships to call for supplies upon request has essentially extended the earlier agreement with a lower profile. U.S. access to Bahraini facilities in the Gulf crisis of 1990-91 was Bahrain's most important contribution to Desert Shield and Desert Storm. The United States completed a defense agreement with Bahrain in September 1991, the provisions of which, as in the agreement with Kuwait, remain secret. It almost certainly includes prepositioning of military equipment, access to naval and air facilities, and joint training exercises.

Qatar. With its small population of not more than 500,000, the bulk of it non-Qatari, Qatar could not defend itself against any probable aggressor. It has relied for its security primarily upon efforts to promote political stability in the Gulf and upon the protection provided by friends. Like Bahrain, Qatar is covered by the Saudi AWACS umbrella and combat aircraft.

The commander in chief of the armed forces is Hamad bin Khalifa Al Thani, the ruler since June 1995 and also the minister of defense. However, the defense establishment, which evolved after independence in 1971 from the Royal Guard, remains heavily dependent on British and other expatriate personnel. The army is a roughly 6,000-man force organized as a single tank battalion and five infantry battalions. The navy, manned by about 700 personnel, has several dozen small vessels, including three French guided missile ships armed with Exocet missiles. Qatar's air force disposes just over a dozen combat aircraft of both French and British manufacture. Among its 800 personnel are seconded British pilots and numerous expatriate technicians. In June 1992 Qatar signed a defense pact with the United States, which was reportedly parallel to those that Kuwait and Bahrain had earlier concluded.

The United Arab Emirates. Of the five countries covered in this volume, the UAE has devoted by far the greatest expenditures, overall and per capita, to the development of its armed forces. The results, however, have not been commensurate with the level of spending. The UAE's armed forces evolved from the Trucial Oman Levies (TOL) later known as the Trucial Oman Scouts (TOS), created by the British in 1951 to maintain order among the tribes of the then Trucial States. By 1971 this was a well-trained, British-officered force of 1,600, drawing 40 percent of its recruits locally, 30 percent from Oman, and the balance from Iran, Pakistan, and India. In that year the TOS became the Union Defense Force (UDF) with its headquarters in Sharjah. From the beginning of independence, however, there were separate forces in each emirate, the Abu Dhabi Defense Force, established in the late 1960s, being the largest. Despite the emirate rulers' pledge in 1976 to merge their forces, effective integration has not been achieved.

The total UAE armed forces manpower is over 50,000, with most of those nominally committed to the UDF. The army comprises five armored battalions, nine mechanized infantry battalions, three artillery battalions, and three air defense battalions. A 1,500-man navy includes a number of missile boats. The air force, of equivalent size, relies upon a main fighter aircraft inventory of 36 French Mirage 2000s. Unlike Bahrain and Qatar, the UAE is not covered by Saudi Arabia's AWACS umbrella. In 1995 the UAE signed a Defense Cooperation Agreement with the United States as Kuwait, Bahrain, and Qatar had done earlier. (Coordinating the views of the seven emirates made reaching an agreement more difficult and time-consuming than in the other states.) Despite efforts to train UAE citizens to fill the ranks of the armed forces, there has been continued heavy reliance on British, Jordanian, and Pakistani officers and technicians, although, following the 1990-91 Gulf crisis, the pro-Iraqi stance of Jordan and Pakistan has apparently led to dismissal of most of their nationals. Large numbers of Omanis continue to serve in the ground forces. Two other factors serve to limit the UDF's effectiveness, a mix of British, French, and U.S. equipment and, most important, the fundamentally divergent political stances of the UAE's two most important members, Abu Dhabi and Dubai.

Attempts to Integrate the Gulf Armed Forces. In 1981 the Gulf Arab states joined Saudi Arabia in forming the GCC. Their action was largely prompted by security concerns, following the Islamic revolution under Khomeini in Iran and the outbreak of the war between Iran and Iraq. The GCC decisions to establish a Gulf Arab arms industry and to coordinate arms purchases have not been realized. There has been some progress toward a third goal, creating a rapid deployment force. In 1983 and 1984 exercises involving elements of all the GCC armed forces participated in joint exercises, and a number of bilateral exercises have been held since. A 7,000-man "Peninsula Shield Force" is stationed at Hafr al-Batin in northeast Saudi Arabia, basically as a symbol of GCC unity against external threat and an earnest indication of its intentions for the future.

More feasible and more immediately useful than joint land forces cooperation or integration would be coordination of air power. As noted, the plans for an integrated air defense system have in part been realized with the extension of the Saudi AWACS coverage to Kuwait, Bahrain, and Qatar. The purchase of different aircraft, despite earlier discussion of GCC acquisition of a common fighter, presents obvious obstacles to interoperability and reflects the divergent political and diplomatic positions of the GCC states, which set limits to the degree of integration or cooperation that can be achieved in the foreseeable future. The aftermath of the 1990-91 Gulf crisis revealed that, whatever the shared sense of danger, the Gulf Arab states (including Saudi Arabia) cannot agree on how best to act in common against military threats. They have indicated a desire to add to their weapons inventories, have made or plan to make agreements with the U.S. for prepositioning of equipment and access to facilities in time of future threat, and continue to see U.S. (and other Western) over-the-horizon forces as their ultimate security guarantee. Beyond that, however, there has been little sense of any greater capacity or disposition to coordinate the development and mission of their armed forces than had been the case before the Iraqi invasion of Kuwait.

Within a short time, post-Desert Storm rhetoric about imposing limitations on the arms build-up in the Gulf area was no longer reflected in the actions of the great powers. The United States, the United Kingdom, and France were engaged in vigorous efforts to promote sales of high-tech weaponry. At the February 1993 Abu Dhabi arms fair, billed as the largest ever in the Middle East, the French won a $4 billion-plus tank sale in fierce competition with the Americans. Russia has begun to look to the Gulf as a potentially important market for weapons produced by the former Soviet Union. In June 1992 Moscow reportedly reached an agreement with the UAE to sell the latter armored vehicles and infantry equipment. In just the first two years following the liberation of Kuwait, the Gulf Arab states (including Saudi Arabia) ordered about $40 billion of arms. *See also* DESERT SHIELD/DESERT STORM, IRAN, IRAQ, *and entries on Gulf Arab states.*

ARTS. In none of the five states covered in this volume have the major arts flourished. This may be attributed to a number of factors, among them the area's pronounced material poverty before oil and the resultant lack of a sophisticated urban culture, the relative isolation of the Gulf region from outside artistic and intellectual stimulus until very recently, and the fairly stringent application of Islamic injunctions in the areas of representational and performing arts. At the same time, minor arts, especially artisan crafts addressing practical needs, played a significant role in Gulf Arab society and achieved a certain refinement. Oral poetry, devoted to religious and, more often, traditional Bedouin themes was and in some quarters remains very popular, as do Bedouin dances. Textiles and jewelry were produced, although generally of lesser quality than elsewhere in the Arab world. Perhaps most impressive among the traditional material arts are those practiced with scarce imported wood, especially in shipbuilding and domestic architecture. The several kinds of ships known collectively as *dhows* are justly celebrated as master-pieces of craftsmanship and are still made today in parts of the Gulf. The art of wood carving as applied to doors and lintels of private residences is no longer practiced, and few examples of this handsome, decorative art form survive. In all of the states, museums and other institutions have been established to preserve and promote traditional arts, with the Arab Gulf States Folklore Center in Doha especially worthy of note.

Only in recent years have modern art forms come to assume a place in the cultural life of these states. Painting has achieved a certain popularity, with both men and women seeking to pursue careers as artists. The state of Sharjah in the UAE is noteworthy in promoting literary culture. It boasts a circle of active poets and short story writers as well as playwrights and actors.

AL-ASLAH. Literally "reform" (also transliterated as *islah*), the term is used to identify a politically influential Islamic current in Kuwait.

AUSTRALIA. Australia is important to the Gulf as a source of raw material imports. The aluminum processing operations of ALBA (Bahrain) and DUBAL (Dubai Aluminum Company) have been dependent upon imports of Australian alumina (although though other less distant sources are now being developed) and the Gulf states import considerable food supplies from Australia, particularly livestock, especially sheep.

AWALI. Just north of the center of al-Awal, the main island of the Bahrain archipelago, Awali is the site where oil was first struck in commercial quantities on the Arab side of the Gulf in 1932. A town of the same name was created to house the employees of the Bahrain Petroleum Company (BAPCO) refinery and other oil-based industry.

AWAMIR, *Sing.* AMIRI. The Awamir are one of the major tribes of Abu Dhabi and have been allied with the Bani Yas since the early 19th century as part of the tribal confederation that has dominated the emirate from that time.

B

BAGGALA. A *baggala* is one of the traditional sailing vessels of the Persian/Arabian Gulf commonly referred to as dhows. It has two masts with lateen sails and a high, squared poop, modeled after Portuguese vessels. Baggalas, ranging up to more than 300 tons with crews of 150 men, were once important in Gulf commerce but are now rare. *See also* BOOM, DHOW, JALBOOT, *and* SAMBOOK.

BAHRAIN. The Arabic name *Al-Bahrain* means "the two seas." The fresh water that still bubbles up from the floor of the saline Gulf led the ancient inhabitants to conceive of the island as resting on a sea of fresh water while surrounded by one of salt.

Geography and demography. The state of Bahrain is an archipelago of 35 islands lying in a shallow western arm of the Arab Gulf, about 15 mi (24 km) from Saudi Arabia (to which it is connected by a causeway) on its west and approximately 18 mi (29 km) from Qatar to the east. The total area is about 250 sq mi (648 sq km), equivalent to the island of Guam and a bit smaller than New York City. Only six of the islands are inhabited. The largest, al-Awal or Bahrain Island, comprises 85 percent of the total area and measures 10 mi (16 km) at its widest and 30 mi (48 km) lengthwise on its almost exactly north-south axis. It holds most of the population, most of the country's arable land, and the bulk of the oil currently produced. Other significant islands include Muharraq, where the international airport and a large urban population are located, and Sitra, connected to the main island by a bridge and site of the nation's oil export terminal. The Hawar Islands, lying just off the coast of Qatar, are claimed by Bahrain in an ongoing dispute with that neighbor.

Bahrain shares the extreme summer climate of the states of the Arab
Gulf littoral, temperatures that regularly range up to 110°F (43°C) and

Bahrain

Persian Gulf

Al Muharraq
MANAMA
Mīnā' Salmān

Sitrah

'Awālī

Gulf of
Bahrain

Hāwar Islands are
in dispute between
Bahrain and Qatar.

10 km

Source: Background Notes
United States Department of State
Bureau of Public Affairs

can reach 125°F (52°C) between June and September, and combine
with extreme humidity. The other months of the year are relatively
comfortable, with winter temperatures generally between 50°F (10°C)
and 70°F (21°C). The 3 to 4 in (8 to 10 cm) of annual rainfall tend to
run off rapidly and are of little benefit.

Bahrain's population is 539,000 (official estimate, 1993). More than
80 percent of the population is urban, concentrated mostly in Manama,
its suburbs, and Muharraq. Native Bahrainis account for about 65
percent of the total. In this respect Bahrain differs from Kuwait, Qatar,
and the United Arab Emirates, where natives are outnumbered by those
of foreign origin. About 60 percent of Bahrain's industrial workers are
expatriates, and most of the foreign workforce is Arab or South and
Southeast Asian. However, fewer than half of the professional and
technical employees are expatriates. All native Bahrainis and most
foreigners are Muslims, but there are significant sectarian and other
divisions within the indigenous population. Although Bahrain has been
under Sunni rule for the past two centuries, up to 70 percent of
Bahrainis are Shias. Sunnis are divided into those of Arabian tribal

origin, including the ruling Al Khalifa, and those called Hawala, the descendants of Arabs who migrated to Iran and entered Bahrain in recent centuries. Shias are both Baharna, who are indigenous and account for the great majority of that community, and Ajam, who are of Persian origin and immigrated over the past three centuries.

History. Bahrain's geographic situation underlies basic continuities in its long history. Centrally located on the Gulf's trade routes and blessed with the vital commodity of fresh water, it has always been a commercial culture, serving as an entrepôt and point of strategic importance. Almost as long ago as 4000 B.C. a trading culture had been established on the Arab side of the Gulf centered on the fabled Dilmun, whose archaeological remains have been excavated since 1953 at the northern end of Bahrain Island. The commerce that enriched Dilmun connected it to the ancient civilizations of Babylonia and those of the Indus valley. Dilmun reached the height of its wealth and power around 2000 B.C., entering a period of decline two or three centuries later when trade routes vital to its prosperity were disrupted. Despite temporary revivals of its fortunes, ancient Bahrain never again achieved its former prominence. It continued to play a significant role in Gulf commerce and came under the influence of such neighboring empires as the Babylonian and the Greek, both Alexandrine and Hellenistic. Fascinating archaeological finds continue to reveal details of the various periods of the ancient era.

Following the arrival of Islam in the seventh century A.D., Bahrain was subsumed successively within the Umayyad and Abbasid empires for some three and a half centuries. A long period of turbulence followed in the Gulf, though Bahrain frequently served as a useful buffer between contending powers, and in the late 15th and early 16th centuries a strong local Arab dynasty restored order and prosperity. The Portuguese dominated the Gulf and Bahrain for the balance of the 16th century. In 1602 a call for Persian assistance against the Portuguese brought annexation by the Safavid ruler Shah Abbas I and Persian domination that lasted for nearly two centuries. It was the establishment of the Al Khalifa as the rulers of Bahrain that ended Persian suzerainty.

The Al Khalifa originally settled in Kuwait as part of the Utbi tribal federation established there in the early 18th century under the Al Sabah. In 1766 they migrated to Qatar, basing their state on the settlement of Zubarah in the northwest part of the peninsula. With the assistance of the Al Sabah they occupied Bahrain in 1782, after which Persian influence ceased to be exercised not only in Bahrain but generally along the Gulf Arab littoral. Just before the end of the 18th century the Al Khalifa moved permanently to Bahrain, continuing to rule their Qatari territories. The Al Thani finally forced recognition of their rule over the peninsula in 1872.

Like the other small Arab Gulf states, Bahrain entered into a series of agreements with Great Britain, specifically the British Government of India, for which the Gulf was an area of intense commercial and strategic concern. These agreements, beginning with the 1820 Treaty of Peace and culminating in an 1892 treaty pledging the Al Khalifa not to enter into any agreement with another state without British consent, solidified the Al Khalifa's rule against various threats, including the Ottoman Empire's attempt to assert its authority in eastern Arabia. Bahrain was, in effect, an independent state under British protection (as distinct from a protectorate), a situation reflected in the permanent residence of a British official in Manama from 1902 on. However, British influence was more systematically exercised in Bahrain than elsewhere in the Gulf, personified by the redoubtable Sir Charles Belgrave, who served as "adviser" (later "secretary") to the ruler for more than three decades, starting in 1926. Thus, well before independence in 1971 Bahrain had the rudiments of a modern state administration, sustained from 1932 by oil export revenues. Moreover, as early as 1938 the first stirrings of Arab nationalist protest and demands for reform were felt. By the mid-1950s these had become intense, fueled by the rise of Egypt's Nasser, the 1956 nationalization of the Suez Canal Company, and the Anglo-French-Israeli invasion of Egypt and its diplomatic/political aftermath. Riots in Bahrain led to the forcible suppression of political groups and activities, forcing the oppositionists underground.

Domestic politics. In anticipation of independence, following Britain's announcement that it would relinquish its role as protector, efforts were made to improve the structure of government. In 1970 a Council of State was established and in 1971, the year of independence, it became the Council of Ministers, though participation continued to be limited to members of the ruling family and a few individuals enjoying close relations with the Al Khalifa. However, in an attempt to establish a more cohesive and popularly based support for the regime, the ruler, Shaikh Isa bin Salman, announced shortly after independence that Bahrain would adopt a constitutional form of government. In December 1972 a constituent assembly with slightly more than half of its members elected by native Bahraini male voters was created and by June 1973 had approved a constitution. That document gave the vote to male citizens age 20 and over, declared the country to be a hereditary monarchy with succession through the ruler's eldest son in perpetuity (a departure from tradition that has not been adopted by any other Gulf Arab country), and established a tripartite government in which the legislature had very limited powers. Members of the National Assembly were to serve four-year terms; they were granted only the power to give advice and consent to laws initiated in the cabinet; and only the ruler could ratify and promulgate laws. The election for the assembly in December 1973, like that which earlier chose the constituent assembly members, produced "leftist" and "religious conservative" blocs, accounting for about half the elected total, the remainder being independents largely from the business and commercial class. No members of the country's social elite stood for election, a new and unsettling concept for most of them, but 10 nonelected members were selected from this class to serve as the cabinet.

Bahrain's parliamentary experiment was brief. It came to grief because the ruling family saw the assembly members' role to be essentially consultative while the latter were determined to be involved in the actual drafting of laws. A general deadlock between cabinet and assembly ensued, with sharp disagreement on three major issues, trade union organization, internal security legislation, and extension of the U.S. Navy's lease of facilities at Jufair. Cabinet opposition to trade unions and assembly opposition to the other measures led the ruler, Shaikh Isa bin Salman Al Khalifa, to dissolve the assembly in August 1975. The government has maintained that the constitution remains in effect, with legislative powers residing in the cabinet, and the assembly has not been reelected. While there were occasional hints of its reestablishment, the threat of a spillover effect from the Iran-Iraq war (underscored by the 1981 coup attempt in Bahrain apparently supported by Iran) reinforced the government's reluctance to return to the experiment.

In keeping with the general move after Desert Storm toward greater political participation for the citizens of the Gulf Arab states, Bahrain's ruler and the prime minister (his brother) Shaikh Khalifa bin Salman Al Khalifa, have expressed support for the "reintroduction of democracy." In reality, however, little movement toward greater political participation has occurred. In January 1993 a new consultative council was formed whose members would be drawn from business, professional, religious, and academic backgrounds, with a number having served in

the earlier assembly. However, the council's role is limited to com-
menting on draft legislation prior to the ruler's approval of it. In mid-
1996 it appeared unlikely that the Bahraini government would soon
adopt a more open political system. At the same time, among intellectuals and many professionals in Bahrain, as elsewhere in the Gulf, there
has been a new sense of urgency concerning the need to change the
political system to permit greater participation. In late 1994 a group of
prominent Sunni and Shia professionals gathered 25,000 signatures on a
petition to restore the Parliament; Shaikh Isa refused to accept the petition. Moreover, throughout 1994, 1995, and in early 1996 Shia restive-
ness erupted in violent riots, especially in December-January 1995
following the arrest and deportation of three of the most prominent Shia
leaders. Shia discontent reflects continued underrepresentation in senior
government positions (as well as total exclusion from the military and
the police) and fact that Shias suffer disproportionately high unemployment in the wake of recent economic problems. The government's fear
of a Shia majority wielding significant political power is exacerbated by
suspicions of Iranian influence or control over Bahrain's Shias.

   Economics.   Bahrain's long tradition of commercial activity has
already been noted. From earliest times it has also derived wealth from
fishing and modest agriculture. The sale of Gulf pearls, before oil, had
long been the nation's principal source of income. Bahrain was the first
Gulf Arab state to develop an oil-based economy, with petroleum
discovered in 1932 and first exported two years later. As a conse-
quence, it was the first to develop a modern economy and a skilled
industrial labor force. At the same time, the relative modesty of its
oil reserves has led it to undertake the first and most serious efforts at
economic diversification. Nevertheless, Bahrain's prosperity remains
closely tied to oil six decades after its discovery there.

   In 1928 Standard Oil of California (SoCal) obtained the concession for oil exploration in Bahrain, forming the Bahrain Petroleum
Company (BAPCO) as a Canadian corporation to evade British stric-
tures against concessions to non-Commonwealth companies. From the
first exports in 1934 oil has been the engine of Bahrain's economic
growth and the principal means by which technology and managerial
skills have been introduced. Oil wealth, fortuitously, was first realized
just as the pearling industry was declining in competition with Japanese
cultured pearls and the impact of the worldwide economic depression
was being felt. The country's oil production peaked at 76,000 barrels
per day (bpd) in 1970, a small fraction of that produced by Saudi

Arabia and its other neighbors, and has been in decline since. Enhanced recovery techniques and shared revenues from an offshore oil field on the Saudi-Bahraini border will continue to ensure at least modest oil income, while offshore exploration holds further promise and significant gas production is underway. Since 1945, Saudi oil has been piped to Bahrain for refining into a large number of products, primarily for export. Until 1975 BAPCO was a subsidiary of Caltex Petroleum Corporation, formed earlier when Texaco joined SoCal (now Chevron) as its owner. In that year the Bahraini government assumed 60 percent ownership, taking over the company entirely in 1980.

Bahrain's moderate oil wealth sustained a steady pace of development that avoided massive dependence on expatriate workers and produced large cadres of actively engaged, skilled Bahrainis. This, added to the long experience of the nation's preoil, commerce-based prosperity, has helped to position Bahrain favorably for the postoil age and it will be the first of the Gulf Arab states to enter. Oil and gas provide less than 20 percent of Bahrain's GDP. An early example of the move toward economic diversification and the largest of several industrial projects is ALBA, which began in the late 1960s and imports alumina from Australia and other raw products from the United States and elsewhere and uses natural gas to generate electricity for smelting. It has generally been a success story, currently producing 460,000 tons of aluminum annually. Other projects include the Arab Shipbuilding and Repair Yard (ASRY), designed to accommodate ships of up to 400,000 tons, and the Arab Iron and Steel Company (AISCO), an ore pelletizing plant. In the mid-1970s, as Bahrain sought to capture some of the financial business driven from Beirut by Lebanon's civil war, the government encouraged the establishment of offshore banking units (OBUs) in the country. These institutions, exempted from requirements imposed on banks with domestic dealings, helped to finance imports into the Gulf region and issued performance bonds for projects undertaken there. The OBUs generated considerable income for Bahrain and made it the major financial and banking center of the Gulf. The general downturn in economic activity in the Gulf caused a slump in OBU operations in the mid-1980s, and the Iraqi invasion of Kuwait in 1990 further damaged Bahrain's position as an offshore banking center. As of 1996 the OBUs and the banking sector had only partly recovered. Bahrain has taken recent initiatives to enhance its economic prospects by permitting 100 percent foreign ownership in many onshore corporations and promoting tourism, now Bahrain's fastest growing industry. As noted previously, however, unemployment is a problem.

The economy with its mix of oil and refined petroleum products exports, heavy and light industry, commercial activity, and agriculture will remain basically sound. At the same time, the price of growing prosperity has been greater dependence on Bahrain's large neighbor Saudi Arabia, whose crude oil represents the great bulk of the throughput in Bahrain's refinery, which is also a major investor in Bahraini industry and a leading customer for its exports. The physical linking of the two countries by the causeway in 1986 underscored the growing closeness of the relationship economically and otherwise.

International relations and security issues. Since independence, Bahrain has pursued a cautious and astute strategy to preserve its security and indeed its independence. Iran has consistently advanced claims to the islands, the shah doing so as Britain prepared to withdraw its protection. This threat was turned aside in 1970 when Iran agreed to accept a UN determination of the wishes of the Bahraini people, who were found to favor independence overwhelmingly. Iranian claims were, however, renewed by the Islamic Republic after the fall of the shah and in 1981 a coup with apparent support from Iran was attempted against the government of Bahrain. While relations between the two countries were subsequently normalized, fear of renewed Iranian claims remains. The other Gulf superpower, Iraq, has also been a major source of concern. From the late 1960s to the mid-1970s Iraq pursued a policy aimed at the radicalization and destabilization of the conservative Gulf Arab states. Both the less forward Iraqi Gulf policy which followed a 1975 treaty with the shah and the 1980-88 Iraqi war with Iran caused the threat from Baghdad to abate. The threat revived dramatically with the Iraqi August 1990 invasion of Kuwait and its aftermath.

Relations with the other conservative Arab Gulf states are generally close, although rivalries and disputes have been common and Bahrain has on occasion played neighbors against one another to help secure its interests. At the time of independence, federation with Qatar and the Trucial States in a single state was seriously considered, failing in the end largely because the others feared domination by the politically stronger and more sophisticated Bahrainis. Relations with Qatar continue to be strained because of the dispute over the Hawar Islands. Ties to Kuwait are especially close and with Oman and the United Arab Emirates (UAE) they are warm. (Reflecting traditional family rivalries, the relationship with Abu Dhabi, dominant member of the UAE, is cordial, while with Abu Dhabi's rival in the UAE, Dubai, it is less friendly.) Although Bahrain has resisted excessive influence by its large, socially and politically more conservative neighbor of Saudi Arabia, it has found unavoidable an ever closer connection in the current uncertain and dangerous environment. The Saudi air defense system extends over Bahrain, and immediately after the 1981 coup attempt a Bahraini-Saudi agreement was reached on exchange and consultation on internal security issues, the first of several such bilateral accords among the Gulf Arab states (excepting Kuwait). In that same year Bahrain had joined with Arabia, Kuwait, Oman, the UAE, and Qatar to form the Gulf Cooperation Council (GCC), a regional grouping with both economic and security aims. Bahrain has been an active participant in various GCC initiatives, contributing to and benefiting from progress toward economic cooperation and integration among the six members. Because of the very modest size of its military establishment, Bahrain's contribution to the joint GCC defense effort is essentially symbolic.

Bahrain is not a member of OPEC because of the slightness of its oil production, but belongs to the Organization of Arab Petroleum Exporting Countries (OAPEC) under whose aegis ASRY and other Bahrain-based, regional enterprises have been established. It is a member of the Arab League and the Islamic Conference Organization (ICO) in whose councils it works closely with the other Arab Gulf states to exert influence on behalf of generally moderate positions.

Bahrain has had a close security relationship with the United States over many years that, in a sense, supplants in part the protecting role that the British formerly played. When Britain terminated that role in 1971, leaving behind a substantial military infrastructure, the small American flotilla, designated U.S. Middle East Force, was permitted to continue to be based as before at Jufair and show the American flag in the area as it had since 1949. In 1973 this relationship was threatened when massive American military assistance to Israel in the October War caused Bahrain to announce its intention to cancel the docking agreement. With the amelioration of strained relations the flotilla was, however, permitted to stay, and in 1977 when the agreement expired, it was replaced by a new one that no longer designated Jufair as home base for the U.S. Middle East Force but permitted American naval vessels to use its facilities on request. In 1987, during the "reflagging" operation in which the United States protected Kuwaiti tankers, Bahrain provided vital assistance in servicing the U.S. warships. In the military operations following Iraq's invasion of Kuwait, Bahrain again played a key role in servicing naval vessels operating in the Gulf. Until the last few years Bahrain's armed forces had remained little more than a constabulary force to maintain domestic order. In the increasingly dangerous environment of the 1980s, however, Bahrain began to acquire significant new weaponry, especially for air defense. F-5 and F-16 fighter aircraft were ordered from the United States together with Stinger surface-to-air missiles and Sidewinder air-to-air missiles. *See also* ISA BIN SALMAN *and* AL KHALIFA.

BAHRAIN NATIONAL OIL COMPANY (BANOCO). The company was formed in 1976 as part of the process of nationalizing the oil industry, taking over in that year the government's recently acquired 60 percent share of the Bahrain Petroleum Company (BAPCO) and acquiring the remaining 40 percent in 1980. BANOCO is also responsible for onshore oil production and refining as well as the exploration and development of offshore fields. *See also* BAHRAIN.

BAHRAIN PETROLEUM COMPANY (BAPCO). The company was formed in 1929 as a subsidiary of California Standard Oil Company (SoCal) and chartered in Canada to comply with British restrictions against non-Commonwealth companies operating in the British-protected Gulf states. In the next year a concession agreement was signed with the ruler, Shaikh Hamad. In 1931 drilling commenced, and in 1932 oil was struck at Jebel ad-Dukhan in the center of Bahrain Island. The export of oil and the development of an integrated oil industry soon followed. The consequences for Bahrain and the world of the Gulf's first oil strike and the creation of its first major, modern industrial enterprise were enormous. Oil income has made Bahrainis wealthier than ever before, and BAPCO has served as an engine of economic growth and modernization for the country. Moreover, the discovery of oil on Bahrain directed the attention of SoCal's geologists to similar underground structures on the Saudi Arabian mainland, leading to the discovery and development of the world's greatest oil reserves and making the Gulf eventually the center of gravity of the world's oil production and export trade. For Bahrain, BAPCO has also had significant social and political consequences. From the early 1950s the large industrial workforce involved in the oil sector was a source of political opposition to the government, feeding the growth of nationalist and radical sentiment. In 1975 the government took over 60 percent of

BAPCO, assuming control of the remaining share four years later. *See also* BAHRAIN *and* BAHRAIN NATIONAL OIL COMPANY.

BALUCHIS. *Also* BALUCH. Immigrants from Baluchistan, the mountainous area of southeast Iran and southwest Pakistan, have played a significant role in the workforce and military of Oman, the United Arab Emirates, and Qatar. Considerable numbers of Baluchis were recruited to serve in the ranks in Oman's army and subsequently provided much of the manpower to the level of noncommissioned officers in the UAE armed forces. Typically Baluchis are employed in the civilian sector in such menial and relatively low-paying jobs as laborers, porters, guards, and domestic servants. Baluchis are predominantly Sunni.

BANI YAS. The Bani Yas came originally from Najd, the central part of the Arabian Peninsula, and by the mid-17th century were the largest tribal confederation in what is now the United Arab Emirates. Then as now they were dominant in the territory of Abu Dhabi. British defeat of their Qasimi rivals in the early 19th century helped the Bani Yas to consolidate their power, based on the oasis settlements of al-Liwa and al-Ain as well as the town of Abu Dhabi on the coast. The Qasimi today rule Sharjah and Ras al-Khaimah, and the legacy of the rivalry with the Bani Yas still significantly colors relations among the members of the UAE confederation. The ruling family of Abu Dhabi, the Al Nuhayyan, one of four families in the Al Bu Falah clan, have long been dominant although numerically one of the smallest subgroups within the Bani Yas. Another Bani Yas subsection, the Al Bu Falasah, seceded from Abu Dhabi in 1833 and settled in Dubai, where they have remained as rivals to the Al Bu Falah. *See also* ABU DHABI, AL BU FALAH, *and* AL NUHAYYAN.

BANKING. There were few banks in the Arab Gulf states before the development of their oil wealth and those were British, most prominently the British Bank of the Middle East (BBME). The BBME was established in Kuwait in 1941 and in Oman in 1948. Eastern Bank (now Chartered Bank) opened in Bahrain as early as 1921. Until 1971 banking was largely controlled by British interests. Now each state has a significant domestic, commercial banking establishment regulated by central banks, and foreign interests are greatly restricted, except in Oman and Qatar. In the former, 14 of 22 local banks are wholly foreign owned. In the latter, 10 are foreign and 5 domestic. A limited American banking presence takes the form of branches of Citibank in Oman, Qatar, and the UAE with First National Bank of Chicago also represented in the UAE.

In 1975 Bahrain sought to take advantage of its well-developed communications and its central geographical location in the Gulf, as the region's wealth burgeoned and Lebanon's civil war undermined Beirut's role as a commercial and financial center, by inviting the establishment of offshore banking units (OBUs). Arab as well as Western banks set up OBUs in Bahrain, generating considerable earnings for the host country through fees and large amounts of foreign exchange brought into Bahrain as the country became the center of regional financial transactions. By the mid-1980s, however, a significant decline had occurred in the activities of the OBUs. This was the result of several developments, among them the general downturn in oil income and the collapse of Kuwait's unofficial stock market, the Souk al-Manakh. Those same developments were also largely responsible for the difficulties that domestic banking experienced in the Arab Gulf states. Overextended loans, a general lack of discipline in the banking systems, and the weakness of central banks greatly exacerbated their impact, reducing the profitability of banking and leading to a number of near failures. The most confused situation was in the UAE, where more than 50 banks with well over 300 branches operated. There the autonomy enjoyed by each member of the federation and the comparative weakness of the Central Bank make the imposition of necessary discipline difficult. A further complication arises from adherence in some parts of the Gulf to the Islamic principle of payment of simple interest only, while elsewhere payment of compounded interest is permitted. Islamic banking is expanding rapidly in the Gulf region, servicing a market that may be as large as $60 billion. Many conventional banks now offer services adhering to Islamic injunctions. In the wake of the difficulties experienced by the banking systems of the Arab Gulf states in the early and mid-1980s, reforms were enacted that have measurably improved banks' performance. After a rather difficult year in 1994, Gulf Arab banks did reasonably well in 1995 and 1996.

BANU or **BANI**. Literally "sons" (the singular is *ibn* or *bin*), the word designates a tribe when used with the name of a real or apocryphal ancestor, for example, Bani Khalid and Bani Yas.

BA'TH. The term ("renaissance" in Arabic) designates a movement founded on Arab socialist ideals enunciated by two Lebanese intellectuals, Michel Aflaq and Salah al-Din Bitar, in the 1940s. Both the Syrian government of Hafez al-Asad and the Iraqi government of Saddam Hussein claim to be its true representatives. While Iraq has sought to exert its political influence in the Arab Gulf states, it is only in Bahrain that a branch of the Ba'th was established, looking to Baghdad for direction.

BATINAH. Literally "belly" in Arabic, the term is applied to the coastal area along the Gulf of Oman, embracing part of the UAE and Oman. It is a plain, varying in width from 6 to 22 mi (9.7 to 35.4 km), with significant cultivation along its entire extent.

BEDOUIN. "Bedouin" is the French rendering and the most common term used in English to refer to the Arab nomad or *bedu* (also *badu*). In Arabic the same word can refer to the desert, the home of the Bedouins. In the Arab Gulf states virtually all the population is now settled. With scarcely significant exceptions elsewhere, only the UAE may be said to continue to have nomadic inhabitants and those are reduced to a comparative handful. Yet in all the Arab Gulf states, and most especially the UAE, tribal affiliations remain politically and socially important and among most elements of the indigenous population traditional Bedouin virtues, such as courage and generosity, continue in large part to define the basic values of the culture.

BELGRAVE, SIR CHARLES D. (1894-1969). Belgrave was a British adviser, employed by the rulers of Bahrain for thirty years, beginning in 1926. In that capacity Belgrave exercised great influence and left a considerable imprint on the country's development. Under his guidance physical infrastructure was improved and the state's administrative structure modernized and made more efficient. The effect of this, especially after the advent of oil income in the mid-1930s, was to consolidate further the position of the Al Khalifa as rulers. Bahrain's central position, politically and strategically, in the British-protected Gulf system and Belgrave's long and forceful tenure caused the country to come more directly and extensively under British direction than the other protected states. By the 1950s, with the increase of anti-government political protest, Belgrave became something of a lightning rod for political radicals. In 1957 he left Bahrain, and his position of adviser to the ruler was abolished.

BINT. *Also* IBNA. *Bint* means "daughter" in Arabic. In conservative, tribal Arab society it is often used as part of a name, identifying the bearer's paternity. As an example, the mother of Zayid bin Sultan, current ruler of Abu Dhabi and president of the United Arab Emirates, was Salmah bint Buti.

BISHARA, ABDULLAH YACOUB (b. 1936). Dr. Bishara was secretary-general of the Gulf Cooperation Council from its inception in 1981 until March 1993. A scholar and skilled diplomat, who earlier served as Kuwait's ambassador to the UN, he played a key role in helping steer the GCC through a decade of consolidation and progress toward greater cooperation among its six members (Bahrain, Kuwait, Oman, Qatar, Saudi Arabia, and the United Arab Emirates) on economic and security matters. *See also* GULF COOPERATION COUNCIL.

BOOM. *Booms* are large, traditional Persian/Arab Gulf sailing vessels, usually motorized and sometimes reaching 120 ft in length and 400 tons displacement. Like early Arab ships, they are pointed at both ends. Booms remain significant in carrying the commerce of the Gulf. *See also* BAGGALA, DHOW, JALBOOT, and SAMBOOK.

BORDERS AND TERRITORIAL DISPUTES. The concept of definitively demarcated borders between states is a recent introduction to the Gulf area, where traditional tribal authority was asserted over pasturage, oases, and settlements, with frequent shifts of fortune. Borders as exact delimitations of political and legal writ came with the Western intrusion into the Gulf, particularly with the discovery and development of the area's oil resources, as there was then an obvious need to determine under whose territory the petroleum wealth lay. Since this occurred when Great Britain was the protecting power for all these states, the boundaries that were established bear a very considerable British imprint. If the British managed to impose a certain order in this way, they also generated sources of dispute and tension that were fully manifested as British power was withdrawn.

The three large Gulf states, Iran, Iraq, and Saudi Arabia, have asserted extensive claims against their smaller neighbors. After World War I Great Britain deliberately drew Iraq's boundaries so as to give it a small and vulnerable window on the Gulf. This has provided a major motive for its claims, at various times, to some or all of Kuwait's territory, the last of those claims being asserted in the form of invasion and occupation in 1990-91. The invasion came after the breakdown of negotiations in which Iraq had demanded that Kuwait cede two islands, Warbah and Bubiyan, and a strip of territory along their common border.

Following the 1991 Gulf conflict a UN boundary commission was established to demarcate the Iraq-Kuwait border. In August 1992 the UN Security Council voted to accept the commission's demarcation and warned the Iraqi government that it was prepared to use military force to defend the border as now defined. Iraq had already rejected the commission's findings, which moved one part of the border slightly north of the line claimed by Baghdad. The new demarcation causes Iraq to lose three oil wells in the Rumailah field, which lies on the border, and places part of Iraq's naval base at Umm Qasr in Kuwaiti territory.

Iran under the shah asserted a historical claim to Bahrain based on its earlier occupation of the island. Although the Iranian Islamic Republic apparently backed a failed coup against the government of Bahrain in 1981, the Iranian claim now appears to be in abeyance. On the eve of the United Arab Emirate's independence, however, Iran forcibly seized the Tunbs, two small islands, from Ras al-Khaimah. The new Iranian government has continued to hold them, and in March 1992, took steps toward more complete control of the island of Abu Musa, which Iran partially occupied also from 1971 through an agreement forced on its owner, Sharjah. Saudi Arabia long claimed large parts of Abu Dhabi, including the Buraimi (al-Ain) area over which it had held sway for most of the 19th century. Only in 1974, three years after the UAE's independence, was an agreement initialed, securing Abu Dhabi's hinterland while compensating Saudi Arabia with a corridor to the Gulf at Khor al-Udaid and gaining formal Saudi recognition for the new country. So sensitive has the issue been, however, that not all the details of the border agreement are public as of 1996. In March 1990 Saudi Arabia and Oman agreed on a common border across the southern portion of the *Rub al-Khali* (Empty Quarter) desert in which the Saudis abandoned longstanding claims to territory under Omani control. In November 1991 Oman and the UAE established a "joint supreme committee" to establish a mutually acceptable border between Oman and the emirates of Dubai, Fujairah, and Ras al-Khaimah. Statements issued in April 1993 appeared to indicate settlement of remaining UAE-Oman border disputes. On September 30, 1992 a clash occurred on the border between Qatar and Saudi Arabia, long one of the most stable in the area. While Qatar reacted sharply to an incursion that killed two Qatari soldiers, it later became clear that it was migrating Bedouins, not Saudi troops, who had strayed across the border. The incident served as a reminder of how easily disputes may occur along inadequately marked frontiers; the 1965 treaty that established the Saudi-Qatari border was never clearly demarcated. The issue began to move seriously toward resolution only in 1996.

Numerous border disputes among the small Gulf states themselves remain unresolved. These extend to the individual members of the UAE. While the armed clashes that occurred between Fujairah and Sharjah and Ras al-Khaimah in the early 1970s have not recurred, the disagreements over demarcation of boundaries that caused them have not yet been settled. The most nettlesome continuing border dispute is that between Bahrain and Qatar, dating back to the 18th century when the Al Khalifa were based in the Qatari peninsula prior to their capture of Bahrain. The Al Khalifa have not relinquished the claim to Zubarah, their ancestral home on Qatar's west coast, and to the adjacent Hawar Islands which may sit atop significant hydrocarbon deposits. In 1982 the issue deeply strained relations between the two countries and threatened the ability of the GCC to function effectively in the face of the threat from the Iran-Iraq war, when Bahrain revived the question by naming a naval vessel after the islands. In 1995 an effort to put the issue before the International Court of Justice foundered on Bahrain's objections.

Because of the rich oil and gas reserves of the Gulf seabed, the drawing of offshore boundaries has also been an important matter and source of considerable contention. Under international law the entire seabed is treated as a continental shelf. Most of the submarine boundaries have been drawn, though, as noted previously, possession of a number of islands remains in dispute. Iran has challenged Qatar's ownership of all of the undersea North Field, a vast natural gas structure.

BRITAIN. *See* UNITED KINGDOM.

BRITISH BANK OF THE MIDDLE EAST (BBME). The BBME is the former British-owned Bank of Iran and the Middle East, renamed when it ceased to operate in Iran during the Mossadeq period of the early 1950s. Established in Kuwait in 1941, in Oman by 1948, and somewhat later in the other Gulf Arab states, the BBME served mainly the financial needs of British, European, and American interests, dominating the banking scene until the independence of the Arab Gulf states and the development of indigenous banks. The BBME currently has a strong representation in Qatar and Oman.

BRITISH EAST INDIA COMPANY. The company was established in 1600 under royal charter to pursue trade with India and the Far East. In 1622 forces of the East India Company aided Persia in retaking Hormuz from its Portuguese captors and, as a reward for the company's assistance, Shah Abbas granted the right to a trading establishment at Bandar Abbas. As the company extended its sway over the Indian subcontinent, its commercial interest in the Gulf grew. British interests in the Gulf remained exclusively commercial through the 18th century, but Gulf Arab attacks on British commerce impelled the company to appeal for intervention by the Royal Navy. This naval intervention led to the establishment of the British imperium, which endured until 1971 in the Gulf.

BRITISH PETROLEUM (BP). The British Petroleum Company is one of the "Seven Sisters," the international oil company majors that dominated the world petroleum markets from just after World War I to the early 1970s. BP began as the Anglo-Persian Oil Company (APOC), formed in 1909 to exploit the Masjid-i Sulaiman oil field, the first major strike in the Gulf area. The British government acquired a majority share in the company in 1914, drawing on its Iranian production to help fuel the Royal Navy in both world wars. In 1935 its name was changed to the Anglo-Iranian Oil Company; in 1951 it was nationalized by the Mossadeq government; and in 1954, in the reorganization of foreign oil interests in Iran under the shah, it acquired its present name. The company had already turned its attention to the Arab side of the Gulf, forming a joint company with the Gulf Oil Corporation to explore and produce in Kuwait, a venture which met success following the 1938 discovery of the vast Burgan field. In 1974-75 Kuwait purchased the Kuwait Oil Company from BP and Gulf, with the former owners continuing to provide technical services and train personnel in return for payment and access to crude oil. BP has a minority interest in Qalingas, the Qatari company established to exploit that country's enormous natural gas reserves. It also holds significant shares of the Abu Dhabi Company for Onshore Oil Operations (ADCO) and the Abu Dhabi Marine Areas Operating Company (ADMA-OPCO). *See also* GULF OIL CORPORATION, KUWAIT, *and* OIL.

AL BU FALAH. The Al Bu Falah are the dominant clan, although one of the smaller subgroups, of the Bani Yas tribal confederation. The rulers of Abu Dhabi have been drawn from one of the four families in the clan, the Al Nuhayyan, for more than two centuries. *See also* ABU DHABI, BANI YAS, *and* AL NUHAYYAN.

AL BU FALASAH. The Al Bu Falasah are the dominant clan of Dubai, whose leaders have ruled the emirate since 1833. Like the Al Bu Falah, the leading tribal faction in Abu Dhabi, they are part of the Bani Yas tribal federation, but in that year seceded from Abu Dhabi and established independent control of Dubai, then a fishing village, and its hinterland. One of the co-leaders of the secession, Maktum bin Buti, established the line of succession that continues to the present and has overseen the emirate's transformation into a wealthy ministate whose affluence derives both from traditional commerce and oil. *See also* BANI YAS, DUBAI, *and* AL MAKTUM.

AL BU SAID. The Al Bu Said have been the ruling dynasty of Oman for almost two and a half centuries. In 1744, following years of civil war and Iranian intervention in Oman, the governor of Sohar in northern Oman, Ahmad bin Said, gained control of the country and shortly thereafter established his family's rule. By the late 18th century his descendants had created an impressive trading empire with territorial outposts that included enclaves in Iran and what is now Pakistan, as well as Zanzibar and coastal settlements in East Africa. The Al Bu Said, themselves members of the Ibadi branch of Islam, followed the pattern of Ibadi Muslim rule, established for a thousand years in Oman, whereby the ruler combined religious and political authority as *imam*. The dynasty, however, developed an increasingly secular character with its commercial success as reflected in both the adoption of the title *sayyid*, then *sultan*, and the transfer of the political capital from the interior, the heart of Ibadi tribal power, to Muscat on the coast, where the bulk of the population is Sunni Muslim. A series of treaties with the British beginning in 1800 secured external help against the Qawasim of Ras al-Khaimah and the Wahhabi forces of the Saudi state. By the late 18th century the Al Bu Said no longer claimed the imamate, which lapsed until it was revived in the later 19th century. Only British military support at critical junctures made possible the sultanate's survival. In 1920 the division between imamate and sultanate was made formal and an uneasy truce lasted until 1954.

In that year Sultan Said bin Taimur, with British assistance, moved against the interior to reunite Oman and Muscat. Full political control of the interior was not established until the accession of his son, the present ruler, Sultan Qabus, through a British-supported coup against his father. Qabus, who was only briefly married without issue, gives no indication of producing an heir, presumably leaving the succession to a collateral branch of the Al Bu Said. *See also* IBADIS, OMAN, QABUS BIN SAID, *and* SAID BIN TAIMUR.

BUBIYAN. A marshy, uninhabited island, 14 mi (23 km) at its widest and 27 mi (43 km) long, Bubiyan is with the smaller neighboring island of Warbah, a Kuwaiti possession, within a mile of Iraq's short Gulf coastline, where its naval base of Umm Qasr is located. Periodically, Iraq has claimed the islands, and indeed occupied them in 1973. Cession of the islands was a key Iraqi demand in the negotiations of July 1990, preceding Saddam Hussein's invasion of Kuwait on August 2.

BURAIMI/BURAIMI OASIS. The name refers specifically to a town in northern Oman, but is broadly applied to the oasis, or cluster of small oases, which it shares with several other settlements on both sides of the Oman-UAE (Abu Dhabi) border. It is the site of Tu'am, one of the oldest archaeological finds in the Gulf area, dating back to the 3rd millennium B.C. In recent history it is associated with a territorial dispute between Saudi Arabia on one side and Abu Dhabi and Oman, as represented by the British, on the other. Prospecting for oil by the Arabian American Oil Company (Aramco) in the area near Buraimi in 1949 reactivated the dispute, which had been quiescent for some time. For most of the 19th century the Saudi rulers had held the oasis, and much of the local population identified itself with the strict Saudi interpretation of Islam generally known as Wahhabism to outsiders. Although Oman and Abu Dhabi had generally controlled the area from the late 19th century, wounded Saudi feelings of injustice (more than prospects of additional oil reserves) led to an armed Saudi occupation of the oasis in 1952. An international tribunal dissolved in acrimony, and the British-officered TOL then seized Buraimi for the rulers of Oman and Abu Dhabi. After UAE independence in 1971 Saudi Arabia withheld diplomatic recognition until the matter was resolved in 1974 in discussions between King Faisal of Saudi Arabia and Shaikh Zayid, ruler of Abu Dhabi and president of the UAE. *See also* ABU DHABI, AL-AIN, *and* BORDERS AND TERRITORIAL DISPUTES.

BURGAN. *Also* AL-BURQAN. When discovered in 1938, Burgan was the world's largest known oil field. It remains the principal field in Kuwait and one of the most productive in the world.

C

CAMEL. The camel was probably first domesticated in southern Arabia, most likely in what is now Oman, in the second or third millennium B.C. Traditionally, the camel has been by far the most important domesticated animal in eastern and southern Arabia, providing a major food source (both milk and meat), the principal means of transporting goods and people, and fuel (in the form of dried dung). Today there are only a few thousand camels in the Gulf Arab states, but they retain a certain cultural and social significance. Camels are still eaten among Bedouins on special occasions, such as weddings, and camel racing is a major sport, especially in the UAE, with large amounts of money lavished on the purchase of the fleetest specimens and wagered on the outcome of races.

CARMATHIANS, *Arabic,* QARAMITA. The Carmathians were a heretical offshoot of Shia Islam, practicing a form of communistic organization. They ravaged eastern Arabia early in the 10th century A.D., after capturing Mecca.

CARTER DOCTRINE. In his January 23, 1980, State of the Union speech, U.S. President Jimmy Carter reacted to the Soviet invasion of Afghanistan, which had occurred four weeks earlier, by warning the Soviets against any incursion into the Gulf. The Carter Doctrine, as it came to be known, declared that the U.S. would regard "any attempt by any outside force to gain control of the Persian Gulf region . . . as an assault on the vital interests of the United States of America" to be countered "by any means necessary, including military force." This gave urgency to the mission of the already established Rapid Deployment Joint Task Force (RDJTF), which was designated the U.S. Central

Command (USCENTCOM) under the Reagan administration. Only Oman granted USCENTCOM access to its bases initially and, in doing so, created a degree of tension with other Gulf Arab states, especially Kuwait which advocated greater neutrality with respect to the U.S. and the USSR. The U.S. response to Iraq's August 2, 1991, invasion of Kuwait was, in a sense, based on an extension of the Carter Doctrine, reacting to the perceived threat of a regional power to control the Gulf and its oil. *See also* OMAN.

CAT (CONTRACTING AND TRADING COMPANY). CAT was established in Lebanon in 1941 and became an important oil company contractor after World War II, dominating the market in Qatar from the 1950s to the mid-1960s. Since then it has declined in importance but has left a significant mark through having trained many of the engineers of Palestinian or Arabian Peninsula origin who worked subsequently in the Gulf.

CHINA. *See* PEOPLE'S REPUBLIC OF CHINA.

CITIES. The states treated in this volume were until recently largely Bedouin societies, and at no time in the past did they develop centers of urban culture as did the Arab countries of Africa and the Fertile Crescent. Until the last few decades one could not properly speak of cities, because the largest settlements were really no more than towns. Nevertheless, the towns tended to dominate political and economic life and developed a certain degree of cosmopolitanism from being communities with longstanding ties to Asia and Africa. By contrast with most urban areas elsewhere in the Arabian Peninsula, their populations often contained nonindigenous elements such as Persians. Only a few have long histories as significant urban establishments, Manama in Bahrain and Muscat in Oman being cases in point. Other towns developed into important commercial centers in more recent times, especially during the Pax Britannica of the 19th and 20th centuries, examples being Kuwait and Dubai. Today the population of the Gulf Arab states is overwhelmingly urban; nearly 100 percent of Kuwait's population lives within a coastal conurbation, and similar concentrations have linked Dubai, Sharjah, and Ajman in the UAE and Muscat and Matrah in Oman. Almost all of the physical urban growth has occurred in the past quarter century (earlier in Kuwait, later in the lower Gulf) as oil wealth made it possible and expatriate worker immigration made it necessary. This has resulted in the sudden creation of large new cities like Abu Dhabi with over half a million people, where a quarter century earlier there had been no more than a few thousand. Moreover, there is little resemblance to traditional Arab cities since development has proceeded in accordance with the logic of late 20th century urban planning and owes little to the influence of Arab urban culture, except where this has been incorporated in architectural detail. At the same time, such features as efficient highways, well-functioning communications systems, and public parks and gardens are noteworthy. (*See also* entries on individual Gulf Arab states.)

CLIMATE. The climate of the Gulf Arab states is generally a harsh one characterized by extreme summer heat and very scanty rainfall. The "summer" is between April and November, and at its height temperatures as high as 115°F (46°C) are frequently recorded together with extreme humidity in the coastal areas. Away from the coast, where humidity is lower, temperatures are even higher. There is some variation throughout the region, with slightly moderated temperatures and a briefer period of high humidity in Kuwait as contrasted with the lower Gulf. The "winters" of the Gulf region, accounting for the remainder of the year, are pleasant, with temperatures generally ranging from the mid-50s to the mid-70s Fahrenheit (low teens to mid-twenties Celsius). In the interior, especially at higher elevations (in parts of the UAE and Oman), winter temperatures can drop to the freezing point. While aridity prevails throughout the region, with most locales not receiving more than 3-4 inches of rain as an annual average (with great fluctuation from year to year), there is significant variation between subregions. Rain-fed agriculture, however, is possible only in Oman in the Jebel al-Akhdar area and in Dhofar, where monsoon rains strike land after crossing the Indian Ocean. In recent years ambitious schemes to plant trees and shrubs, most extensively in Abu Dhabi, have coincided with somewhat wetter and more temperate conditions. Although weather modification is theoretically possible through such a "greening" of the desert, these changes are almost certainly the result of natural, short-term fluctuations occurring in the weather pattern.

Wind is a significant factor influencing the climate of the Gulf area. In June and July northerly winds, the *shamal* (also *shimal*) may be strong, generating sandstorms. At other times of the year, before or after the shamal, winds from the south, generally called *gaws*, prevail. Usually less intense, they, like the shamal, can be threatening to mariners, and both reinforce the effect of the area's heat, making desiccation even more intense.

COMMUNICATIONS. *See* NEWS MEDIA.

COMPAGNIE FRANÇAISE DES PETROLES (CFP). CFP is one of the major international oil companies. It has been a significant concessionaire and producer in the Gulf area as a result of its acquisition in 1925 of a 23.75 percent share in the former Iraq Petroleum Company. CFP has shares in the Abu Dhabi National Oil Company (ADNOC), Qalingas (Qatar's gas exploration and production company), and Petroleum Development Oman.

CONSTITUTIONS. Bahrain, Kuwait, Qatar, and the United Arab Emirates have adopted written constitutions. While Oman has not done so, its creation of a consultative council implies a constitutional arrangement between ruler and people. Constitutions were introduced only with political independence in recent years and represent an essentially Western notion of an explicit contract between ruler and ruled. This contrasts with the implied relationship between political authority and subjects reflected in Islamic law, the *Sharia*, which embodies the concept of sovereignty resting with God (Allah) rather than with the people. Each constitution affirms the position of the ruling family and makes Islam the official religion, while introducing the concepts of separation of powers and representative government. Kuwait's constitution entered into force in 1962 and, while not challenging the hereditary status of the Al Sabah, went further than the constitutions subsequently adopted elsewhere in qualifying the ruler's authority. The Kuwaiti constitution stipulated that the emir would share legislative power with a national assembly. Indeed, the latter could overrule the emir's veto. Bahrain's constitution, adopted in 1973, was patterned after Kuwait's, also establishing separation of executive, legislative, and judicial powers and shared legislative authority between ruler and national assembly. In the case of Bahrain the assembly met for only a few months before being suspended and has not been reconvened, while the Kuwaiti Parliament has twice been suspended, most recently being reelected in October 1992. Qatar adopted a provisional constitution in April 1970 that remains in effect. The document provides for a consultative council that can debate draft laws and budgets and question ministers, but legislative as well as executive power is effectively vested in the emir. At independence in December 1971 the UAE adopted a provisional constitution that became permanent in 1996. With minor changes, it is the document drafted in 1970 for a nine-member federated state that was to have included Bahrain and Qatar as well as the seven members of the UAE. The UAE constitution assures very extensive powers to the members of the federation, making them, in effect, self-ruled entities. *See also* LAW.

CONSULTATIVE COUNCIL. In some of the Gulf Arab states consultative councils have been established, echoing the concept of the traditional *majlis*, where a ruler received petitions and advice from subjects, and represent a modest step toward modern representative government. These may be understood to include Oman's State Consultative Council, Qatar's Advisory Council, and the United Arab Emirates' FNC. In all cases members are appointed or confirmed by rulers with a view to representing the significant constituencies in the state. While their powers are only advisory, their views and and opinions are seriously heeded and help to shape state policy. *See also* MAJLIS *and* entries on individual states.

COUNCIL OF MINISTERS. Apart from Kuwait, which has a cabinet of ministers sharing executive power with the ruler and a national assembly with real legislative powers, councils of ministers serve as instruments of both executive and legislative power in the Gulf Arab states. In Bahrain, since the suspension of the National Assembly in 1975, the Council of Ministers has assumed that body's legislative powers. Oman's Council of Ministers serves as the principal executive body, prepares draft legislation for the sultan, in whom both ultimate executive and legislative power are vested, and oversees government policies and programs. The corresponding body in Qatar is described in that state's constitution as "the highest executive organ of the State." It assists the ruler as executive and recommends to him laws that he promulgates. In the case of the UAE, the Council of Ministers is a federal cabinet, headed by a prime minister, where most federal laws are initiated pending discussion in the Federal National Council and approval and ratification in the Supreme Federal Council. The Council of Ministers is also charged with general oversight of the nation's domestic and external affairs.

COUNCIL OF NATIONAL UNITY. The council, also called the Committee for National Unity, was established in 1956 by the ruler of Bahrain, Shaikh Salman, following a period of unrest on the island that began with Shia-Sunni riots in 1953. It represented an attempt to give voice to political dissent without threatening the authority of the ruler. However, a protest organized by the CNU against the French and British, following the Anglo-French-Israeli invasion of Egypt in October-November 1956, turned violent and led to the council's dissolution and the arrest and banishment of its leaders. The next experiment in popular political representation did not occur until the election of a national assembly in 1973, two years after independence. *See also* BAHRAIN *and* NATIONAL ASSEMBLY.

COUNCIL OF RULERS. In 1952 Great Britain created the Council of Rulers as a mechanism bringing together the emirs of the seven Trucial States for consultation on issues of interest to all of them. In the two decades preceding the creation of the United Arab Emirates the council's deliberations helped to produce useful habits of working together on common problems. The same name is sometimes used to refer to the present grouping of the rulers of the UAE's member states.

COURTS. *See* LAW.

COX, SIR PERCY (1864-1937). Cox was an extremely able and energetic British official who played an important part in the affairs of the Gulf before and after World War I. From 1899 to 1904 he was British Agent in Muscat, where he was active in solidifying British-Omani relations. As British Resident or senior representative in the Gulf from 1904 to 1913, his principal concern was with events in central Arabia, where the Saudi and Rashidi clans were contending for supremacy. As British High Commissioner in mandate Iraq after World War, I he played the key role in settling the Iraqi-Saudi and Kuwaiti-Saudi boundaries. *See also* SAUDI ARABIA.

CRIME. Both petty and serious crime have been virtually unknown in recent history in the Gulf Arab states, in part because of the severe punishments prescribed by the *Sharia* or Islamic law, but more generally because of the cohesion of their conservative Islamic society and the strength of its behavioral norms. This has begun to change somewhat under the impact of large populations of expatriate workers and new tastes and modes of behavior that they have helped to introduce. Particularly in the United Arab Emirates there has been a growing incidence of crime, including drug dealing, theft, and occasional rapes and murders, within the largely male expatriate population, which accounts for upward of 80 percent of the total population. While statistics are not available, the crime rate is almost certainly a small fraction of that in the United States and most European countries. Nevertheless, it is a disturbing new phenomenon for the Gulf Arab states and symptomatic of potent, socially disruptive forces whose impact will grow. *See also* LAW.

CURRENCY. Reflecting the role of the (British) Government of India in the affairs of the Gulf Arab states, the currency generally in circulation from the begining of the 20th century until well after India's independence was the Indian rupee. Kuwait introduced its own currency, the Kuwaiti dinar, when it became independent in 1961. Bahrain followed suit in 1965, replacing the rupee with its own dinar. Qatar and the emirate of Dubai jointly issued a currency in riyals beginning in 1966, which, together with the Bahraini dinar, circulated in the Trucial States. It was only in 1978 that this arrangement was superseded, when the currency boards of Qatar and the UAE began issuing national currencies denominated in riyals and dirhams, respectively. Backed by considerable bank reserves and reflecting strong economies, the Gulf Arab state currencies are strong and stable. Those of Qatar, the UAE, and Oman are pegged, formally or practically, to the U.S. dollar.

CURZON, LORD GEORGE NATHANIEL (1859–1925). Lord Curzon (born into the nobility, he was made an earl and, later, a marquess) served as viceroy of India from 1898 to 1905. The embodiment of imperial hauteur, he grandly described British domination of the Gulf as "the most unselfish page in history." In another context, however, he asserted that continued British control of India depended on maintaining British supremacy in the Gulf. Curzon was the first senior British official to view the Gulf as a unit and to pursue British interests there in that light.

D

DARWISH. A leading Qatari merchant family of Iranian origin, the Darwish fortune dates to the 1930s when Abdullah Darwish became the local agent of the Anglo-Iranian Oil Company (AIOC), then exploring in Qatar, and formed a close business relationship with Hamad ibn Abdullah Al Thani, the second son of the ruler. In the 1950s and 1960s, when Abdullah was the ruler's petroleum representative, the family company dominated the construction market in Qatar and, indeed, exercised a controlling influence over the government during the rule of Ali ibn Abdullah Al Thani. After the seizure of power by Shaikh Khalifa, younger brother of Ali, who was less well disposed to the Darwish, their business declined. While no longer dominant in Qatar, the Darwish family business interests remain significant.

DAS ISLAND. Das is an island of about one square mile located approximately 70 mi (113 km) off the coast of western Abu Dhabi. Formerly uninhabited, it was selected in 1955 as the base of operations for the Abu Dhabi Marine Areas Operating Company (ADMA-OPCO). Abu Dhabi's first crude oil exports were shipped from Das in 1962. On the island some 4,000 oil company personnel oversee a complex of gathering facilities that brings in crude oil from three offshore fields, Umm Shayf, Zakum, and Bunduq (jointly owned with Qatar). From 1977 Das has also received gas from offshore fields, converting it to liquefied natural gas (LNG) for export.

DATES. Evidence suggests that the date palm was first domesticated about 4000 B.C. in the Arabian Peninsula. Traditionally, dates have been the most important agricultural crop in the Gulf Arab states. Their extremely high nutritional value makes them a principal source of nourishment, either fresh or preserved. Other parts of the date palm have served numerous important uses. The pits of the fruit were a major source of fodder for camels; from the fronds a variety of household implements were fashioned, as were the barasti huts in which many townspeople lived; and the trunks provided beams for the construction of more substantial houses. The wood was also used as a fuel. Date cultivation is less important today than formerly but remains significant, especially in the United Arab Emirates and Bahrain.

DEFENSE. *See* ARMED FORCES.

DEIRA. *Also* DAIRA *and* DAYRA. Deira is that part of the city of Dubai that lies on the east bank of the creek that divides the city into rough halves, with Dubai proper on the west side. The two sides of the creek, Dubai's traditional harbor, are now joined by two bridges, a tunnel, and water taxis known as *abras*. Dubai's *suq*, the principal shopping area generally regarded as the city's center, is located in Deira as are most of the major hotels and commercial offices.

DESALINATION. All the Gulf Arab states depend heavily on desalted water for drinking and, with the exception of Oman, for agricultural and industrial use as well. Kuwait, with the most acute shortage of natural fresh water, has been a pioneer in developing large-scale desalination plants, generally run by locally produced gas, sometimes in conjunction with the generation of electric power.

DESERT SHIELD/DESERT STORM. Operations Desert Shield and Desert Storm were the American names for the buildup of allied armed forces in the Gulf-Arabian Peninsula region following Iraq's August 2, 1990, invasion of Kuwait and for the military offensive of January 17-February 28, 1991, which liberated that country. On the day of Iraq's invasion President Bush reacted with the imposition of economic sanctions against Iraq, but stated initially that there was no intention to intervene militarily. Later that day, following a previously scheduled meeting with British prime minister Margaret Thatcher, the position was changed to one of keeping options open. Also on the first day of the crisis the UN Security Council voted 14 to 0 (with Yemen abstaining) to impose mandatory economic sanctions against Iraq if it did not immediately withdraw from Kuwait. On August 6 the council imposed sanctions (with Yemen and Cuba abstaining). On that same day, King Fahd of Saudi Arabia, following a meeting with U.S. secretary of defense Dick Cheney, requested the stationing of U.S. forces in Saudi Arabia to guard against a possible Iraqi attack, following the massing of Iraqi troops on the Saudi border. The Saudi request for non-Muslim military forces to be placed on its soil to protect the kingdom was altogether unprecedented. It paved the way for the massive American and allied buildup of forces in Saudi Arabia, continuing until the following January. At the same time, the UN Security Council Established the basis for a strategy of forcing Iraq from Kuwait through the application of economic sanctions. President Bush and Secretary of State Baker skillfully orchestrated the structuring and maintenance of the anti-Iraq coalition to make credible the military card and allow it to be played if and when it were agreed to be necessary. In this they enjoyed the great advantage of an inept and clumsy opponent in the person of President Saddam Hussein of Iraq, whose brutalization of Kuwait, seizure of Western hostages, and unwillingness to contemplate compromise positions, for example withdrawal from Kuwait in exchange for border readjustments, helped to hold the allies together and force a military showdown that he could not win.

Events continued to move rapidly in the days immediately following the Iraqi invasion. On August 8 Iraq annexed Kuwait, the UN Security Council unanimously declared the annexation null and void, and President Bush portrayed U.S. policy in the Gulf crisis as based on "four simple principles," complete and unconditional Iraqi withdrawal from Kuwait, restoration of Kuwait's legitimate government, Gulf security and stability, and protection of Americans abroad. On the same day deployment of U.S. air and naval forces, ordered the evening of August 6, was formally announced. On August 10 the Arab League voted to commit troops to the defense of Saudi Arabia. Twelve states voted for the resolution; Iraq, Libya, and the PLO opposed it; Jordan, Sudan, and Mauritania voted for it with reservations; Algeria and Yemen abstained; and Tunisia was absent. A few days later the U.S. sought to put teeth into the UN sanctions by imposing a blockade on August 16 (implementing a presidential order of August 12) to interdict ships going to or from Iraq with commercial or military cargoes. (The British government had already taken similar action.) While this initially drew criticism from UN secretary general Perez de Cuellar and the French, Soviet, and Chinese governments, on August 5 the Security Council voted 13 to 0 (with Yemen and Cuba abstaining) to permit allied ships to use force in ensuring compliance with the sanctions.

Financial contributions were a key factor in implementing Operations Desert Shield/Desert Storm. On September 6, 1990, Saudi Arabia pledged some $500 million a month to help cover the costs of U.S. military deployments and Shaikh Jabir, emir of Kuwait, pledged $2.5 billion to defray expenses of U.S. military operations in the Gulf region through the remainder of the year. Germany and Japan, which for constitutional and political reasons had refused to contribute military resources, pledged financial assistance as well. On September 14 Japan promised $3 billion in addition to an earlier $1 billion commitment, and on September 15 the German government announced a $2 billion aid pledge. Each made additional pledges to support the war effort in late January 1991, after military operations had begun. Premier Kaifu of Japan promised the contribution of an additional $9 billion to the Gulf war effort and Germany another $2.5 billion.

Soviet cooperation was secured when President Bush and Soviet president Mikhail Gorbachev met in Helsinki on September 9, issuing a joint statement condemning the Iraqi invasion of Kuwait and calling for the Soviet Union to play a major role in the Arab-Israeli peace process. Generally, Soviet policy continued to support the anti-Iraq coalition, though during hostilities Moscow tried to play an independent peacemaking role. Two days later Bush sought to secure his domestic flank by speaking to Congress about the importance of preventing Iraqi domination of Gulf oil reserves and reiterating that military action might be necessary if economic sanctions did not have their intended effect. Most Democrats continued to press for sustaining economic sanctions rather than resorting to arms, but on November 29, following heavy U.S. lobbying, the UN Security Council voted 12-2 to authorize coalition forces to use "all necessary means" to expel Iraq from Kuwait if it did not withdraw by January 15. (Yemen and Cuba were opposed and China, which could have exercised a veto, abstained instead.) On January 12 a reluctant Congress gave the president authority to use military force against Iraq, the Senate by a vote of 52 to 47 and the House by 250 to 183.

Through the fall and early winter the massive deployment of U.S. and other coalition forces had continued. By early November over 200,000 U.S. troops had been deployed, together with significant numbers from other allies in the anti-Iraq coalition. On November 8 President Bush announced that the number of U.S. personnel would be essentially doubled to 430,000. The other major non-Arab troop deployments were those of Great Britain with 35,000 and France with 17,000. They and other European and Third World countries contributed aircraft, ships, tanks, and other materiel. Saudi Arabia committed 20,000 troops to the front lines, while its five GCC partners joined with it in committing a combined 10,000-man force. Egypt deployed 30,000 troops to Saudi Arabia and Syria 19,000 (with another 50,000 on the Syrian-Iraqi border). With the passing of the January 15 deadline for Iraqi withdrawal from Kuwait, the allied forces commenced air operations against Iraq on the early morning of January 17 (local time). After more than five weeks of intensive air strikes against targets in

Iraq and occupied Kuwait, a ground attack was launched on February 24, leading to a crushing Iraqi defeat with acceptance of a cease-fire on February 28. The brief duration of military operations helped to avert anti-Western popular Arab demonstrations on the scale many had predicted. Saudi sensitivities had been addressed in a US-Saudi military command agreement on November 5, 1990, which stipulated that Saudi Arabia would be in overall command of the defense of its territory while the U.S. would be in overall command of an offensive against Iraq, and any such attack would have to be approved by both countries. Since U.S. and other Western forces, including significant numbers of female personnel, were overwhelmingly deployed away from population centers, their presence gave less offense to conservative Muslim sensibilities than some had feared.

On February 6, 1991 Secretary of State James Baker outlined five Bush administration postwar goals: a new security arrangement among the Gulf states; an arms control agreement to check Iraq's ability to restart its nuclear, biological, and chemical weapons programs; an economic reconstruction program between poor and wealthy Middle East countries; a renewed effort to promote Arab-Israeli peace; and reduction of U.S. dependence on imported oil. More than five years after the conclusion of Operation Desert Shield/Desert Storm only two of those goals had been met. Iraq's weapons of mass destruction, its chemical and biological weapons and production facilities, and nuclear facilities that could be used for future weapons development were being destroyed under UN supervision in accordance with the cease-fire agreement, although Saddam Hussein remained in power and prevention of future Iraqi development of such weapons could not be assured. Peace talks between Israel and the Arabs were initiated and, on September 13, 1993, resulted in an Israel-PLO agreement to establish Palestinian self-rule in Gaza and Jericho as the first step toward self-rule throughout the occupied territories. The other three goals that the secretary had enunciated appeared beyond reach, for the moment. Nevertheless, a major war aim of the Bush administration, namely progress toward more representative government in the Gulf Arab states, appeared to have begun with the October 5, 1992, election of the Kuwait National Assembly and with modest expansion of the scope of consultative councils elsewhere. Finally, the original political and security goals of the military operation, that is liberation of Kuwait and the prevention of Iraqi control, either direct or indirect, of the oil of Saudi Arabia and the other Gulf Arab states, were accomplished. In

October 1994 Iraq made menacing moves toward Kuwait, drawing a rapid U.S. response. Within days over 60,000 troops and hundreds of aircraft were sent to the Gulf. Iraq pulled back its troops. *See also* ARMED FORCES, KUWAIT, SAUDI ARABIA, *and* UNITED STATES.

DESERTS. All of the Gulf Arab states lie in the geographical zone that includes the Sahara and whose climate is dominated by a subtropical high-pressure belt of hot air. Only a few, small areas in parts of Oman and the UAE receive more than 3 to 4 in (8 to 20 cm) average annual rainfall, the rest of the land is desert or semidesert. Contrasting varieties of desert landscape are found, including the generally flat coastal *dikaka* and its *sabkhas* or salt flats, gravel plains, and the great dunes of the *Rub al-Khali*, or Empty Quarter, the world's largest sand desert, which extends across southern Saudi Arabia into Oman and the UAE. Plant growth is scanty, although hardy species such as the acacia tree and some sedges thrive, supporting a population of wildlife now significantly reduced through excessive hunting.

DHAFRAH. The *Dhafrah* is an area comprising a large part of the western interior of Abu Dhabi. For at least three centuries it has been a significant part of the domain of the Bani Yas, Abu Dhabi's dominant tribal confederation, and their Manasir tribal allies.

DHAHIRAH. *Also* ZAHIRAH. The *Dhahirah* is the large plain in the west of the Hajar Mountains, the "back" in Arabic, which is divided by the mountains from the narrow *Batinah* or "belly" on the mountains' eastern flank facing the Gulf of Oman.

DHAID. *Also* DHAYD. Dhaid, located in the emirate of Sharjah, is one of the major towns in the interior of the UAE. It is an oasis settlement traditionally significant because of its agricultural production.

DHAWAHIR. A group of 15 subtribes near Al-Ain, the *Dhawahir* (whose identity derives from the *Dhahirah* area) have been closely allied to the dominant Bani Yas of Abu Dhabi for over a century. They are now largely settled, beneficiaries of Abu Dhabi's oil wealth.

DHAYD. *See* DHAID.

DHOFAR. *Also* DHUFAR. Dhofar is the southernmost part of Oman and is one of two areas in that country (the other being the Musandam Peninsula) organized as a province and administered by a governor. This reflects Dhofar's distinctly different character from the other regions of Oman. It consists of a coastal plain and rugged, mountainous terrain in the interior that receive monsoon winds and rains from South Asia. In this cooler, moister climate crops such as coconuts and bananas are produced, and significant herds of cattle have been introduced in recent years. The region's distinctiveness extends to its people, numbering perhaps 50,000, many of whom speak a tongue of ancient South Arabian origin, closely related to Arabic from which it has significantly borrowed. The Al Bu Said rulers asserted their claim to Dhofar in the 1820s, with effective control established in the late 19th century, although at some later times authority was largely confined to the provincial capital of Salalah and the nearby coastal area. Several of Oman's oil fields are in Dhofar, and Sultan Qabus, whose mother was a Dhofari and who spent much of his early life in Salalah, has vigorously pressed the economic and social development of this part of the sultanate, following the defeat of the separatist Dhofar Liberation Front in the mid-1970s. *See also* DHOFAR LIBERATION FRONT, OMAN, POPULAR FRONT FOR THE LIBERATION OF THE OCCUPIED ARAB GULF, POPULAR FRONT FOR THE LIBERATION OF OMAN, POPULAR FRONT FOR THE LIBERATION OF OMAN AND THE ARAB GULF, *and* SALALAH.

DHOFAR LIBERATION FRONT (DLF). The DLF was established in 1965 by Dhofaris opposed to the oppressive rule of Sultan Said bin Taimur. The front mainly comprised tribal separatists but, with the active support of the independent, Marxist state in neighboring South Yemen from 1969, the movement came under radical leftist leadership. External support from Arab nationalists was largely supplanted by money, weapons, and training from the Soviet Union, the People's Republic of China, and other Communist states. A corresponding enlargement of the movement's territorial goals caused it to be renamed the Popular Front for the Liberation of the Occupied Arab Gulf (PFLOAG). (Confusingly, the same acronym represents a later alteration of the name to Popular Front for the Liberation of Oman and the Arab Gulf.) By 1970 the front controlled most of Dhofar, and Sultan Said, who had responded to the threat with further repression rather than urgently needed economic development, was overthrown by his son, Qabus, acting in concert with British advisers. Qabus pressed an effective strategy of combined military, political, and economic initiatives carried out with the assistance of several interested neighbors, including Saudi Arabia, Iran, and Jordan, as well as Britain, which supplied both seconded and contract military personnel. By 1974 the impact of the counteroffensive was reflected in the rebels' adoption of the more modest designation of Popular Front for the Liberation of Oman (PFLO) and by 1975 Dhofar had been effectively pacified. Qabus has lavished large amounts of investment in Dhofar and gone far toward integrating it effectively for the first time with the rest of the country. *See also* DHOFAR, OMAN, POPULAR FRONT FOR THE LIBERATION OF THE OCCUPIED ARAB GULF, POPULAR FRONT FOR THE LIBERATION OF OMAN, and POPULAR FRONT FOR THE LIBERATION OF OMAN AND THE ARAB GULF, *and* SALALAH.

DHOW. The term (of Swahili origin) applies to ships of traditional design, built of imported teak and rigged with a (triangular) lateen sail. In the heyday of Gulf Arab commerce, between the eighth and 15th centuries, these vessels regularly carried goods to and from ports as far away as China. Now outfitted with powerful engines, they still play an important role in intra-Gulf trade. During the Iran-Iraq war such vessels, largely from Dubai, carried on lucrative smuggling across the Gulf. *See also* BAGGALA, BOOM, JALBOOT, *and* SAMBOOK.

DHUFAR. *See* DHOFAR.

DIBBA. Dibba is a major town on the eastern side of the Musandam Peninsula, facing the Gulf of Oman. Its fine natural harbor helped to make it a leading seaport in ancient times. The rejection of Islam in southeastern Arabia after the Prophet Muhammad's death brought Islamic armies into the area, and their triumph in a climactic battle fought at Dibba assured Islam's sway. Situated at the point where the emirates of Sharjah and Fujairah and the small, northern exclave of Oman all meet, Dibba has three divisions, Dibba Hisn in Sharjah, Dibba Muhallab in Fujairah, and Dibba Bayah in Oman.

DICKSON, H. R. P. (1881–1959). Dickson served as a political officer of the British government for two decades in Iraq and the Gulf, during World War I and afterward. His name is most closely associated with

Kuwait, where he was principal local representative of the Kuwait Oil Company after retirement from government service in 1936. He wrote two books about Kuwait and its surroundings, *The Arab of the Desert* and *Kuwait and Her Neighbors*. The first remains a minor classic.

DIGDAGA. *Also* DIQDAQAH. Digdaga is the site of an important agricultural trials station in Ras al-Khaimah in the UAE, where several varieties of fruits and vegetables have been successfully cultivated and a dairy herd established.

DILMUN. Dilmun is the name of an ancient indigenous civilization in eastern Arabia and its principal settlement in Bahrain, which developed in the beginning of the third millennium B.C. Dilmun's prosperity was based on commerce, which linked it to the Sumerian culture to the north and the Indus civilization to the east. The location of Dilmun in Bahrain was established by a Danish archaeological expedition in the 1950s. Extensive investigation of other sites in Kuwait, Saudi Arabia, Qatar, and the UAE has revealed the extent of the trading civilization based on Dilmun.

DIRAH. A *dirah* is the range within which a tribe maintains its grazing rights. Control of wells and access to vegetation for camels and other livestock are of paramount importance in establishing the limits of a dirah. The concept of precisely drawn boundaries and actual ownership, as opposed to control of territory, is an innovation of European origin in the Gulf Arab states. *See also* BORDERS AND TERRITORIAL DISPUTES *and* TRIBES.

DIWAN. The term *diwan* generally describes a traditional administrative structure of government in Middle Eastern states. In the Gulf Arab emirates it has comprised a body of advisers appointed from dominant elements of society by the ruler to assist him in the exercise of authority. Despite the evolution of more modern structures of government, the diwan still plays a significant role in the political life of the Gulf Arab states.

DOHA. Doha is the capital and largest city of Qatar, situated roughly half way up the east side of the Qatari Peninsula. One meaning of this Arabic word is "branch," which here refers to the inlet from the Gulf around which the town grew up. Before the advent of oil wealth in the

late 1940s, it was a fishing port with a few thousand inhabitants. With
its suburbs, Doha is now a modern, planned city of a quarter million or
more, over half of Qatar's total population. Its general plan follows that
of Kuwait City, with concentric roadways marking the city's growth
outward.

DRESS. The dress of Gulf Arab men and women remains largely
traditional, with the style of garments determined both by practical
dictates of a harsh climate and considerations of Islamic modesty,
conservatively defined. The principal exceptions are to be found in
industrial or military settings, where utility and safety require specific
forms of modern garb. Men and boys generally wear the *thobe* (*thawb*),
a loose-fitting cloak, or a similar garment called a *dishdasha*, with
sleeves and buttons up to the neck. In cool weather a *bisht*, a cloak of
wool or camel's hair, may be worn, especially by men of elevated social
standing. On the head a square cloth generally called a *ghutra* is worn
folded and secured with the ropelike *iqal* (or *igal*). (Somewhat
confusingly, in other parts of the Arab world the ghutra is referred to as
a *kuffiyah* [also *kaffiyeh*], which in the Gulf refers to the skullcap worn
under the head cloth.) In Oman the ghutra is generally wound like a
turban and worn without the iqal.

While young girls now often wear Western-style dresses, from
puberty onward they are usually fully covered in public with a layer of
clothing that begins with the pajamalike *sirwal*. Over that is worn the
kandura, a loose dress, then a thobe, and finally an *abaya,* a large,
black cloak covering the wearer from head to feet. Frequently, women
may wear Western-style dress under an abaya when in public. Veiling
of women is common in the Gulf Arab states, although in Kuwait and
Bahrain it is increasingly less practiced. In parts of Qatar, the UAE, and
Oman, the *burqa*, a rigid mask, rather than an actual veil, is worn.

DUBAI. The name Dubai refers to the emirate, second to Abu Dhabi in
area, population, and wealth in the UAE, and to the capital city in which
the great bulk of the emirate's population resides, and to the principal
section of the city on the west side of the creek that forms the old
harbor.

The modern history of Dubai dates from 1833, when the Al Bu
Falasah subsection of the Bani Yas occupied a small village on that site
and declared themselves independent of Abu Dhabi. From that point the
hitherto insignificant settlement of Dubai developed under its Maktum

rulers into an important trading and pearling center. In the late 19th century and early 20th century the town grew into a major commercial center where numerous Persian, Baluchi, and Indian merchants settled, lending Dubai a less tribal and much more cosmopolitan character than its rival and former master, Abu Dhabi. Prosperity in part reflected good fortune in the possession of the best natural harbor on the Arab side of the lower Gulf and the capture of the considerable entrepôt trade relinquished by Iranian ports when their government imposed high import/export duties in 1902. At the turn of the century, Dubai was a community of several thousand people. The continuation of an enlightened laissez-faire ethos has served the emirate well. As early as 1938-39 a reform movement, directed against then-ruler Said Al Maktum, called for more open government, schools, and various social services. The political pretensions of the reformers were defeated, but subsequently under Said's son, Rashid, the essence of the reforms was realized, promoting Dubai's further orderly development. With the added income from oil after the 1960s, Dubai launched a number of ambitious ventures such as the Gulf's largest drydock, the international trade center, and the new Jebel Ali port and industrial zone. Despite widespread predictions that these would be ambitious failures, all have proven successful. Dubai is the Gulf's most important trading entrepôt and its airport the busiest in the Middle East. The success of its recently established international airline, Emirates Air, reflects its continuing spirit of enterprise.

To the present day Dubai and Abu Dhabi remain rivals. As recently as 1948 a Dubai raiding party killed 52 men on the Abu Dhabi side of a conflict over the emirates' joint border. That issue is now essentially resolved, but differences over the nature of the UAE federation, which they both dominate, continue. From the UAE's inception in 1971 Dubai under Rashid favored a loose structure that would leave to each emirate very substantial autonomy. Dubai, in fact, largely succeeded, since Zayid bin Sultan Al Nuhayyan of Abu Dhabi, as UAE president deferred on several crucial issues, effectively granting Dubai parity within the federation, despite its much smaller size and slighter resources, in order to ensure the UAE's survival. Crises arose in 1976 and 1979 over attempts to promote a stronger central government. Nevertheless, as in 1968, when the two emirates came together to promote the idea of a federation, Dubai and Abu Dhabi submerged their differences sufficiently to surmount the threat of dissolution. At the same time, the different character of the two remains, one sophisticated and business-oriented, the other traditional and tribal in its outlook, and the rivalry persists. With the death of Rashid in 1990 and Zayid's fairly advanced age (in his late 70s, and older by some accounts), there is reason for some concern, as the quality of leadership in each emirate will almost inevitably decline with the passing of the patriarchs. Thus far, however, Dubai has appeared to be well served by the leadership provided by Rashid's eldest son and successor, Maktum, who has worked closely with his brothers, Muhammad, Hamdan, and Ahmed to continue with the successful policies of their father. The long, disabling illness of Rashid from 1981 meant that the sons had, in effect, governed on their own for almost a decade before his death. *See also* ABU DHABI, RASHID BIN SAID AL MAKTUM, UNITED ARAB EMIRATES, *and* ZAYID BIN SULTAN AL NUHAYYAN.

DUBAI ALUMINUM COMPANY (DUBAL). DUBAL was established in 1979 at the Jebel Ali industrial port using, like its rival ALBA, imported raw materials and management expertise. It has a capacity of 245,000 tons and exports 95 percent of its production. It is run by natural gas produced by the Dubai Gas Company (DUGAS). After a shaky start, DUBAL has provided profits as well as large quantities of heat for use in a major desalination facility, which produces 30 million gallons of water per day.

DUGONG. The dugong is a marine mammal, closely related to the North American manatee, which was a significant Gulf food source in ancient times. Recent counts have indicated a population of about 7,000 in the Gulf, though several hundred are known to have perished from the 1983 oil slick generated by military action in the Iran-Iraq war, and there were further losses from the much more massive oil spill that occurred during the 1990-91 Gulf crisis, the result mostly of deliberate Iraqi action.

DUTCH EAST INDIA COMPANY. A trading company founded in 1602, the Dutch East India Company was armed with extensive military and political authority by the state to advance the Dutch Republic's imperial ambitions. It contended with the British East India Company for ascendancy in the Gulf through most of the 18th century, after the two had cooperated in ending the Portuguese imperium in the Gulf.

E

EDUCATION. Up to the very recent past, education in the Gulf Arab states, aside from the imparting of practical skills, meant almost exclusively Quranic instruction, conducted in schools called *kuttabs*, where elementary reading and writing skills were taught. Higher scholarship was confined to study of the *Sharia*, the corpus of Islamic law. This was pragmatically inspired by the need to educate *qadis*, or "judges," to interpret and apply the law. Girls sometimes attended the kuttabs and also were taught what was necessary to carry out household duties.

In the past few decades no changes have been more dramatic than those made in education. Today each of the Gulf Arab states offers free public education to its nationals and, generally, the children of other residents as well. The great majority of school-age boys and girls are being educated, and large numbers continue their studies through college and beyond, both at the new national universities in each country and overseas.

Bahrain and Kuwait were the first Gulf Arab states to establish modern schools. In the former, Western missionaries opened private schools for both boys and girls in 1905, and in the latter, in 1912, merchants set up a school called Al-Mubarakiyya to teach clerical skills. By 1921 Bahrain had its first modern public school, in 1937 its first technical school, and had secondary schools for boys and girls by 1940 and 1950, respectively. In 1936 Palestinian teachers, shortly joined by other Arabs, opened public secondary schools in Kuwait, and by 1937 girls' education had begun. In Qatar the first elementary school for boys was opened in 1952, that for girls in 1955. Secondary education for both followed shortly. Sharjah was the site of the first successful modern school in the Trucial States (later the United Arab Emirates) in 1953, established by the British and run by the Kuwaitis. Initially, Kuwait and subsequently Egypt played leading roles in helping to establish a system of education in the preindependence period of the UAE. In Dubai strong emphasis was placed on technical education from the 1950s on. In Oman there were only three boys' schools before 1970, reflecting the generally reactionary outlook of Sultan Said bin Taimur. Since then, under Sultan Qabus, expansion of public education has been, as elsewhere in the Gulf Arab states, extremely rapid. Primary and secondary education in all these states are free to all students and generally compulsory for nationals. Their quality has improved significantly in the past few years. The general aim of creating a literate population (in addition to Arabic, English is widely taught) has not yet been fully met. According to recent U.S. State Department estimates, adult literacy rates for native populations were 74 percent in Bahrain, 71 percent in Kuwait, 65 percent in Qatar, 60 percent in the UAE, and about 20 percent (other estimates are significantly higher) in Oman.

In higher education Kuwait and Bahrain have also led the way. Kuwait University opened in 1966; by the late 1980s its enrollment had grown to over 18,000, of which 25 percent were non-Kuwaiti. The university facilities were severely damaged during the Iraqi occupation of Kuwait from August 1990 to February 1991, but by 1993 operations were back to normal. In 1968 Bahrain opened both Gulf Technical College and Gulf Polytechnic. The latter merged in the mid-1980s with the University College of Bahrain (established in 1979) to form the University of Bahrain, with a current enrollment of over 4,000. Bahrain was also the site of the Arabian Gulf University, envisioned as an institution in which graduate students from all the Gulf Arab states would enroll, to avoid costly duplication of facilities. An attractive campus with colleges of medicine, applied sciences, and education was established and operated briefly with a small student enrollment. The university is not currently operating, however, because of the failure of the GCC states to contribute their shares of financial support. It has, for the meantime at least, been absorbed by the University of Bahrain.

In Qatar separate colleges of education for men and women, established in 1973, merged in 1977 to form the University of Qatar, with over 5,000 students. The UAE opened its National University in 1977, with about 8,000 students currently enrolled. An independent university was established in the emirate of Ajman from which the first class graduated in June 1992. A university emphasizing the arts and humanities is currently being started in the emirate of Dubai. Oman launched the Sultan Qabus University in 1986, which is now attended by about 1,000 students. The national universities are state-controlled institutions. While the University of Bahrain is described as being autonomously controlled, the minister of education chairs its board of trustees. In Qatar the ruler is the university's "supreme head," and the chancellor of the UAE's university is a member of the ruling family of Abu Dhabi. The universities are largely modeled on the American system with fairly diversified curricula, except in the case of Oman's very new university. Arabic is the principal language of instruction, with English generally the medium for courses in the physical sciences. Faculty members are largely drawn from other countries, mostly Arab, with Egyptians very strongly represented. Many have degrees from U.S. universities. The student body in each university is about evenly divided between men and women. Foreign enrollment is significant in Kuwait and the UAE, where it is about 25 percent of the total, with Palestinians (at least until the Gulf crisis of 1990-91) forming the largest group among the non-nationals. The establishment of local universities has reduced the numbers of students going overseas for their higher education. However, many continue to do so, especially for graduate studies, with the United States the most popular destination and Great Britain and Egypt following. Academic standards, as one might expect in newly created universities in societies where modern education has just recently been introduced, are well below those of most universities in the United States and Europe, though improving. Kuwait University is clearly the leader in quality of instruction. It has published the respected *Journal of Palestine Studies*, although following the 1990-91 Gulf crisis that activity was suspended. It established the Institute for Gulf Studies to promote serious scholarship on historical and contemporary matters in the Gulf area and publishes *The Journal of Gulf and Arabian Peninsula Studies*. A continuing challenge for all these universities is to draw more students into the sciences and other disciplines that impart the requisite skills to reduce their societies' dependence on foreigners.

EGYPT/EGYPTIANS. Egypt and Egyptians have played a significant role in the Gulf Arab states since before their independence. The political influence of Egypt under Gamal Abdel Nasser in the late 1950s and 1960s was pronounced, especially in Bahrain, where it excited strong nationalist sentiments. Egypt has for nearly four decades supplied the greatest numbers of foreign teachers in the Gulf states, playing a major role in the education of students at all levels. Egyptians are also found in significant numbers in midlevel bureaucratic positions and in private sector white-collar positions. In the post-Nasser era, Egypt came to be a natural ally for the Gulf states against the more radical states of the Arab world. Nevertheless, all but Oman felt obliged to abide by the Arab League decision calling for the breaking of diplomatic relations with Egypt after Camp David and the Egyptian-Israeli peace treaty. The Gulf states, including Saudi Arabia, took the lead a decade later in promoting Egypt's reintegration into the Arab world. Egypt's significant participation in the Desert Shield/Desert Storm coalition against Iraq helped to cement further its ties to the Gulf states, although residual differences in perspective and mutual expectations helped to undermine the projected joint Syrian-Egyptian security force for the Gulf following the conflict. The number of Egyptian expatriates working in the Gulf appears to have increased as Palestinians have been expelled from Kuwait and to some extent from other Gulf Arab countries.

EMIR. *Also* AMIR. The word is an Arabic title variously translated as "commander" or "prince." It has been used by the rulers of the states covered in this volume, except for the ruler of Oman, whose title is "sultan."

EMIRATE. *Also* AMIRATE. This is an English language neologism, absorbed into Arabic as *imarat*, referring to the territory under the rule of an emir. *See also* SHAIKHDOM.

EMIRI DIWAN. An *emiri diwan* is a secretariat or council of appointed advisers who assist an emir in carrying out his policies. With the evolution of more modern forms of government, this traditional political institution has lost some of its importance.

EMIRATES AIR. In 1985 Dubai launched its own airline to compete with Gulf Air, which is owned by Abu Dhabi, Bahrain, Oman, and Qatar. Emirates Air expanded rapidly and currently flies to 30 destinations, serving several new routes in Europe and East Asia. With passenger traffic now grown to well over two million, it is another dramatic success story for Dubai's business enterprise.

EMPTY QUARTER. *See* DESERTS *and* RUB AL-KHALI.

ENGLAND. *See* UNITED KINGDOM.

ENTERTAINMENT. Traditional indigenous entertainments were, until very recent years, the only kinds practiced in the Gulf Arab states (excluding foreign communities). These persist, notably in the form of camel racing, horse racing, falconry, Bedouin dances, and social rituals which accompany the giving and receiving of hospitality. Aware of the danger that folk arts may soon be lost, each state has begun programs to ensure their survival, and the GCC has established a folklife center in Doha. Modern Western entertainments have made their mark, though many, such as cinemas and nightclubs, found, for example, in Bahrain and the United Arab Emirates, exist overwhelmingly for expatriates. Videocassettes have brought a new form of entertainment consistent with the strong emphasis on family privacy but introducing new tastes and values. Team sports, particularly soccer, have become highly popular, and auto racing is now second to soccer as the leading sports entertainment, both in the Gulf Arab states and in the wider Middle East. One of the most celebrated sports figures in the Arab world today is Saeed al-Hajri, a Qatari race car champion.

EUROPEAN UNION (EU). The EU (European Community before 1994) served as a model for the GCC formed in 1981 by Bahrain, Kuwait, Oman, Qatar, Saudi Arabia, and the UAE with the stated purpose of eventual economic (and other) integration. To promote GCC-EU relations, a cooperation agreement was reached in 1990. The Gulf states have run a continuous deficit in their trade with the EU and look especially to increased sales of petrochemical products to redress the imbalance. This has engendered EU fears of threats to its own petrochemical industry, a difficulty which may be surmounted in part through further promotion of joint ventures both in Europe and the Gulf.

F

FAILAKAH. *Also* FAYLAKAH. Located at the mouth of Kuwait Bay and measuring about 10 mi (16 km) long by 3 mi (5 km) wide, Failakah is the only one of Kuwait's islands that is inhabited. Archaeological research indicates its habitation in ancient times and its linkage to the Dilmun civilization centered on Bahrain.

FAKHRO. *Also* FAKHRU. The Fakhros are a prominent Bahraini merchant family of Hawala origin, that is, Arabs who left the Arabian Peninsula several centuries ago to settle in Iran and returned to the Arab side of the Gulf in recent times. Notable members of the family include Yusuf Fakhro, a leading merchant in the early 20th century, and Dr. Ali

Muhammad Fakhro, until recently Bahrain's energetic and progressive minister of education.

FALAH, AL BU. *See* BU FALAH, AL.

FALAJ. A *falaj* is an irrigation channel. *Aflaj* (the Arabic plural) were introduced into southeast Arabia from Iran in ancient times and form elaborate irrigation systems in the interior of Oman and the area around Al-Ain in the UAE, where they bring water as much as 20 mi (32 km) from the Hajar Mountains. Smaller systems, no longer in use, were built in Bahrain as well. The aflaj are of two types, the *ghayl*, or open channel, and the *qanat falaj*, or underground canal. The latter starts at an *umm al-falaj*, or mother well, at the base of mountain slopes where rainfall runoff collects beneath the surface. Vertical shafts connect the tunnels to the surface at frequent intervals, permitting removal of rock and earth during initial construction and providing access for cleaning and repair.

FALASAH, AL BU. *See* BU FALASAH, AL.

FALCONRY. Falconry, although fairly widely practiced, may be described as the sport of shaikhs, a traditional pastime indulged in by rulers of Gulf states both as relaxation from affairs of state and as a means of preserving and strengthening ties with their Bedouin population. Shaikh Zayid, ruler of Abu Dhabi and president of the UAE, has sponsored an international conference on falconry and written a book on the subject. Such promotion of the sport has helped to advance general support for conservation and protection of the environment by demonstrating how such measures have increased once severely depleted numbers of falcons and their quarry. The falcons, generally the peregrine (Arabic, *shahin*) or saker (*hurr*), are captured along the Gulf coast during annual migrations (as they have grown scarcer and more expensive, some have been imported), and are tamed and taught to return prey to their handlers. The most prized game is the *houbara*, a species of bustard, with desert hares also frequently hunted.

FAMILY. *See* AHL, A'ILAH, *and* AL.

FASHT. *Fasht* (a Persian word) refers to a coral reef or shoal, often associated with islets in the Gulf. Though territorially not significant, some, such as the Fasht al-Dibal contested by Bahrain and Qatar, are the subject of potentially serious disputes.

FAUNA. Despite the severity of the eastern Arabian climate there is a remarkable diversity of wildlife in the Gulf Arab states, although the density of the animal population is low because of extreme aridity. The Arabian gazelle has been preserved through conservation efforts after near extinction following the introduction of motor vehicles and modern weapons to the desert. The oryx almost certainly survives only in Arabian zoos. Mountain goats, wolves, foxes, and, occasionally, leopards are found in remote areas, and smaller mammals such as hares, hedgehogs, jerboas, and gerbils are common. Between 250 and 300 bird species are encountered, most in migratory passage. Especially noteworthy are waterfowl, including herons, cormorants, and flamingos. Numerous reptiles have adapted to desert conditions, among them several varieties of lizard and about 40 species of land snakes, a few poisonous. The most notable among the arachnids is the scorpion, found throughout the region. Modern insecticides have brought under control mosquitoes and flies, once significant disease carriers, as well as locusts, which formerly devastated vegetation.

Marine life in both the Persian/Arab Gulf and the Gulf of Oman is extensive and varied, with one study identifying four thousand species. Fish abound, including perch, mackerel, and a tasty grouper called *hamour,* and are taken commercially and for sport. Among crustaceans, shrimp are important; hawksbill turtles are found; and the dugong, a relative of the North American manatee, frequents the waters around Bahrain and farther south. It remains to be seen how extensive the damage to wildlife resulting from massive dumping of oil into the Gulf during Operation Desert Storm will be. Waterfowl have clearly been affected severely, many shrimp will undoubtedly be lost, and all surface breathing animals are at risk. That some forms of marine life, like the dugong, survived a smaller oil spill in 1983 better than expected may offer some modest hope. *See also* FALCONRY *and* FISHING.

FEDERATION OF ARAB EMIRATES. *See* UNITED ARAB EMIRATES.

FEDERAL NATIONAL COUNCIL (FNC). The council, sometimes referred to as the Federal National Assembly, is made up of 40 members drawn from the seven emirates that compose the UAE. Abu

Dhabi and Dubai each have eight seats, Sharjah and Ras al-Khaimah six apiece, and Ajman, Fujairah, and Umm al-Qaiwain each have four. While each emirate may choose the manner of selecting its members, they tend to be picked by the rulers and generally represent the merchant class. Members serve two-year, indefinitely renewable terms and sit in ordinary sessions of not less than six months, beginning in November. All federal legislation is referred to the FNC, but its powers are only advisory as its recommendations on draft legislation may be overridden by the Supreme Federal Council (sometimes referred to as the Supreme Council of the Union), made up of the seven emirate rulers. Nevertheless, debates are often intense, and the FNC's advice is regarded seriously. A move to a stronger federal government as envisioned in the unadopted, revised constitution of 1976 would accord the FNC powers that would make it a true legislative body.

FISHING. Traditionally, fishing has employed a large part of the workforce in all the Gulf Arab states and was an important economic activity for both local and export markets. The oil boom and inefficient, outmoded methods of fishing have reduced the role of the industry in their economies. It is a minor income-earner and fewer than 5 percent of the economically active population is engaged in fishing and agriculture combined; indeed, only in Oman is that figure exceeded and in the UAE closely approached. Nevertheless, surveys have indicated a considerable potential for the fishing industry in both the Persian/Arab Gulf and the Gulf of Oman with plentiful fish such as grouper, tuna, perch, mackerel, and snapper as well as shrimp and varieties of shell-fish. The governments of all the Gulf Arab states, especially the UAE and Oman, are making considerable efforts to promote fishing, including fish farming. By the mid-1980s those two countries were harvesting more than 80,000 tons of fish apiece. For Oman fishing is a distant second to oil as an export earner.

FLORA. The severity of the eastern Arabian climate has limited plant life to a few hundred adaptive species, mostly halophytes and xerophytes (plants tolerant of salt and drought). Hardy shrubs, sedges, and grasses grow in desert areas where even modest rainfall at long intervals engenders a profusion of floral color. Along the coasts from Bahrain south, mangroves are found, providing a habitat for significant marine life, and in semidesert areas hardy trees such as tamarisk and acacia are found. Extensive irrigation, especially in Abu Dhabi, has made possible cultivation of additional plants such as bougainvillea and eucalyptus. The date palm is the native plant with the most food and economic value.

Oman, as in many other ways, presents an interesting contrast to its neighbors in its distribution and variety of plant life. In the Jebel al-Akhdar area (Arabic for "green mountain") junipers, oleanders, and asparagus are found and, to the south, in Dhofar, coconut palms and pomegranate trees. *See also* AGRICULTURE, DATES, *and* FOOD.

FOOD. Before the oil boom, the Gulf Arab states were virtually self-sufficient in food and exported some food products. Now, although government efforts have enabled domestic needs to be met in some areas, foodstuffs remain the third or fourth largest import account. Traditional dishes featuring lamb, fish, dates, and other indigenous foods, as well as imported rice, are favored as well as dishes introduced from other parts of the Arab world such as *tabbouleh* (combining chopped parsley, mint, tomatoes, and onions), *hummos* (ground chick-peas mixed with sesame seed paste), and *laban* (yogurt). The serving and consumption of food remain an important social ritual in a part of the world where the giving and receiving of hospitality are of special importance. In this respect coffee plays a particularly significant role

FOREIGN AID. The wealthy Gulf Arab states of Kuwait, the UAE, and Qatar have been among the world's most generous donor states in percentage of national income devoted to foreign aid (in 1981 the UAE's foreign grant and loan assistance peaked at 8 percent of GDP). Some of the aid (including Saudi assistance) goes to Bahrain and Oman in the form of GCC defense funds. Most is provided to other Arab and Islamic countries to support carefully studied and monitored projects. Foreign aid is often used to advance political ends. Kuwaiti and UAE assistance to the People's Democratic Republic of Yemen (now merged with the former Yemen Arab Republic to form the Yemen Republic) in the 1970s and early 1980s played a significant part in moderating that country's policies, specifically ending its threats against neigh-boring Oman. Together with Saudi Arabia, those two Gulf states sup-ported Iraq with perhaps $50 billion in "loans" in that country's war with Iran, a form of aid paid out to buy insurance against Iran (and Iraq itself). The Palestine Liberation Organization (PLO) and Jordan have been major recipients of aid from the Gulf Arab states. Nevertheless, they and other Arabs have called for a sharing of the oil wealth as an

Arab world resource, not merely the possession of individual states to be meted out at their pleasure. These calls were issued anew at the time of Iraq's invasion of Kuwait by many who resented what they saw as Kuwaiti and other Gulf Arab indifference to the plight of their less fortunate Arab brothers. As a reaction to their alignment with Iraq, however, the Gulf Arab states cut off aid to both Jordan and the PLO. At the same time, in April 1991, the Gulf Arab states, including Saudi Arabia, approved a $10 billion aid program for Egypt, Syria, and perhaps other states that had contributed to the military effort to end Iraqi occupation of Kuwait. For both economic and political reasons the Gulf Arab states and Saudi Arabia will henceforth provide foreign aid at a more modest level than during the previous two decades, when they dispensed $78 billion of such assistance. However, following the dramatic September 13, 1993, signing of the Declaration of Principles between Israel and the PLO, paving the way to Palestinian self-rule in Gaza and Jericho as a step toward a peace settlement, the Gulf Arab states, except for Kuwait, have pledged financial support for the fledgling Palestinian entity. *See also* FUND FOR ARAB ECONOMIC DEVELOPMENT *and* KUWAIT FUND FOR ARAB ECONOMIC DEVELOPMENT.

FOREIGN RELATIONS. *See entries for individual countries.*

FOREIGN WORKERS. The transition from traditional subsistence to modernizing, oil-based economies in the Gulf Arab states has necessitated importation of foreign labor to perform technical and managerial jobs that trained indigenous personnel are lacking for, and menial tasks which are shunned by the native labor force as low-paying and socially unacceptable. In Kuwait, the UAE, and Qatar, the dependence on expatriates exceeds that in Bahrain and Oman because of their greater and more rapidly acquired wealth. Kuwait's preinvasion work force totaled about 600,000 of which almost 540,000 (81 percent), were non-Kuwaiti, and the total population was nearly 73 percent foreign by one estimate in the mid-1980s (others placed it at about 65 percent). Some 60 percent of the foreign workers were other Arabs (mainly Palestinians, followed by Egyptians). These typically have filled technical, managerial, and professional jobs in teaching and in government, while Kuwaitis tend to hold positions in the bloated government bureaucracy. By the 1980s a growing number of East Asians had entered the workforce, especially to carry out major construction projects. The

1990-91 Gulf crisis led to the flight or expulsion of most of the large Palestinian community with Egyptians and South or East Asians largely replacing the Palestinians.

In the UAE the reliance on foreign labor is similarly great, although in those emirates lacking significant oil wealth the numbers of expatriate workers are low. Both in Abu Dhabi and Dubai the labor force is about 90 percent foreign, and the indigenous population of the UAE as a whole is not more than 15 percent-20 percent. Most skilled and unskilled workers come from South Asia, and many Indians and Pakistanis operate small retail businesses. Other Arabs, especially Palestinians and Egyptians, are teachers, professionals, and civil servants. As in Kuwait, there was a pronounced turn to increasing reliance in the 1980s on East Asians, especially Filipinos and Koreans, to carry out construction projects and fill other needs. Since the recent Gulf crisis the numbers of Palestinian and Jordanian workers have significantly decreased. In Qatar's much smaller labor market the foreign labor force is probably about 90 percent of the total and, as in the UAE, the largest element of the workforce and general population is of South Asian origin.

In all these cases the massive dependence on foreign intellect and brawn to promote rapid economic development has brought painful and dangerous dilemmas. The conservative Gulf Arab regimes have been fearful that other Arabs, especially Palestinians, would bring with their needed skills dangerous political ideas to infect the local population. The Iran-Iraq war also heightened fears of the large Shia populations in the Gulf states, excepting Qatar. (Much of the Shia population, especially in Bahrain, where it forms the majority, has long been resident on the Arab side of the Gulf; indeed, much of it is Arab, not Iranian.) While Arab and other immigrants have been granted wide access to medical, educational, and other benefits on much the same terms, usually free, as Gulf state nationals, citizenship is available to very few. This reflects an obvious fear by Gulf Arabs both of diluting and altering their own societies and, in the cases of Kuwait, the UAE, and Qatar, of simply being overwhelmed by the more numerous expatriates. At the same time, cause for resentment is equally obvious among those whose work has built and continues largely to sustain the prosperity of these countries, yet who are still denied basic civil rights, even though they may be second or third-generation residents of the host country. After terrorist bombings and an attempted assassination of the emir in 1987 and 1988, respectively, Kuwait expelled several thousand Shia residents. Following the occupation of Kuwait in 1990-91, when major Palestinian groups supported Iraq and some Palestinians in Kuwait collaborated with the occupiers, Palestinians suffered physical mistreatment, exclusion from state-operated schools, and expulsion from the country.

As noted, the UAE and Kuwait have increased their reliance on East Asian workers, including Filipinos, Koreans, and Thais (typically employed on construction projects and in medical and other services), and correspondingly reduced the need for Arabs or South Asians, who tend to bring families and settle more permanently. This strategy, however, has engendered its own problems, raising in many minds the danger of cultural deracination from large numbers of foreign workers of non-Islamic cultures, especially when many, such as nannies, come into intimate social contact with the indigenous population. Moreover, this strategy merely defers implementation of the policy of moving toward self-reliance, a policy boldly enunciated but thus far honored only in the breach. Iraq's invasion of Kuwait and the events that followed led to further calls for reduced reliance on expatriate labor. Kuwaiti officials spoke, after liberation, of barring the return of most expatriates who had fled, expelling some who had remained, and altogether halving the nation's population and restoring a Kuwaiti majority. Yet there is still no evidence of real progress toward significant "Kuwaitization" of the labor force.

Bahrain and Oman have developed major dependence on foreign labor, but not to the extent of reducing their own populations to minorities, as is true of their wealthier neighbors. In Bahrain foreigners account for about a third of the population and nearly half of the labor force, with the construction, trade, and services sectors dominated by non-Bahrainis. Perhaps a third of Oman's population is foreign, mostly from South Asia, with expatriates heavily represented in all fields including professions and civil administration, as in the other Gulf states. Despite dramatic gains in educating their populations to meet the needs of developing societies, all the Gulf states have become profoundly habituated to an indefinite dependence on foreign skills.

FRANCE (Official name, FRENCH REPUBLIC). In the 17th and 18th centuries France was an active contender for strategic and commercial ascendancy in the Indian Ocean and had a significant interest in Oman and the lower Persian Gulf. However, Britain's mastery in the area was secured after the defeat of Napoleon's expedition to Egypt in 1798. In the late 19th and early 20th century some French efforts were made to breach the dominant British position, especially in Oman, but these failed, and no significant French involvement on the Arab side of the Gulf occurred until British protection was withdrawn from the Gulf Arab states (1961 in Kuwait and 1971 in Bahrain, Qatar, and the UAE).

French commercial and economic involvement in the Gulf Arab states remains fairly modest; France does not rank among the top trading partners of any, though it has significant trade with each. In recent years the French involvement in the area's security affairs has grown with major arms sales to Kuwait, Qatar, and the UAE, whose air force adopted the Mirage-2000 as its main fighter plane. France's prominent role in the anti-Iraq alliance in Desert Shield and Desert Storm, diplomatically and militarily, has assured that country of a continuing and significant role in the region. Moreover, as a key member of the European Union (formerly the European Community), France will play an important role in determining terms of trade between the EU and the GCC, for example, on the issue of GCC exports of petrochemicals to the EU. *See also* ARMED FORCES, COMPAGNIE FRANÇAISE DES PETROLES, DESERT SHIELD/ DESERT STORM, *and* EUROPEAN UNION.

FRUIT. *See* AGRICULTURE *and* FLORA.

FUJAIRAH. *Also* FUJAYRAH. Fujairah has the third smallest land area (450 sq mi or 1,166 sq km) and second smallest population (54,000) of the seven emirates that constitute the UAE. It is the only one whose territory lies entirely on the east (Gulf of Oman) side of the Musandam Peninsula and, with Ajman and Umm al-Qaiwain, is one of the emirates lacking significant exploitable oil or gas. Fujairah possesses potentially valuable mineral ores including chrome, iron, copper, and uranium in the Hajar Mountains; it has modest agriculture and fishing; and its attractive beaches offer some scope for development of a tourist industry. There is little prospect, however, for an end to Fujairah's dependence on federal economic support. Lack of wealth has kept the numbers and percentage of its expatriate population low, and a very large part of its indigenous population retains strong tribal identities, with the Al Sharqi tribe dominating. Its ruler, Hamad bin Muhammad, from the dominant section of that tribe, is energetic and university-educated. Fujairah acquired formal status as a separate emirate only in 1952, when the British recognized it as such. It had earlier been part of the powerful federation of the Qawasim, who still rule the emirates of Sharjah and Ras al-Khaimah, but it enjoyed de facto independence under the Al Sharqi from the late 19th century. *See also* AL SHARQI.

FUTTAIM. The Futtaims are a leading Dubai merchant family. Majid Futtaim directs one of the largest import businesses in the UAE.

G

GALADARIS. The Galadaris are one of the principal merchant families of Dubai and, like many of the others there, of Iranian origin. Their wealth came from the gold trade that flourished in Dubai up to the early 1970s, with merchants transshipping gold to India (where its purchase was illegal) by fast dhows. In 1986 the family's fortunes suffered a severe reversal after accumulation of excessive indebtedness, in turn sending shock waves through the Dubai banking sector.

GENERAL TREATY OF PEACE. The treaty was imposed by the British Government of India on the Qawasim shaikhs based on the Arab side of the southern Persian/Arab Gulf (the "Pirate Coast") in January 1820, following British military action against Ras al-Khaimah. In the same year Bahrain also became a party to the treaty, which ended piracy and curtailed the Qawasim's maritime dominance of the lower Gulf. Subsequent treaty agreements in 1853 and 1892 strengthened and expanded the earlier agreement. Apart from making the Gulf safe for commerce and confirming British primacy there, it also froze contemporary power relationships among the tribes of what came to be called the Trucial Coast (now the United Arab Emirates). Tribal shaikhs evolved into rulers of territorial entities, laying the basis for the constituent states of today's UAE. *See also* EXCLUSIVE AGREE-MENT, TREATY OF MARITIME PEACE IN PERPETUITY, *and* UNITED KINGDOM.

GERMANY, FEDERAL REPUBLIC OF. Its late entry into the 19th century colonial scramble kept imperial Germany from having much impact on the Gulf region except for one significant event. In 1896 the ruler of Kuwait discussed with German representatives the possible extension of the Berlin-Baghdad railway to a Gulf terminus in Kuwait, which prompted the British government to reconsider its earlier refusal to extend protection to Kuwait. More recently, the involvement of the Federal Republic of Germany in Gulf affairs has been modest. In none of the five small Gulf Arab states does Germany provide as much as 10 percent of total imports, and its purchases of their exports are even less. In political and strategic terms the German role is similarly slight and largely exercised indirectly through its role in the EU. Germany does not export arms to the Gulf Arab states, but supported the Desert Shield/Desert Storm operation with financial contributions.

GHAFIRI. *Ghafiri* (Arabic collective, *Ghafiriyya*) is the name of a tribal confederation that continues to be an important source of identi-fication for tribesmen in Oman and the UAE. Those so identified trace their origins back through the Nizari Arabs to the Adnani or northern Arabs as distinguished from the Yamani (Qahtani) or southern Arabs, a mytho-historical division reaching back to earliest Arab memory. A ninth century A.D. civil war in Oman pitted Nizaris against the Yamanis, who had first settled there. In a similar conflict of the 18th century Nizari tribes followed the Bani Ghafir, or Ghafiri tribe, against Yamani tribesmen, who followed the Bani Hina, or Hinawi tribe. Since then the division has assumed those identities and helped shape rivalries and divisions in Oman. In the UAE, formerly the Trucial States, the Bani Yas, which became the dominant tribal federation in the mid-19th century, are Hinawi, and their Qawasim rivals are Ghafiri. *See also* ADNAN, NIZARI, *and* QAHTAN.

GHALIB, IMAM. Ghalib bin Ali al-Hinai was the last of the imams of Oman, ending the imamate established in 750 A.D. by the Ibadi sect of Islam, which still predominates in Oman. In 1954 the respected imam Muhammad bin Abdullah al-Khalili died, and Ghalib was chosen as his successor. Shortly before, oil explorations by a British-owned oil company had begun in Oman, and both the sultanate of the Al Bu Said, based in Muscat on the coast, and the imamate in the interior of Oman were determined to realize any profits from a concession. In 1955 the British-supported Sultan Said bin Taimur took control of the interior from the Saudi and Egyptian-supported imam, and the latter resigned his position, leaving the country reunited under the rule of the sultan. In 1957, however, Ghalib's supporters, again with Saudi assistance, rose against the sultan and proclaimed Ghalib imam once more. Sultan

Said was obliged to request British military intervention to defeat this threat, which was finally suppressed in January 1959, with a dramatic assault on the Jebel al-Akhdar, stronghold of the imam's last defenders. Ghalib went into exile in Saudi Arabia, refused the offer of Sultan Qabus, Said's successor, to return to Oman as a purely religious figure, and died in Riyadh. *See also* AL BU SAID, IBADIS, *and* IBADI IMAMATE.

GREAT BRITAIN. *See* UNITED KINGDOM.

GULF (ARAB, ARABIAN, *or* PERSIAN). The Gulf is a large body of water lying between Iran to the east and the Arabian Peninsula to the west. It extends about 500 mi (805 km) in a southeastward direction from the Shatt al-Arab to the Strait of Hormuz. Measuring just over 200 mi (322 km) across at its widest, it has an area of 88,000 sq mi (227,979 sq km). It is noteworthy for its shallowness, seldom exceeding 300 ft (91 m) in depth, with the deeper part generally on the Iranian side, where mountains rise up from a narrow coastal plain. Its shallow waters and many reefs and islands make the Gulf hazardous in places for navigation and generally uninviting for the maneuvering of large naval craft. The summer brings extreme heat, with temperatures reaching 115°F and more. Water temperatures of over 100°F are recorded, and in places the Gulf's waters are extremely saline.

From earliest times the Gulf has been an important artery of commerce. As long ago as the early part of the third millennium B.C. a trading civilization with settlements along the Arab side of the Gulf connected Sumer in the Tigris-Euphrates Valley and the Indus Valley civilization of Mohenjo-Daro. In the early Islamic era Arab ships from the Gulf came to dominate the trade routes to India and East Asia, establishing the most extensive maritime network known to that time. The subsequent decline of that trade was confirmed and hastened by the development of trade routes from Europe to Asia around the Cape of Good Hope and resultant European domination of the Indian Ocean and the Gulf itself. The Gulf remained a commercial backwater (unless an exception is made for the pearl trade, which reached its heyday in the 19th and early 20th century) until the production and export of oil assumed important dimensions by the mid-20th century. By 1980 the great bulk of total world oil exports was carried on tankers from the Gulf, and the location of some two-thirds of the world's oil reserves in the eight littoral Gulf states ensured the region's vital importance indefinitely. In the late 1970s and 1980s oil and the intensified Soviet-American regional rivalry elevated perceptions of the Gulf's geostrategic importance to the highest point ever. The Iran-Iraq "tanker war" in the Gulf raised Western fears commensurately, leading to the extraordinary step of the U.S. "reflagging" of Kuwaiti tankers and commitment of significant naval forces in the Gulf, ostensibly to protect free passage generally, but in actuality to thwart Iranian attacks on Kuwaiti and Saudi shipping. The ending of the Iran-Iraq war in 1988 and shortly thereafter of the threat from the East Bloc momentarily lessened preoccupation with Gulf security. This changed dramatically with the Iraqi invasion of Kuwait on August 2, 1990, and the subsequent unprecedented involvement of U.S. and Western European as well as various Arab military and naval forces to drive the Iraqi forces from Kuwait.

Contemporary Gulf nomenclature is a sensitive matter. The Greeks gave the name "Erythraean Sea" to all the bodies of water surrounding the Arabian Peninsula. In the medieval Islamic period the Gulf was generally referred to as the "Sea of Fars" (Persian Sea), and the term "Persian Gulf" entered into use at the same time. In the 17th and 18th centuries the designation "Gulf of Basra," reflecting that port's great importance, challenged but failed to supplant the earlier term of reference. The rise of Arab nationalism has led to the general use of "Arab Gulf" or "Arabian Gulf" in the Arab world. Cautious scholars and diplomats frequently take refuge in the use of the unmodified "Gulf." *See also* DESERT STORM/DESERT SHIELD, FAUNA, FISHING, IRAN-IRAQ WAR, OIL, *and* PEARLING.

GULF AIR. Gulf Air is a regional airline, jointly owned and operated by four states of the lower Gulf, Bahrain, Oman, Qatar, and Abu Dhabi. It is headquartered in Bahrain, where its predecessor, Gulf Aviation Company Limited, was established in 1950.

GULF COOPERATION COUNCIL. *Also* ARAB GULF COOPERATION COUNCIL (GCC). The Gulf Cooperation Council links the six conservative patriarchal Gulf Arab states— Bahrain, Kuwait, Oman, Qatar, Saudi Arabia, and the UAE— in an organization designed to promote coordination in the areas of economic and security concerns. It was established in 1981 with Saudi Arabia taking the initiative, following a significant history of efforts to establish such an organization, especially to provide defense coordination. In 1975 the shah of Iran proposed a security pact, and in the following year the present emir, then prime minister, of Kuwait called for a Gulf union covering economic, political, and other areas of concern. Indeed, under Saudi leadership, cooperation in both internal and external security among the Gulf Arab states was promoted in the late 1970s. It was a series of traumatic events in 1979-80 that provided both the impetus and the opportunity to create the GCC. The December 1979 Soviet invasion of Afghanistan enhanced Moscow's threat and that of its regional proxies, especially the People's Democratic Republic of Yemen, and the subsequent promulgation of the Carter Doctrine raised Gulf fears of superpower intervention. However, what proved to be the most powerful motive was the Iranian Revolution which toppled the shah in January 1979, removing a government that had shared the Gulf Arab states' basic interests (despite important points of difference and dispute) and established a new leadership publicly committed to the overthrow of their rulers. The outbreak of the Iran-Iraq war in September 1980 added another source of threat and, equally important, enabled the six states to act independently of their two dominant neighbors.

A February 1981 meeting of the foreign ministers in Riyadh drew up the GCC's charter and the rulers met in Abu Dhabi in May to establish the organization formally. The charter is somewhat ambiguous, setting forth the member states' desire to pursue "coordination, cooperation, and integration," their commitment to working within the larger framework of Arab and Islamic interests, and their intention to pursue cooperation in all areas of common concern. The GCC is organized in four constituent parts: (1) the Supreme Council, composed of the heads of state, empowered to determine general policy and make binding decisions, and required by the charter to convene a regular session annually; (2) the Commission for the Settlement of Disputes, which makes recommendations to the Supreme Council on disagreements over interpretation of the charter or disputes between member states; (3) the Ministerial Council, made up of cabinet-level representatives of the member states who propose to the Supreme Council the means of implementing GCC programs; and (4) the Secretariat General, headquartered in Riyadh, with a secretary general who oversees six directorates, political, economic, legal, financial/administrative, environmental/human resource affairs, and information. The secretariat prepares studies and monitors GCC decisions. At the first meeting of the Supreme Council, Dr. Abdullah Bishara, a distinguished Kuwaiti diplomat who had long been his country's UN ambassador, was selected as secretary-general. and served in that post for 12 years. At the GCC summit of December 1992, in Abu Dhabi his resignation was accepted. The Supreme Council elected Shaikh Fahim bin Sultan Al Qasimi, a member of the ruling family of Ras al-Khaimah and an experienced diplomat, who served as secretary-general for three years. At the December 1995 GCC summit a veteran Saudi diplomat, Jamil Ibrahim al-Hejailan, was chosen to succeed him. The choice led Qatar's ruler, Shaikh Hamad bin Khalifa Al Thani, to leave the summit meeting, in an unprecedented action, because his own Qatari candidate for the position was snubbed.

At the outset there was division among the member states as to whether the GCC's orientation should be more toward economic or security concerns. Kuwait, neutral in the U.S.-Soviet cold war and nonconfrontational in Gulf and Arab politics, represented the former position; Oman, having just survived a dangerous rebellion abetted by a proxy of Moscow with external, including British, assistance and faced with special responsibility for safeguarding the Strait of Hormuz, emphasized security; the others were ranged in between. Partly because agreement was easiest among them on economic matters, these were given prominence, as reflected in adoption of the Unified Economic Agreement, announced immediately after establishment of the GCC and aimed at eventually establishing a common market along the lines of the EU. The oil glut provided a further boost to economic cooperation. While progress has not been as dramatic as was hoped, there has been movement toward eliminating intra-GCC customs duties, establishing a common external tariff, providing for free movement of people and capital within the GCC, and establishing a unified investment strategy, the last given practical form in the Gulf Organization for Industrial Consultancy. While coordination of oil policies has not been a notable success, the GCC continues to take a lead in pressing its members' access to U.S., European, and Japanese markets for GCC petrochemical exports, a critical issue in their economic development.

If economic issues were given public emphasis early on, security matters were the most pressing for the GCC. A September 1981 meeting of GCC military chiefs of staff took up defense planning and security concerns that were intensified when an Iran-supported coup attempt in Bahrain was thwarted. While envisioned GCC pacts on both defense and internal security have failed to materialize, there has been modest progress. The GCC has set up a joint rapid deployment force, which in 1983 and 1984 carried out exercises code-named "Peninsula

Shield" and "Gulf Shield II," but exercises since then have tended to be bilateral. The force is stationed at Saudi Arabia's Hafr al-Batin base, but its limited size has thus far made it mainly a symbolic entity. Although agreement was reached in 1982 to set up a common GCC air defense system, to enhance the effectiveness of the most crucial elements in the members' means of defense, this has been thwarted by the considerable lack of interoperability in weapons systems, especially those dealing with command, coordination, and communication functions. The GCC's military weakness was evident in August 1990, when it was utterly incapable of meeting Iraqi aggression against member state Kuwait. In the aftermath of the crisis it soon became apparent that the March 1991 Damascus agreement, calling for Egyptian and Syrian forces to remain in the Gulf area as the nucleus of an Arab peace force to guarantee regional stability, would not be implemented. Effective integration of the GCC's military forces also remains elusive, with the Saudis rejecting an Omani proposal for an enlarged GCC army under unified command and preferring a looser arrangement. What does seem clear is that the GCC states will have to continue to look to external protectors, especially the U.S., if again threatened by powerful enemies.

If the GCC has not produced dramatic progress toward economic and defense integration, it has achieved modest success in these and other areas. In taking a measured, pragmatic approach to the achievement of attainable goals, it has survived, where more grandiose and ideological Arab efforts to achieve cooperation or unity have failed. The strongly shared cultural heritage of the societies as well as the similar values, interests, and concerns of the ruling families, some of them linked by intermarriage, when added to the sense of shared threat still menacing them, appear sufficient to sustain the GCC and its deliberate progress toward greater integration. *See also* ARMED FORCES, DESERT SHIELD/DESERT STORM, EUROPEAN UNION, IRAN, *and* IRAQ.

GULF INVESTMENT CORPORATION (GIC). The Gulf Investment Corporation, (GIC), established in November 1982, with a capital of $2.1 billion, later raised to $3 billion, with equal shares paid in by each of the Gulf Cooperation Council states, was the first GCC joint venture. It became operational in May 1984, with a general aim of promoting the economic development and integration of the shareholding states, principally by identifying and supporting new ventures (with either private or public partners) and by developing a capital market in the

Gulf. The GIC has earned a healthy return on its investments and helped a number of significant projects through loans and purchase of equity.

GULF NATIONAL FORUM. The forum was established in May 1992 at a meeting of professionals and businessmen from Bahrain, Kuwait, Qatar, Saudi Arabia, and the UAE convened in Kuwait. The organization's goals are to promote and protect democracy, human rights, and basic freedoms in the GCC countries.

GULF NEWS AGENCY. The most notable Gulf-wide cooperative program in communications, the Gulf News Agency, was begun in 1976 when Bahrain, Iraq, Kuwait, Saudi Arabia, and the UAE created it to serve the needs of the press in each state.

GULF OIL CORPORATION. The Gulf Oil Corporation was established by the Mellon banking family of Pittsburgh in 1907 (its name is taken from the Gulf of Mexico) and became one of the "seven sisters" or major international oil companies. In 1927 Gulf was thwarted, as a signatory to the Red Line Agreement, from acquiring a concession to explore and produce oil in Bahrain and turned its attention to Kuwait. Initial British government opposition to an American concession gave way to a compromise, following negotiations with the U.S. government, whereby Gulf and the Anglo-Persian Oil Company (APOC) formed the Kuwait Oil Company (KOC), each with a 50 percent share, in February, 1934. A concession was obtained later that year. In 1938 the oil of the vast Burgan field was discovered (weeks before the discovery of oil in Saudi Arabia), and, following the shutting down of operations during World War II, oil was first exported in 1946. In 1951 Gulf agreed to a 50/50 profit-sharing arrangement with the Kuwaiti government, which followed similar agreements between American concessionaires and the governments of Venezuela and Saudi Arabia. In 1974 the government acquired 60 percent participation in KOC, leaving 20 percent each to British Petroleum (BP), (as successor to APOC) and Gulf, and in the following year took complete control. In 1984 the Kuwait Petroleum Corporation (KPC), which oversaw all the government's oil operations, purchased Gulf facilities in several European countries. In 1985 Gulf ceased to exist as an independent corporation when it was purchased by Chevron, the former Standard Oil Company of California. *See also*

ANGLO-PERSIAN OIL COMPANY, KUWAIT OIL COMPANY, *and* KUWAIT PETROLEUM CORPORATION.

GULF OF OMAN. The Gulf of Oman is an arm of the Arabian Sea whose northern extremity is the coast of southern Iran and whose southern and western limits are defined by the northern coast of Oman and the eastern coast of the UAE. It is separated from the Persian/Arab Gulf by the Strait of Hormuz.

GULF ORGANIZATION FOR INDUSTRIAL CONSULTANCY (GOIC). The GOIC was established in 1976 to gather data, generate proposals, and evaluate potential projects. Part of its purpose is to rationalize industrial development in the Gulf Arab states and avoid costly duplication. Headquartered in Doha, Qatar, it is jointly owned by Iraq, Kuwait, Qatar, Saudi Arabia, and the UAE (with shares of 17 percent each) and Bahrain and Oman (each holding 7.5 percent of the GOIC's equity).

GULF WAR. *See* IRAN-IRAQ WAR *and* DESERT SHIELD/DESERT STORM.

GWADAR. *Also* GWADUR. Gwadar is a small seaport in Pakistani Baluchistan on the Arabian Sea. In 1797 Sultan bin Ahmad, ruler of Muscat, obtained the port and its hinterland in an agreement with the Khan of Kalat. Gwadar became a prime source of recruits for the rulers of Muscat (later of all Oman). Gwadaris and other recruits from Baluchistan formed the largest part of the army's ranks until outnumbered by Omani Arabs in the mid-1980s. Gwadar remained an Omani possession until 1958, when Sultan Said bin Taimur, faced with budgetary constraints, sold Gwadar to the government of Pakistan for £3 million.

H

HAJAR MOUNTAINS. The Hajar ("rock" in Arabic) Mountains are the most prominent geographic feature of the northern emirates of the UAE and of northern Oman. Formed of both igneous rock and limestone, they extend from the tip of the Musandam Peninsula at the Strait of Hormuz almost to the Ras al-Hadd headland, the easternmost point of the Arabian Peninsula. Divided into the Western and Eastern Hajar by the Wadi Sama'il in Oman, the mountains in the UAE reach over 6,000 ft (1,829 m) and rise to 10,000 ft (3,048 m) in Oman to form the Jebel al-Akhdar ("green mountain"), an elevated plateau. Apart from the Jebel al-Akhdar the range is largely barren rock, but limited agriculture is made possible in the valleys by rainfall runoff, which also replenishes a water table extending many miles from the mountains. Modest mineral deposits, including copper and chrome, have been discovered in the Hajar. The mountains have provided a refuge or protective barrier for various groups throughout history, notably for the Ibadi community, which broke away from mainstream Islam A.D. the late seventh century.

HAMAD BIN ISA AL KHALIFA (b. 1950). Shaikh Hamad is the eldest son of Isa bin Salman, the present ruler of Bahrain, and is the heir apparent. He studied at the military academy at Mons, Belgium and serves as the minister of defense.

HAMAD BIN KHALIFA AL THANI (b. 1950). Shaikh Hamad became the ruler of Qatar on June 26, 1995, when he deposed his father, Shaikh Khalifa bin Hamad Al Thani, who had ruled since 1972. Since 1992, when his father gave him responsibility for managing Qatar's day-to-day affairs, Hamad was the country's de facto ruler. In that capacity the energetic 45-year-old ruler chartered a more independent foreign policy than had Khalifa, befriending Iran, reestablishing diplomatic relations with Iraq, and going further than other Gulf Arab states in pursuing normal ties with Israel. Khalifa's disagreement with both the substance and style of his son's leadership created friction that led to the deposition of the former ruler. The action proceeded in an orderly and peaceful manner with pledges of support to Hamad from leaders in the Al Thani family, the National Advisory Council, government bureaucracy, and armed forces. It also won crucial, speedy acceptance from the other GCC states including Saudi Arabia, long Qatar's closest ally and protector, which had been unhappy with Qatar's assertively independent new stance. Domestic and foreign support for the new ruler thwarted Khalifa's attempt to reassert his authority in the weeks after Hamad's accession and made possible a smooth transition.

Hamad's education and career provided solid preparation for his full assumption of the responsibilities of ruler. Following primary and secondary education in Qatar, he graduated from Sandhurst Military

Academy in Great Britain. Commissioned as a lieutenant colonel in command of a mobile battalion, he rose to the rank of major general and was appointed commander in chief of Qatar's armed forces. In that position he oversaw extensive modernization and upgrading of the country's military and brokered the defense pact with the United States, which calls for prepositioning military equipment at a base being constructed on Qatar's western coast. In the early 1980's Hamad headed the Supreme Planning Council, which establishes the country's economic and social policies. He also helped to establish municipal councils as a means of promoting popular participation in local government. *See also* KHALIFA BIN HAMAD AL THANI, QATAR, *and* AL THANI.

HAMDAN BIN ZAYID. The fifth son of Zayid bin Khalifa Al Nuhayyan ("Zayid the Great") and the second to succeed him, Hamdan ruled Abu Dhabi from 1912 to 1922. His tightfisted attitude toward other members of the ruling family created enmity that led to his murder by his brother Sultan, initiating a series of assassinations that ended in 1928 with the installation of Sultan's son Shakhbut as ruler.

HAWALA. The Hawala (probably from the Arabic verb "to move to a new residence") are Arabs who migrated from central Arabia to Persia, shortly after its seventh century A.D. conquest by the armies of Islam. Among those who returned to the Arab side of the Gulf were the Qawasim, who now rule the emirates of Sharjah and Ras al-Khaimah, and a large number of the leading merchants of Bahrain.

HAWALI. Hawali is a suburb to the southeast of Kuwait City and the principal city of one of four governorates of Kuwait to which the same name is given. The city of Hawali was developed in the 1950s for the residence of non-Kuwaitis and became one of the most densely populated settlements in Kuwait.

HAWAR ISLANDS. Located just off the west coast of Qatar and about 15 mi (24 km) from the southern tip of Bahrain, the Hawar Islands are in dispute between the two countries and a source of continuing acrimony in their relations. Bahrain's claim reflects its former suzerainty over Qatari territory and its current rulers, the Al Thani. The possible existence of large gas and oil deposits under the islands lends further urgency to the dispute. In 1982 the semiquiescent issue was revived when Bahrain named a naval vessel after the islands. In 1995 Qatar supported but Bahrain opposed an effort to place the issue before the International Court of Justice. Only the largest island, about 11 mi (18 km) long and 1 mi (1.6 km) wide, is inhabited. The other, much smaller islands, some accessible by wading from the Qatari shore at low tide, are home to considerable wildlife, especially migratory birds.

HEALTH. In the 20th century the Gulf Arab states have made the transition from what one observer has called "premedical societies," ravaged by endemic diseases, to countries with the most modern, comprehensive health services, enjoying standards of health comparable to those of the contemporary industrialized nations. The first modern health care in the Gulf was introduced by the Arabian Mission of the Dutch Reformed Church of the United States, which established hospitals in Kuwait, Bahrain, and Oman in the early years of this century. Bahrain was the first, in 1925, to establish free medical services for its citizens. As oil wealth has permitted, each of the Gulf Arab states has created a complete health care system of hospitals, clinics, and other facilities with free care for all nationals. With the decline of oil revenues in the early 1980s, fees were introduced for most health services for expatriates. Although Gulf Arabs pursue medical studies abroad or in recently established medical schools in Bahrain, Kuwait, and Oman, 75 percent or more of the physicians and an even higher percentage of nurses are of expatriate origin. Kuwait has relied heavily on Egyptian doctors, the other Gulf Arab states on South Asians. Nurses in all five states come largely from South Asia with, in recent years, significant numbers from the Philippines.

The eradication or effective control of formerly prevalent diseases such as trachoma and malaria has introduced a pattern of morbidity and mortality more typical of the modern industrial world, with higher incidence of cancer and heart attacks occurring at more advanced ages. Life expectancy is close to Western European and American levels except in Oman, where it is probably about 50 years. In that country lack of sanitation and insufficient knowledge of personal hygiene remain significant problems, because modern health care came later and rural areas are more difficult to access.

HINAWI. See GHAFIRI and OMAN.

HOLMES, MAJOR FRANK (1874–c.1940). Holmes was a mining engineer from New Zealand who, while on military service in the Middle East during World War I, learned of oil seepages on the Arab side of the Persian/Arab Gulf, convincing him that great oil wealth lay beneath the Arabian sands. In 1920 he established the Eastern and General Syndicate and obtained exploratory concessions from Gulf Arab rulers, including Abdul Aziz bin Saud, then emir of Nejd and al-Hasa, later king of Saudi Arabia. Holmes's vision had to contend with general skepticism as to possible oil discovery and with a degree of British opposition to entry by American oil companies, which alone had a serious interest in acquiring his concessions, into the British-protected Gulf states. He did manage to sell his Bahrain concession to the Standard Oil Company of California (now Chevron), the success of which led to the Saudi Arabian concession that became Aramco. Since he also represented Gulf Oil in securing a half share in the Kuwait Oil Company (KOC), he was in great measure responsible for the greatest oil discoveries in the Gulf, today representing over 30 percent of the world's reserves. Holmes never gained great wealth from his prophecy and perseverance, but the ruler of Kuwait gave him the sinecure of a lifetime appointment as London representative of the KOC. *See also* BAHRAIN PETROLEUM COMPANY, GULF OIL COMPANY, *and* KUWAIT OIL COMPANY.

HORMUZ, STRAIT OF. The Strait of Hormuz, connecting the Persian/ Arab Gulf and the Indian Ocean (via the Gulf of Oman), passes between Iran and Oman, narrowing to 28 mi (45 km). The shipping channels are within the Omani 12-nautical-mile limit. The strait was the focus of intense concern as a potential "choke point" during the Iran-Iraq war (1980-88). Iran threatened to close it on several occasions, and both the Carter and Reagan administrations stated that it would be kept open, even if that should require naval action. Despite the general skepticism of military experts that Iran could block the strait, the fact that nearly 90 percent of the Gulf's oil exports passed through it prompted anxiety. Iranian attacks against Saudi and Kuwaiti tankers, in response to Iraqi attacks on Iranian and other tankers carrying Iranian oil, added to fears of possible closure of the strait and led to the upgrading and further construction of pipelines across Arabia to Red Sea outlets. Construction of a pipeline from the UAE across Oman to the Gulf of Oman has been discussed, but no action yet taken.

I

IBADIS. While most of the Gulf Arab states' Muslims, indigenous and expatriate, are Sunnis or Shias, the third and smallest of the significant branches of Islam, the Ibadi sect, has dominated Oman since the eighth century A.D. The Ibadis are a moderate offshoot of the Kharijites (Arabic, *Khawarij*), a radical sect that split from mainstream Islam over the question of succession to leadership of the Islamic community. In the latter part of the seventh century A.D. this group, centered on Basra in present-day Iraq, came under the leadership of Abdullah bin Ibad, a native of Najd in central Arabia, whose name the movement continues to bear. Shortly after his death those who had followed him were exiled to Oman, where the great majority of Ibadis have since resided, with small numbers also in parts of North and East Africa and Iran.

Ibadi doctrine specifies election of an imam on the basis of his capacity to provide spiritual and temporal leadership to the community, with the choice made by senior religious and other leaders and confirmed by public support. The somewhat ambiguous definition of the manner of choosing an imam led to frequent disputes. The community was at various times without an imam, a situation for which its doctrines provided guidance as they did for periods of special endangerment, when Ibadis resorted to concealment (Arabic, *kitman*). Ibadis are characterized by a puritanical adherence to the ethical norms of Islam, although friendly relations and marriage with other Muslims are permitted.

Ibadis have always been concentrated in the interior of Oman, where their imamate has always been centered, while the large Sunni and small Shia communities of Oman are prominent in the coastal areas. The ruling family in Oman, the Al Bu Said, is Ibadi but has based its power on Muscat and the coast for two and a half centuries. After the death of the dynasty's founder, the Al Bu Said rulers did not lay claim to the imamate. It was revived in the interior in the later part of the 19th century, formally restored in 1913, and finally overthrown in the 1950s by Said bin Taimur, father of the present sultan. *See also* IMAM/ IMAMATE, ISLAM, KHARIJITES, *and* OMAN.

IJMA. *Ijma* is the Arabic term for "consensus." In the Gulf Arab states important political and other decisions are made in accordance with the tradition of unanimous agreement. In the religious context ijma refers to the consensus of Islamic authorities on a legal issue and constitutes one of the four *usul* or foundations of Islamic law (*Sharia*). It is particularly stressed by the Shafi'i school of Islamic jurisprudence.

IMAM/IMAMATE. The term "imam" denotes a prayer leader in Islam. After the death of the Prophet Muhammad it also referred to his successor in his capacity as leader of the Islamic community, more generally designated as caliph (Arabic, *khalifa*) in the dominant branch of Sunni Islam. The term has been more particularly associated with the other two significant branches of Islam, Shi'ism and Ibadism. The dominant movement within Shi'ism, the "Twelvers" (Arabic, *Ithna'ashari*), prevalent not only in Iran but also among the Shias on the Arab side of the Gulf, hold that the line of legitimate imams began with Ali, cousin and son-in-law of Muhammad. The line continued through his descendants to a twelfth imam in the 9th century A.D. who disappeared to remain "hidden" until the day of final judgment. The Ibadis, who remain the dominant Islamic sect in Oman, date back to a seventh century A.D. rejection of Ali's leadership. Their imamate was established A.D. 750, founded on the belief that the imam, temporal as well as prayer leader of their community, should be selected by prominent religious and lay figures with reference only to merit, relationship to the family or tribe of Muhammad being deemed unnecessary. Ibadis do not regard the leadership of an imam as an absolute necessity, although for most of the 1,200 years after the first imam's election the position was occupied. The last Ibadi imam was elected in 1954, and the imamate dissolved in the following year, when Sultan Said bin Taimur extended his rule from Muscat over the interior of Oman. It was briefly reestablished in the late 1950s, but suffered final defeat in 1959. *See also* IBADIS, ISLAM, *and* SHIAS.

IMMIGRATION. *See* FOREIGN WORKERS.

IMPERIAL AIRWAYS. Between 1932 and 1936 the British reached agreements with Trucial States rulers to establish facilities for military and civilian air routes to India, with Imperial Airways building an airdrome in Sharjah. The opening of the Gulf air route was significant in two ways: it established for the first time a physical British presence on the coast, which would be expanded during and after World War II, and it created a new, closer relationship between the British and the

Gulf rulers, strengthening them politically and providing them with a new source of (preoil) income.

INDIA, REPUBLIC OF. Ties between India and the Arab side of the Gulf are as old as history, dating back 5,000 years to the commerce that linked the Dilmun civilization of the Gulf with the contemporary Indus Valley culture. Seaborne trade between the two areas continued to the modern era, and it was the depredations of lower Gulf "pirates" against the commerce of British India in the early 19th century that led to British intervention in the Gulf and the establishment of a Pax Britannica through treaties imposed to protect shipping. An essential task of the Anglo/Indian government was to maintain order in the Gulf as a key part of the imperial route linking Great Britain and the jewel of its imperial crown. With India's independence in 1947 and the vesting of all responsibility for British interests in the Gulf in the Foreign Office in London, the India-Gulf relationship reverted to a primarily commercial one. As the oil of the Gulf Arab states began to be developed, great numbers of Indians came via illegal entry, especially to the lower Gulf, in search of employment, dramatically altering the demographic map. Much of Dubai's preoil wealth was derived from smuggling, that is, the reexport of gold to India, where the government had forbidden its sale. Currently, India maintains significant trading relationships with the Gulf Arab states, importing petroleum-derived fertilizers among other products. The most important economic factor, however, is the billions of dollars of remittances that Indian workers send back to India each year. Political and diplomatic relations are generally friendly. *See also* INDIANS *and* UNITED KINGDOM.

INDIANS. Indians are a very key element of the Gulf Arabs states' demographic makeup, forming overall the largest expatriate community in the Gulf. Trade first brought Indian settlers, both Hindus and Muslim Shias, to the Omani coast in the 16th century, and they dominated Omani commerce until 1970. From the mid-19th century Hindu and Muslim Indians settled in the Trucial States (now the UAE), favored because of their status as British subjects, to control the pearl trade. It was the economic development fueled by oil production, however, which brought the present numbers of Indians, beginning in Bahrain in the early 1930s, when the British encouraged their displacement of Iranian workers to weaken Iran's claim to the island. Indians are to be found in a variety of white-collar positions, such as accountants, engineers, skilled workers, and shopkeepers. The number of Indians in each Gulf Arab state is substantial, ranging from under 5 percent of total population in Kuwait to 20 percent or more in the UAE (larger than the indigenous population) and constituting in all cases a significant part of the workforce. *See also* FOREIGN WORKERS.

INDUSTRY. All the Gulf Arab states have as an economic policy priority the establishment of industries that will sustain economic well-being after their petroleum and gas reserves have been exhausted. Most Gulf Arab industrial activity, however, remains in or closely connected to the oil sector. Apart from extraction, transporting, processing, and refining facilities for oil and gas, each state has established petrochemical plants to manufacture such products as urea, ammonia, and some plastics for domestic use and export. All had established cement plants by the 1970s to serve the local construction industry at a time of rapidly expanding infrastructure, and they have created extensive food processing facilities, including flour mills. Bahrain, with its much earlier oil production, trained work force, and dwindling petroleum reserves, was the first to venture into heavy industry, with the establishment of ALBA in 1968. Since then Dubai has also established an aluminum processing plant (Dubai Aluminum Company or DUBAL), Bahrain has set up, under the aegis of the GCC, an iron ore pelletizing plant, and Qatar produces half a million tons of steel reinforcing bars annually, mainly for sale to Saudi Arabia and the UAE. In the service industry area Bahrain also led the way with the establishment of the OAPEC-funded Arab Ship Repair Yard (ASRY) in 1977, subsequently trumped by the larger Dubai Drydocks, with each struggling over several years toward eventual profitability. The UAE has taken the lead in developing container port services, and Dubai has created a large industrial and free trade zone at its port of Jebel Ali. Despite the efforts of the GOIC to promote rational regional industrial development, there continues to be some duplication of facilities. More fundamentally, the limit to economically justifiable development of nonoil industries seems to have been reached, constrained by the paucity of raw materials other than hydrocarbons, shortage of indigenous labor, and difficulty of matching the price and quality of competitors. It appears likely that industry not directly or indirectly dependent on oil will remain a minor part of the Gulf Arab states' economies, contributing less than 5 percent of GDP, except in Bahrain and, perhaps, Oman. *See also* ALBA, ARAB SHIP REPAIR YARD,

DUBAI ALUMINUM COMPANY *and* GULF ORGANIZATION FOR INDUSTRIAL CONSULTANCY.

IRAN, ISLAMIC REPUBLIC OF. Iran is one of the Gulf's two dominant powers, and together with Iraq looms very large for all the Gulf Arab states. Although Iran and the Gulf states share the common religion of Islam, Iran is dominated by its majority Shia population and currently a revolutionary Shia leadership, while the Gulf Arab states, except Bahrain, have Sunni majorities and are all ruled by Sunni elites.

Ancient Iran or Persia occupied at one time or another much of what is now the Gulf's Arab littoral, and in the sixth century B.C. the Achaemenid rulers of Iran colonized what is now Oman. The later Sassanids reasserted Iranian sway over the Arab shore, especially Oman, until defeated by Arab Muslim arms in the seventh century A.D. In Oman the imprint of long Persian occupation may be seen in such things as varieties of food crops and the irrigation system. In more recent times Iranian authority has rarely been extended to the Arab side of the Gulf. From 1602 to 1783 Iran controlled Bahrain, generally through Arab governors, and in the mid-18th century briefly intervened in an Omani civil war. By that century, however, Iranian weakness had permitted the Qawasim rulers of Sharjah to exercise de facto control over Iranian ports, most notably Lingah, until the 1930s, when Reza Shah forced them out. His son, Muhammad Reza Shah, sought to reassert Iranian hegemony over the Gulf in the 1960s and 1970s, especially following the 1968 Labor government announcement of British withdrawal from its security obligations east of Suez. The withdrawal prompted assertion of Iranian claims to Bahrain, relinquished when a UN mission determined that popular sentiment favored independence. The shah then pressed for Iranian control of three strategically placed islands in the lower Gulf, Abu Musa and the Tunbs, long held by Sharjah and Ras al-Khaimah, respectively. An agreement on shared ownership was reached with Sharjah, but the Tunbs were seized by force on the eve of UAE independence. If, however, the shah's Iran was an overbearing and domineering neighbor, it nevertheless shared the basic domestic and international political values of the Gulf Arab states as a pro-Western bulwark against the Soviets, their allies, and proxies. Indeed, Iran's military assistance in Oman against the Dhofari uprising of the 1960s and 1970s was important in defeating that radical threat. Thus the overthrow of the shah and the establishment of the Islamic Republic of Iran were troubling developments for the

Gulf Arab states. Iran's revolutionary government has urged the overthrow of their ruling families and has been linked to hostile acts against their governments. These acts include the encouragement, if not active assistance, of a coup attempt by Shia Arabs against the Bahraini government in December 1981 and the bombing of Kuwaiti oil facilities early in the Iran-Iraq war, as well as several Shia terrorist operations, including an attempt on the life of the emir of Kuwait, between 1983 and 1985. The ending of the Iran-Iraq conflict, in which the Gulf Arab states rendered support to Iraq, helped make possible some warming of relations. In the wake of the 1991 Gulf war this process went further with Iran and its Arab neighbors pursuing cooperative policies in OPEC and at one point discussing common measures for Gulf security (although little progress has been made in that latter respect). In 1992 and 1993, however, Iran's further assertion of control over Abu Musa and its arms acquisitions, together with the divided Iranian government's ambiguous and conflicting signals as to its intentions in regional policy, generated further unease among the Gulf Arabs in the mid-1990s. Nevertheless, Qatar and Oman have continued to pursue a pragmatic course of friendly relations with Iran. *See also* IRAN-IRAQ WAR, OMAN, *and* POPULAR FRONT FOR THE LIBERATION OF OMAN AND THE ARAB GULF.

IRAN-CONTRA SCANDAL. In 1985 the Reagan administration authorized three shipments of U.S. antitank and antiaircraft missiles from Israel to Iran in an effort to gain release of American hostages held in Lebanon by pro-Iranian groups. In January 1986 President Reagan approved a covert American diplomatic initiative to Iran to try to free remaining hostages in Lebanon and promote the development of a more moderate Iranian government. With Israeli assistance more weapons and spare parts for military equipment were sold to Iran. This initiative was revealed in November 1986 as was the fact that officials in the National Security Council had used some of the proceeds from the sales to support the Contra rebels in Nicaragua in violation of American law. The American arms shipments to Iran were in apparent contradiction to the U.S. policy of a pro-Iraq tilt in the Iran-Iraq war and thus created considerable unease among moderate Arab states, especially those of the Gulf.

IRANIANS. Iranians are a significant part of the social and economic fabric of the Gulf Arab states. In Bahrain, Dubai, Kuwait, and Oman

(Muscat) there are old established communities, with many prominent merchants among them. Many of the older, settled Iranian families on the Arab side of the Gulf are known as *hawwala,* or *muhawwala,* those who migrated to Iran from the Gulf Arab littoral and later returned. Most of them, as well as the Baluchi Iranians, are Sunni, while most of the other Iranian residents are Shia. More recent Iranian arrivals, drawn by the oil boom, are professionals, small merchants, and skilled and semiskilled workers. Security considerations in the 1980s led the Gulf Arab states, especially Kuwait and Bahrain, to replace Iranian workers with South Asians. *See also* FOREIGN WORKERS.

IRAN-IRAQ WAR. The war between the Gulf's two regional super-powers presented the small Gulf Arab states with a painful dilemma and the threat that hostilities, by design or accident, would spill over onto their territory and shipping. There was fear of Iraq, with its record of hostile propaganda and attempted subversion against their governments, but the threat projected by Iran's revolutionary Shia regime was the greater of the two evils and led to general support or "tilted neutrality" in favor of Iraq. Two days before the Iraqi initiation of full-scale hostilities on September 21, 1980, the rulers of Bahrain, Kuwait, Qatar, and Saudi Arabia pledged financial support for Iraq in the impending conflict. The UAE remained divided through the war, with Dubai and Sharjah preoccupied with maintenance of close trading links to Iran while Abu Dhabi supported Iraq from immediately after the September 19 meeting. The war preoccupied the Gulf's dominant powers and provided the opportunity to establish the GCC, for which the Iranian revolution had supplied the primary impetus. When the war turned in Iran's favor, 1981-83, the Gulf Arab states began to press their efforts at conciliation through the Arab League, the Organization of the Islamic Conference, the Nonaligned Movement, and the UN. These initiatives continued but were overshadowed by the tanker war from the spring of 1984, when Iraq struck at ships carrying crude oil from Iranian ports and Iran retaliated by striking at Kuwaiti and Saudi tankers. This in turn led to the 1987 Kuwaiti request to both the U.S. and USSR for protection, giving rise to the "reflagging" operation which brought U.S. Navy protection and a dramatic turnabout from the Gulf Arab states' and especially Kuwait's own earlier position against American or Soviet intervention in the Gulf. "Loans" to sustain Iraq in the war totaled $40-$50 billion, principally from Saudi Arabia and Kuwait. Disagreement over the forgiving of Iraqi indebtedness by Kuwait was a factor in provoking Iraq's August 1990 invasion of Kuwait. *See also* IRAN *and* IRAQ.

IRAQ, REPUBLIC OF. From its independence in 1932 Iraq's relations with the Gulf Arab states were relatively slight as long as they remained under British protection. The first Iraqi initiative toward an independent Gulf neighbor was assertion of a claim to Kuwait immediately after the latter's independence in June 1961. Thwarted by British dispatch of troops and subsequent Arab League action, Iraq acknowledged Kuwait's sovereignty and independence in 1963. Further demands, however, were made in 1973 and 1975, underscored on the first occasion by an Iraqi attack on a Kuwaiti border post, for access to or cession or lease of Kuwait's islands of Warbah and Bubiyan, which abut the approach to Iraq's naval base at Umm Qasr. Similar demands were made during the Iran-Iraq war. The breakdown of the Taif talks of July 1990 over cession or lease of territory and other issues led to Iraq's August 2 invasion of Kuwait. Informed opinion overwhelmingly rejects Iraq's claim to Kuwait, but Iraq maintains that it has never accepted a de jure determination of the common border. The border has been demarcated by the UN commission that was established to do so by the terms of the agreement that ended the hostilities between Iraq and the coalition that drove it from Kuwait. Iraq has denounced the results of the commission's work, which had the effect of giving Kuwait a part of the Iraqi naval base of Umm Qasr and several oil wells formerly on the Iraqi side of the border.

Iraq's relations with the other Gulf Arab states have been less conflicted but uneasy. After the establishment of Ba'th rule in 1968, Iraq provided money, arms, and training to Ba'thist cells in the Gulf Arab states, especially Bahrain. Even after British withdrawal in 1971 these had little impact, and the failure of the radical challenge in the Gulf region was symbolized by the final rout of the Popular Front for the Liberation of Oman and the Arab Gulf in Oman's Dhofar Province in 1975. In that same year Iraq signed the Treaty of Algiers with Iran, settling their principal outstanding differences and signaling a period of Iraqi preoccupation with internal affairs during which relations with Iraq's conservative southern neighbors were more friendly. Generally, these relations were reinforced by Iraq's need for their support in its war with Iran, although the lower Gulf states attempted to adopt a sufficiently neutral stance to deflect Iranian wrath and allow themselves to attempt mediation of the conflict. Iraq's invasion and occupation of

Kuwait represented a massive and overwhelming threat to all of them, which brought alignment with Saudi Arabia in opposing Iraq. That alignment meant their agreement to an unprecedented degree of military cooperation with the United States and other Western states as well as with Arab allies to drive Iraq from Kuwait. Since Desert Storm, Oman and Qatar have moved toward normal relations with Iraq, though menacing Iraqi troop movements in fall 1994 reawakened fears in Kuwait and elsewhere. *See also* BORDERS AND TERRITORIAL DISPUTES, IRAN-IRAQ WAR *and* DESERT SHIELD/DESERT STORM.

IRAQ PETROLEUM COMPANY. The Iraq Petroleum Company (IPC) was created in 1928 as successor to the Turkish Petroleum Company, which had been established before World War I to explore for oil in the part of the Ottoman Empire later to become Iraq. Its shares were held by the Anglo-Persian (later Anglo-Iranian) Oil Company, the Compagnie Française des Petroles, Standard Oil Company of New Jersey, the Socony-Vacuum Oil Company, and Calouste Gulbenkian ("Mr. Five Percent"). The partners agreed in 1928 to the Red Line Agreement, which pledged each not to seek a concession in an area including all of the Arabian Peninsula, except in cooperation with the others. IPC opted not to seek a concession in Bahrain, where Standard Oil of California (SoCal), through a Canadian subsidiary, developed the first oil strike on the Arab side of the Gulf. After SoCal had struck what was to become the Aramco bonanza in Saudi Arabia, IPC secured seven concessions in Qatar, Oman, and all of the Trucial States. Subsequently some of these concessions became producers, though most of the oil wealth in these states was developed by other concessionaires. *See also* OIL.

IRRIGATION. *See* AGRICULTURE *and* FALAJ.

ISA BIN ALI AL KHALIFA. Shaikh Isa's rule in Bahrain covered almost the last third of the 19th century and first quarter of the 20th. He was placed in power by the British in 1869, then forced to abdicate in favor of his son Hamad in 1923. *See also* BAHRAIN *and* AL KHALIFA.

ISA BIN SALMAN AL KHALIFA (b. 1932). Shaikh Isa is the current ruler of Bahrain, having succeeded his deceased father as emir in December 1961. Isa had been designated as heir apparent in 1958 and had already begun to assume official responsibilities in preparation for his rule. His performance as president of the Municipal Council of Bahrain's capital and largest city, Manama, in the wake of political disruption in the mid-1950s, and in other positions, served to demonstrate his leadership skills. In the two years before he became emir, Isa had assumed considerable responsibility for the country's domestic and foreign affairs owing to the poor health of his father.

Generally, Shaikh Isa has presided over three decades of dramatic change in Bahrain with great skill and coped with daunting external threats as tumultuous events have overshadowed the Gulf. In anticipation of independence, declared on August 14, 1971, Isa devoted considerable attention to creating a new government structure, including an appointed cabinet. In late 1971, acting against the advice of some members of the Al Khalifa, Isa called for elections to choose just over half the members of a constituent assembly that would prepare a draft constitution for the state. This led to a difficult parliamentary experiment of less than two years that ended in August, 1975, after members of the National Assembly openly criticized the government's public security regulations and its close ties to the US. Although the experiment in elected government has not been repeated, Isa's pragmatic tolerance as well as the relative honesty and efficiency of his government, with his brother Shaikh Khalifa, the prime minister, in charge of day-to-day affairs, have buffered the impact of an authoritarian government dominated by the Al Khalifa and their allies among the great merchant families. His promotion of economic and social welfare and his reputation as a moderate have been of key importance in maintaining Al Khalifa rule, a challenge for a Sunni Muslim ruler in a country that is 70 percent Shia. In late 1994, 1995, and 1996 Shia riots, caused largely by high unemployment, were firmly put down. Isa and his government have proven adept at aligning themselves with regional and international powers to preserve Bahrain's independence and security. After quashing a December 1981 coup attempt, the ruler moved Bahrain to a delicate course of accommodation with Tehran, while ostensibly supporting Baghdad in the Iran-Iraq war. In recent years he has also promoted very close economic and security ties to Saudi Arabia. He was careful in the mid-1970s to help preserve the U.S. Navy's Bahrain presence through the lowest of low profiles, so that Bahrain was able to play a key role in providing logistical support, both during the 1987-88 Kuwait "reflagging" exercise and in the 1990-91 Gulf crisis, thereby cementing relations with Bahrain's ultimate source of security against external threat. *See also* BAHRAIN *and* AL KHALIFA.

ISA TOWN. Isa Town is a planned, government-financed community in Bahrain, southwest of the capital, Manama. It received its first families in 1968 and now has a population of about 40,000. Isa Town served as the model for two still more ambitious projects, Hamad Town and Fasht al-Adham, being built on reclaimed land.

ISLAM. Islam was introduced to the Arab side of the Gulf within the Prophet Muhammad's lifetime. Since then, for nearly 14 centuries, it has been the most important cultural factor in shaping and regulating society. The entire indigenous population of the Gulf Arab states is Muslim as is the great majority of the expatriate workforce. Islam is declared to be the official religion in each state, and Islamic law, the *Sharia*, continues to regulate such matters as marriage, divorce, and inheritance, and to deal with at least some criminal offenses. It is not too much to say that being Muslim is an essential part of any Gulf Arab's identity.

Generally, Islam is observed in a more traditional way than in the more Westernized parts of the Arab world, such as the great urban centers in Egypt, Syria, and Iraq, with its impact on social and cultural life immediately apparent. Close identification with Islam and its behavioral norms has been a key factor in confirming the legitimacy of Gulf Arab rulers. In the 1980s, in reaction to rapid modernization and the secularizing Western values it introduces and, to some extent, inspired by the Islamic revolution in Iran, there has been a resurgence of religious sentiment and calls for more rigorous adherence to Islamic standards of public and private behavior. To some extent this "populist Islam," typically of strong appeal to university students and young professionals, is directed against the ruling establishments. While such a challenge has been contained or deflected, the Al Khalifa rulers of Bahrain face the challenge of ruling a population that is 70 percent Shia. The apprehension of Shia plotters against the government in December 1981 greatly weakened the principal militant Shia group. Fairly lenient sentences for the plotters helped to blunt further threats and the excesses of the Iranian revolution dampened the enthusiasm of Shias on the Arab side of the Gulf for accepting it as a model for their own political ambitions. However, in 1994-95 an economic downturn prompted violent Shia antigovernment protests.

Although in the other states Shias are a minority, their numbers are significant, in recent years reaching over 20 percent of the population in Kuwait and Qatar. In Bahrain and elsewhere considerable numbers of them are of Arab origin, while those from Iran have come at different times for different reasons. Shias of Iranian origin include wealthy merchants and taxi drivers. Most Arab Shias are *Ithna'asharis*, or "Twelvers," the sect that is the established religion of Iran.

The Gulf area is also home to the third and smallest of the significant branches of Islam, the Ibadi sect, concentrated in Oman, where Ibadism is practiced by more than half the population. An outgrowth of the seventh century A.D. Kharijite movement, it is not far removed from majority Sunni Islam in essential principles, but combines austere adherence to those principles with belief in an elected imam or spiritual and temporal leader. Ibadism's stronghold was traditionally the inaccessible interior of Oman, but in the 1950s the last Ibadi imam was defeated by Sultan Said bin Taimur with British help.

Among the majority Sunnis of the Gulf Arab states there are differences of belief and practice, but these are not large. Qatar's Sunni population follows the same strict Wahhabi interpretation of Islam as do the Sunnis of Saudi Arabia. Together with the Wahhabis, other Sunnis adhere to the strictest school of Islamic law, the Hanbali. Of the three remaining schools, the Maliki is the most widely represented. *See also* IBADIS *and* IMAM/IMAMATE.

ISLAMIC BANKING. *See* BANKING.

ISLAMIC CONFERENCE ORGANIZATION. (ICO). *Also* ORGANI-ZATION OF THE ISLAMIC CONFERENCE (OIC). The Islamic Conference Organization came into formal existence in 1972, two years after King Faisal of Saudi Arabia had gained international Islamic support for a permanent Islamic political organization with its secretariat in Jidda. Originally intended primarily as a means of opposing Soviet and radical Arab influence in the Middle East, the ICO has become a significant forum for dealing with major political and diplomatic issues. The Gulf Arab states are active members and sought to use the ICO, together with other forums, to try to bring the Iran-Iraq war to a negotiated close.

ISRAEL, STATE OF. The Gulf Arab states share with the rest of the Arab world the conviction that the creation of Israel was an unjust usurpation of the rights of the Palestinian Arabs. Together with other moderate Arab states, they support a peace settlement based on UN resolutions 242 and 348, with Israel yielding the remaining territory occupied in the June war of 1967. They call for establishment of an independent Palestinian state and have been prepared to accept terms of settlement acceptable to the Palestinian political mainstream.

For many years Israel and the Arab-Israeli conflict were not overriding concerns of the Gulf Arab states. This reflected their physical distance from Israel, the insulating interposition of British protection, and the failure despite Saudi and other efforts to link European and American access to their oil with the Arab-Israeli question. What changed this dramatically was the October 1973 Arab-Israeli war, when a massive U.S. military resupply effort on behalf of Israel caused King Faisal of Saudi Arabia to call for progressive reductions in oil exports and a cutoff of all oil to the U.S. and the Netherlands pending Israeli withdrawal from occupied Arab territories. The Gulf Arab states (including both Abu Dhabi and Dubai in the UAE) joined the embargo. Moreover, the large numbers of Palestinians in the Gulf helped generate a more active support of their cause against Israel, both from genuine sympathy for that cause and through fear of what they might do to threaten and destabilize Gulf Arab governments if support were not given. Thus these governments observed the Arab economic boycott of Israel and, with the exception of Oman, broke relations with Egypt in the wake of the Camp David Accords (1978) and the Egyptian-Israeli Peace Treaty (1979). Oman, facing the threat of its then-Marxist neighbor, the People's Democratic Republic of Yemen, and far removed from Israel, backed Egyptian president Anwar Sadat's settlement with Israel. It should also be noted that a significant Palestinian presence in the Gulf Arab press tended to lend an added stridency to anti-Israel expressions. In addition to the threat of political destabilization by Palestinian groups or radical Arab states demanding various kinds of anti-Israel actions, the possibility of direct menace from Israel was itself taken seriously after the Israeli air raid against Iraq's nuclear reactor at Tuwaitha in June 1981 and threats by Israeli hardliners to bomb Gulf oil facilities in any future Arab-Israeli conflict. Through the 1980s and into the 1990s the immediate dangers of the Iranian revolution, the Iran-Iraq war, and the crisis precipitated by Iraq's August, 1990, invasion of Kuwait have overshadowed the threat represented by Israel. Indeed, it was clear that even if Israel had retaliated against Iraqi Scud missile attacks, the Gulf Arab states would have continued to cooperate with their U.S. and other Western and Arab allies to defeat the Iraqi threat. The de facto alignment of Gulf and other Arab states with Israel against a common threat led some observers to see victory over Iraq and Israeli self-restraint as helping to mute fears and antagonisms between Israel and moderate Arab states, especially those of the Gulf, while generating new momentum for an Arab-Israeli peace settlement. In late 1991 and 1992 Arab-Israeli peace talks were launched, and the Gulf Arab states signaled their support for this U.S. initiative. Indeed, by January 1992 they had joined the "multilateral phase" of the peace talks dealing with functional problems in the Middle East, such as the sharing of water resources. Further, the Gulf Arab states gave their support to the Israel-PLO Declaration of Principles of September 13, 1993, calling for Palestinian self-rule in Gaza and Jericho as a first step toward an Israeli-Palestinian peace settlement. In September 1994 the GCC states voted to end the secondary economic boycott against Israel (the refusal to deal with companies that do business with Israel). The election of the Likud coalition candidate, Binyamin Netenyahu, in May 1996, halted progress in the peace process and chilled the economic and other relations that were developing between Israel and the Gulf Arab states. *See also* PALESTINIANS *and* ARAB-ISRAELI CONFLICT.

ITALY (Official name, ITALIAN REPUBLIC). Italy has not had significant historic associations with the Gulf Arab states. A curious footnote to World War II was an Italian bombing mission launched from the island of Rhodes against the oil refinery in Bahrain and (by navigational error) the oil facilities at Dhahran, Saudi Arabia, in October 1940, which did little damage. Its present relations are mainly limited to modest trade with them, importing oil and exporting various industrial products including arms. Italy contributed modestly to the 1987 US-European naval build-up in the Gulf in conjunction with the U.S. "reflagging" of Kuwaiti tankers to counter the Iranian threat to shipping, and assigned 10 small naval vessels and eight combat aircraft to the multinational coalition that drove Iraqi forces from Kuwait in January-February 1991.

ITHNA'ASHARIS. *See* ISLAM.

J

JABIR AL-AHMAD AL-JABIR AL SABAH (b. 1926). Jabir al-Ahmad al-Jabir Al Sabah has been the emir or ruler of Kuwait since December 1977, guiding that state through the most threatening period of its modern independent history. He was educated at the Mubarakiyya School to the age of 10, and subsequently by private tutors. Although his eventual selection as emir could not be foreseen, both the senior Al Sabah and Kuwait's British protectors recognized Jabir as having leadership qualities. From 1949 to 1959 he served as the director of security for Ahmadi, the city that grew up around Kuwait's oil operations, and in 1959 became director of the country's financial department. After independence, in 1961, he became minister of finance, establishing centralized control over Kuwait's finances. In 1962 Jabir was passed over in favor of Sabah al-Salim, brother of the emir, Abdallah al-Salim, in the selection of an heir apparent. The decision broke the pattern of alternation between the Salim and Jabir branches of the ruling family. In 1965 Abdallah died and was succeeded by Sabah. Jabir then became heir apparent and prime minister, in which role he increasingly exercised control of the government, capping a long apprenticeship for his role as emir since late 1977. In the following year he designated Saad al-Abdallah, Kuwait's foreign minister, as heir apparent, thereby restoring the established family pattern of succession.

In the first 13 years of his rule Jabir maintained reasonable stability at a time of threat, both internal and external. He kept relative peace among the often contentious members of the Al Sabah and maintained the general support of the Kuwaiti populace by continuing the generous social welfare system established when the country's oil wealth began to be realized. Kuwait's National Assembly, the only parliamentary body among the Gulf Arab states, was suspended before he became ruler. Despite his reputation for favoring more political representation, Jabir did not assent to assembly elections until 1981. The assembly was again suspended in 1986 when, at a time of great external danger, Al Sabah ministers came under political attack. Despite these problems and the economic-political difficulties created by the collapse of the Suq al-Manakh, Kuwait's unofficial stock market, in 1982, the greatest threats during Jabir's rule have been external. Given Kuwait's proximity to Iraq, he saw no alternative to providing massive financial support to Iraq in its war with Iran as well as permitting Kuwait to be used as a principal transit point for the shipment of military and other goods to Iraq. This drew Iranian air attacks against Kuwaiti oil facilities and helped inspire Shia terrorist attacks in Kuwait, one of which narrowly missed in its aim of assassinating the emir in 1985. In the later phases of the war, when Iran attacked Kuwaiti shipping, Jabir deftly played his established policy of neutrality between the superpowers by gaining Soviet promises of support in order to induce the U.S. to "reflag" Kuwaiti oil tankers.

When Iraq invaded and occupied Kuwait in August, 1990, Jabir and most of the Al Sabah fled and a government-in-exile was set up in Saudi Arabia. Although he and the Al Sabah retained general support among Kuwaitis, many, especially among those who remained behind to endure and resist the brutal Iraqi occupation, have demanded greater political freedom. Jabir's rather leisurely return from comfortable exile and his deferral of elections for a new assembly to October 5, 1992, engendered substantial frustration and anger. However, the holding of a free election, the seating of an antigovernment majority, and the government's invitation to members of the opposition to participate in the cabinet have helped to engender trust in the government. Jabir retains the broad support of the Al Sabah and the general Kuwaiti public, but faces a considerable challenge in the more assertive assembly, major economic problems, and daunting security concerns. *See also* KUWAIT *and* AL SABAH.

JA'LAN. The Ja'lan is a subregion of Oman that includes the eastern-most headland of the country. Situated at the eastern end of the Hajar Mountains, it comprises a valley leading to the Gulf of Oman. Its port of Sur once played a major role in Oman's commerce with East Africa and India. The modernized ports of Muscat and Salalah have greatly reduced Sur's significance as a commercial port, but it remains an important fishing port where traditional ships are still built for fishing and local trade. Ja'lan was one of the areas first settled by the initial wave of Arab settlers from western Arabia in the first century A.D.

JALBOOT. *Also* JALBUT *and* JALIBUT. The *jalboot* is one of the several Gulf sailing vessels (most now have engines as well as sail) collectively referred to as *dhows*. Its name and shape indicate that it was probably modeled on the British Navy's "jollyboat," a small, open boat carried at the stern of a large vessel. *See also* BAGGALA, BOOM, DHOW, *and* SAMBOOK.

JAPAN. Japan's first significant, albeit indirect, contact with the Arab states of the Gulf was in the 1930s, when the introduction of Japanese cultured pearls devastated the Gulf states' pearling trade, then the most important factor in their economies. By the 1980s Japan had become the major trading partner of the Gulf states, accounting for a very large part of their oil exports (up to half of each state's production) and providing the lion's share of imports, including heavy industrial goods, motor vehicles, and television sets.

The switch from coal to oil as its principal energy source after World War II led Japan to rely heavily on oil from Iran and the Gulf Arab states. Although Japan's late entry into the Gulf oil market effectively precluded major direct participation in oil production, a Japanese business consortium did establish the Arabian Oil Company that, in 1957, obtained a joint Saudi-Kuwaiti concession for offshore production. Together with later concessions for oil and gas in the UAE, and oil in Oman, it has provided an independent source for at least part of Japan's Gulf oil supply that, in turn, amounts to about 75 percent of the country's total oil imports. The Arab oil embargo of 1973-74 and the outbreak of the Iran-Iraq war in 1980 caused great Japanese concern for the security of its oil supplies and led to an intensified search for other oil and nonoil energy sources. However, it discovered that no real alternatives to its dependence on Gulf oil existed and turned to a renewed emphasis on cultivating strong, positive relations with the Gulf Arab states, resulting in a new phase of close interdependence. The Gulf states wish to draw more direct Japanese investment and gain access to Japanese markets for their increasing petrochemical production and energy-intensive products such as refined aluminum, in addition to crude oil and gas. Despite its massive and intensive economic involvement in the Gulf, Japan has remained aloof politically and militarily, a position dictated by a stringent interpretation of its constitution and prevailing public opinion. To deflect criticism of its lack of direct involvement in the allied military effort to oust Iraqi forces from Kuwait during the 1990-91 Gulf crisis, Japan pledged $11 billion in financial aid to the United States and $3 billion to several Middle East nations.

JASIM (QASIM) BIN MUHAMMAD AL THANI (?–1913). Jasim bin Mohammed Al Thani ("Qasim" is the correct transliteration of the name, while "Jasim" reflects the regional pronunciation) was a leading figure of the Al Thani clan and was in large measure responsible for securing its rule over Qatar and establishing the latter's independence. Jasim took advantage of the Ottoman Turks' occupation of Hasa in eastern Arabia in 1871 by accepting their suzerainty in exchange for recognition of him as *qaim maqam* (chief administrator of a district) in Qatar. Ottoman recognition served to establish independence from the Al Khalifa of Bahrain, who had originally occupied and continued to claim Qatar. Through patience, tenacity, and occasional boldness Jasim extended Al Thani authority throughout Qatar, frequently playing off the British and the Ottomans to maintain and solidify his position. The capstone to this process was a Qatari victory over Ottoman forces in 1893, when the Turkish *vali* (governor) of Basra came with troops to enforce Ottoman authority, which Jasim had flouted. Turkish rule continued de jure until World War I, but Jasim had secured Qatar's independence in fact. In the same month and year that Jasim died, July 1913, an Anglo-Turkish convention (never ratified because of the outbreak of World War I) brought Ottoman occupation of Qatar to a formal end. *See also* QATAR *and* AL THANI.

JAWF. The Arabic word *jawf*, used in a geographic sense, means "interior" or "center." In Oman the Jawf region is an inland area of the central Hajar Mountains, to the southwest of Muscat, which recent archaeological work indicates was the heart of ancient civilization in Oman.

JEBEL. *Also* JABAL. Literally a "mountain," the word *jebel* as used on the Arab littoral of the Gulf may denote an elevation much more modest than what is ordinarily understood by the term.

JEBEL AKHDAR *or* AL-JABAL AL-AKHDAR. Literally the "green mountain" in Arabic, the *Jebel Akhdar* is a group of 10,000-foot mountains in the western Hajar Mountains of northern Oman that form a lofty plateau. While vegetation is less luxuriant than the name might imply, it is substantial and includes juniper trees, grasses, grapes, pomegranates, and asparagus. The Jebel Akhdar and the almost equally inaccessible neighboring mountains and valleys offered refuge from early times to groups fleeing oppression. Among these were the Ibadi

Muslims, a minority sect that in the eighth century A.D. settled in Oman as an independent imamate or community led by an imam with religious and political authority. The imamate survived. although with occasional vagaries until the modern era.

JEBEL ALI. Located on the coast of Dubai, about 20 mi (32 km) southwest of Dubai City, Jebel Ali (named for a slight prominence on the low, flat coastline) is the site of an ambitious industrial center and free trade zone served by the world's largest man-made port. Begun in 1976, the Jebel Ali major industrial components were in place by the early 1980s and include DUBAL, run by natural gas from DUGAS. Heat from the DUBAL smelter is used to run the desalting plant, which provides Dubai City water. Among other ancillary industries is Dubai Cables (DUCAL), which exports power cables. In 1985 the Jebel Ali Free Trade Zone opened with a large area set aside for various kinds of foreign enterprises to operate exempt from income taxes and the usual requirement of a local sponsor. Companies operating in the zone may also expatriate profits for at least 15 years. Despite the disruptions of the Iran-Iraq war and the Gulf crisis of 1990-91, Jebel Ali has generally met the expansive economic expectations vested in it.

JEBEL DHANNA. Situated on the coast of Abu Dhabi, about 140 mi (225 km) south-southwest of Abu Dhabi City, Jebel Dhanna is the export terminal for all of Abu Dhabi's onshore oil production. The name refers to a prominence of over 350 ft (107 m) created geologically by a "salt plug" and selected as a gathering point for the oil so that the flow to waiting tankers offshore is assisted by gravity. Adjacent to Jebel Dhanna, which was constructed beginning in 1962, the industrial city of Ruwais was subsequently created to produce a variety of refined oil products from a portion of the oil production. *See also* RUWAIS.

JEBEL DUKHAN *or* JABAL AL-DUKHAN. Rising more than 400 ft (122 m), Jebel Dukhan, part of a limestone escarpment, is the highest point in Bahrain. Its name "Mountain of Smoke" comes from the mists that often appear upon it. Situated in the center of Bahrain Island, it marks the area of most onshore Bahraini oil production, thus giving its name to Bahrain's main oil field.

    The same name is given to a limestone ridge on the western edge of

the Qatar Peninsula. Like Bahrain's Jebel Dukhan, its name also identifies a producing oil field.

JEWS. On the Gulf side of the Arabian Peninsula there are only scanty
indications of a Jewish community in antiquity. However, there was for
some time in Kuwait a prosperous Jewish community and, to the
present, there is a small Jewish merchant community in Bahrain, whose
leading family, the Nanoos, has several business interests, including
offshore banking.

JIDDA. The island of Jidda is part of the Bahrain archipelago and is the
site of the state prison. The name is shared by Saudi Arabia's largest
port city, located on the Red Sea.

JOASMEE. *See* QAWASIM.

JORDAN, HASHEMITE KINGDOM OF. In the years since the Gulf
Arab states began developing their oil wealth, Jordan and many of its
citizens have played a key role in both the civilian and military spheres
of those countries. Jordanians have served as teachers and in a variety
of other white-collar positions, both in the public and private sectors. In
the UAE Jordanians served as judges and as officials in the Ministry of
Justice during the first years after independence. Perhaps the most
significant role that they have played was in helping the Gulf states to
develop their internal and external security services. Numerous
Jordanian military and internal security officers have been seconded to
serve, particularly in the UAE and Oman. Moreover, Jordanian military
personnel played a direct and key role in helping Oman to defeat the
Dhofar Rebellion in 1975. Jordan committed officers, NCOs, military
engineers, and briefly a combat battalion. The economic benefit to
Jordan of this Gulf Arab state involvement was very substantial. By the
early 1980s expatriate Jordanians were sending about $1.25 billion
annually back to their country, virtually all of it coming from the
Arabian Peninsula (much of it from Saudi Arabia as well as the states
covered in this volume). The subsequent severe downturn in the international oil market had a pronounced negative impact on employment
opportunities for Jordanians in the Gulf Arab states and thus on
remittances to Jordan.
    Jordan's sympathetic position toward Iraq during the 1990-91 Gulf
crisis further undermined its economic relationship and for a time

severely compromised its political and security relations with all or most of the Gulf Arab states. By 1995 relations had warmed. However, most of the Jordanians who worked in Kuwait left after the Iraqi invasion or were later expelled, while the other states reduced the numbers of Jordanian expatriates in their work forces. *See also* FOREIGN WORKERS.

JUFAIR. Jufair is a settlement on Bahrain, now part of the capital of Manama. In 1828 it was the site of a battle in which a Bahraini force defended the islands against an Omani attack. In the post-World War II era a British naval base was established at Jufair. From 1949 a small American flotilla, designated U.S. Middle East Force, was stationed there to show the American flag in the Gulf-Peninsula area. When British naval forces were withdrawn in 1971, it remained there under the Jufair Agreement, which granted the U.S. the use of the facilities in exchange for a $4 million annual payment. U.S. support for Israel in the 1973 October war and opposition in Bahrain's short-lived National Assembly in 1975 challenged, but did not upset, the arrangement. In 1977, however, the executive agreement between Bahrain and the U.S. expired and was replaced by an agreement under which Jufair was no longer considered a home base, but U.S. Middle East Force ships were permitted to call at Jufair upon request. This allowed a further lowering of an already low American profile with little practical effect on the use of facilities at Jufair. During the U.S. Navy buildup in the Gulf attendant on the 1987-88 "reflagging" of Kuwaiti tankers and the 1990-91 Gulf crisis, the facilities at Jufair played a key role. *See also* MIDDLE EAST FORCE.

JUFAIR AGREEMENT. *See* JUFAIR.

JULANDA. Originally the term *Julanda* referred to the Arab leader in Oman who served as the vassal of the Sassanian Persians. It was subsequently the name of a ruling family that produced A.D. 750 the first Ibadi imam of Oman, Julanda bin Mas'ud. The Julandas fell from power in the next century.

JULFAR. Julfar was an important port, located just to the north of the present city of Ras al-Khaimah in the UAE, at least as early as the Achaemenid period, when it was occupied by the Persians. In the early Islamic period it served as a landing point for the proselytizing Muslim armies. It remained an important port up to the 17th and 18th centuries, when it underwent Portuguese and Persian occupation and was superseded by Ras al-Khaimah.

K

KALBA. The name refers to a town and its surrounding area at the southern limit of the UAE Gulf of Oman coast. It has been a possession of the Qawasim rulers of Sharjah since the early 19th century, although disputed for some time with the sultans of Muscat. In 1936 the British recognized Kalba as an independent emirate under a member of the Qawasim clan, to facilitate the securing of landing rights for British aircraft. In 1952, with the death of the last of the line of Qawasim rulers in Kalba, the territory reverted to the direct governance of Sharjah.

KANOO. The Kanoos are one of the Gulf's great merchant families, centered in Bahrain, with a business empire throughout the Arabian Peninsula, based on services that include shipping and banking. The business began with Yusuf Kanoo, who supplied goods to pearling captains, then invested in the pearl business, subsequently branching into banking. His astute cultivation both of the ruling Al Khalifa family and the British Agent enhanced his success, but the company barely survived the collapse of the natural pearl market in the 1930s. Eventual payment of all the company's debts helped to restore its prestige and Yusuf's arrangement for transfer of its operations to his nephews, Jasim and Ali and, eventually, to the grand nephews who run it today, ensured its success. In the 1950s Abdullah Kanoo established a branch of the business in Saudi Arabia, and in the following two decades branches were set up in Abu Dhabi, Dubai, and Oman.

KHALID BIN MUHAMMAD AL QASIMI. Shaikh Khalid was ruler of Sharjah when the UAE became an independent federation on December 2, 1971. On the eve of independence he reached an agreement with the shah of Iran to share sovereignty and oil revenues of the island of Abu Musa. In January 1972, a cousin, Saqr bin Sultan, who had been removed as ruler in 1965 by the British in favor of Khalid, assassinated Khalid and tried to use popular resentment over the perceived surrender of Abu Musa to regain power. The UAE federal government thwarted the attempted coup and installed the deceased ruler's brother, Shaikh Sultan, as ruler.

KHALID BIN SAQR AL QASIMI. Shaikh Khalid is the son of the ruler of Ras al-Khaimah, Shaikh Sultan bin Muhammad, and his designated successor. He has frequently acted as his father's deputy in UAE and Gulf affairs since creation of the federation.

KHALIFA, AL. The Al Khalifa have been the ruling family of Bahrain since 1783. They were part of the Utub, a tribal grouping of clans claiming to be from the great central Arabian Anaizah confederation, who migrated to Kuwait in the early 18th century. Toward the 1760s the Al Khalifa left Kuwait and tried to settle on Bahrain in whose waters they had already established extensive pearling operations. Rebuffed by the Omani tribe that controlled the islands as a Persian fiefdom, they settled at Zubarah on the western coast of the neighboring Qatari Peninsula. Subsequent rivalry led to an attack by Bahrain's rulers against Zubarah, which was repulsed, opening the way to the Al Khalifa's occupation of Bahrain, thereby ending Persian suzerainty over the islands. The Al Khalifa continued to exercise at least a measure of control over Qatar through the 19th century. Although claims to the mainland have been abandoned, they still dispute with the Al Thani rulers of Qatar ownership of the Hawar Islands and artificial islets on the shoal of Fasht al-Dibal.

Conflict within the family marked its rule through much of the 19th century until, in 1869, a strong ruler, Shaikh Isa bin Ali, inaugurated the orderly exercise of Al Khalifa authority. Since that year the rule of primogeniture has regulated succession, in a departure from traditional Arab practice, and was made law by inclusion in the 1971 constitution. Isa bin Ali was deposed by the British political resident in 1923, but the general impact of British dominion in the Gulf, beginning with the 1820 General Treaty of Peace, signed by the ruler of Bahrain as well as the rulers of what came to be called the Trucial States, was to strengthen the position of the rulers. The Al Khalifa benefited from recognition by the unchallenged power in the area and gained modest but significant material rewards for various services rendered, which gave them an advantage over the powerful merchant families that became still more pronounced when oil revenues commenced in the 1930s. British assistance in modernizing the administration of Bahrain, especially during the three-decade tenure of Sir Charles Belgrave, from 1926 on, further strengthened the position of the ruling family.

The Al Khalifa have lacked two sources of legitimacy enjoyed by the other Gulf Arab ruling families: they do not share the sectarian identity of the majority of their subjects, since they are Sunni Muslims although 70 percent of the population is Shia, and they originally imposed themselves as rulers by conquest from outside the territory and society they have since ruled. In spite of these disabilities and notwithstanding past and continued reliance on autocratic force at various junctures, the Al Khalifa have maintained their authority and essential legitimacy in the face of severe challenges. In the 1950s labor unrest and political protest stirred by the rise of Arab nationalism threatened the regime's stability. A mix of repression and conciliation met the threats, which continued into the mid-1970s. The 1973-75 experiment with representative government failed largely because the Al Khalifa were not prepared to accept the National Assembly's questioning of basic policy issues, specifically on organizing trade unions and on internal security issues. The assembly's refusal to ratify the U.S. Navy's lease of facilities at Jufair helped persuade the ruler, Shaikh Isa bin Salman, to dissolve it. The Al Khalifa have managed political discontent through wide distribution of economic benefits. In 1994-95, however, rising unemployment brought violent protest from the hard-hit Shias. An appropriately low profile toward the United States, when its Middle East policies generated strong Arab hostility, as during and after the October 1973 Arab-Israeli war, has enabled the Al Khalifa to maintain close US-Bahraini relations during a period of dangerous regional threats. Shaikh Isa has maintained reasonable harmony within the family, and the Al Khalifa keep effective control of the key positions in government. The ruler's brother, Shaikh Khalifa, serves as prime minister, running the day-to-day affairs of government, and Isa's son, Shaikh Hamad, is minister of defense and under the constitution heir apparent. Other members of the family hold cabinet posts or serve in the civil service and military, helping to broaden the base of the Al Khalifa's rule. *See also* BAHRAIN.

KHALIFA BIN HAMAD AL THANI (b. 1932). Shaikh Khalifa became the ruler of Qatar in 1972 and was deposed by his son, Shaikh Hamad bin Khalifa, on June 26, 1995. He was the son of Shaikh Hamad bin Abdullah Al Thani, who was heir apparent but who did not live long enough to become ruler. Although only the fourth among eight sons, Khalifa was favored by both his father and his grandfather, Shaikh Abdullah (r. 1913-49). His education by tutors was traditional and Islamically oriented. By the 1950s he began to assume governmental responsibilities as a civil court judge, then was director of education and from 1960 was in the key post of finance minister. When his cousin, Shaikh Ahmad, was made ruler in that same year, Khalifa was designated heir apparent. Since the former's general indifference and laziness were matched by the latter's dedication and energy in discharging official duties, he had become de facto ruler well before his official accession in February 1972. Khalifa championed the union of Qatar, Bahrain, and the seven Trucial States following the 1968 announcement of British withdrawal from the Gulf. He has remained a strong proponent of Gulf Arab cooperation since the failure of that union. As ruler he undertook major governmental reforms, including the abolition of the Al Thani practice of retaining three quarters of the state's oil revenues, establishment of Qatar's first 10-year development plan, and formation of the state Advisory Council. By 1992 Khalifa had given management of the country's day-to-day affairs to his energetic son and heir apparent, Shaikh Hamad. The latter pushed Qatar toward a more independent policy within the GCC and the wider Arab world, moving the country toward normal relations with Iran, Iraq, and Israel. Continued disagreement between father and son over the direction of Qatar's foreign policy led Hamad to depose his father. The action took place smoothly with the support of the senior members of the Al Thani and civilian and military authorities. By early 1996, after trying for several months to regain his position, Khalifa appeared to accept his overthrow as irreversible. *See also* HAMAD BIN KHALIFA AL THANI, QATAR, *and* AL THANI.

KHALIFA BIN SALMAN AL KHALIFA. Shaikh Khalifa is the younger brother of Shaikh Isa, the ruler of Bahrain. As prime minister he presides over the day-to-day affairs of government. He also maintains extensive commercial interests, a source of some resentment by Bahrain's commercial middle class.

KHALIFA BIN ZAYID AL NUHAYYAN. Shaikh Khalifa is the eldest son of Shaikh Zayid, ruler of Abu Dhabi and president of the UAE. He is prime minister of Abu Dhabi's government, deputy prime minister of the federal government, deputy supreme commander of the UAE armed forces, and heir apparent to his father as ruler of Abu Dhabi. In recent years Zayid has increasingly turned over day-to-day official responsibilities to Khalifa, who has demonstrated a significant capacity for governance, although he displays a certain reluctance for his destined role and lacks his father's special natural talents for leadership.

KHARIJITES. The Arabic *khawarij* (singular, *khariji*) means "seceders," referring to those who withdrew their support from Ali, the fourth caliph (Arabic, *khalifa*) of the Islamic community, when he agreed to an arbitration between himself and his rival, Mu'awiya, the governor of Syria, who had challenged Ali's claim to the caliphate. A Kharijite assassinated Ali and some of the Kharijites carried on the struggle against the authority of the Umayyad Empire founded by Mu'awiya. They have continued to survive in the form of a moderate branch, the Ibadis, who remain the dominant sect in Oman. *See also* IBADIS.

KHOR. *Also* KHAWR. The term is in common use on the Arab littoral of the Gulf, denoting an inlet or small bay.

KHOR ABDALLAH. *Also* KHAWR ABDULLAH. The Khawr Abdallah is the inlet from the Gulf that leads between Kuwait's Bubiyan and Warbah Islands and the Fao (Faw) Peninsula of Iraq to the latter's naval base at Umm Qasr. Iraq has long sought to acquire or lease the islands, because they dominate the entrance to that country's only port that is not immediately adjacent to Iran.

KHOR FAKKAN. *Also* KHAWR FAKKAN. Khor Fakkan refers to the natural deep water harbor and town that grew up around it in an enclave of Sharjah on the east (Gulf of Oman) coast of the UAE. It was a significant holding of the Portuguese in the 16th and 17th centuries and is today an important container port, launched in 1979, that can accommodate the world's largest vessels. The Iran-Iraq war confirmed Khor Fakkan's importance as the UAE's only deep water port outside the Arab/Persian Gulf.

KHOR AL-UDAID. *Also* KHAWR AL-UDAYD. Located at the base of the Qatari Peninsula on its east side, Khor al-Udaid is a protected bay with a narrow inlet from the Gulf. Abu Dhabi has long claimed that its western borders extend to this point, a claim disputed both by Qatar and Saudi Arabia, the latter having a strong interest in obtaining access to the Gulf south of the Qatari Peninsula. In 1974 an Abu Dhabi (UAE)-Saudi accord granted this land corridor to Saudi Arabia in exchange for Saudi recognition of UAE sovereignty over the long-disputed al-Ain oasis and surrounding area. The terms of this agreement, however, have never been made public, and most maps continue to show the Qatari-UAE boundary at Khor al-Udaid. It is also the site of a significant archaeological discovery of a settlement dating back to the early history of the Arab side of the Gulf.

KHUFF FORMATION. The Khuff is a geological formation in Bahrain's and Qatar's territorial waters that contains gas reserves expected to sustain production well into the 21st century.

KURIA MURIA ISLANDS. *Also* KHURIYA MURIYA ISLANDS. These are a group of small islands off the coast of southern Oman, governed as a part of Dhofar province.

KUWAIT. *Also* KUWAYT (*Full name,* DAWLAT AL-KUWAIT *or* STATE OF KUWAIT).
   Land and People. The name "Kuwait" is the diminutive of the Arabic word for "fort" and probably derives from a structure built in the late 16th century. Kuwait is located at the northwestern extreme of the Persian/Arab Gulf, its land borders of almost 300 mi (483) shared nearly equally with Iraq on the north and Saudi Arabia on the south.
   Its area of 7,800 sq mi (20,207 sq km) includes several islands of which the most important are Bubiyan, Warbah, and Failaka. Only the last is inhabited. There are few distinguishing features in a largely flat landscape that rises to just under 1,000 ft (305 m) in the southwest plateau. While Kuwait lacks permanent surface water and has only a few small oases, it possesses significant amounts of groundwater, much of it brackish but usable for agricultural and industrial purposes. Kuwait has still found it necessary to build the greatest single complex of desalting facilities in the world to satisfy its need for fresh water. The country's most striking geographical feature is Kuwait Bay, a very large, natural harbor and the only good one in the northern reaches of the Gulf. There are no significant natural resources except for the enormous petroleum reserves which have been conservatively estimated at 92 billion barrels.

Although its high summer humidity is of briefer duration and its average temperatures less extreme than in the southern parts of the Gulf, Kuwait's climate is harsh from late spring to fall. Midsummer temperatures regularly reach 110°F and not infrequently 120°F. The rest of the year is pleasant, with generally sunny weather and temperatures from 45°F to 60°F. Subfreezing temperatures may occur inland. The scant rainfall averages from 3 to 6 inches per year, although fluctuating year to year from virtually nothing to 12 inches or more. Winds from the northwest tend to reinforce the cooling effect of winter

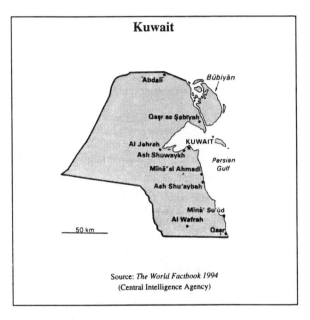

Kuwait

Source: *The World Factbook 1994*
(Central Intelligence Agency)

temperatures. Summer winds, generally southerly, are mostly hot and dry. Sandstorms can occur in summer or winter.

Kuwait's population, before Iraq's August 1990 invasion, was 1.9 million, although some estimates placed it as high as 2.2 million, of which 42 percent were Kuwaiti. Nearly 49 percent of the total was made up of non-Kuwaiti Arabs, with Palestinians (some holding Jordanian passports) by far the largest single expatriate Arab community, accounting for about 21 percent of the country's population. Two years after Kuwait's liberation, the population was 1.45 million, with the number of Palestinians perhaps not much over a tenth of the preinvasion total of 400,000 and the number of other Arabs reduced from

250,000-300,000 to about half that number. By 1996 the estimated population was 1.9 million, with Asian workers representing most of the increase. Virtually 100 percent of the country's population is urban.

History. Although continuous settlement in Kuwait dates only from the early 18th century, it has a significant ancient past dating from the third millennium B.C., as revealed by archaeological investigations on Failaka Island. The settlement of that period, located midway between Sumer in Mesopotamia and Dilmun in Bahrain and eastern Arabia, was part of the trading culture represented by those high civilizations. Its prosperity in that earliest historical period, during the Hellenistic period, and in later times derived from its position near the intersection of important land and sea trade routes and the existence of its superb natural harbor.

The modern history of Kuwait began in the early 18th century when several clans from the Utub tribal grouping, claiming to be part of the great Anaizah tribal confederation to which the Al Saud also belong, established a settlement there after extended drought and famine had driven them from central Arabia. Early on, the Al Sabah emerged as leaders in a grouping of several clans that included the Al Khalifa who were later to become rulers of Bahrain. In 1756 the clans formally established the Al Sabah as rulers by electing Sabah bin Jabir of that clan to be the Utbi shaikh. The Al Sabah directed Kuwait's affairs in close consultation with the other leading merchant families of the shaikhdom, ruling, in effect, as *primus inter pares*. In the later 19th century the Al Sabah developed sources of wealth that enhanced their power, and in the 20th century oil revenues gave the ruling family dominant authority. Although in the 18th and 19th centuries Kuwait was not the wealthy target it later became, the Al Sabah, from an early date, proved their adeptness at countering powerful external threats through deft maneuvers and opportune solicitations of great power protection. From central and northern Arabia came the threat of the religious reformist state of the Al Saud, to the north was the Ottoman Empire with shifting designs, and southward in the Gulf was a growing British presence that was eventually to predominate.

At the end of the 19th century the strong Kuwaiti ruler Mubarak bin Sabah ("Mubarak the Great") sought to play the British and Ottomans against each other. The British, alarmed by Russian designs (and, later, by German schemes) to use Kuwait as a coaling station and possible terminus for a railroad from the Mediterranean, reached an agreement with Kuwait in January 1899, similar to those with the other Gulf states, whereby Britain assumed responsibility for Kuwait's security and foreign relations, while Kuwait obligated itself not to deal directly with any other foreign powers. A 1914 agreement affirmed Kuwait's independence under British protection, and the arrangement remained essentially unchanged until the 1961 withdrawal of British protection. The British, in effect, determined the present boundaries of Kuwait at the Uqair Conference of December 1922, where Sir Percy Cox, British High Commissioner in Iraq, pressed terms that reduced the extent of Kuwait's territory under an unratified 1913 Anglo-Ottoman agreement to the advantage of Abdul Aziz Al Saud (Ibn Saud) and his expanding realm, later to become Saudi Arabia. In 1923 the High Commissioner declared the Kuwaiti-Iraqi border to be that of the 1913 agreement, a border in dispute to the present.

Internally, Kuwait experienced both political and economic shocks between the world wars. Strains between the ruler and the merchant families led the latter in 1921 to present a set of demands in the form of a political charter to the leading Al Sabah candidate for succession at that time, Shaikh Ahmad Al-Jabir. He accepted the charter, which included a provision for election of representatives of both the Al Sabah and the merchants to direct the affairs of state. The ruler, once installed, simply disregarded this first initiative to establish formal, representative government in Kuwait. A more serious effort to do so occurred in 1938, in parallel with similar reform movements in Bahrain and Dubai that were prompted by Arab nationalism aroused by strife in Palestine. It was also a reaction to the threats of King Ghazi of Iraq to annex Kuwait. The merchants forced the ruler's acceptance of a National Legislative Council of 14 elected members, presided over by a member of the Al Sabah. It was authorized to oversee the domestic affairs of the state and empowered to ratify treaties. The council embarked upon an ambitious program of legal, economic, and educational reforms, but it survived for only six months, with Shaikh Ahmad then able to reassert his prerogatives and dissolve the *majlis*. It was undermined by some of the same weaknesses as the National Assembly, which was established in 1962, especially internal divisions and a very small electoral base that excluded participation by the bulk of the population.

On the economic front three blows struck Kuwait in the 1920s and 1930s. In 1921 a disagreement with Abdul Aziz over collection of customs duties led that ruler to impose a damaging economic blockade, not lifted until 1940. The introduction of Japanese cultured pearls in 1930 undermined the single most important economic activity, pearling, and the simultaneous impact of the worldwide economic depression completed the subversion of Kuwaiti prosperity. In the meantime, however, the 1938 discovery of oil established the basis for Kuwait's emergence as a welfare state with one of the world's highest per capita incomes.

Economy. Oil production began in 1946 with 5.9 million barrels and revenues of under $1 million, but after just seven years, following Iran's nationalization of its oil industry and the consequent Western boycott against Iranian oil, annual production reached almost 300 million barrels and revenues climbed to $169 million. Production peaked at just over 3 million barrels per day (bpd) in 1972 and annual income at just under $18 billion in 1980. Even before independence Kuwait had, in 1960, established the Kuwait National Petroleum Company (KNPC), an integrated oil company. In 1975 it nationalized the Kuwait Oil Company (KOC) (a jointly held concession of Gulf Oil and British Petroleum), and shortly thereafter the remaining smaller concessionaires, thereby becoming the first Gulf Arab state to achieve total ownership of its oil sector. In addition to creating a diversified domestic oil and gas industry Kuwait had, by the 1980s, developed an extensive international set of holdings including, among others, Santa Fe International Corporation (U.S.) and several thousand service stations in Europe. Most of Kuwait's earnings have been consigned to overseas investments, much of it in the United States., and the greater part managed by Kuwaiti institutions, in particular Kuwait Investment Organization (KIO), Kuwait Foreign Trading, Contracting and Investment Company, and Kuwait International Investment Company. By the early 1980s Kuwait, as an advanced example of a rentier state, derived as much income from investments as from exports of crude and refined oil products.

Political and social development. It was Kuwait's good fortune, during the challenging period of transformation ushered in by this vast wealth, to be ruled by Shaikh Abdallah al-Salim Al Sabah (r. 1950-65), the most able and admired of Kuwait's emirs in recent history. Shaikh Abdallah, by his control of the state's new wealth, was the first ruler to enjoy full financial independence. In the course of his rule he oversaw the establishment of the most complete welfare state in the world. Kuwaitis thenceforth enjoyed social security and unemployment benefits, subsidized housing, free education, health services, and utilities, and paid no income taxes. In a breathtakingly brief span of time, virtually all Kuwaiti boys and girls were receiving modern educations previously limited to sons of the wealthy; in 1966 a university was established whose enrollment exceeded 10,000 by the 1980s; and Kuwaitis came to enjoy one of the highest ratios of physicians and nurses to residents in the world (as late as 1940 there had been only four medical doctors in the country). In 1976, to ensure that later generations of Kuwaitis would continue to receive these benefits, a Reserve Fund for Future Generations was set up, to which set allocations of state revenues were to be added annually. In addition to these benefits, which had the effect of blunting potential opposition to the Al Sabah, the government, from 1957 to 1981, distributed billions of dollars through land acquisition from private citizens at inflated prices. While this largely benefited already wealthy and powerful families, it also helped to enrich Kuwaitis of modest status and, with other benefits and incentives, helped to broaden prosperity and create a new social-economic context in which bright and energetic Kuwaitis of any rank could advance their prospects.

With its obvious advantages, the sudden acquisition of great wealth also brought dramatic changes of a problematic nature. The old Kuwait disappeared physically, economically, and socially. The old town and its wall gave way to a rapidly expanding metropolis of modern structures pushing outward through a series of concentric ring roads. The old occupations, such as boat-building, lost all economic rationale and were no longer pursued. Kuwait became an almost entirely urbanized culture, the most liberal and sophisticated in the Gulf. One of the most striking changes was the growth and shift in the composition of Kuwait's population. The decision to use oil revenues for rapid development necessitated the importation of the wide range of human skills required to run both an economy and bureaucracy characterized by rapid growth and enormously increased complexity. In 1946 fewer than 100,000 people inhabited Kuwait, virtually all native. Within a decade the population had more than doubled and 45 percent was expatriate. By the early 1960s Kuwaitis were in the minority in their own country, and by 1970 they accounted for only about 40 percent, a situation that continued up to the Iraqi invasion of August 1990. Considerable numbers of Iranians, Egyptians, Iraqis, Lebanese, and other Arabs came to fill jobs ranging from unskilled labor to employment as technicians, teachers, health care providers, government administrators, and so on, but by far the most important were Palestinians, many with Jordanian passports. Among the best educated in the Arab world, and displaced by the Arab-Israeli wars beginning in 1947, the Palestinians came to form the next-largest community after the native Kuwaitis.

The Kuwaitis confronted early the dilemma of whether to offer citizenship to immigrants, with Shaikh Abdallah and his advisers deciding not to do so except in the rarest of cases. It was apparent that granting political power to a nonnative majority would soon reduce Kuwaitis to a secondary status in their own country. At the same time, the decision meant that foreign workers and their families could never aspire to enjoy the full political, legal, and social rights of citizens, however much they might contribute to the country's development and however great their demonstrated loyalty to their adopted home might be. The resentments thus engendered among Palestinians and other immigrants with, sometimes, three generations of families resident in Kuwait, were exacerbated by the fact that only a small percentage of Kuwaitis worked and those who did generally monopolized the most prestigious and best-paying jobs. Conversely, the significant employment opportunities of Kuwait induced political quiescence among the immigrants, especially among stateless Palestinians who knew that they had nowhere else to go.

From the beginning of independence in 1961 Kuwait has been preoccupied by external threats to its security. Almost immediately following the declaration of independence, President Kassem of Iraq declared Kuwait to be part of Iraq, and Shaikh Abdullah (very likely at British prodding) requested British help. A small military force was sent, later replaced by an Arab League force for several months. A considerable monetary transfer from Kuwait to Iraq ended the threat, at least temporarily. The establishment in 1962 of the Kuwait Fund for Arab Economic Development (KFAED) provided a mechanism to help purchase security but also channel funds into development projects extending eventually beyond the Arab world. Although other Arabs complained that Kuwait failed to share its wealth generously enough, Kuwait has given more economic aid as a percentage of GNP than any other country.

The creation of the National Assembly, also in 1962, was in large measure a reaction to rising Arab nationalism. However, Shaikh Ahmad, who had headed the 1938 assembly, was sympathetic to a limited experiment in representative government. The 1962 constitution affirmed the Al Sabah as Kuwait's hereditary rulers, but circumscribed the emir's powers. While the emir and cabinet ministers hold executive power, the ruler shares legislative power with the assembly, which can override his veto by a two-thirds vote. The assembly has been a mixed success, suspended twice by the emir, in 1976 and 1986, when its attacks on the ruling family became pronounced. Moreover, the severely limited electoral franchise is restricted to male Kuwaiti citizens with family residence established since at least 1920. The result is that only about 15 percent of the Kuwaiti population may vote, which breeds cynicism about Kuwait's venture in parliamentary government.

In regional and international politics Kuwait's preoccupation with security led to careful cultivation of a middle-of-the-road, neutralist stance. In both the Gulf-Arabian Peninsula and wider Arab world contexts the country assumed a fairly low profile. Partly out of conviction and partly for self-protection Kuwait adopted a strongly supportive position on Palestinian rights, especially toward the dominant mainstream Fatah organization and the Palestine Liberation Organization (PLO) of which Fatah formed the main element. Both organizations were founded in Kuwait, and Yasir Arafat, Fatah's founder and the PLO's president after 1967, lived and worked as an engineer in Kuwait. The government of Kuwait imposed a 5 percent tax on the incomes of all Palestinian workers with the revenues going directly to the PLO. Kuwait was a founding member of OPEC and OAPEC and joined the Arab oil embargoes of 1967 and 1973. In 1963 it established diplomatic relations with the Soviet Union, two decades before any other Gulf Arab state except for Iraq, and pursued a neutral policy with a pro-West tilt for the balance of the cold war. It was the Iranian revolution of 1979 and the Iran-Iraq war breaking out the next year that presented Kuwait with a still more threatening regional environment and challenged its approach to maintaining its security.

With the outbreak of war in September 1980, Kuwait saw little option to a very pronounced pro-Iraqi tilt, permitting use of its ports and highways to transport war materiel to Iraq and providing billions of dollars in "loans" as well as through consignment of oil for sale. The Iranian revolution and the war provided the impetus and the opportunity for the Gulf Arab states to band together in a regional organization, the Gulf Cooperation Council (GCC). With characteristic caution Kuwait insisted on emphasizing the economic over the security aspects of the GCC agreement. On the international level Kuwait maintained a neutralist stance with arms purchases both from the West and the Soviets. This changed in the later phases of the Iran-Iraq war when Iraq's devastating Exocet missile attacks against Iranian oil shipments prompted the Iranians to attack tankers carrying Kuwaiti and Saudi oil.

Kuwait promptly and decisively turned to the United States for security assistance with the 1988 purchase of 40 F-18 fighter-bombers. In 1987 Kuwait had approached both the Soviet Union and the U.S. to help protect its shipping, but it was the latter that assumed the burden of this "reflagging" operation, whereby Kuwaiti vessels were put under the U.S. flag and escorted by U.S. Navy vessels.

Threats to internal security during the course of the war also helped to alter Kuwaiti attitudes and approaches to sources of danger. Terrorists inspired, if not directed, by the Khomeini government carried out a series of bombings in December 1983, and in May 1985 an Iraqi Shia narrowly failed in an attempt to assassinate the emir with a car bomb. Finally, in April 1988 members of an apparently pro-Iranian Shia group from Lebanon hijacked an Air Kuwait plane to try to force release of the terrorists convicted and imprisoned after the 1983 bombings. Not only did Kuwait stand fast in the wake of these threats, refusing to release any of the prisoners, but it tightened security against further possible Shia violence and expelled many Shias who were considered suspect.

The end of the war, in August 1988, offered Kuwait respite to deal with economic and financial problems that had emerged in the 1980s. Together with other oil exporting countries, Kuwait suffered from the fall in oil prices, its oil revenues declining from $17.9 billion in 1980 to $4.3 billion in 1984. In 1982 its unofficial stock market, the *Suq al-Manakh*, crashed, causing a financial crisis not yet wholly resolved. By the end of the decade of the 1980s, however, Kuwait, which had drawn on its ample reserves to cover budget deficits, had experienced significant economic recovery. Oil prices rose modestly, and OPEC in November 1989 agreed to raise Kuwait's production quota to 1.5 million bpd, which the Kuwaitis had demanded in connection with their claim to possess the world's fifth largest oil reserves. Even then, Kuwait continued to overproduce for some months, in part driven by the concern for supplying its large overseas downstream marketing net-work. This overproduction was a major element in the bill of particulars that Iraq directed against Kuwait in the months before the August 2, 1990, invasion. Together with alleged Kuwaiti cheating in production from the shared border field of Rumailah, President Saddam Hussein of Iraq perceived this as a deliberate attempt to deprive Iraq of revenues badly needed to meet Iraq's postwar reconstruction needs. Added to these grievances were Kuwait's refusal to forgive formally its war "loans" to Iraq and to cede or lease the islands of Bubiyan and Warbah, adjacent to Iraq's naval base at Umm Qasr.

   The August 2, 1990, Iraqi invasion and its aftermath. Although
Kuwaitis were keenly aware of Iraq's hostility, the country and its
leadership remained complacent, with the level of military alert actually
downgraded and army officers on leave as Iraqi forces massed on the
border. The complacency may have reflected hope for compromise
through Saudi-sponsored talks, the history of previous Iraqi threats
successfully rebuffed, and the conveyance of American military
assurances. Little Kuwaiti military resistance was offered, and the
senior members of the Al Sabah fled, with the exception of the emir's
brother, Shaikh Fahd al-Ahmad, who fought and was killed. A
government-in-exile under the emir was set up in Taif in Saudi Arabia.
Approximately a third of the country's 600,000 citizens also fled, an
equivalent number was already overseas, and 200,000 remained in
Kuwait, some offering resistance to the Iraqi occupiers.

   The shock of the invasion was intensified for Kuwaitis by the
indifference or actual approval of brother Arabs with respect to Iraq's
action, especially in Jordan, Yemen, and Tunisia as well as among
Palestinians, including some of those in Kuwait (other Palestinians
risked their own lives to help Kuwaitis during the occupation). Kuwaiti
disillusionment was such that postliberation polls showed that a
plurality of Kuwaitis no longer saw the Palestinian cause as the Arab
world's most important issue, and a large majority favored Western
over Arab security guarantees, positions unthinkable before the Iraqi
invasion. Another dramatic move away from an earlier position was
Kuwait's suspension, beginning without formal announcement in 1993,
of the secondary economic boycott against Israel that had banned
American firms having business in or with Israel from doing business in
the Arab world. Most Kuwaitis clearly approved the state's cutoff of aid
to those Arab states that had sympathized with Iraq, and Palestinians in
Kuwait bore the brunt of Kuwaiti anger, with many beaten and forcibly
detained and as many as a thousand, by some estimates, executed
without trial. The many Palestinians who had worked in the public
sector lost their jobs. Moreover, the Kuwaiti government refused
enrollment for students who remained in school during the occupation,
effectively eliminating private employment for Palestinians with school-
age children. Kuwait, together with the other Gulf Arab states, signaled
its support of the September 13, 1993, Israel-PLO Declaration of
Principles, which calls for Palestinian self-rule in Gaza and Jericho.

However, Kuwait did not join them in pledging financial support for the new Palestinian entity.

Sentiment toward the Al Sabah was more negative after the occupation, especially among those left to fend for themselves while the ruling family fled to comfortable exile. Many of the political opposition felt increased antipathy, especially when the emir and prime minister made a leisurely postliberation return to Kuwait and deferred assembly elections to October 1992. Until then, the National Council, elected in January 1990, and lacking legislative powers, functioned in place of the National Assembly. Although the legality of parties is ambiguous under Kuwait's constitution, a group of mostly Western-educated liberals announced formation of Kuwait's first open political party in December 1991, calling for free speech. In the following month the government lifted the prepublication censorship of the country's newspapers.

The October 5, 1992, parliamentary elections marked a dramatic step in Kuwait's political history. In a free exercise of the franchise Kuwait's limited electorate gave the opposition factions 35 seats in the 50-member body, with 19 antigovernment winners running on religious platforms. Formal political parties continue to be prohibited. The Islamist candidates cooperated with secularists in the preelection campaigning, and the new assembly will provide an interesting test case of whether Islamist leaders can work within an elected system to try peacefully to effect desired social and political changes. The new 16-member cabinet includes six oppositionists, twice as many as ever before. At the same time, the key portfolios of defense, interior, foreign affairs, and information remain in the hands of the Al Sabah, and the position of prime minister remains the preserve of the crown prince. If the assembly has failed thus far to grapple with fundamental issues, such as the country's restrictive citizenship law, it has addressed significant concerns, establishing stronger penalties for official corruption and overturning the secrecy law that kept many government documents from public view. Even more significant, it has passed a law forcing public investment companies to issue semiannual reports. This was in response to the discovery of losses of large sums through poor management and embezzlement from the formerly respected KIO. While it remains to be seen how far the assembly can expand its political authority, it now seems certain that parliamentary rule is permanently established in Kuwait.

The most dramatic postliberation problem, although in a sense the most easily addressed, was the physical econstruction of Kuwait. Iraqi sabotage was less thoroughgoing than first thought, with reconstruction costs in the $20-$30-billion range, rather than the $100 billion of initial estimates. Key work was completed by late 1991 under the supervision of the U.S. Army Corps of Engineers, although some further reconstruction will continue for a number of years. The oil wells sabotaged by Iraq were capped in a remarkable 8 months, with the last of the oil well fires snuffed out in early November 1991, far sooner than most had predicted. Less than a year later oil production had already reached a million bpd, two-thirds of the preinvasion level, and by February 1993, Kuwait was pumping two million bpd. In all, more than a billion barrels of oil were lost through wellhead spills or fires, and studies indicate that damage to pressure in the oil fields will reduce by 1.3 billion barrels the amount of eventually recoverable oil. Together these losses represent not more than about 2.5 percent of Kuwait's oil reserves. The damage to the environment will be enormous and long-lasting to Kuwait and to the waters and countries of the Gulf, including Iran on the opposite side. Kuwait's financial empire, what Saddam Hussein in his impatience and ignorance apparently thought could be taken by invading Kuwait, remained intact during the occupation, the lion's share managed by the London-based KIO. However, the financial contributions to the Gulf war effort, infrastructure replacement costs, and the continued decline in oil prices very rapidly reduced Kuwait's financial reserves from a prewar level of about $100 billion to probably less than $30 billion. Foreign investment income was severely reduced: for 1993 it was under $1.5 billion. Some of the losses came from mismanagement including possible malfeasance in the handling of Kuwait's overseas investments. As disturbing as the financial loss was, the injury to the reputation of the KIO, hitherto the leading symbol of Kuwait's financial strength and acumen was severe. Management of the country's financial assets has become an important subject of National Assembly debate.

What will remain more difficult than physical and financial recovery will be reaching and implementing fundamental decisions about the future nature of Kuwaiti society. Mistrust of other Arabs led Kuwaiti leaders to declare that Kuwaitis would never again be a minority in their own land. (By the mid-1990s, however, that was again the case.) While the other Gulf Arab states have made efforts to normalize their relations with the Arab states with which they broke over the Gulf crisis of 1990-91, Kuwait has found it less easy to forgive what it considers betrayal. Indians and other South Asians are being brought in to take the place of former Arab expatriates, and Palestinians will, according to some reports, be limited to 40,000, a tenth of their former number.

Moreover, some 150,000 or more people called *bidounis*, short for *bidoun jinsiyya* ("without nationality"), Arabs who have, in many cases, lived for generations in Kuwait but lack citizenship, have been denied reentry into the country. Since Palestinians staffed half the bureaucracy's positions and bidounis filled many of the military and police ranks, it is difficult to see how these former key elements of the workforce will successfully be replaced. In the wake of their traumatic ordeal, Kuwaitis take both a more inward-looking and a more dependent approach toward the central issue of security. There is little disposition to resume its former neutrality and low profile, and Kuwait has indignantly refused to listen to fellow GCC member pleas to consider normalization of relations with Iraq. The Iraqi occupation and the American-led liberation have confirmed Kuwait's dependence on U.S. military force for its external security. Indeed, Kuwait rejected the March 1991 plan for stationing Egyptian and Syrian troops on its soil. In September 1991 Kuwait and the U.S. initialed a security agreement providing for periodic joint exercises (one of which was held the following December), training, and also stockpiling of U.S. equipment. In late January, 1992, the first consignment of the U.S. F-18 fighters ordered before the invasion was delivered. The prompt American response to Iraq's threatening troop movements of October 1994 offered further reassurance. All of this, however, fell short of the Kuwaiti desire for the security that would be inherent in a large, permanent American military presence on its soil. *See also* ARMED FORCES, DESERT SHIELD/DESERT STORM, FOREIGN WORKERS, GULF COOPERATION COUNCIL, IRAN-IRAQ WAR, OIL, PALESTINIANS, PETROCHEMICAL INDUSTRY, *and* AL SABAH.

KUWAIT BAY. The state of Kuwait grew up around Kuwait Bay, the only significant natural harbor in the northern part of the Arab side of the Gulf. Kuwait City is located on the southern side of the bay.

KUWAIT CITY. The city proper is situated at the southern entrance to Kuwait Bay; in its metropolitan extension it embraces most of the population of the state of Kuwait. The area of the old walled town is now the central business district from which the city extends outward to the south, its growth marked by semicircular ring roads. The modern city has been divided into planned sectors and separate residential sections house native Kuwaitis and foreign workers and their dependents. An example of the latter is the large suburb of Hawalli, where a large community of Palestinians resided before the Iraqi invasion in August 1990.

KUWAIT FUND FOR ARAB ECONOMIC DEVELOPMENT (KFAED). The fund was established at the time of Kuwait's independence in 1961 to provide economic development assistance to Arab countries. In 1974 its charter was amended to permit loans to non-Arab countries. By the end of 1988 it had made 222 loans in support of 173 projects in 17 countries. The loans totaled nearly $3.5 billion. *See also* KUWAIT.

KUWAIT INVESTMENT AUTHORITY (KIA). The KIA was established in 1982 by Kuwait's elected national assembly to serve as a watchdog to oversee the country's investment policy, which has largely been carried out by the London-based KIO. In fact, the KIA has been dominated by the more dynamic KIO.

KUWAIT INVESTMENT ORGANIZATION (KIO). The KIO, established in 1962, is the largest of Kuwait's state investment institutions, handling the lion's share of the country's overseas investments, which in 1990 stood at roughly $100 billion, from offices in London. Two years after Kuwait's liberation the KIO was reported to have lost $5 billion through mismanagement and fraud. As a result, the assets of five Kuwaitis, including two members of the ruling Al Sabah family, were frozen in 1993. Some reports indicated that Kuwaiti overseas investments had shrunk to $30 billion or less because of costs associated with the Gulf conflict, large sums paid out to cover bad bank debts, and the money lost through KIO mismanagement.

KUWAIT NATIONAL PETROLEUM COMPANY (KNPC). KNPC was established in 1960, the year before Kuwait's independence, to provide Kuwait with its own integrated oil company.

KUWAIT OIL COMPANY (KOC). The KOC was formed by the Gulf Oil Company of the U.S. and the Anglo-Persian Oil Company (later British Petroleum, BP) in 1932 and struck oil in 1938. In two stages, in 1974 and 1975, the government purchased KOC, with Gulf and BP continuing to provide technical services and personnel in exchange for service fees and access to crude oil. It remains the major producer of Kuwaiti crude oil. *See also* KUWAIT.

KUWAIT PETROLEUM COMPANY (KPC). Kuwait's government created the KPC in 1980 to bring together the Kuwait Oil Company, Kuwait National Petroleum Company, and the other major elements of the country's oil industry. It is one of the world's largest corporations, with joint ventures and downstream facilities overseas. *See also* KUWAIT.

L

LABOR. Until the post-World War II era, economic activity in the Arab Gulf states was almost entirely of a traditional nature, the exception being Bahrain, where oil revenues had begun to be realized in the 1930s. The rapid transition to modern economies in the absence of significant numbers of trained managers and workers forced heavy reliance on foreign labor, including unskilled laborers, technicians, and managerial personnel in both private and public sectors. In recent years the effective workforce in Kuwait, Qatar, and the United Arab Emirates has become 90-95 percent foreign. Oman, where the discovery and exploitation of oil has come later and in fairly modest amounts, continues to have a significant traditional labor force in fishing, agriculture, and crafts amounting to perhaps 50 percent or more of the total. Similarly, in Bahrain indigenous labor remains at half or a bit more of the total workforce. Because of its more than half a century of modern economic development, Bahrain has a sophisticated native labor force, and it is there that labor has played a significant role in national politics. With the acceleration of economic development after World War II, a kind of "industrial proletariat" had developed, with some unrest in the late 1940s and significant opposition to the government by the 1950s, in large part over the employment of large numbers of Asians in the petroleum sector. The Bahrain labor movement, linked by the mid-1950s with Arab nationalist sentiments, generated major strikes and, after the Anglo-French-Israeli invasion of Egypt in the Suez war of 1956, incited riots against the government and British interests in Bahrain. Once the more radical forces in the labor movement had been suppressed and BAPCO had turned to a policy of of local purchase of supplies, more moderate elements split from the radicals, the latter continuing an underground existence as the Bahrain Workers' Union. Following the failure of Bahrain's parliamentary experiment in 1975, a general labor law was promulgated that provided for arbitration of disputes and prohibited the formation of unions and the calling of strikes. Both were either declared illegal or discouraged in the other Gulf Arab states.

Labor laws have been enacted in all the Gulf Arab states to provide protections and benefits to workers. A GCC policy enunciated in 1985 set goals for manpower development, calling for improved education, including vocational programs, as well as better working conditions and a reduction in the numbers of foreign workers. The number of women in the workforce has been increasing despite continuing conservative social prejudices against that development. Most female employment has been confined to situations that ensure gender separation, with women either in occupations traditionally confined to women or in offices set up specifically to conduct banking or other business exclusively with other women. Gradually, however, women are beginning to work alongside men or in public occupations. In the UAE women have begun to be accepted in federal ministries; in the early 1980s an Emirian woman had achieved the position of assistant deputy minister of education. In the wake of the 1991 Gulf war Abu Dhabi established a female military security force, and a female branch of the Oman Royal Police has already earned a significant measure of respect. In Kuwait and Bahrain a number of women have begun to make a mark in the professions, notably in education.

LANGUAGES. The indigenous language of the Gulf Arab states is Arabic. The spoken Arabic of the Gulf varies slightly from state to state and between subregions. The only exception to Arabic as the indigenous language is the isolated surviving pre-Arabic languages found in parts of Dhofar in Oman. Other languages are important. Farsi remains significant as the language of some of the leading merchants as well as of considerable numbers of workers coming from Iran in recent years, and immigrant worker languages heard in many quarters include Baluchi, Urdu, Hindi, Tagalog, Thai, and Korean. English is important, having acquired a special status by virtue of long British involvement in the Gulf as well as from the international commercial and technical status of the language, because many Gulf nationals have studied in the United Kingdom or the United States and because English is the second language of many of the non-U.K. and non-U.S. expatriates working in the Gulf countries. It is in fact the second language of the Gulf, widely studied in schools and used at the university level for instruction in scientific and technical subjects.

LAW. Legal systems of the Gulf Arab states reflect both their Islamic identity and the influence of Western law as the need to regulate complex contemporary commercial, social, and political realties has been thrust upon them. They have in recent years moved toward a great increase in formal regulations and legal codification.

Traditionally, tribal law has prevailed in the inland areas largely inhabited by Bedouins. These are unwritten, based on custom, and upheld by tribal elders. In the towns Islamic law was applied through the *Sharia* courts. The *Sharia* as interpreted by the four principal schools of jurisprudence (Hanafi, Hanbali, Maliki, and Shafi'i) is based on the Quran and the *hadith*, or documented sayings of the Prophet Muhammad and, depending on the particular interpretation, to some extent on *ijma* or "consensus," and *qiyas* or "analogy." In the *Sharia* courts the *qadi*, or "judge", plays an active role with no jury involved in legal procedures. Punishments tend to be strict, but are matched by equally strict rules of evidence. Expatriates in the Gulf Arab countries are subject to the *Sharia* and many are tried and convicted on charges involving consumption or distribution of alcohol and drugs or sexual misconduct.

British law was introduced in the 19th century to provide extra-territorial jurisdiction for British subjects, especially Indians who were under the protection of the British Government of India. Following independence, the Gulf Arab states turned largely to non-British sources, especially Arab civil law, particularly as represented in Egyptian models, which were strongly influenced by French law. All the Gulf Arab states now have formalized independent legal systems (all but Oman under a written constitution) that combine *Sharia* and law derived from outside sources. In each state a hierarchical structure of courts has emerged, and in the United Arab Emirates courts exist at both the federal and emiral levels. (Reflecting its generally independent stance, Dubai's courts remain outside the federal system.) A significant corpus of written laws has emerged. Commercial codes have an obvious importance in light of the Gulf Arab states' role in the international economy and apply generally accepted international practices in harmony with the *Sharia*.

The GCC has attempted to promote similar systems of legislation in its member states with some limited success, as in laws on tariffs and preferential treatment to GCC nationals in commercial transactions. A uniform labor law is among the envisioned elements of a unified system of GCC law.

LEAGUE OF ARAB STATES. *See* ARAB LEAGUE.

LEBANON. Relations between Lebanon and the Gulf Arab states are not of great direct significance. Small numbers of Lebanese are to be found in business positions, often as managers of companies, and some Lebanese construction firms are involved in the Gulf. Lebanon's civil war had an economic impact, especially in Bahrain, as the Gulf assumed some of the financial and business management functions previously carried out in Lebanon. The GCC strongly condemned the Israeli invasion of Lebanon in 1982.

LIBYA. The monarchy of King Idris maintained friendly relations with the Arab Gulf states. Libya was a founding member of OAPEC with Saudi Arabia and Kuwait in 1968, establishing that organization as a conservative oil producers' club. Libya's 1970 revolution dramatically altered its nature. Libya as a politically radical state with limited oil reserves has been a leading OPEC hawk at odds with the Gulf Arab states over oil export policy as well as other issues. Thus relations have been generally strained, if not hostile. Libya under the rule of Colonel Qaddafi provided support to the Dhofar Rebellion which aimed to overthrow the Sultanate of Oman and eventually the traditional regimes in the Gulf. It also supported Iran in its war with Iraq, then supported Iraq in the 1990-91 Gulf crisis.

LITERACY. *See* EDUCATION.

LIWA. The Liwa oases are located in the southwest part of Abu Dhabi, forming an arc of some four dozen small oases extending 40 mi (64 km) from east to west. (The name comes from the Arabic word for "curve.") There is sufficient water in shallow aquifers to permit limited date culture, but only a small population can be sustained in its villages, generally migrating seasonally to the coast. In the past the men of the oases spent summers with the pearling fleet. Liwa is the ancestral home of the Bani Yas and of that tribal confederation's dominant subsection, the Al Bu Falah and its ruling clan, the Al Nuhayyan. In 1793 the center of Al Bu Falah power moved to Abu Dhabi on the Gulf coast, but Liwa remained an important part of the Bani Yas realm and the emirate of Abu Dhabi, which it dominated. Today a major afforestation project is centered on Liwa.

LORIMER, J. G. Colonel Lorimer was an officer of the Indian Political Service whose *Gazetteer of the Persian Gulf, Oman and Central Arabia* remains the preeminent reference work on the Gulf Arab states. The Gazetteer, which appeared in six large volumes between 1908 and 1915, draws together an enormous mass of information, divided into historical and geographical sections. It was prepared for British officials and was not publicly available until the 1950s.

LUCE, SIR WILLIAM. Sir William Luce served as British Political Resident, the senior British representative to the protected Gulf Arab states, from 1961 to 1966. Luce was called from retirement in 1970 to act as the foreign secretary's special adviser on the Gulf. Prior to the June 1970 British election, the Conservative Party had opposed British withdrawal from east of Suez, advocated by the Labour Party. Post-election uncertainty, with the Conservatives back in power, led to Luce's appointment to sound out the government of the shah of Iran and the Gulf Arab rulers concerning British withdrawal and advise Her Majesty's Government accordingly. Between August 1970 and February 1971, Luce made three trips to the Gulf and, following his report, Foreign Secretary Sir Alec Douglas-Home announced on March 1 the decision to withdraw remaining British military forces by the end of the year. Luce subsequently undertook additional visits to the Gulf to try to find compromise agreements between Iran and the emirs of Sharjah and Ras al-Khaimah over Iranian claims to the islands of Abu Musa and the Tunbs. *See also* ABU MUSA, IRAN, KHALID BIN MUHAMMAD AL QASIMI, RAS AL-KHAIMAH, SHARJAH, TUNBS, *and* UNITED KINGDOM.

M

MAGAN. *Also* MAKAN. Magan was an ancient kingdom in what is now northern Oman, flourishing in the second millennium B.C. It was an important part of the network of commercial city-states in the Gulf region and provided a number of significant Mesopotamian imports, most notably copper.

MAJLIS. Derived from the verb "to sit," *majlis* refers both to a meeting room and the gatherings or sessions held there. It may be formal or informal, for social, business, or political purposes and, in all these cases, represents a traditional means of reaching decisions by consensus. The term is also used, somewhat confusingly, to refer to the very different national councils established in the five Gulf Arab states dealt with in this volume. In that usage it covers both an elected parliament, in the case of Kuwait, and purely advisory councils, as in Qatar. *See also* IJMA, NATIONAL ASSEMBLY, *and* individual country entries.

AL MAKTUM. The Al Maktum are the ruling family of the emirate of Dubai. They are part of the Al Bu Falasah faction of the Bani Yas tribal federation that has traditionally dominated Abu Dhabi. In the 1830s the Al Maktum led the Al Bu Falasah out of Abu Dhabi to establish themselves independently in Dubai. They have since remained the rivals of the Al Nuhayyan, for two centuries the rulers of Abu Dhabi. *See also* ABU DHABI, BANI YAS, AL BU FALAH, AL BU FALA-SAH, *and* AL NUHAYYAN.

MAKTUM BIN BUTI. Maktum bin Buti was one of two leaders who took the Al Bu Falasah out of Abu Dhabi and set up an independent emirate in Dubai. He ruled from 1832 to 1852 and established the Al Maktum as the ruling family in Dubai.

MAKTUM BIN HASHAR AL MAKTUM. Maktum bin Hashar was the ruler of Dubai, 1894-1906, under whose enlightened leadership Dubai grew into a major entrepôt in the Gulf. Key to that commercial success was the capture of much of the trade of the Persian port of Lingah, following the Persian government's imposition of high customs duties on imports and exports in 1902.

MAKTUM BIN RASHID AL MAKTUM (b. 1940) The present ruler of Dubai, Shaikh Maktum, assumed that position on the death of his father, Shaikh Rashid. As the eldest son he formally became crown prince in 1985 and essentially ran the affairs of Dubai during his father's long, incapacitating illness from 1981 until his death in 1990, in close cooperation with his three full brothers, Hamdan, the United Arab Emirates' minister of finance and industry, Muhammad, the UAE defense minister, and Ahmad, commander of military forces in the UAE's central region. With them he shares a passion for horse breeding and racing. Maktum was born in 1940. He received a traditional Quranic education in schools in Dubai, but between 1961 and 1964 studied English at Cambridge University. He shares his father's strong interest in sustaining Dubai's role as a commercial hub in the Middle East, establishing the Dubai Commerce and Tourism and Development Board and promoting Dubai as a center for foreign investment. At the same time he gives evidence of being somewhat more committed to cooperation in federal affairs than Rashid was. As UAE vice president and prime minister he worked closely with Shaikh Zayed, UAE president and ruler of Abu Dhabi, during the 1990-91 Gulf crisis. *See also* DUBAI *and* AL MAKTUM.

MANAMA. Manama is the capital of Bahrain and its largest city. Located in the northeast corner of the archipelago's main island, it contains over a fourth of the nation's half-million population, and more than half the city's population is non-Bahraini. Although adjacent to the site of Dilmun, which was an important trading community by the early third millennium B.C., Manama dates back only to the 15th century A.D. It is mostly a modern city, reflecting its position as the banking and commercial center and transportation hub of the Gulf area.

MANASIR. The Manasir form a leading tribe in Abu Dhabi, residing mostly in the Dhahirah area in the central part of the emirate. Together with the Awamir and the Al Dhawahir, the Manasir have been allied to the Bani Yas, the dominant tribal grouping in Abu Dhabi, since the early 19th century.

MARRIAGE. In the conservative Islamic societies of the Gulf Arab states marriage is a civil contract arranged between families. Marriage with a first cousin or other close relative in the patrilineal kinship group is preferred, both to preserve wealth within the extended family and to help ensure a socially appropriate alliance. The preference for marriage at a young age (generally late teens) survives, but the impact of great wealth on these societies has created more liberal attitudes, giving to contemporary brides and grooms somewhat greater freedom of choice in a partner. Inflated dowries and increasing numbers of marriages with foreigners, both Arab and non-Arab, are among significant social problems in the Gulf states today. Polygamy is little practiced, especially in the cities, in large part because of economic constraints.

MASFUT. Masfut is the most important of the several enclaves of the emirate of Ajman in the UAE. Located in the Hajar Mountains, it has a modest agricultural production.

MASIRA ISLAND. Masira is the largest island possession of Oman, 40 mi (64 km) long and 10 mi (16 km) wide, located off the coast of central Oman in the Arabian Sea. It was used by the British in World War II as a base for antisubmarine patrols and in the 1970s played a significant role in the campaign against the Dhofar Rebellion. In 1976, with the antiregime forces defeated, the British withdrew, leaving what was, together with Salalah in Dhofar, their last base in the Middle East. Since 1980, the United States has had access to the air base at Masira, together with other Omani facilities.

MATRAH. Matrah is an important city and port in Oman, located adjacent to Muscat. Like the latter, it developed centuries ago around a fine natural harbor; it is now a center of commerce with upgraded port facilities. Because of its location in the capital area, Matrah houses government offices and benefits from a generous portion of the government's development funds.

MERCHANTS. Merchants emerged in the Persian/Arab Gulf over 4,000 years ago and have since played a key role in its affairs. Today's important merchant families have benefited enormously from oil and the wealth it has brought, but trace their fortunes to the preoil era. Merchant enterprises tend to be family-owned and run, and most fortunes have been made through import activities. Before the realization of oil wealth, merchant families were often close to the rulers and exercised considerable influence on them, especially in Kuwait, Bahrain, and Dubai, with several still significant in this respect. With the general modernization of Gulf societies merchants are adopting more Western-style approaches to doing business, but the way in which transactions are conducted is still largely in the traditional *majlis* style with a strong emphasis on personal contact. *See also entries under names of individual merchant families, notably* DARWISH, FUTTAIM, GALADARIS, KANOO, *and* AL-NABOODAH.

MIDDLE EAST FORCE (MIDEASTFOR). The Middle East Force is a small U.S. Navy force (usually a small flagship and two destroyers) assigned to the Gulf since 1949. Before the British withdrawal from the Gulf, it had access to port facilities in Bahrain through an informal arrangement with the United Kingdom. Access was maintained under the independent government of Bahrain, although in 1977 an exchange of diplomatic notes had the effect of continuing the arrangement while ending formal "homeporting" in order to enable the Bahraini government to weather political attacks over the U.S. presence. *See also* ARMED FORCES, BAHRAIN, *and* JUFAIR.

MILES, COLONEL S. B. Miles, an official of the British Government of India and the Political Agent in Muscat from 1872 to 1886, was the author of *Countries and Tribes of the Persian Gulf,* which remains a classic among studies of the Gulf region. Completed at the same time as Lorimer's *Gazetteer* in the years just before World War I, it was, in contrast to that other classic, published for the public rather than restricted to official use and was a work of original, sympathetic, and informed scholarship, not a compilation of others' observations.

MILITARY. *See* ARMED FORCES.

MINA. *Mina* is the Arabic word describing a port or harbor. Several significant Gulf ports are given this designation. In Kuwait, Mina al-Ahmadi is the site of an important oil loading terminal, while in Oman, Mina Qabus is a modern port facility at Matrah, serving the capital area. Also in Oman, Mina al-Fahl is a specialized oil port near the capital, and Mina Rasyut, in the south of the country, serves the Dhofar area as a general cargo port. Mina Salman is Bahrain's principal port and, in the United Arab Emirates, Mina Saqr, Mina Zayid, and Mina Rashid are the principal ports of Ras al-Khaimah, Abu Dhabi, and Dubai, respectively, the last named being the largest in the UAE.

MOROCCO, KINGDOM OF. Morocco, as a hereditary monarchy, is a natural friend and ally of the patriarchal Gulf Arab states and has enjoyed generally friendly relations with them. Because of its distance from the Gulf and lack of economic complementarity, however, its substantive relations with the Gulf states have been relatively slight. In the past the UAE has employed a number of Moroccans in air force support capacities. In 1990 Morocco joined the coalition against Iraq after the latter's invasion of Kuwait, contributing 2,000 troops. The government's decision met with widespread popular disapproval in Morocco, provoking significant public demonstrations against it.

MOSQUE. A mosque is a place of public Muslim worship. The word is from the French *mosquée*, in turn derived from the Arabic *masjid* (as it is pronounced in the Egyptian dialect), and means literally a "place of prostration." In the Gulf, mosques have traditionally varied from small structures of very modest building materials to large "Friday mosques" often built by wealthy merchants. Oil wealth has made possible the construction of large and elaborate mosques in all the Gulf Arab states.

AL MUALLA. The Al Mualla are the family that has ruled the emirate of Umm al-Qaiwain, one of the seven members of the United Arab Emirates, since entering into a treaty arrangement with the British in 1820.

MUBARAK BIN SABAH AL SABAH. Shaikh Mubarak, known as "the Great," became ruler of Kuwait by murdering his half brother, Muhammad bin Sabah, in 1896 and ruled until his death in 1915. Mubarak was recognized, like his predecessors, as a *qaim maqam*, or "district head," within the Ottoman Empire. Anticipating, however, that extension of Ottoman control would end Kuwait's autonomous position, he petitioned the British to extend their protection to Kuwait. Initial British reluctance yielded to fears of Russian railway schemes using Kuwait as a terminus and in 1899 a treaty agreement was signed that, like the earlier agreements with Bahrain and the Trucial States, conferred upon Great Britain the responsibility for Kuwait's protection and the conduct of its foreign relations. Mubarak in turn pledged to have no direct relations with other states or to yield any part of Kuwait's territory to a foreign power. Following the outbreak of World War I, in November 1914, Mubarak received assurances from Great Britain that it recognized Kuwait as an independent state, in return for which it was understood he would cooperate in the British campaign against the Turkish forces in Iraq. *See also* KUWAIT, AL SABAH, *and* UNITED KINGDOM.

MUHAMMAD BIN RASHID AL MAKTUM (b. 1950). Muhammad is one of the three full brothers of Maktum bin Rashid, ruler of Dubai. He has served as defense minister of the UAE and has cooperated closely with his brothers in managing the affairs of Dubai during the long illness of their father, Rashid bin Said, from 1981 to 1990, and since his death.

MUHARRAQ. Muharraq is the name of both the second largest island and city in the Bahrain archipelago. Connected to the capital city of Manama on Bahrain Island by a 1.5 mi (2.5 km) causeway, it has about one-half that city's 150,000 people, with the combined population of the two accounting for nearly half the country's total. By contrast with Manama's more mixed population, that of Muharraq is largely made up of Sunni Muslims who represent the minority among native Bahrainis overall. Bahrain's international airport is in Muharraq, but the city is less developed and less affluent than Manama.

MUHAWWALA. The term *muhawwala*, from the Arabic verb "transfer" or "return," in the Gulf Arab states context refers to a population of Arabs that crossed to the Iranian side of the Gulf several centuries ago, retained the Arabic language, and returned to the Arab side of the Gulf in the late 19th or early 20th century. Their numbers include both workers and wealthy merchants.

MUSANDAM (MASANDAM) PENINSULA. Also referred to as *Ras Musandam*, or Musandam Cape, and as *Ru'us Jabal*, or "Mountain Headlands," the Musandam Peninsula is the tip of the Oman promontory terminating at the Strait of Hormuz and forming a small exclave of Omani territory separated from the rest of Oman by UAE territory. Possession of this northernmost territory thrusts Oman directly into regulation of or threats to the strait, because its main shipping lanes lie within Omani territorial waters. Iran periodically threatened to close the strait during the Iran-Iraq war. Physically, Musandam is dramatic. Running from the northern end of the Hajar Mountains, it is a barren, rugged area with stark cliffs dropping to the sea and forming fjordlike inlets. The majority of its isolated population is Shihuh, a tribe of mainly Arab origin but with strong social and linguistic elements of Iranian origin. Musandam, like Dhofar in the south, is governed as a province, reflecting its remoteness and strategic importance. Its governor holds cabinet rank and reports directly to the ruler, Sultan Qabus. *See also* OMAN *and* SHIHUH.

MUSCAT. The name "Muscat" refers both to the capital city of the Sultanate of Oman and, during a certain period of Omani history, to the territories ruled by the sultan from the city. The name in Arabic means literally "the place where a falling object lands," by extension denoting an anchorage. Its small but well-protected natural harbor, one of the few on the Omani coast, made it an important port from pre-Islamic times. In the medieval period it was generally under Persian control and became a significant entrepôt, attracting the attention of the Portuguese who captured it in 1507 during the expansion of their naval power into the Indian Ocean, and held it for nearly a century and a half. The forts, Jalali and Mirani, which the Portuguese built to protect the harbor, remain as landmarks.

The Ya'aribah dynasty united Oman by the mid-17th century, driving the Portuguese from Muscat in 1649, but dissolved in a civil war in the early part of the 18th century, during which intervening Persian forces briefly controlled the city. By 1749 the Al Bu Said family, rulers to the present day, left the Omani interior to its fractious tribes and turned their attention to developing a commercial empire in the Indian Ocean, controlling territories on the Indian and African coasts, with the city of Muscat as its prosperous entrepôt hub. The Ibadi, religiously-based imamate of the interior kept its identity and became Oman, while the commercially oriented Al Bu Said sultanate, which controlled the coast and was increasingly allied to and protected by the British, developed separately and became Muscat. This remained the case until 1954, when Oman was reunited under Sultan Said bin Taimur, the father of the present ruler, Sultan Qabus. Today the city of Muscat, physical expansion precluded by the surrounding mountains, retains its symbolic importance, but government and private activity have overflowed into Matrah to the immediate west and the new town of Ruwi to the south. *See also* AL BU SAID, IBADIS, and OMAN.

N

AL-NABOODAH. The Al-Naboodah family is one of several large merchant families of Iranian origin in Dubai. From a small shop in the

1950s the family's interests had by the mid-1980s grown into a diversified enterprise that included importing, distributing, and construction, with some 3,000 employees.

NATIONAL ASSEMBLY. Both Kuwait and Bahrain have established national assemblies, the only institutions in the Gulf conferring legislative powers on elected members. Bahrain's assembly functioned only briefly in the mid-1970s, while that of Kuwait has twice been suspended and was reelected on October 5, 1992.

Kuwait's assembly was established by the constitution of 1962. The first election of members was held in January 1963. Its 50 members are chosen by a small, all-male electorate and serve four-year terms. Although the ruler can dissolve the assembly, it has significant powers. It shares legislative power with the emir. Ministers are subject to no-confidence votes, the assembly approves each year's national budget, and bills may be initiated in the assembly as well as in the executive branch. The intention of the government in launching Kuwait's legislative experiment, foreshadowed by a 1937-38 legislative assembly, was to strengthen its legitimacy. In providing a forum for often vigorous criticism of the government, the National Assembly has no doubt defused antiregime sentiment that might have found more dangerous expression. Political parties are in principle not permitted (although in December 1991 a party was formed, devoted to promoting free speech and the right of political assembly), but groupings developed early on, both pro and antigovernment, representing Kuwaiti and Arab nationalists, secular liberals, and those who stressed Islamic reform. However, it has twice exceeded the bounds that the Al Sabah ruling family has been prepared to accept and has been suspended as a result. This occurred in 1976 when personal attacks on cabinet members and fear of exacerbating divisions within Kuwaiti society, among other reasons, led the emir, Shaikh Sabah, to suspend the assembly. It was restored by his successor, Shaikh Jabir, in 1981. A second suspension followed in 1986, prompted also by vocal assembly criticism at a time of economic recession and complicated by the collapse of the unofficial stock market, the Suq al-Manakh, to which the government had responded with insufficient energy. In June 1990 elections were held to establish a consultative assembly to discuss restoration of the legislature. This was overtaken by the Iraqi invasion two months later and, following Kuwait's liberation, the emir promised elections to a new National Assembly in October 1992. That event produced a political watershed, with 35 of the assembly's 50 seats won by candidates running on antigovernment platforms. Nineteen of those oppositionists ran on religious platforms. Six opposition members were chosen to sit in the 16-member cabinet, twice as many as ever before, but key portfolios such as defense, interior, and foreign affairs remain securely in Al Sabah hands. The new assembly has taken up sensitive issues such as the state's restrictive citizenship law, has already revoked the secrecy law that prevented public scrutiny of many government documents, and has passed a law, in the wake of the Kuwait Investment Organization's mishandling of state funds, requiring public investment companies to issue semiannual reports. The government appears committed to working with the new assertive assembly, offering some hope that Kuwait's political system will become more effectively participatory and more truly representative.

Bahrain's 1973 constitution, closely modeled on Kuwait's, was approved by a constituent assembly chosen in December 1971 by an all-male electorate. It called for 30 elected members to serve four-year terms. As in Kuwait, parties were forbidden, but blocs of secular nationalists and reformers (including two Marxists) as well as religious conservatives made up the assembly, which was elected in December 1973. In the aftermath of the October 1973 Arab-Israeli war the assembly operated in a tense atmosphere, with strong opposition to continued American naval presence in Bahrain a key issue. The decisive issue was a public security bill, seen by the government as a necessary measure against a violent leftist threat and by the opposition as an attempt to suppress freedom of expression. This led Shaikh Khalifa, the prime minister, to submit his resignation to his brother the ruler, Shaikh Isa, and the latter both dissolved the National Assembly and suspended the article of the constitution requiring a new election. Despite frequent rumors of plans to reestablish the assembly, it has remained suspended. *See also* BAHRAIN *and* KUWAIT.

NATIONAL DEMOCRATIC FRONT FOR THE LIBERATION OF OMAN AND THE ARAB GULF (NDFLOAG). NDFLOAG was a small group of Omani dissidents, formed in 1970, that carried out unsuccessful attacks against Sultan Said bin Taimur. However, the effect of their activities in the northern part of Oman, combined with the rebellion in Dhofar by the Popular Front for the Liberation of the Occupied Arab Gulf (PFLOAG), precipitated the British-supported move against Said and the accession of his son Qabus to the position of

Sultan in September 1970. The two fronts merged in 1971 under the name Popular Front for the Liberation of Oman and the Arab Gulf. *See also* OMAN, POPULAR FRONT FOR THE LIBERATION OF THE OCCUPIED ARAB GULF, POPULAR FRONT FOR THE LIBERATION OF OMAN, POPULAR FRONT FOR THE LIBERATION OF OMAN AND THE ARAB GULF, *and* QABUS BIN SAID AL BU SAID.

NATIONALISM. National consciousness came fairly late to the Gulf Arab states, because of their relative isolation from the rest of the Arab world until recently. It remains generally less pronounced because of their great oil wealth and other powerful sources of identity. Arab nationalism did begin to influence the Gulf initially with the 1936-39 Arab revolt in Mandate Palestine and later with the rise of Nasser, progressively affecting young men susceptible to calls for an end of British control and the traditional regimes to which it was allied. Bahrain was especially vulnerable to this because its ruling family was not of indigenous origin, and indeed was part of the island nation's Sunni Muslim minority, not its Shia majority, and because the ethnic and sectarian divisions militated against establishment of a national identity. Bahrain's early development of its oil resources had created an industrial working class whose immediate economic grievances helped generate a phase of "liberal nationalism" in the early- to mid-1950s, which gave way to a phase of radical nationalism. At about the same time a similar enthusiasm for identification with Arab nationalism marked the Kuwaiti experience. The government adopted a strongly Arab nationalist stance as a self-protective mechanism. In contrast to Bahrain, the relative homogeneity of Kuwait's native population also allowed for the development of a Kuwaiti national consciousness that embodied elements of superiority, with Kuwaitis suggesting that their model of development defined the future for their laggard Gulf brothers. Qatar's religious conservatism and Wahhabi identity with Saudi Arabia have slowed growth of nationalist sentiment, while the UAE's history is too short to have overcome emiral rivalries that forestall a real national identity. Oman's national identity in the past has been centered on the imamate, not the sultanate that now rules. There and in all the other Gulf Arab states, government programs are aimed at promoting stronger national identities through the preservation of folkloric arts and the support of research and documentation centers to gather and interpret the record of the past.

Support of Iraq in its war with Iran helped to diminish the role of radical nationalism, generally existing underground, a diminution that had already begun in the mid-1970s. Then Iraq's invasion of Kuwait in August 1990, and its aftermath, ended whatever lingering impulses of Arab nationalism might have remained in the Gulf, at the same time strengthening, at least in Kuwait, state nationalism. Recent surveys suggest a certain confusion of identity, with Islam often cited as an individual's primary focus of loyalty. However, subnational particularisms also remain strong as well with tribalism still a potent force in the UAE and Oman. *See also* TRIBALISM and entries on individual countries.

NATURAL GAS. The Gulf Arab states generally are less dramatically endowed with natural gas than petroleum but do have significant associated reserves (gas found together with oil) as well as unassociated gas. Indeed, Qatar owns the world's largest gas field, located off its northern shore and containing over 4 percent of the world's natural gas. In addition to Qatar, Kuwait and Abu Dhabi (the latter controlling almost 3 percent of the world's reserves) are significant gas exporters; in Bahrain and Dubai gas is used to generate electricity for refining aluminum from bauxite; and in Oman it is used for a variety of domestic purposes.

NEUTRAL ZONE. The 1922 Treaty of Uqair established a Neutral Zone between Kuwait and Saudi Arabia and another between Iraq and Saudi Arabia, because seasonal movement of Bedouins and their herds in the area in question made establishment of a settled boundary impractical. In 1948 J. P. Getty's Pacific Western oil company won the Saudi concession in the Neutral Zone, shared with Aminoil, the Kuwaiti concessionaire. In 1969 Kuwait and Saudi Arabia established a single border in place of the Neutral Zone with the ownership and exploitation of resources in what came to be known as the Divided Zone left unaffected. Onshore production in the zone was halted by the Gulf crisis hostilities of 1991, but within a year and a half had resumed at its prewar level of approximately 150,000 bpd.

NEWS MEDIA. As elsewhere in the Arab world, both print and broadcast media in the Gulf Arab states are government-controlled or heavily censored. The greatest freedom of expression has existed in Kuwait (although it was curtailed with suspension of the National

Assembly) and in the UAE. In January 1992 formal prepublication censorship in Kuwait was lifted. Despite the fact that Gulf Arab culture is much more oral than literary, the UAE has nine newspapers including probably the best in the Gulf, *Al-Khalij* (The Gulf) of Sharjah. Popular in other Gulf states as well as the UAE, it has a generally leftist, Arab nationalist stance (like other Gulf papers its staff includes non-Gulf Arabs). It features the work of local and other Arab writers and intellectuals. It published in September 1991 the results of a symposium of Gulf scholars in Sharjah that undertook a vigorous discussion of political issues in the aftermath of the Gulf crisis.

The quality of the broadcast media is generally slighter. Local television is available in all the Gulf Arab states but does not play an important role as a source of news. Some surveys suggest that television viewers in the Gulf relied for news much more on CNN than on local programming during the 1990-91 Gulf crisis.

NIZARI. The term "Nizari" refers to the grouping of Arab tribes that came to Oman from northern and central Arabia centuries after the southern Arabian, or Yamani, tribes had arrived. These identities go back to the Arabs' ancient past and the establishment of a fundamental dichotomy between northern and southern tribes, mythically descended from the eponymous Adnan and Qahtan. The terms *Ghafiri* and *Hinawi* (from Omani tribes named Ghafir and Hina) have since the 18th century defined this division in Oman and the UAE. In the former particularly, the identities continue to have potential political importance. *See also* ADNAN, QAHTAN, *and* GHAFIRI.

NIZWA. Nizwa is the major town in that part of Oman that gives its name to the country as a whole. Located in a relatively fertile area between the Hajar Mountains and the Rub al-Khali desert sands, it supports sufficient agriculture to satisfy local needs. In the mid-eighth century A.D., Nizwa, because of its strategic location vis-à-vis the tribes of inner Oman, became the principal seat of the Ibadi imamate, established by a moderate branch of the Kharijites, or "seceders" from the main Islamic community, who to the present account for the majority of Muslims in Oman. Noted for its artisans, especially silversmiths, the town is now the site of light industry. *See also* IBADIS, IMAM/ IMAMATE, ISLAM, KHARIJITES, *and* OMAN.

NOMADS. *See* BEDOUIN.

NU'AIM. *Also* NA'IM. The Nu'aim constitute one of the largest tribes in southeast Arabia, with members scattered from Oman to Bahrain. A branch of the Nu'aim is the dominant tribal group in Ajman, one of the seven emirates of the UAE, whose ruling family bears the same name. *See also* AJMAN.

AL NUHAYYAN (*Also* NAHYAN). The Al Nuhayyan constitute the leading family within the Al Bu Falah, in turn the preeminent clan of the Bani Yas tribal federation that has dominated the emirate of Abu Dhabi for more than two centuries. During that time the Al Nuhayyan family has provided the emirate's rulers. The current ruler, Shaikh Zayid bin Sultan, has held that position since 1966 and has been president of the UAE since its birth in 1971. *See also* ABU DHABI, BANI YAS, AL BU FALAH, *and* UNITED ARAB EMIRATES.

O

OASES. All the Gulf Arab states possess oases, but the only ones of major significance are found in the UAE and Oman. Two among these are worthy of note. On the border of Oman and the emirate of Abu Dhabi is an agglomeration of oases and the 10 settlements that grew up around them, seven in Abu Dhabi and three in Oman. The area is known in Abu Dhabi as al-Ain, after its principal settlement, and in Oman is, in similar fashion, identified as al-Buraimi. On the Abu Dhabi side of the border the settlements have merged into a city of over 100,000, seat of the national university. In southwestern Abu Dhabi a string of small oases called al-Liwa is located, with a population in the thousands, symbolically important as the ancestral home of the Al Nuhayyan rulers of Abu Dhabi. *See also* ABU DHABI, AL-AIN, BURAIMI OASIS, *and* LIWA.

OFFSHORE BANKING UNITS (OBUs). *See* BANKING.

OIL. It is oil and its location in the Persian/Arab Gulf area that makes the Gulf so important. If Iran, Iraq, and Saudi Arabia were included with the states covered in this volume, the oil estimated to lie under the waters and adjoining territories of the Gulf would account for about two-thirds of the world's total. The five small Gulf Arab states possess as much as one-fifth of global reserves.

The first oil strike in the Gulf region was in Iran in 1908. A world oil glut after World War I and British desires to keep foreign interests out of the states under its protection delayed exploration in the Gulf Arab states. A New Zealand entrepreneur, Major Frank Holmes, intrepidly pursued concessions along the Gulf's Arab littoral, leading eventually to the securing of a concession for Standard Oil of California (SoCal) in Bahrain, where oil was found in 1932. Six years later the huge bonanzas of Kuwait and Saudi Arabia were struck, and in 1940 Qatar's first successful well was drilled, although with the exception of slight Saudi production, no oil was commercially produced until after World War II. The enormous reserves of Abu Dhabi and the slighter ones of Dubai and Oman were first exploited in the 1960s. (Details of oil concessions and explorations as well as company–producer country relations and reserve and production figures are provided under individual country and company entries.)

Even before oil was struck in the Gulf Arab states it had begun to exercise a profound impact upon them. Exploration concession payments to the local rulers, modest as the amounts were, represented an enormous infusion of wealth, elevating them economically above the merchant class for the first time. Also for the first time, borders of the European kind were introduced to the Gulf when it became essential to determine whose oil was being discovered. The borders were largely defined by British diplomats. Uncertain or disputed frontiers continue to cause tension, the Iraq-Kuwait border being a prime example. Perhaps most important, the discovery of oil really opened the Gulf Arab states to the outside world for the first time in modern history with all the momentous consequences that followed. With breathtaking speed the Gulf Arab states ceased to be an impoverished backwater, hitherto of real concern only to the British as part of a strategic imperial lifeline, and acquired astonishing wealth while being caught up in the politics of the Middle East and the international arena. Oil and its consequences brought independent nationhood to states long insulated by British protection. It caused these societies to be suddenly exposed to events, ideas, and tastes from the outside world as education (at home or in overseas universities), new communications, and a massive influx of Arab and other expatriates decisively ended their long and somnolent isolation.

Because the oil concessionaires were exclusively American and British until the 1950s, and remained overwhelmingly so after that, the Gulf Arab states were tied closely to those economies, with oil exports paid for and denominated in U.S. dollars and British pounds. Subsequently, Japan and Western Europe became major oil importers. The Gulf states' acquisitions of technology, economic consumption patterns, and political-security alignments have, in large measure, followed in the wake of the oil connection. There have, of course, been countervailing forces within these states and the relations between them, and the oil companies and importing countries have evolved through dramatic confrontations and crises. In 1950 the adoption of a 50/50 profit-sharing formula in Saudi Arabia led to a general reordering of company-exporting country relations. That process began in earnest, however, when the Organization of Petroleum Exporting Countries (OPEC) was formed in 1960, with Kuwait as a founding member and Qatar as an observer, to try to counteract oil company reductions in the posted price of oil at a time of international oversupply, thus lowering producing country incomes. The balance of power was such that the producers could do little more than compel observance of the posted price until a combination of factors profoundly altered the power equation and the relationship in the early 1970s.

The new situation was inaugurated when "independent" oil companies sought to challenge the position of the "seven sisters," the large internationals that dominated Middle East oil production, by agreeing to deals that were more favorable to the host countries. This initiated a rapid rise in prices that, in the course of the October 1973 Arab-Israeli war, were ratcheted further upward. At the same time, King Faisal of Saudi Arabia, angered by the massive U.S. military resupply of Israel, which he believed betrayed assurances made to him by President Nixon, persuaded most Arab oil exporters to impose an embargo. This involved cutbacks in the general level of exports and a complete embargo on shipments to the U.S. and the Netherlands, to remain in place until Israel withdrew from occupied Arab territory. This invocation of the "oil weapon," bringing near panic and long gasoline lines to the United States, marked the end of the era in which the oil companies had been the dominant actors in the largest international business. The Gulf Arab states then proceeded to negotiate "participation" agreements with the companies, in effect nationalization, signaling the new balance of power. (The UAE and Oman continued to permit companies to hold equity in oil concessions.) By the late 1980s and early 1990s the new relationship, in which the companies have purchase preferences and service agreements, appeared to work to the satisfaction of all concerned. Interestingly, however, in the 1990s it appears that some of the earlier nationalizations may be reversed as Middle East producers, including some of the Gulf Arab states, expand their production capacity and accept company investment in exchange for equity.

The Gulf Arab states, except for Bahrain and Oman, belong to OPEC. With the severe downturn in world demand for oil and the depressed prices of the early and mid-1980s, the Gulf Arab members of OPEC, to stretch the commercial life of their large reserves and dampen development of alternative energy resources, came into conflict with Iran, Libya, and other OPEC producers with smaller reserves relative to production who wished to maximize current earnings by cutting production. The Gulf states won out, forcing higher production and preserving their market shares. The current price levels, with likely gradual future price rises, constitute their favored scenario. Uncertainties and problems do remain. As Iran recovers from the ravages of its long war with Iraq, it presses harder to market more oil for urgently needed revenues. When Iraq is again permitted to produce its OPEC quota, difficult decisions probably involving some Gulf Arab production cutbacks will have to be made. In the longer run the key questions concern fundamental issues such as preparation for the post-oil era and the degree to which the Gulf Arab states will remain dependent on foreign labor and skills. Kuwait's Reserve Fund for Future Generations is one (partial) answer. Economic diversification is another, but most of that, like production of aluminum from imported bauxite, cannot be sustained when the oil runs out. Although the Gulf crisis of 1990-91 led Kuwaitis and others to pledge to reduce their dependence on expatriate workers and develop correspondingly greater self-reliance, it remains for the Gulf Arab states to demonstrate the will and capacity to do this. *See also* INDUSTRY *and entries on individual Gulf Arab states and oil companies.*

OMAN (*Official name,* SULTANAT OMAN *or* SULTANATE OF OMAN). Oman shares with the other Gulf Arab states a generally arid climate with extremely hot summers and temperate winters, a conservative Islamic culture, a system of traditional hereditary rule, a long history of maritime commerce, possession of hydrocarbon deposits that have brought recent wealth, and the urgent concerns of a region beset by a decade of conflict and crisis. It is also in a number of ways distinctively different, beginning with its geographic orientation. Virtually all its coastline is on the Gulf of Oman and Arabian Sea, arms of the Indian Ocean, with corresponding influences on its economic, military, and political history. Technically, Oman is a Persian/Arab Gulf state only by its few miles of Gulf coastline of its Musandam Peninsula exclave. Parts of Oman receive sufficient rain, some from the Indian Ocean monsoons, to support a much more extensive agriculture than is possible in the other Gulf Arab states. Separated from central Arabia by the daunting sands of the Rub al-Khali desert, Oman was much less influenced by events in that quarter than were the other Gulf Arab states. Indeed, its remoteness from the political centers of the Arab world and its rugged and extensive hinterland (Oman has between two and three times the combined area of the other states) has made it a natural refuge throughout history for oppressed minorities. Such a group, the Ibadi Muslims, product of an early schism in Islam and distinct from both Sunni and Shia Islam, constitute the majority of Omanis and have in large measure defined Oman's national identity.

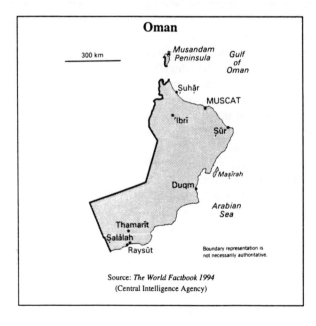

Oman

300 km

Musandam Peninsula

Gulf of Oman

Suhār

MUSCAT

'Ibrī

Sūr

Maṣīrah

Duqm

Arabian Sea

Thamarīt

Salālah

Raysūt

Boundary representation is not necessarily authoritative.

Source: *The World Factbook 1994*
(Central Intelligence Agency)

Land and people. Oman occupies the southeast corner of the Arabian Peninsula, its area variously estimated from a bit over 80,000 to 120,000 sq mi (207,000 to 311,000 sq km). (The discrepancy reflects uncertainty over demarcation of borders.) Its coastline extends over 1,100 mi (1,771 km), from just inside the Strait of Hormuz to the border with the Yemen Republic. In addition to Yemen, it shares borders with Saudi Arabia on its west and the UAE both to the west and north, where territories of Sharjah and Fujairah separate the small but strategically important Omani exclave of the Musandam Peninsula from the rest of the country. None of these borders is yet fully and definitively delineated. Roughly the northern two-thirds of Oman, the region from which the country takes its name, contain the bulk of the population in several distinct areas. From the UAE border the Batinah, a narrow coastal plain between the Hajar Mountains and the Gulf of Oman, runs over 150 mi (242 km) to the town of Sib, just west of Muscat. Its alluvial soils, irrigated by mountain water runoff, constitute the country's most important agricultural area and the most heavily populated. Inland to the west is the mountainous Western Hajar region, including the 10,000-foot-high Jebel al-Akhdar plateau. Further to the west are the Dhahirah and Inner Oman, between the mountains and the Rub al-Khali, with a series of significant towns, among them Nizwa, traditional seat of the Ibadi imamate. This area sustains a modest agriculture, and the country's principal oil fields are found here. Less fertile and less populated is the rugged Eastern Hajar area, divided from the Western Hajar by the Sama'il Valley, which meets the Gulf of Oman at Sib and from which the capital area of the cities of Muscat and Matrah is separated by a purely political boundary. To the south this area meets the Ja'lan, a narrow valley at whose Gulf of Oman terminus the port of Sur is located, and the Wahiba Sands. Due west of the eastern Hajar is the Sharqiya, an arid, little-populated region. To the south and southwest of the areas described above is Central Oman, a barren, ill-defined area that merges imperceptibly into Dhofar Province. Dhofar's narrow coastal plain and the mountains behind it are watered by monsoon rains, making possible agriculture including coconut palms and beef production. Significant islands are the Khuria Muria group off Dhofar and Masirah off central Oman, with significant military facilities located on the latter.

The size of the population, as no census has ever been taken, is subject to the same conjecture as the country's area, with estimates ranging from around 750,000 to 1.5 million. Between a quarter and a third are resident aliens, most from the Indian subcontinent. By contrast with the other Gulf Arab states, Oman is largely rural, with nearly half its people in the towns and villages of Inner Oman and the Dhahirah and about a third on the Batinah coast. There are no large cities. The capital of Muscat and its neighbor Matrah may each approach 50,000 while Salalah, capital of Dhofar, has about 30,000.

History. Oman's history dates back to the early third or late fourth millennium B.C., with evidence of commercial and cultural linkages with ancient Mesopotamia. A fairly advanced, agriculturally based civilization existed in Oman, centered in the western Hajar Mountains and favored by a climate estimated to have been considerably wetter than today. By about 2000 B.C. camel nomadism had begun to reduce the sphere of settled agriculture which recovered only in the subsequent millennium. The renewal of settled agriculture coincided with Persian domination of this part of Arabia, its imprint still evident in the irrigation systems that, down to modern times, have been key to the prosperity of interior Oman. By early in the first century A.D. Arab tribes began to move into Oman, coming initially from western Arabia, later from the north. At the same time the Sassanids reasserted Persian control of the area, eventually evolving a system of indirect rule through an Arab leader called a *julanda*.

The coming of Islam just before the death of the prophet Muhammad (A.D. 632) ended Persian rule and affirmed Oman's Arab character. Just over a century later, the establishment of an Ibadi imamate in Oman had profound consequences for the way Oman developed. The Ibadis, distinct from both Sunni and Shia Muslims, are a moderate branch of the Kharijites, or "seceders," who rejected the authority of the caliphs after Omar, the second successor to Muhammad. They adhere to a strict form of Islam that rejects limiting selection of a caliph or imam to a particular family or clan, holding that he should be chosen for his moral and religious virtue and leadership ability. The establishment of the Ibadi imamate with its seat at Nizwa ended rule by the Julandas; with significant interruptions the imamate survived to 1959. In the 12th century it gave way to rule by a tribal dynasty in the interior, the Nabahaniyah, and Persian rule in the coastal areas. Although it was revived in the 15th century, it was eclipsed by the establishment of Portuguese authority from the early 16th to the mid-17th century, when it again flourished under the Ya'aribah dynasty, extending Omani authority and influence to East Africa, Iran, and the Persian/Arab Gulf. By the mid-18th century, however, Ya'aribah rule collapsed in catastrophic civil war along tribal lines harking back to the pattern of Arab settlement, that is, Qahtani tribes from Yemen and Adnani (also referred to as Nizari) from central Arabia. In the 18th century these were grouped, respectively, into Hinawis and Ghafiris, which define the basic alignments of Omani tribes to the present day.

From the civil war in 1749 emerged the Al Bu Said dynasty to which the present ruler Sultan Qabus belongs. The Al Bu Said revived, at least for some decades, the maritime power that the Ya'aribah had established. However, divisions within the family, which in 1856 separated Zanzibar and other East African territory from Oman, also contributed to a split between inner Oman and the coastal areas. Only the first Al Bu Said rulers claimed the title of "imam." Their successors, based in Muscat, turned their greatest energies toward maritime ventures, leaving the tribes of the interior mainly to their own devices. Threats from the Qawasim naval power of Ras al-Khaimah in the early 19th century and from the Saudi state to the north subsequently helped to push the Al Bu Said into dependency on British support for survival. After the imamate was revived formally in 1913 it threatened the town of Muscat, whose capture was averted only through the intervention of British Indian forces. In 1920 the Treaty of Sib gave formal effect to the division of authority between the Al Bu Said sultanate in Muscat and the imamate tribal confederation of the interior. This situation continued until the 1950s, when Petroleum Development Oman, prospecting in the interior, created an armed force, the Muscat and Oman Field Forces, and seized the imamate town of Ibri. Sultan Said bin Taimur then moved against the imamate, whose collapse was hastened when the British-trained-and-led Trucial Oman Scouts drove the imamate's Saudi allies from Buraimi. The reunication of the Sultanate of Muscat and Oman was soon jeopardized when the deposed Imam Ghalib and his supporters in Saudi exile planned and executed a campaign which was defeated only with significant British help, when the imam's final stronghold on the Jebel Akhdar was stormed by a detachment of British Special Air Services in January 1959.

The reclusive Said withdrew to Salalah in Dhofar, and his general neglect of the population came to be exacerbated by the petty restrictions that he imposed, as well as Omanis' awareness of the benefits that their neighbors were beginning to enjoy as oil incomes were invested in economic development. Through the 1960s, rebel groups in Dhofar carried out acts of violence with Saudi and Egyptian encouragement. By the late 1960s what had begun as a Dhofari tribal rebellion against the sultan had been transformed into a radical leftist, Arab nationalist movement styled the Popular Front for the Liberation of the Occupied Arab Gulf (PFLOAG) with greatly expanded aims, as the name implied. It received material support from Iraq, the Soviet Union, and the People's Republic of China and was sustained by a base in neighboring Marxist South Yemen (the People's Democratic Republic of Yemen, PDRY, which in 1990 merged with the Yemen Arab Republic to form the Yemen Republic). Though lacking widespread popular support, the rebellion's organized military strength enabled it to control much of Dhofar and emboldened other regime opponents, organized as the National Democratic Front for the Liberation of Oman and the Arab Gulf (NDFLOAG), to attempt the overthrow of Sultan Said and his government in 1970. This prompted disaffected members of the government to conspire with key British advisers to remove Said and install Qabus as sultan in July 1970. The country's name was then changed from Sultanate of Muscat and Oman to Sultanate of Oman.

As ruler, Qabus turned urgent attention to defeating the Dhofari insurgency, which by late 1971 had merged PFLOAG and NDFLOAG as the Popular Front for the Liberation of Oman and the Arab Gulf (somewhat confusingly retaining the acronym of its principal parent). This was accomplished over the course of five years with a combination of effective military and social-economic action. Oman received important assistance from neighbors who feared contagion from the radical forces promoting rebellion in Dhofar, in addition to key British support that included seconded and contracted military officers. Iran supplied men and materiel, the UAE and Saudi Arabia provided financial support, and the UAE and Jordan loaned some military personnel to free up Omani forces from duty elsewhere, allowing their dispatch to Dhofar. By 1975 the reorganized rebellion, restyled the Popular Front for the Liberation of Oman (PFLO), had been confined to isolated pockets in the bush, and by 1976 Oman was united and at peace. Crucial to success in Dhofar was the lavishing of generous aid on that part of the country as pacification proceeded and in the years following. Rapid development of transportation and communications networks throughout the country, together with establishment of other infrastructure largely neglected by Sultan Said, helped to consolidate the position of Qabus and his government. Schools, clinics, and hospitals (some planned, but not built during Said's rule) were rapidly constructed. A national university opened its doors in 1986 with faculties in education, Islamic studies, agriculture, medicine, and other specializations. In undertaking these ambitious schemes Qabus benefited greatly from Oman's expanding oil production, which had reached over 300,000 bpd in 1970, the fourth year of production. Reserves, though modest by Arabian Peninsula standards, have been steadily enlarged through exploration, and production rose through the 1980s to 685,000 bpd in 1990. Most of its oil exports go to the Far East, principally to Japan and South Korea, and in 1990 generated about $5 billion in revenues. Oil accounts for about half of the GDP. Modest natural gas production is used for the generation of electric power, water desalination, and other industrial purposes. Not a member of OPEC, Oman is a founding member of the non-OPEC producers group, the Independent Oil Producing and Exporting Countries (IOPEC).

Economics. Although Oman suffered from the price downturn of the mid-1980s, it had already built most of its essential physical infrastructure. Recently, increased attention has been turned to development of the nonoil sector, including traditional economic pursuits such as agriculture and fishing, which generate just over 3 percent of GDP but employ up to 60 percent of the economically active indigenous population. Light industry, aimed largely at import substitution, has also been emphasized. Oman's expatriate workforce, largely from the Indian subcontinent, is estimated to be a bit less than half of the nation's total labor force of slightly more than 500,000. The policy of "Omanization" aims not at replacing all or most expatriates but at ensuring employment for the more than 12,000 Omanis who enter the labor market each year. One area that it is hoped will produce employment opportunities for Omanis is tourism, being developed cautiously to serve up to 100,000 visitors annually.

This reflects Oman's concern to preserve its traditions and its environment. In the latter regard Oman is unique among the Gulf Arab states in having a minister of environment who, with the support of Sultan Qabus, has placed environmental concerns high on the development agenda. All new economic projects must have approval from the minister of environment before implementation.

The environmental policy is one example of the close, personal involvement in government affairs of Sultan Qabus, the one Gulf Arab state ruler who most closely approximates an absolute monarch. Qabus enjoyed great popularity during his first years in power as increasing oil revenues and the reversing of his father's parsimonious approach brought sudden and enormous material improvement to most Omanis. That popularity has waned somewhat as reduced revenues and other problems affect his highly personalized authority. The sultan has kept in his own hands the key government posts of prime minister, minister of defense, minister of foreign affairs, and minister of finance. In 1981 he established the State Consultative Council (SCC), embodying a tradition of consultation closely associated with the Ibadi imamate but new to the Al Bu Said sultanate. Its powers have since been expanded.

Although it remains an advisory institution and is not empowered to deal with the sensitive areas of foreign and defense issues or oil policy, the SCC has provided useful advice to the sultan on a range of social, economic, and legal issues. The selection of SCC members from the country's principal geographic regions, its inclusion of members selected by the chamber of commerce, and the televising of some of its sessions represent at least a modest move toward greater institutionalization of political power. Sultan Qabus has shown solicitude for a politics of inclusion, geographically and socially. His special concern for development in Dhofar has been extended to other outlying areas, although the capital area around Muscat and Matrah continues to draw a large part of new investment. He has also made special efforts to expand opportunities for youth and women in Oman's economic and social life. Despite the general conservatism of the country, women have achieved considerable advancement in several fields, including government service.

Political dynamics and issues. Oman under Sultan Qabus has enjoyed general stability, but political problems exist. One is the issue of corruption, especially the large fortunes made by a small circle of men close to the palace, with a number of foreigners among them. Despite a declared policy of "Omanization," Qabus continues to rely significantly on expatriate, especially British, advisers, thereby incurring a certain unease on the part of Omani nationalists. The number of resident aliens is another concern, and non-Arabs such as Baluchis, Indians, and Zanzibaris have been alienated to one degree or another by discriminatory practices. Other domestic concerns are traditional sources of challenge to the government, including tribal disaffection and conservative Ibadi disapprobation of the Al Bu Said who, though Ibadi themselves, have not been viewed as supportive of Ibadi values. On these fronts Qabus seems to have acted effectively, on the whole, to check political opposition. Perhaps more serious is the question of succession, as the sultan's marriage to his cousin Kamilla was brief and without issue, and he has since displayed no matrimonial inclinations. While several capable members of the ruling Al Bu Said family serve in various government capacities, and the family has apparently made plans for a succession if Qabus should unexpectedly pass away, the Al Bu Said are a small family with no other dominant member. Presumably, as Qabus is in his mid 50s, the question of succession will not soon become urgent.

As in the other Gulf Arab states, the Gulf crisis of 1990-91 helped to promote movement toward greater political participation. In 1981 Oman had established a Consultative Assembly (*majlis al-istishar*) of 45 (later 55) members appointed by the sultan and drawn from the tribes, merchant families, and the government. It advised the sultan on public issues, excluding the sensitive areas of defense and foreign policy. In late 1991 a new Consultative Council (*majlis al-shura*) was created. Each of the country's 59 districts presents three nominees from which a single delegate to the council is selected by the government, subject to the approval of the sultan. (In 1995 the majlis was expanded to 80 members.) While the first assembly could do little more than discuss government policies and offer suggestions, the new one is empowered to review all social and economic legislation drafted by various ministries before they are enacted, participate in the creation of development plans and help oversee their execution, and propose ways of developing and improving public services. Ministries are required to submit their annual reports to the council, which can summon ministers at any time to discuss any issues that fall within their purview. Council members serve three-year terms and may succeed themselves. While the new council is, of course, still far short of a full-fledged legislature, it represents a significant advance toward broader representation in the affairs of government for the Omani population.

Internationally, Oman seems to have weathered several threats and emerged reasonably secure, pursuing a somewhat maverick foreign policy line in Gulf Arab terms. In its immediate neighborhood the greatest danger has come from the west, in the form of PDRY support for the rebellion in Dhofar, as noted previously. The rebellion was defeated by 1975 and subsequent UAE-Kuwaiti diplomatic initiatives, backed by economic aid to impoverished South Yemen, led to a normalization of Oman-PDRY relations in 1982. The 1990 absorption of the former Marxist state into a Yemeni union seems to assure tranquillity on that border, for which demarcation is now settled. Memories of hostile contention on the UAE border a relatively few years ago, and longstanding fears of Saudi claims to territory where important oil fields lie, still generate Omani unease, but are not likely to flare into real crises in the foreseeable future.

Oman is a member of the Gulf Cooperation Council, along with Saudi Arabia and the other Gulf Arab states and, although it has differed with other GCC states on security issues and has received fewer than anticipated economic benefits through its membership, it plays an active role in the council. In September 1991 it hosted a meeting of the GCC chiefs of staff to advance GCC military cooperation. The Iranian Revolution and Iran-Iraq war were obvious sources of concern, but Oman's fairly small Shia minority is largely of South Asian origin and generally quiescent, and Oman currently enjoys reasonably good relations with Iran. Close ties with the United States, including the conclusion of agreements for American access to military facilities in Oman in the late 1970s and early 1980s, as well as failure to join the rest of the Arab world (except Morocco) in breaking diplomatic relations with Egypt in 1979 following its peace treaty with Israel, made Oman something of an odd-man-out. Events have overtaken the negative effects of these forward Omani positions, as they did its somewhat controversial action in establishing diplomatic relations with both the PRC and USSR before most of the other Gulf Arab states had done so. *See also* AL BU SAID, DHOFAR, IBADIS, IMAM/IMAMATE, NATIONAL FRONT FOR THE LIBERATION OF OMAN AND THE ARAB GULF, POPULAR FRONT FOR THE LIBERATION OF OMAN AND THE ARAB GULF, QABUS BIN SAID, *and* SAID BIN TAIMUR.

ORGANIZATION OF ARAB PETROLEUM EXPORTING COUNTRIES (OAPEC). In 1968 Kuwait joined with Saudi Arabia and Libya (then a conservative monarchy) to establish OAPEC as a mechanism to unify Arab oil policy. Libya's 1969 coup and the subsequent addition of states with conflicting ideologies and political aims undercut the original intent, although OAPEC did serve as the mechanism for implementing the 1973 embargo. The organization has proved useful in disseminating and exchanging information among members on oil-related issues, training Arab petroleum technicians, and promoting joint ventures like the Arab Shipbuilding and Repair Yard in Bahrain. All the Gulf Arab states are members of OAPEC.

ORGANIZATION OF THE ISLAMIC CONFERENCE (OIC). *See* ISLAMIC CONFERENCE ORGANIZATION.

ORGANIZATION OF PETROLEUM EXPORTING COUNTRIES (OPEC). Kuwait was one of the five founding members of OPEC in 1960 that, at Saudi Arabian and Venezuelan initiative, was established to counteract oil company reduction of posted prices. Abu Dhabi and Qatar later joined; Bahrain's small production did not qualify it for membership; and Oman has opted not to join, although generally it abides by OPEC pricing decisions. Over the first decade of its existence OPEC accomplished little more than prevention of further price cuts. In the early 1970s events conspired to give it ascendancy in its relations with the international oil companies. Entry by the "independents" in a significant way into Middle East oil operations, by offering deals more favorable to host governments than those earlier established with the international oil companies then identified as the "seven sisters" (British Petroleum, Gulf, Royal Dutch Shell, Standard Oil of California, Standard Oil of New Jersey, Mobil, and Texaco) plus the Compagnie Française des Pétroles, started to shift the balance. In 1971-72 several OPEC members began moving assertively to nationalize oil company operations, and Saudi Arabia began the process of "participation," purchasing company assets, which was emulated by the other Gulf Arab states. The process was accelerated by the October 1973 Arab-Israeli war, which unleashed the Arab "oil weapon" at Saudi initiative through the Organization of Arab Petroleum Exporting Countries, in response to President Richard Nixon's massive military resupply of Israel. General production cuts were implemented with a total embargo against the United States and the Netherlands. The Gulf Arab states' members of OPEC have been active and, in the 1980s, frequently prominent in the organization's deliberations and decisions. Generally, they have acted as a bloc over the past several years to press policies designed to maximize their market shares and to support moderate, slowly rising prices to delay development of substitute energy sources and ensure production from their large reserves well into the future. *See also* OIL and entries on individual countries, and oil companies.

P

PAKISTAN. Gulf Arab states' relations with Pakistan have generally been close and cordial; this was especially so with the more Islamically conservative among them during Zia ul-Haq's presidency. There are significant trade relations, and Pakistan has received economic aid from Abu Dhabi, Kuwait, and Qatar. In several instances Gulf Arab states' rulers have had a close relationship. Shaikh Zayid Al Nuhayyan, ruler of Abu Dhabi and president of the UAE, has long maintained homes in Pakistan, where he and other wealthy Gulf Arabs spend hunting holidays. Pakistani relations with Oman have been warm, with a significant network of cultural, economic, and other ties. Recent events, however, have caused something of a strain in Gulf Arab-Pakistan relations as the latter failed to support Kuwait and its allies against Iraq, following the invasion of Kuwait.

PAKISTANIS. Pakistanis have long played an important role in the Gulf Arab states, especially in the lower Gulf. Their country's strong Islamic identity and consistently pro-Arab position in the Arab-Israeli dispute have helped to engender trust (although strains have recently entered the relationship, as noted in the previous entry). In addition to large numbers of Pakistanis who filled skilled and semiskilled positions in the workforce, some are engaged in retail trades. Most of the emirates in the UAE and Oman have used Pakistanis in their security forces, and Kuwait has employed Pakistanis as military instructors.

PALESTINE LIBERATION ORGANIZATION (PLO). The Gulf Arab states have long supported the Palestinian cause of self-determination, dating back as far as the 1936-39 disturbances in Mandate Palestine. The PLO was established in 1964 and initially was closely allied to Egypt under Gamal Abdel Nasser. In 1967, following the devastating Arab defeat in the June war, the Palestinian movement Fatah, which had been established in the 1950s, emerged under the leadership of Yasir Arafat as a powerful, militant Palestinian movement and soon dominated the PLO. Arafat has continued to lead Fatah and the PLO to the present. Until 1990, Kuwait, Qatar, and the UAE backed diplomatic and political support of the PLO with generous subventions, although these were reduced somewhat in the mid-1980s because of budgetary constraints. Support of Yasir Arafat and the PLO reflected both sympathy for the Palestinian cause and concern for acts of disruption and hostility by resident or other Palestinians. Support for the PLO in the Gulf Arab states was cut off as a result of its pro-Iraqi position following Saddam Hussein's invasion of Kuwait in August 1990. The Gulf Arab states have, however, supported the September 13, 1993, Israel-PLO Declaration of Principles calling for limited Palestinian self-rule in Gaza and Jericho and the May 1994 agreement signed in Cairo by Egypt, Israel, and the PLO that set out the details for establishment of a nominated Palestine National Authority (PNA) to implement that rule. On January 20, 1996 Arafat was elected President of the Palestine Council, an 88-member elected body, representing the legislative arm of the PNA. All the Gulf Arab states except Kuwait have pledged support to promote the economic development of the new Palestinian entity, seen as the first step toward self-rule for the whole West Bank as well as Gaza. *See also* ARAB-ISRAELI CONFLICT, ISRAEL, *and* PALESTINIANS.

PALESTINIANS. Large numbers of Palestinians have resided and worked in the Gulf Arab states since the 1948-49 Arab-Israeli war, with by far the largest concentration in Kuwait. They played a critically important role in the development of the Gulf states, most especially Kuwait, as civil servants and as professionals in a number of key fields. Palestinians have also been prominent in journalism, particularly in Kuwait and the UAE. The Gulf Arab states have always harbored somewhat ambivalent feelings toward the Palestinians, combining sympathy for their plight with unease over their potential for causing disruption in their politically and socially conservative host countries. Gulf Arabs have typically viewed Palestinians as hired hands who are insufficiently grateful for the opportunity to earn a good living, while Palestinians have regarded themselves, most especially in Kuwait, as the true builders of a new nation who have, in spite of their vital contribution, been treated as second-class citizens. (Not more than a tiny handful of Palestinians has ever been granted citizenship by any Gulf Arab country.) Virtually all Palestinians in the Gulf have been careful to keep a low profile because of their vulnerable position. The 1990-91 Gulf crisis has profoundly altered their situation, most obviously in Kuwait, where the PLO embrace of Saddam Hussein caused a deep sense of betrayal. The majority of the over 350,000 Palestinians in prewar Kuwait fled to Jordan or the West Bank and, by contrast with Kuwaiti citizens, have not been permitted to return. Scores, perhaps hundreds of Palestinians were executed in a venting of Kuwaiti rage after the country's liberation, many beaten, and, by one credible account, some 6,000 placed in detention. Less than a fourth of the original population remains, and the employment of all Palestinians in the public sector has been terminated. Fewer than 40,000 Palestinians are reportedly being permitted to stay. While their situation is less desperate elsewhere in the Gulf, the place of the Palestinians in the Gulf Arab states in the future appears uncertain. *See also* FOREIGN WORKERS, ISRAEL, *and* PALESTINE LIBERATION ORGANIZATION.

PARLIAMENTS. *See* NATIONAL ASSEMBLIES.

PEARLING. Historical records suggest that as early as the ninth century A.D. pearling was a major activity among the Arabs of the Gulf. It acquired its greatest importance in the 19th and early 20th centuries when British-imposed treaties, especially the 1853 Treaty of Perpetual Peace, provided the necessary degree of security for pearling to flourish. At its height, around the turn of the 19th century, the pearling fleets totaled about 3,500 vessels and, by one estimate, some 70,000-100,000 men were involved in the enterprise, sailors, divers, merchants, and shipbuilders. As many as 60 million pearls were sold annually, largely to merchants in India, and many found their way to eventual sale in the United States. The yearly income generated in the Gulf has been estimated at £1.5 million. The pearling fleets were out from as early as mid-May until as late as the end of September, leaving many villages virtually without men for four months of the year. For divers the occupation was dangerous and debilitating and, while merchants and tribal shaikhs who organized the labor acquired modest wealth, for most who were involved in pearling it represented a kind of impoverished servitude. The Gulf pearling industry was effectively destroyed by the worldwide depression of the 1920s and 1930s and by the introduction of the Japanese cultured pearl in 1930. Today the collection of traditions about pearling is an important part of the effort to preserve the Gulf Arabs' folkloric heritage, and pearl diving is a dominant theme of Gulf Arab film, theater, and other art forms.

PEOPLE'S DEMOCRATIC REPUBLIC OF YEMEN (PDRY). While it existed, the PDRY was the Arab world's only Marxist state and, as such, a source of special concern to the conservative Gulf Arab states. From the late 1960s to 1975 the Aden government provided active support, including men and materiel, to a radical military rebellion in Oman's adjoining southern province of Dhofar aimed at overthrowing the government of Sultan Said and subsequently that of Sultan Qabus. Following the defeat of the rebellion, the PDRY continued its efforts to foment unrest until diplomatic efforts led by Kuwait and the UAE, sweetened with economic aid to the impoverished Aden regime, brought a normalization of Omani-PDRY relations. The PDRY's continued, if uneven, progress toward moderation, and the May 1990 union with the Yemen Arab Republic (North Yemen) to form the Yemen Republic, ended the threat from this quarter to Oman and the Gulf Arab states. *See also* POPULAR FRONT FOR THE LIBERATION OF THE OCCUPIED ARAB GULF.

PERSIA. *See* IRAN.

PERSIANS. *See* IRANIANS.

PERSIAN GULF. *See* GULF.

PETROCHEMICAL INDUSTRY. *See* INDUSTRY.

PETROLEUM. *See* OIL.

PIRACY. Pirates were present in Gulf waters from earliest historical times, and by the 18th century their numbers even included a few American buccaneers. By the early 19th century the fleet of the Qawasim federation, centered on Ras al-Khaimah, dominated the waters of the Gulf and Indian Ocean as far as Bombay. The contemporary British, whose India trade was severely disrupted, denounced the depredation as piracy, but today's Arab historians, including descendants of the Qawasim themselves, view it as maritime warfare carried out in the spirit of Arab nationalism. This distinction derives from cultural perspectives, not from the facts of the case. Whichever viewpoint one takes, the depredation probably derived from at least three causes: a desire to seize some of the rich Indian Ocean trade long dominated by the neighboring Omanis, Wahhabi sectarian enthusiasm carrying over from the Qawasim's landward alliance with the first Saudi state, and reaction to European intrusion. What is significant is that British intervention, initially in the form of naval expeditions, had by 1819 checked the Qawasim, and subsequently in treaties between 1820 and 1853 established a largely self-enforcing truce in the Gulf that benefited all parties by permitting peaceful conduct of trade and pearling. The name "Trucial Coast" derived from this treaty system, which created a British imperium in the Gulf for a century and a half, and the basis for the Gulf Arab states that exist today. *See also* QAWASIM, RAS AL-KHAIMAH, *and* UNITED KINGDOM.

POPULAR FRONT FOR THE LIBERATION OF THE OCCUPIED ARAB GULF (PFLOAG). PFLOAG, established in 1968, grew out of an earlier movement, the Dhofar Liberation Front (DLF), an essentially tribal rebellion seeking to throw off the rule of the Al Bu Said in Oman's southern province. The new organization enlisted international leftist support from Iraq, the People's Republic of China (PRC), and the USSR to promote the broader aim of its title. It operated from a base in neighboring, newly independent, Marxist South Yemen (PDRY), adopted an anti-Islamic stance, and sought to impose a collectivist, socialist regime in the area of Dhofar that it controlled. PFLOAG's ideology and repressive tactics denied it extensive popular support, but its significant external support (including very considerable weaponry) and Sultan Said's ineffective response enabled it to extend its sway over most of Dhofar. With the accession of his son Qabus by a coup in 1970 the tide began to turn, as notable Iranian, British, and other military aid to Oman began to have an impact and especially as generously supported civic action programs became effective in Dhofar. In 1971 the front linked with another rebel group, the National Democratic Front for the Liberation of Oman and the Arab Gulf, adopting the name Popular Front for the Liberation of Oman and the Arab Gulf, thus retaining its original initials. *See also* DHOFAR, OMAN, NATIONAL DEMOCRATIC FRONT FOR THE LIBERATION OF OMAN AND THE ARAB GULF, POPULAR FRONT FOR THE LIBERATION OF OMAN, *and* POPULAR

FRONT FOR THE LIBERATION OF OMAN AND THE ARAB GULF.

POPULAR FRONT FOR THE LIBERATION OF OMAN. The PFLO was formed in May 1974 by the militant faction of the Popular Front for the Liberation of Oman and the Arab Gulf (PFLOAG), with the name reflecting the reduced scope of the revolt, which was then a year and some months from its final defeat.

POPULAR FRONT FOR THE LIBERATION OF OMAN AND THE ARAB GULF. In 1971 the National Democratic Front for the Liberation of Oman and the Arab Gulf (NDFLOAG) merged with the Popular Front for the Liberation of the Occupied Arab Gulf (PFLOAG) to form the Popular Front for the Liberation of Oman and the Arab Gulf (PFLOAG). It thus united dissident movements in the north and south of Oman to oppose the government of Sultan Qabus who had replaced his father, Sultan Said, as ruler the year before. Armed opposition to the sultan's government continued under this name until 1974, when the front's setbacks caused it to adopt the more modest name Popular Front for the Liberation of Oman. *See also* NATIONAL DEMOCRATIC FRONT FOR THE LIBERATION OF OMAN AND THE ARAB GULF, OMAN, POPULAR FRONT FOR THE LIBERATION OF THE OCCUPIED ARAB GULF, POPULAR FRONT FOR THE LIBERATION OF OMAN, *and* QABUS BIN SAID AL BU SAID.

PORTS. *See* MINA, DOHA, JEBEL ALI, KHOR FAKKAN, MANAMA, MATRAH, MUSCAT, *and* RAS AL-KHAIMAH.

PORTUGUESE. Following the rise of Iberian power in the 15th century, the Portuguese burst into the Indian Ocean at the opening of the 16th, seeking to monopolize trade with the Indies by using the Cape of Good Hope route, which they had just pioneered to outflank the older trade routes linking Europe with the East. The Portuguese commander Alfonso de Albuquerque saw the Strait of Hormuz as a critical strategic prize and set about seizing key positions inside the Gulf on both sides and in Oman. For over a century the Portuguese retained these possessions, driven out finally by growing Dutch and English power and a resurgent Oman by the mid-17th century. *See also* GULF *and* OMAN.

PRESS. *See* NEWS MEDIA.

Q

QABUS BIN SAID AL BU SAID (b. 1940). Sultan Qabus, the current ruler of Oman, was born in Salalah, capital of Oman's southern province, of a Dhofari mother. His childhood was spent there and he was educated in a British public school and at Sandhurst, Britain's military academy. From the time of his return to Salalah in 1964, Qabus was kept under virtual house arrest by his suspicious father, Sultan Said bin Taimur. By 1970, Said had shown himself incapable of coping with the rebellion that had engulfed Dhofar and threatened to spread to the rest of Oman, and the British, who were historically committed to supporting the sultanate, were preparing to end their military presence in the Gulf the following year. To save the situation, Qabus moved to depose his father in July 1970, working with both Omani and British allies. The new sultan proceeded effectively to end the rebellion, which was then led by the Popular Front for the Liberation of Oman and the Arab Gulf. In addition to reorganizing the Sultan's Armed Forces (SAF), he expanded the number of seconded and contract British and other officers as well as noncommissioned officers, and benefited from the commitment of a very considerable number of Iranian men and weapons. Equally important was Qabus's astute proclamation of an amnesty for rebels who surrendered with their arms and the generous application of a very large part of Oman's growing oil revenues to developmental programs for Dhofar, consti-tuting a highly effective "minds and hearts" campaign that was key to stamping out the rebellion by late 1975. This carried over into a general program of rapid, social, infrastructure development for schools, hospitals, and other institutions throughout Oman, helping to generate considerable popularity for Qabus.

Upon his accession the inexperienced young sultan relied heavily on an advisory council largely made up of expatriate Britons. At the council's suggestion Qabus's uncle Tariq bin Taimur, half brother of Sultan Said, was invited to return from a lengthy absence in Europe to serve as prime minister. Philosophical and other differences led to a break between the two. After Tariq's departure from the government

Qabus instituted a more autocratic government than his uncle had favored. A reconciliation was later effected (the sultan was briefly married to Tariq's daughter), but Tariq did not subsequently play more than an advisory role, and his death removed from the scene the one other member of the ruling family with real leadership capabilities. This circumstance, combined with the sultan's apparent disinclination to remarry and produce an heir, makes succession a matter of concern, although Qabus is healthy and still comparatively young. A more immediate problem has been heavy reliance on the close circle of advisers, already noted, some of whom have harmed the sultan's image and diminished his considerable popularity by their greed in exploiting their positions. To the extent that "Omanization" and broadened representative government become realities rather than mere rhetoric, this source of concern will be effectively addressed. Qabus and Oman emerged from the Gulf crisis of 1990-91 largely unscathed, with ties to neighbors, including Iran, in a favorable state as were relations with Oman's important overseas partners, including the United States. The economic benefits generated by enhanced oil revenues seem to assure positive prospects for both ruler and country in the foreseeable future. *See also* AL BU SAID, DHOFAR, NATIONAL DEMOCRATIC FRONT FOR THE LIBERATION OF OMAN AND THE ARAB GULF, OMAN, POPULAR FRONT FOR THE LIBERATION OF THE OCCUPIED ARAB GULF, POPULAR FRONT FOR THE LIBERATION OF OMAN AND THE ARAB GULF, *and* TAIMUR BIN FAISAL AL BU SAID.

QADI. A *qadi* is a judge, appointed by a ruler or government, to apply Islamic law, or *Sharia*. In the conservative Gulf Arab states this position remains an important one.

QAHTAN. The name *Qahtan* came to be applied to the "old" or "South" Arabs by Arab genealogists of the early Islamic era, differentiating them from the "new" Arabs, grouped under the name *Adnan*. The dichotomy reflects less the actual history of tribal society in the Arabian Peninsula than a device to impose a certain definition and order on that society. In parts of Oman and the UAE, the Hinawi-Ghafiri division, which retains a contemporary social and political significance, parallels the Qahtani-Adnani split. *See also* ADNAN, GHAFIRI, *and* HINAWI.

QANAT. *See* FALAJ.

QATAR (*Full name*, DAWLAT QATAR *or* STATE OF QATAR).

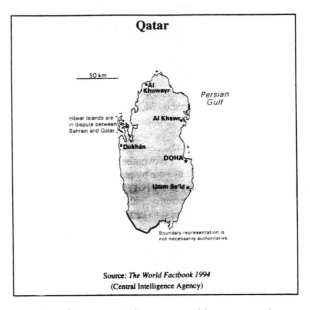

Qatar

Source: *The World Factbook 1994*
(Central Intelligence Agency)

Geography. Qatar occupies a roughly rectangular peninsula extending some 120 mi into the Persian/Arab Gulf about midway along its Arab (western) littoral. It is about 50 mi wide and has an area of 4,247 sq mi (11,003 sq km). Land borders are shared with Saudi Arabia and the UAE. Qatar is separated by about 30 mi of water from Bahrain to the west. Its land surface is largely barren desert with limestone outcroppings and *sabkha*, or "salt flats", on the coasts. The harsh environment of the interior prevented significant settlements there until technology made them possible. It shares the severe summer weather of its neighbors, with temperatures reaching 122°F (50°C) and oppressive humidity in the coastal settlements. Winters, by contrast, are moderate and pleasant, with temperatures averaging 63°F (17°C). Rainfall, occurring in the winter, is scanty and groundwater slight, sustaining only the sparsest natural vegetation and agriculture. Its only significant natural resources are hydrocarbons, but these suffice to generate one of the highest per capita incomes in the world. Oil reserves of 3.2 billion barrels will run out in about two decades, but its natural gas reserves amount to 163 trillion cubic feet, a bit over 4 percent of the world's total, the great bulk of it contained in Qatar's North Field, the world's largest reservoir of nonassociated gas, guaranteeing national wealth for generations to come.

Demography. Qatar's population, only a few thousand early in this century, grew rapidly with the exploitation of its oil revenues after World War II. Today most estimates place the total population of Qataris and expatriates at around 450,000, with natives comprising only about 20 percent of the total. Even before oil wealth brought in various alien groups, the population was mixed. A significant population of Persians migrating across the Gulf had settled in Qatar by the early years of this century as had Hawwala Arabs, descendants of Arabs who had migrated centuries earlier to the Persian side of the Gulf. Another large group is made up of East Africans brought as slaves, the last of them freed by the mid-20th century. Today other Arabs account for about a quarter of the population, Iranians a sixth, and South Asians a third. Over 92 percent of the population is Muslim, the great majority Sunni along with an estimated 16 percent Shia.

History. There is evidence of settlement since prehistoric times and of outposts connected with the third and second millennium B.C. mercantile culture centered on Dilmun in neighboring Bahrain. Qatar is little mentioned in extant records, however, until recent times. In the 1760s the Al Khalifa clan, part of the Utub migration from central Arabia to Kuwait slightly earlier, settled in Qatar with their principal base at Zubarah, a town on the west coast that became a significant center of the pearl trade and other commerce. An attack on Zubarah by Bahrain's rulers, tributaries of Persia, was repulsed, and, in a reversal of fortunes, the Al Khalifa occupied Bahrain and have ruled it since. The Al Thani established themselves as rulers much later than the other Gulf Arab state ruling families, doing so after a long, confused period of contention encompassing the first two-thirds of the 19th century, during which time the Al Khalifa maintained control of at least the western side of the peninsula. In 1867 a joint Al Khalifa-Bani Yas attack on Qatar's east coast led to British diplomatic intervention, which recognized Muhammad bin Thani as representative of the Qatari community and, at least implicitly, independent of Bahrain. His son, Qasim Al Thani (the new name stylization indicating establishment of a ruling house), accepted troops and the title *qaim maqam* ("governor") from the Ottoman Turks in 1871, during their campaign to establish their authority in eastern Arabia, thus gaining insurance against the Al Khalifa. By 1893, determined to be free of Ottoman suzerainty, Qasim precipitated a crisis with the Ottomans and defeated their superior forces, confirming his leadership and Qatar's autonomy, if not de facto independence. Twenty years later Saudi forces under Abdul Aziz Al Saud reconquered the Hasa Province of eastern Arabia from the Ottomans, permanently ending the Turkish threat. (In that same year the Ottoman government renounced its claims to Qatar in the Anglo-Turkish Convention of July 1913, which was never ratified because of the outbreak of World War I.) Qatar's status was further defined by a 1916 agreement between Abdullah bin Qasim Al Thani and Sir Percy Cox, British Political Resident in the Gulf, closely resembling the 1892 treaty arrangements with the Trucial Shaikhdoms. It conferred British protection, prohibited establishment of foreign relations with or cession of any territory to other states without British consent, and provided special rights to Britain and British subjects. These developments effectively ended Al Khalifa claims to Qatar, although the Al Thani did not physically occupy Zubarah until 1937. Indeed, to this day the Al Khalifa remain unreconciled to the loss of their old capital.

Political developments and independence. Qatar, like the other Gulf Arab states, suffered the nearly total loss of its pearling industry in the 1930s as a result of the worldwide depression and the introduction of Japanese cultured pearls. Like them, it was able to recover by granting an oil concession, in this case to Petroleum Concessions Ltd., a subsidiary of the Anglo-Iranian Oil Company (later British Petroleum) in 1935, generating income that enabled the ruler, Abdullah bin Qasim, to strengthen his position against the intrigues of family rivals. At the same time a political agreement was concluded with the British government, granting certain privileges to British subjects and reaffirming and extending British protection of Qatar. Oil was struck as World War II was breaking out, so that production did not begin until 1949. As wealth began to accrue, the general pattern of developments occurring earlier in Kuwait, and subsequently in the UAE, was followed: the position of the ruling family was further consolidated, a social welfare state rapidly evolved, and a large and complex governmental administrative structure soon grew to oversee matters once directly handled in the ruler's *majlis* or by his handful of retainers.

The rapid march to oil-based wealth subsumed the still more rapid move to political independence, following Great Britain's decision in 1968 to withdraw its military forces east of Suez and end its protective relationship with Qatar, Bahrain, and the Trucial States. In February 1968 Qatar proposed that it join Bahrain and the seven Trucial States in a federation of nine and in 1970 drew up a provisional constitution reflecting that proposal. When agreement could not be reached on a union of all nine emirates, and Bahrain gravitated toward a go-it-alone stance once the shah's government had relinquished Iran's claim to that state, Qatar moved toward independence on its own as well, adopting a constitution modified to reflect that fact on September 3, 1971. Among its provisions were confirmation of the position of the Al Thani ruling family with Qatar's head of state always to be drawn from their number but, by contrast with Bahrain, having no preestablished order of succession; establishment of a Council of Ministers to assist the ruler; and creation of a Consultative Council to offer recommendations on policy issues. The last was never elected, but an Advisory Council was established in 1972, its members appointed and selected so as to reflect the merchant community, religious leaders, and other significant constituencies within Qatar. While the ruler's power is not formally limited, he must respond to the concerns of various Al Thani factions as well as the religious establishment, merchants, and others.

Many Qataris, like other Gulf Arabs, saw a need for wider and more effective participation in the political process as a result of the Gulf crisis of 1990-91. In January 1992, 50 leading citizens presented a petition that demanded an assembly with legislative powers. The document also called for economic and educational reforms and claimed that there was an abuse of political power. Later that year, as an indirect response, the Council of Ministers was reorganized. There were signs in 1995, moreover, that Shaikh Hamad, after seizing power in June from his father, Shaikh Khalifa, was committed to evolution toward a more open and liberal government.

The Al Thani are far and away the largest ruling family in the Gulf Arab states, their philoprogenitive propensities by some accounts causing their numbers to reach as many as 20,000. Their size and wealth have firmly established the family's dominant position, and, while the quality of the rulers has varied markedly, the family has been able to ensure that those whose talents are unequal to the position are replaced before excessive damage is done. Quarrels erupt within the family, but its instinct for collective survival and its wealth keep these from doing irreparable harm. Externally, the Al Thani have displayed a pronounced talent for playing threatening outside factors against one another, whether Ottoman Turks and the British in the past or contemporary Gulf powers. Other factors that have assisted Qatar's survival and security are its relative marginality in Gulf affairs and, until recently, its relations with the Al Saud. Qatar developed as a state largely apart from the rivalries and conflicts of the Gulf, indeed, often serving as a place of refuge for losers in those rivalries. From the early 19th century the neighboring Saudi state, in its first and later manifestations, has exercised a powerful influence, reflected in Qatar's allegiance to the same Wahhabi (*Muwahhidun* or "unitarian") doctrine of conservative Islam.

However, traditionally the Saudis have seen the writ of the Al Thanis as confined to the people on the coasts and not the tribes that migrated seasonally from eastern Arabia into the Qatari Peninsula. During Abdul Aziz Al Saud's reassertion of Saudi claims in the 1920s, there was fear that Qatar might be swallowed by its large neighbor. Great Britain's assertion of its role as protector averted that danger and border disputes generated by development of oil concessions were amicably settled. Qatar has generally aligned its external policy closely with Saudi Arabia's, and generally enjoys particularly close relations with Riyadh. A September 1992 border clash troubled those normally close relations. Bilateral talks began in 1993, and in 1996 the issue appeared to be headed toward resolution.

Foreign relations. Relations with other neighbors are somewhat mixed. Those with Bahrain reflect the latter's previous history as overlord of Qatar and its as yet incomplete reconciliation to the loss of its former possessions. Disputes over the ownership of Fasht al-Dibal and the Hawar Islands continue to trouble their relations despite the efforts of GCC allies to mediate. Relations with the UAE vary by emirate. A history of claims by the Al Nuhayyan, rulers of Abu Dhabi, to Qatari territory has continued to chill somewhat relations between the two states. Relations with Dubai have long been close, strengthened by intermarriage between the ruling houses and with other members of the UAE, as well as with Kuwait and Oman. Qatar has been an active member of the GCC, OPEC, and the Arab League. As indicated previously, it closely followed Saudi Arabia's lead in its foreign relations, in the Gulf, the Arab world, and the international arena until the 1992 border clash. Qatar contributed troops to the effort to liberate Kuwait from Iraqi occupation, placing them under Saudi command as did the other Gulf Arab states, and has made available facilities for future access by U.S. and other Western forces in the event of threat. In June, 1992, Qatar signed a security pact with the United States that called for a greater level of cooperation in deploying U.S. air power. An issue of concern for the future is Iran's claim to a portion of Qatar's North Field gas reserves. In 1993 Qatar made diplomatic efforts to deflect that danger by placing its relations with Iran on a friendlier footing.

Economic and social development. Qatar's small population and enormous wealth have made possible rapid economic development and the creation of a full-fledged welfare state. Even the economic downturn of the mid-1980s had little effect on Qatar, whose per capita income remains one of the highest in the world (currently over $20,000). Al Thani rule has been solidified by a wide distribution of wealth. (A central reason for the 1972 removal of Ahmed Al Thani in favor of his cousin, Khalifa bin Hamad, who ruled until 1995, was the former's extreme venality.) Public education for boys and girls began in a serious way in the mid-1950s, with the great majority now completing secondary school and many continuing on to universities, including Qatar's own national university. Modern health facilities are available to the population, and the same array of modern transportation, communications, and other amenities associated with the other wealthy Gulf Arab states is to be found in Qatar. Development is largely centered on Doha, the capital, a modest town based on fishing and pearling before World War II, now a modern metropolis with more than half of the country's population. Qatari society is conservative, reflecting its Wahhabi heritage shared with Saudi Arabia. However, Qatar is somewhat less austere. For example, women are permitted to drive.

Qatar's oil may run out in the next few years, but its vast gas reserves will generate great wealth for another century. It enjoys the great advantage that its gas is unassociated, so that gas production is not affected by the level of oil production, as is generally the case elsewhere in the Gulf. The gas will be exported, used for domestic energy needs and as feedstock for petrochemicals, and utilized by Qatar's cement and steel industry as well as its desalination facilities. Hydrocarbon wealth has created a significant, affluent middle class engaged in construction, banking, and other businesses. The once dominant Darwish family has lost its commercial primacy, but remains important, while the Jaidah and Manai families as well as members of the Al Thani have developed large business interests. The country's great wealth has discouraged serious efforts to displace the foreign workers, the largest single group coming from South Asia, who make up the great bulk of the workforce. A major social issue is how, under these circumstances, to employ the skills of educated young Qataris.

In recent years Qatar has aimed at "self-sufficiency" in agriculture. While this goal is probably out of reach, Qatar has managed to grow more than 70 percent of its summer vegetables and over 40 percent of the winter variety. Dairy and poultry production meet an increasing percentage of local consumption, and fishing remains an important industry (even if scarcely significant in terms of the amount of national income produced). Recently, a modest tourist industry has been developed to further strengthen and diversify the economy.

Altogether, Qatar's prospects seem good. Its enormous hydrocarbon wealth and its $15 billion overseas investments that are secure in the United States, United Kingdom, and Far East assure its economic future. Continued political stability seems reasonably certain despite the overthrow of the ruler, Shaikh Khalifa bin Hamad, by his son, Shaikh Hamad bin Khalifa, on June 26, 1995. Since 1992 Khalifa had left to his son the management of the day-to-day affairs of the country. Hamad moved Qatar to a much more independent external policy in the Gulf and beyond than that which his father favored, and the resulting friction between father and son led to Hamad's formal assumption of the position of ruler. His careful preparation of the move, securing first the support of important Al Thani family members as well as the military and civilian bureaucracy, helped to assure a smooth transition. *See also* DOHA, FASHT, HAWAR ISLANDS, HAMAD BIN KHALIFA AL THANI, KHALIFA BIN HAMAD AL THANI, AL THANI, *and* ZUBARAH.

QAWASIM. The Qawasim (sing., Qasimi) are a tribe to which the ruling families of the emirates of Sharjah and Ras al-Khaimah in the UAE, also bearing the tribal name, belong. By the late 18th century the Qawasim had established a powerful tribal confederation that ruled the lower Gulf coast from Sharjah to the Musandam Peninsula. Allied on land with the burgeoning power of the first Saudi state, their ships, numbering in the hundreds and manned by some 20,000 skilled, tough sailors, dominated the lower Gulf and contested Oman's mercantile supremacy. It was Qasimi attacks on British vessels and British Indian subjects (contemporary British reports, reflecting the pronunciation of the local dialect, referred to "Joasmees") that drew the British deeply into Gulf affairs in the early 19th century. First came a series of naval expeditions against the Qawasim, then the imposition of a series of treaty agreements on them and the other local Gulf Arab powers to preserve maritime peace.

For the first two-thirds of the 19th century, the Qawasim, centered on Sharjah and Ras al-Khaimah, contested with the Bani Yas tribal confederation of Abu Dhabi for primacy in what came to be called the Trucial Coast. In part because the Bani Yas commanded the greater land resources and the Qawasim's Saudi allies suffered Egyptian invasion, the former prevailed. The greatest of the Qawasim chiefs, Sultan bin Saqr, ruled Sharjah and Ras al-Khaimah from 1803 to 1866 and strove to restore their earlier position. After his death, however, a pattern of family intrigue and internal contention severely weakened the Qasimi state and led to Ras al-Khaimah's split from Sharjah, not officially recognized by the British until 1921. Two branches of the Qawasim continue to rule these emirates to the present day, and in Sharjah the tradition of intrafamily contention has continued. The Qawasim remain proud of their former ascendance in the southern Gulf and betray a certain resentment at having to play a secondary role in the UAE behind Abu Dhabi, on whose largesse Ras al-Khaimah has been heavily dependent. *See also* RAS AL-KHAIMAH, SHARJAH, *and* UAE.

QUOINS. The Quoins, whose Arabic name is *Salma wa Banatha* ("Salma and her daughters"), are small uninhabited islands belonging to Oman and are important because of their strategic position in the Strait of Hormuz.

QURAN (KORAN). In Arabic *Al-Quran* means "the recitation," which for Muslims is the word of God (Allah) as revealed to the prophet Muhammad approximately in 610 A.D. Its language, reflecting the refined usage of Mecca at that date, has since provided the basis of classical Arabic. In the conservative Gulf Arab states the Quran has not only been revered as Islam's sacred scripture but also was central to such formal education as was available in the premodern era when memorization of Quranic passages was the essential curriculum of the *kuttabs*, or "traditional schools."

R

RADIO AND TELEVISION. *See* COMMUNICATIONS.

RAINFALL. *See* CLIMATE.

RAPID DEPLOYMENT FORCE (RDF). The term "rapid deployment force" has been applied both to the U.S. strike force created during the administration of President Jimmy Carter to counter an external military threat to the Gulf, particularly that of the Soviet Union following its 1979 invasion of Afghanistan, and to a small GCC force based at Hafr al-Batin in Saudi Arabia, which has carried out military exercises since 1983. The American RDF, headquartered at MacDill Air Force Base in Florida, subsequently became in January, 1983, a unified, multi-service command designated U.S. Central Command (USCENT-COM). *See also* ARMED FORCES.

RAS AL-KHAIMAH.
  Geography and Demography. Ras al-Khaimah is the northernmost of the seven United Arab Emirates, consisting of two separate parcels of territory totaling about 650 sq mi (1,684 sq km). Despite its small area, comprising less than 3 percent of the UAE's total, it exhibits greater topographical diversity than any other part of the country. The Gulf coastal plain continues in a narrowed extension past Ras al-Khaimah town until, at the village of Sha'am, the mountains of the Musandam Peninsula dramatically meet the water. Inland the Jiri Plain receives sufficiently greater rainfall to permit cultivation, including date palms, acacia, and eucalyptus trees as well as vegetable and fruit production. Ras al-Khaimah extends into the Hajar Mountains on Musandam, sharing with Oman the population of the Shihuh, a distinctive, isolated people of mixed Arab-Iranian origin. The whole population of Ras al-Khaimah is less than 100,000, with the town of the same name accounting for most of the total. Because of its comparative lack of wealth, Ras al-Khaimah presents a striking demographic contrast to Abu Dhabi and Dubai; whereas up to 90 percent of the population is expatriate in the latter emirates, almost exactly the reverse is true for Ras al-Khaimah. The emirate has had a long and eventful history which continues to weigh heavily on it,

shaping attitudes and perspectives.

History. From the late third millennium B.C. to the mid-19th century, Ras al-Khaimah enjoyed a position of wealth and power in the lower Gulf. In the early Islamic era dhows sailed from Julfar, just to the north of the present town of Ras al-Khaimah, to destinations as far away as China. A key element in the Portuguese imperium of the 16th and 17th centuries, Julfar was superseded in the 18th century by Ras al-Khaimah, whose name, "top" or "headland of the tent," derives from a local legend about a tent pole light displayed as a signal to sailors. The 18th and early 19th centuries were the heyday of the Qawasim (sing., Qasimi), a Hawwala Arab tribe whose power extended to both sides of the lower Gulf and whose scores of ships, sailing principally from Ras al-Khaimah and manned by thousands of ferocious fighters, ravaged the commerce of the Gulf and the northern Indian Ocean to the vicinity of Bombay. The threat to British India's trade brought a military reaction against what London and Bombay viewed as "piracy," and the imposition in 1820 and thereafter of a series of treaties that established a truce in the Gulf. As a part of the Trucial Coast the Qawasim state's former dominance was eclipsed and its fortunes further reduced when the ruling family of the same name split in the late 19th century. In 1869 Ras al-Khaimah effectively established independence from Sharjah, which had become the principal seat of Qawasim power, although the British government did not accord it formal recognition as an independent emirate until 1921. Development of the oil wealth of Abu Dhabi and Dubai, where branches of the rival Bani Yas tribal confederation ruled was, in effect, a final reversal of fortune, confirming Ras al-Khaimah's secondary economic and political status.

This eclipse of fortunes has not been easily accepted and helps to explain Ras al-Khaimah's often uncooperative attitude toward its British protectors before UAE independence and toward its federal partners subsequently. The transition to independence was a compounded trauma for Ras al-Khaimah. The shah of Iran, having relinquished his claim to Bahrain, felt compelled to assert his claims to the Tunb Islands, long held by Ras al-Khaimah, and seized them on the eve of the withdrawal of British protection against the resistance of Ras al-Khaimah police. Arab applause for Shaikh Saqr bin Muhammad's defiance was not accompanied by any material assistance, Arab or British, and the islands were lost. Moreover, oil explorations led to disappointment. By late 1971 these had been expected to yield a source of wealth that might sustain a separate independence or at least enable Ras al-Khaimah to enter the new federation with a status more nearly equal to that of Abu Dhabi and Dubai. This reinforced Saqr's inclination to remain outside the federation at its birth on December 2, 1971. (So strong was that disposition that he even offered the United States a military base in Ras al-Khaimah in an effort to secure the economic support that would enable him to go it alone.) Failure to strike oil compelled Saqr to join the UAE on February 10, 1972, accepting the political dominance of the wealthy emirates.

Since joining the federation, Ras al-Khaimah has benefited from Abu Dhabi's largesse, which has funded much of its development. It has developed a modest modern economy including production of stone aggregate, cement, and other construction materials alongside the traditional pursuits of fishing and agriculture. The last activity has been impressively expanded, with a major dairy operation and an Agricultural Trials Station at Digdaga. Ras al-Khaimah now produces significant quantities of food for local consumption and for export to its sister emirates and beyond. Finally, in late 1983, oil was struck offshore and modest production began early the next year.

As ruler since 1948, Saqr has exhibited both impressive strength of purpose and political adroitness. Ras al-Khaimah's modest economic wealth and strongly tribal society have kept the emiral government a fairly simple and traditional affair, with most formal government machinery devoted to running the Ras al-Khaimah municipality. The ruler's capable son Khalid, heir apparent and deputy ruler of Ras al-Khaimah, who received his higher education in the United States, may be expected to continue in that mold. His nephew Shaikh Fahim was chosen to be the second secretary-general of the Gulf Cooperation Council in 1993. *See also* JULFAR, QAWASIM, SAQR BIN SULTAN, *and* UNITED ARAB EMIRATES.

RASHID BIN SAID AL MAKTUM (?–1990). Ruler of the emirate of Dubai from 1958 until his death in 1990, and an active and powerful regent from 1939 to 1958, Shaikh Rashid was one of the most astute and impressive rulers in the Gulf. Cunning and ruthless in advancing his ambitions and those of Dubai, which were largely indistinguishable, Rashid was reminiscent of a Renaissance merchant prince. It was Rashid and his bold and strong-willed mother, Shaikha Hussa, who saved his father Said's rule and that of the Bani Hashar line of the Al Maktum against the threat of two rival branches in 1939. Throughout his regency and rule, Rashid's single-minded aim was to expand his emirate's wealth, building on Dubai's position as an important lower Gulf entrepôt. To that end he was a practical reformer who promoted modern education and other innovations calculated to enhance the efficient governance of the emirate. As a young man he welcomed to Dubai merchants from the Iranian side of the Gulf, many of whom have since amassed great fortunes, and later encouraged the profitable sale of gold to Indian purchasers (referred to as "smuggling" but legal until it reached Indian territorial waters). Development of its oil deposits from 1962 raised Dubai's prosperity to new levels, although the advent of oil production in the Trucial States meant that Abu Dhabi's wealth would outstrip that of Dubai.

Rashid was an interesting contrast to Shaikh Zayid, ruler of Abu Dhabi, Dubai's traditional rival. While Rashid's concerns were limited to Dubai and its prosperity, Zayid, endowed with Bedouin magnanimity, was most at home with tribesmen in the desert, and he sought to create a strongly unified UAE and to play an active role on the wider Arab stage. When Great Britain announced in 1968 its intention to withdraw from the Gulf, Rashid joined Zayid in promoting the concept of federation, agreed to serve as the UAE's vice president at its establishment in 1971, and joined Abu Dhabi in opposing early threats to the new union's government. However, he drove a hard bargain with Zayid in gaining for Dubai a near equivalence of authority in the UAE with Abu Dhabi, despite his emirate's far slighter territory, wealth, and military strength. Rashid favored a much looser federation than Zayid and lost few opportunities to criticize the federal government for its inefficiency and waste. He preserved the autonomy of Dubai's military forces and declined OPEC membership, thus disregarding production quotas, while also invariably failing to contribute his share to the UAE's federal budget. Reluctantly, in 1979, he accepted the UAE's premiership to avert possible dissolution of the union, but his opposition to a strong federal government has probably assured the continuation of the weak federal government of his preference. When Rashid was incapacitated by a stroke in August 1981, the heir apparent, Maktum bin Rashid, and his brothers took over the running of the emirate's day-to-day affairs with little observable change. Rashid's principal legacy of a prosperous, well-run, laissez-faire state appears likely to endure. *See also* DUBAI, AL MAKTUM, UNITED ARAB EMIRATES, *and* ZAYID BIN SULTAN AL NUHAYYAN.

RED LINE AGREEMENT. The Red Line Agreement was an accord reached after World War I among the companies that formed the Iraq Petroleum Company (IPC), namely Anglo-Persian Oil Company (APOC) (now British Petroleum, BP), Compagnie Française des Pétroles, Calouste Gulbenkian ("Mr. Five Percent"), Royal Dutch-Shell, and Standard Oil Company of New Jersey (now Exxon), committing them to operate only through IPC within the former territory of the Ottoman Empire. The accord had a significant impact on the pattern of development of oil concessions in the Gulf area until it was rescinded after World War II.

RELIGION. *See* ISLAM.

ROYAL DUTCH-SHELL. The British-Netherlands international oil company, one of the "seven sisters," was a partner in the IPC and a concessionaire in Qatar and Oman. In Qatar its holdings were taken over by the government, but it remains an operating company; in Oman, since 1980, it has held 34 percent of Petroleum Oman and is the country's principal oil producer.

RUB AL-KHALI. The UAE and Oman, together with Yemen, share the *Rub al-Khali* or "Empty Quarter" with Saudi Arabia, to which the lion's share of its 250,000 sq mi (648,000 sq km) belongs. Its vast sandy wastes have been an important barrier to the movement of people, helping Oman to ward off absorption by Saudi Arabia in the past.

RUSSIAN FEDERATION. The dissolution of the Union of Soviet Socialist Republics (USSR), which ceased to exist formally as of January 1, 1992, removed a major international actor from the Gulf region. As the principal successor state, Russia retains a serious interest in the area but lacks the means to challenge the primacy of American influence. Moscow views the Gulf Arab states as significant markets for weapons sales that earn desperately needed foreign exchange. At the same time, its weapons transfers to Iran and Iraq are a major cause of concern to the Gulf Arab states and to the United States. Russia has pursued agreements for major new projects in Iraq, anticipating that country's renewal of oil exports, and has sought preferential treatment in the repayment of the $7 billion that Iraq owes to it. As the intensification of Russian nationalism promotes a more assertive foreign policy, Moscow will doubtless seek to reassert a position of significant influence in the Gulf. See also UNION OF SOVIET SOCIALIST REPUBLICS.

RU'US *or* RAS AL-JIBAL. *See* MUSANDAM PENINSULA.

RUWAIS. Situated on the coast of Abu Dhabi, about 150 mi west of Abu Dhabi City, Ruwais is an industrial town where a complex of petroleum-based operations has been established, starting with a refinery.

S

SAAD AL-ABDALLAH AL-SALEM AL SABAH. Saad al-Abdallah is Kuwait's heir apparent and prime minister. He was minister of defense and interior when the ruler, Jabir al-Ahmed, made the choice in early 1978, a few months after his own accession as emir. The somewhat controversial choice restored the pattern of alternating rule between the two Al Sabah branches, Jabir and Salem, and reflected the ruler's judgment as to who was the most competent candidate available to follow him. *See also* KUWAIT *and* AL SABAH.

SABAH AL-SALEM AL SABAH. Sabah was the emir of Kuwait from 1965 to 1977, his selection breaking the pattern of alternation between the ruling family's two branches. Illness toward the end of his rule caused his heir apparent, Jabir al-Ahmed, to become ruler in fact before his formal accession. *See also* KUWAIT *and* AL SABAH.

AL SABAH. The Al Sabah have been the rulers of the state of Kuwait since its inception. They were part of the Utub, a group of clans claiming membership in the central Arabian Anayzah confederation, which migrated in the early 18th century to the northern Gulf where, in the second decade of the century, a permanent settlement, which came to be called Kuwait, was established. Initially, the Sabah clan exercised loose authority under the Bani Khalid overlords of the area, but by 1756 Kuwaiti independence was established and Sabah bin Jabir was elected as Utbi ruler; his descendants have ruled ever since. His son,

Abdullah, ruled from 1762 to 1812 and consolidated friendly relations with the British, who were to play a crucial role in the country's history. A distinguishing feature of the Al Sabah is the general lack of violence in their history, contrasting with most of the other Gulf Arab ruling families. The significant exception was Mubarak the Great, who assassinated his half brother, Muhammad, in 1896 and ruled from that date until 1915. Mubarak placed the state under British protection to avoid possible absorption in the Ottoman Empire. Only his male descendants are eligible to rule Kuwait; in fact, only those from the Al Jabir and Al Salim branches, descended from two of his sons, have been emirs. In the 20th century the Al Sabah have generally provided capable leadership. This was notably the case with Abdullah al-Salim, emir between 1950 and 1965, who guided the state to independence, social welfarism, and a constitutional system of government. Although he presided over the establishment of a parliament, he also oversaw the process by which vast oil wealth enormously strengthened the position of the thousand-strong Al Sabah. The family's policies have been vigorously challenged in the National Assembly, leading to that body's suspension for lengthy periods of time, but the Al Sabah's right to rule has never been seriously challenged. This remained true during the Iraqi invasion and occupation in 1990-91. However, the country's lack of military preparedness, the flight of virtually all the Al Sabah, the emir's unhurried return from comfortable exile in Saudi Arabia, his postponement of elections for a new assembly until October 1992, and the disinclination of the senior Al Sabah to embrace liberalization of the political system engendered significant criticism of the ruling family. Shaikh Jabir has worked reasonably well with the new, reform-minded assembly in its first four years. *See also* KUWAIT.

SABKHA. A *sabkha* (Arabic pl., *sibakh*) is a salt flat caused by the upwelling and evaporation of underground salt seepages. Such flats are encountered along the UAE's Gulf coast and in the interior of Oman. In dry weather their hard crust provides a surface on which vehicles may be driven, but which is hazardous when softened by rain.

SABKHAT AL-MATTI. The largest of the salt flats along the UAE's coast, the Sabkhat al-Matti is a considerable plain, measuring about 35 mi (56 km) at its widest and some 65 mi (105 km) in length, located in the westernmost portion of Abu Dhabi.

SAID BIN TAIMUR AL BU SAID (1910–1972). Said was sultan of Oman (Muscat and Oman before the country's reunification) from 1932 to 1970. His father, Sultan Taimur, a reluctant ruler, abdicated in favor of Said on his son's twenty-first birthday, by which age he had already begun to exercise authority. Part of his education was in India, which may have contributed to his disposition to rule in an absolutist rather than collegial fashion, the general Gulf Arab style. In the early years of his rule his principal aims were to restore Oman's solvency and reduce the role of the British, who had propped up several weak Al Bu Said rulers in Oman. In these aims he was generally successful initially. Developments in the 1950s and 1960s, however, bringing both opportunities and dangers, finally overwhelmed Said. He had been determined to bring the interior of Oman back under Al Bu Said rule and saw his opportunity when Petroleum Development Oman (PDO), a subsidiary of Royal Dutch-Shell, sent in an armed exploration party. In 1954 he thus drove the imam, Ghalib bin Ali al-Hinai, and his followers from Oman and reunited coast and interior. The Saudi-supported imam returned in 1957 with Saudi and Egyptian help, and it was only with significant British military assistance that the imam's forces were routed in January 1959 and Oman's reunification secured. However, Said's continued parsimony, at a time when oil-fueled development was proceeding rapidly in neighboring states, some of it carried out by Omani expatriate workers, bred resentment in economically stagnant Oman. Said isolated himself in Salalah, capital of the southern Province of Dhofar. It was there that the most serious opposition to his rule arose in the form of the Dhofar Liberation Front, formed in 1965 and reorganized as the Popular Front for the Liberation of the Occupied Arab Gulf in 1968, acquiring an extreme leftist complexion and support from Arab radicals, the USSR, and the PRC. The spread of disorder to northern Oman persuaded Said's 29-year-old son Qabus and key Omani and British advisers to the government that his continuation in power was untenable and Said was forced to abdicate in July 1970. Some revision of the almost wholly negative image of Said has recently been attempted. It is true that some of his eccentricities have been magnified to make him an object of ridicule and that some developmental projects for which Qabus received credit were initiated under Said. Nevertheless, there can be little doubt that by the time of his overthrow, Said had lost touch with contemporary realities and lacked the will or capacity to deal effectively with them.

See also AL BU SAID, DHOFAR, IBADIS, OMAN, POPULAR FRONT FOR THE LIBERATION OF THE OCCUPIED ARAB GULF, QABUS, *and* SALALAH.

SALALAH. Salalah is the capital and largest town in Dhofar Province, the southernmost area of Oman, situated on the coast with a narrow plain as hinterland. From the late 1950s until his deposition in 1970 Sultan Said bin Taimur made Salalah his chief place of residence. Since the accession of Qabus as sultan in that year, Salalah has benefited from the generous investment of development funds. Its port facilities have been improved, both for commercial and military purposes. Site of a former British Royal Air Force base, the U.S. has access to its military facilities with Omani consent in the event of a security threat to the area. *See also* DHOFAR, OMAN, POPULAR FRONT FOR THE LIBERATION OF OMAN, *and* SAID BIN TAIMUR.

SAMBOOK. *Also* SAMBUK. The sambook is one of the traditional types of Gulf sailing vessels referred to as "dhows." It has two masts, a tapered bow, and high, squared stern. Sambooks were widely used in pearling and continue to be used for fishing and commerce, usually with diesel engines added. *See also* BAGGALA, BOOM, DHOW, *and* JALBOOT.

SAQR BIN MUHAMMAD AL QASIMI. Saqr bin Muhammad has been the ruler of Ras al-Khaimah since 1948, when he seized power from his uncle Sultan, who himself had deposed Saqr's father, Muhammad, in 1921. His strong will and political wile have enabled him to survive and ensure the continuity of the Bani Muhammad line of the ruling family and to confirm his U.S.-educated son Khalid as heir apparent. Saqr has always been a bit of a maverick, frequently defying British authority before UAE independence in 1971 and often appearing somewhat obstreperous in dealing with the UAE's other rulers. Saqr refused to yield the Tunb Islands to Iran on the eve of UAE independence, hoping for Arab, particularly Iraqi, support against the shah. His anticipation of an oil strike in late 1971 and his anger at being slated to play second fiddle in the new federation to the rulers of traditional rival states Abu Dhabi and Dubai, Zayid bin Sultan Al Nuhayyan and Rashid bin Said Al Maktum, caused Saqr to delay joining the UAE for some 10 weeks after its launching. His keen awareness of the dominant position of his ancestors in the lower Gulf makes dependence on Abu Dhabi's largesse and his own secondary political role in federation particularly painful. *See also* AL QAWA-SIM *and* RAS AL-KHAIMAH.

SAQR BIN SULTAN AL QASIMI. Saqr bin Sultan (cousin of the ruler of Ras al-Khaimah who bears the same name) was ruler of Sharjah and head of its branch of the Qasimi tribe between 1951 and 1965, until forced out by the British because of his Arab nationalist scheming. In January 1972 trying to capitalize on antipathy toward his nephew and successor, Khalid bin Muhammad, who had reached an accommodation with the shah of Iran compromising Sharjah's sovereignty over Abu Musa Island, he led a coup attempt. Although the ruler was killed, the coup failed and Saqr was arrested by the new federal government of the UAE. This reversion to violence in a ruling family presented a keen dilemma to the leaders of the federation, Shaikh Zayid bin Sultan of Abu Dhabi and Shaikh Rashid bin Said of Dubai. The new federal constitution called for the death penalty in this case, but its imposition against the leader of a rival tribe and emirate could also have excited tribal jealousies and animosities, thereby endangering the new federation. Thus Saqr was confined to house arrest in Abu Dhabi, and the murdered Khalid's younger brother, Sultan bin Muhammad, succeeded him as ruler. *See also* AL QAWSIM *and* SHARJAH.

SAUDI ARABIA, KINGDOM OF. By virtue of its size, wealth, and military strength, Saudi Arabia looms very large in the affairs of all its small Gulf Arab state neighbors. Moreover, memories of past Saudi expansion, driven by reformist Islamic zeal into parts of what are now the UAE and Oman, together with dependent relationships on the part of Bahrain and Qatar and Saudi succor of Kuwait in its recent crisis— all tend to sustain a conviction among the Saudis that they are destined to play a naturally dominant role in the Arabian Peninsula and to create a corresponding sense among the others of a sometimes overbearing posture on the part of Riyadh. At the same time, bilateral relations are all distinctively different and each deserving of a brief description.

Kuwait, Bahrain, and Qatar are all linked to Saudi Arabia through ruling houses that originated in clans claiming membership in the same central Arabian tribal confederation, the Anayzah, as did the Al Saud (although the Al Thani of Qatar emerged as a ruling family a century or more later than the others). Kuwait, by virtue of the Al Sabah's long eminence, wealth, and leadership role in developing a modern, oil-driven economy, has been next to Saudi Arabia in the scope of its regional role. The relations of all three states with Saudi Arabia have, in this century, passed through different stages. After Abdul Aziz Al Saud extended his sway over eastern Arabia in 1913, those states began to feel Saudi encroachment. In 1922 a British-brokered agreement at Uqair gave the Saudi leader two-thirds of the territory claimed by Kuwait, and tension between the two states rose when a dispute caused Abdul Aziz to impose a damaging embargo against Kuwait. In Qatar he worked to undermine the ruler's authority and forced payment of a secret subsidy from that neighbor. Statements made at the time indicate the Saudi ruler's view that the territory of his lesser neighbors was properly part of his realm and that he simply deferred to the practical necessity of honoring Britain's protective agreements with them. However, events modified his perspective. Consolidation of Saudi power, represented by the establishment of the Kingdom of Saudi Arabia in 1932, gave Abdul Aziz greater security. External threats to Kuwait from Iraq and to Bahrain from Iran, as well as internal threats in the form of domestic reform movements, led him to be more solicitous of their welfare and Qatar's as well. Relations between the three states and Saudi Arabia have since been generally friendly, although the Saudis have been concerned about the impact of Kuwait's and Bahrain's experiments in greater political representation and their generally more liberal social climate. Kuwait's neutralist international policy, pursued up to the late 1980s, was at odds with Saudi policy. Increasingly, Saudi Arabia has adopted a protective attitude toward Qatar and Bahrain, drawing them under its security shield, and a very close economic relationship has evolved with Bahrain, symbolized by the causeway that has linked the two countries since 1986. Saudi-Qatari relations were troubled, however, by a border clash in September 1992. In 1993 bilateral talks commenced and by 1996 the issue appeared to be moving toward resolution.

Saudi border disputes with Abu Dhabi and Oman caused troubled relations into the 1970s. In each case the dispute arose from oil exploration and the need for border delineation, but reflected the Al Saud's conviction that their 18th-19th century occupation of territory, centered on the Buraimi/al-Ain Oasis and driven by religious fervor and military power, entitled them to its possession. British support for

Abu Dhabi and Oman, then under Great Britain's protection, thwarted Saudi efforts to assert these claims in the 1950s, and Saudi recognition of the UAE was withheld until 1974, when an agreement on the Abu Dhabi-Saudi border was reached. Although some ambiguities remain (the Abu Dhabi-Saudi border agreement has never been published), these do not seriously trouble their relations.

From the mid-1970s Saudi Arabia's attitude toward the smaller Gulf Arab states has been generally friendly and cooperative. Saudi financial support helped Sultan Qabus to defeat the Dhofari insurgency. Even before the GCC was established, the Saudis were active in promoting various joint ventures and undertook to invest in Bahrain's new aluminum industry rather than proceed to establish their own. Saudi Arabia has played a positive leadership role in the GCC, its relations with Kuwait reflected in establishment of the GCC's secretariat in Riyadh balanced by selection of Dr. Abdullah Bishara, a Kuwaiti diplomat, as the organization's first secretary-general (he resigned in 1993). Saudi Arabia took the lead with the Gulf Arab states to coordinate their military efforts with the U.S. and other allies against Iraq to liberate Kuwait, in Operation Desert Storm in 1991. In 1995, Qatari-Saudi friction resulted when each country advanced its own candidate for the GCC's third secretary-general at the December 1995 GCC summit. Briefly, Qatar's new ruler, Shaikh Hamad bin Khalifah Al Thani, threatened to withdraw his country from the GCC. By summer 1996, however, Qatar was reconciled to the election of the Saudi candidate, Jamil Ibrahim al-Hejailan, and, as already noted, there was progress toward resolution of the Saudi-Qatari border dispute. *See also* entries on each Gulf Arab state, AL-AIN, BURAIMI/BURAIMI OASIS, GULF COOPERATION COUNCIL, *and* WAHHABIS.

SAYYID SAID BIN SULTAN. Said bin Sultan is generally remembered as the greatest of the Al Bu Said rulers of Muscat. Said's rule began in 1806, when he assassinated his cousin Badr, and continued for half a century to 1856. Anxious to reestablish Oman's maritime position in the Gulf, which had been disrupted by the Qawasim "pirates," he joined with British forces to defeat them. Thwarted by the British-imposed truce in his ambition to dominate the Gulf, he turned his attention to East Africa. Said reasserted neglected Al Bu Said rule in Zanzibar and the adjacent coast and, through most of his rule, neglected his domains in Oman. He did add Dhofar to his empire, but on his death it was divided between his two sons. *See also* OMAN *and* AL BU SAID.

SHAIKH. *Also* SHAYKH.The basic meaning of *shaikh* is "elder." It is widely used to refer to the chief of a clan or tribe, connoting authority that comes from demonstrated leadership ability and, especially, mediatory skills. The title of "shaikh" is conferred in principle by democratic means, although in practice the position is generally hereditary. The rulers of the Gulf Arab states, excepting Oman, are customarily referred to as shaikhs (Arabic pl., *shuyukh*). Oman's Al Bu Said rulers earlier styled themselves as *sayyid* or "lord," but more recently adopted *sultan*, an Arabic term whose usage, in this case, was initiated by the British.

SHAIKHDOM. *Also* SHAYKHDOM. The term "shaikhdom," an English-language neologism, refers to the territory ruled by a shaikh.

SHAKHBUT BIN SULTAN AL NUHAYYAN. Shaikh Shakhbut bin Sultan ruled the shaikhdom of Abu Dhabi from 1928 to 1966. His rule began after his father, Sultan bin Zayid, and Sultan's three brothers were assassinated in office in the space of 11 years. Upon Shakhbut's accession, his mother, Shaikha Salama, demanded of him and his three brothers a vow that none would resort to violence against the others. The promise was kept, even though Shakhbut was himself deposed. In a turn of events parallel to that played out four years later in Oman, when Qabus replaced his father, Said, as sultan, Shakhbut proved unable to cope with the challenge of managing new oil wealth, and his younger brother, Zayid, worked with Abu Dhabi's British protectors to engineer his removal. Initially exiled to Beirut, Shakhbut later returned to Abu Dhabi, where he lived for the balance of his life. *See also* ABU DHABI, UNITED ARAB EMIRATES, *and* ZAYID BIN SULTAN AL NUHAYYAN.

SHARIA. *See* ISLAM *and* LAW.

SHARJAH. *Also* SHARIGAH *and* SHARIQAH. The name of the UAE's third largest emirate is most correctly transliterated from written Arabic as *Shariqah*, but *Sharjah* comes closest to the local pronunciation. The city of Sharjah lies just north of Dubai on the Persian/Arab

Gulf coast, where the emirate has about 10 mi of coastline, but three exclaves on the Batinah coast along the Gulf of Oman are also part of Sharjah: Dibba, Khor Fakkan, and Kalba. This territorial fragmentation makes Sharjah the only emirate sharing borders with all the others. It has an area of about 1,000 sq mi (2,590 sq km) and a population of more than 150,000, most of which lives in the city of Sharjah. The city forms a coastal conurbation with the city of Dubai. The emirate shares the extreme summer heat, aridity, and coastal humidity of its neighbors, but some agriculture is possible in the Dhaid Oasis and the territories on the Batinah coast.

Sharjans share with their neighbors in Ras al-Khaimah the legacy of the Qawasim lower Gulf empire of the late 18th to early 19th centuries, taking considerable pride in their past and, like the Ras al-Khaimans, out of sorts with the hand that fate has dealt them. Sharjah has even more to lament than Ras al-Khaimah, beginning with its loss of the latter's territory, made formal through British recognition of Ras al-Khaimah as an independent emirate in 1921. Later, having been the local World War II base of Great Britain's Royal Air Force (RAF) and subsequently of the TOS, its creek became silted, undercutting its commerce, and the British Political Resident decamped for Dubai in 1954, so that Sharjah abruptly lost its centrality and importance in the lower Gulf. With its oil and gas yet to be discovered when the UAE was formed, Sharjah fared poorly in the distribution of federal power. While Dubai achieved near parity with Abu Dhabi in the new union, Sharjah was placed on a par with its much poorer neighbor, Ras al-Khaimah, which had initially declined to join. Moreover, Sharjah had been forced to yield its sovereignty over Abu Musa Island to the shah's Iran, with which it arranged to share administration and oil revenues. Within weeks this had helped to precipitate a coup in which former ruler Saqr bin Sultan sought unsuccessfully to regain power, though his erstwhile successor, Khalid bin Muhammad, was killed in the attempt.

Sharjah has since struggled, with some success, to recoup its fortunes, although the course has not been smooth. The onset of modest oil wealth led to excessive spending on such costly showpieces as luxury hotels and an international airport, 10 mi from that of Dubai, and contributed to a prolonged downturn in the early and mid-1980s. This helped lead in 1987 to an attempted coup against Sultan bin Muhammad, who had succeeded his brother Khalid in 1972. An older brother, Abdul Aziz bin Muhammad, bypassed in the earlier succession, justified his attempted takeover by citing Sultan's failed economic policies. A compromise left Sultan as ruler but made Abdul Aziz heir apparent and increased his role in the emirate's daily affairs. In February 1990 this agreement was undone when Sultan dismissed his brother as deputy ruler and revoked his right of succession. The ruler is, in fact, more a scholar than a politician. He holds an engineering degree from the College of Agriculture of the University of Cairo and, after becoming ruler, earned a Ph.D. from the University of Exeter. His doctoral dissertation, later published as a book, was an attempt to refute the claim that his Qasimi ancestors were pirates. His intellectual bent is reflected in Sharjah's leadership in developing modern education and in its unrivaled primacy in the arts in the UAE. Sharjah's press is the most unfettered in the Gulf, with *Al-Khaleej* (The Gulf) the most respected newspaper in the region. *See also* KHALID BIN MUHAM-MAD AL QASIMI, SAQR BIN SULTAN, SULTAN BIN MUHAM-MAD, *and* SULTAN BIN SAQR.

AL SHARQI. The Al Sharqi are the ruling family of Fujairah, the most recently established and the poorest of the seven United Arab Emirates. Together with most of the inhabitants of the emirate they belong to the tribe of the same name. The Al Sharqi have a long history of enmity with the Al Qawasim rulers of both Ras al-Khaimah and Sharjah from whom they seized and established effective control over territory on the east side of the Musandam Peninsula by the 1930s. Great Britain, however, did not recognize Fujairah as an independent member of the Trucial States until 1952. *See also* FUJAIRAH.

SHELL. *See* ROYAL DUTCH-SHELL.

SHI'AS/SHI'ISM. *See* ISLAM.

SHIHUH. The Shihuh are a tribal group who inhabit the rugged, mountainous tip of the Musandam Peninsula, subsisting traditionally on limited agricultural production and goat herding. Their extreme isolation led to fanciful speculation as to their origins until recent anthropological research conclusively indicated that the several tribes are for the most part of Arab origin, although one speaks a Farsi dialect. Most live in Omani territory, with some in Ras al-Khaimah, and in recent years increasing numbers have migrated to parts of the UAE in search of jobs.

SHIMAL. *Also* SHAMAL. The Arabic word for "north" is used to describe the strong wind that blows down the Gulf in the early summer, sometimes reaching sufficient force to be a maritime hazard, especially for smaller craft.

SHURA. *Shura*, "consultation," is practiced in Gulf Arab societies as a time-honored tribal principle and a Quranic injunction. It governs, at least in theory, the exercise of political authority in the Gulf Arab states and is embodied in the several *majalis* (sing., *majlis*) *al-shura*, "consultative councils," established or projected in the Gulf Arab states.

SIB, TREATY OF. The Treaty of Sib, an exchange of letters in September 1920 under the aegis of the British Political Resident at Muscat, gave formal effect to the division of Oman between the imamate, ruling the tribes of the interior, and the sultanate, ruling the coastal region from Muscat. The treaty ended civil war and initiated a *modus vivendi* of some 34 years between imamate and sultanate.

SITRA. The island of Sitra is part of the Bahrain archipelago, attached to Bahrain by a causeway, and the site of the country's oil export terminal and oil refinery.

SOHAR. *Also* SUHAR. Sohar is a major port town located on Oman's northern, Batinah, coast. It achieved prominence in the tenth century A.D. when instability in the Persian/Arab Gulf made it a favored home port for ships trading with both India and Africa. It was an important Portuguese port during their 16th-17th-century occupation of the coast and for the Persians during their mid-18th century occupation. It is the site of a copper deposit that today provides ore for a smelting and pelletizing complex.

SOUTH YEMEN. *See* PEOPLE'S DEMOCRATIC REPUBLIC OF YEMEN.

SPORTS. Traditionally, sports have been limited to falconry and camel racing, with team sports competition an alien concept. In recent years this has begun to change. Soccer has achieved great popularity, with Gulf Arab teams having gained considerable respect in international competitions. Other Western sports, including auto racing, are also gaining popularity.

STANDARD OIL OF CALIFORNIA (SoCal). Through a Canadian-registered subsidiary, the Bahrain Petroleum Company (BAPCO), SoCal made the first oil strike on the Arab side of the Gulf in 1932. This led to its subsequent discovery and development of Saudi Arabia's massive oil reserves through the concession that became the Arabian American Oil Company (Aramco). SoCal's name was later changed to Chevron. It has since absorbed the Gulf Oil Corporation. *See also* OIL.

SULTAN. The Arabic meaning of the word *sultan* is "power," "dominion," or "mandate" and thus by extension a "ruler." Little used in the Arab world as a title, it was applied by the British to the Al Bu Said rulers of Oman in the 19th century and continues to be used by them.

SULTAN BIN MUHAMMAD AL QASIMI. The present ruler of Sharjah, one of the seven United Arab Emirates, Sultan (here used as a name, not a title) acceded to the throne in January 1972, replacing his assassinated older brother Khalid. The latter had been killed in the attempt of a cousin, Saqr bin Sultan, a former ruler earlier deposed by the British, to regain his position. Sultan has the distinction of being the one university graduate among the seven UAE rulers. Indeed, he earned a Ph.D. degree in Middle East Studies from Exeter University, an accomplishment of some note in the emirate, where intellectual and artistic achievements have been held in high esteem. However, his leadership, especially in economic matters, has been widely criticized. Following large expenditures on projects of dubious merit and the painful pinch that came afterward, an older brother of the ruler, Abdul Aziz, attempted to depose Sultan. The Supreme Council of the UAE rulers supported Sultan, but a compromise arrangement made Abdul Aziz heir apparent and gave him an increased say in Sharjah's governance. This arrangement was, however, undone in February 1990, when Sultan removed Abdul Aziz from his posts as deputy ruler and heir apparent, thus revoking his right to succession. *See also* KHALID BIN MUHAMMAD AL QASIMI, SAQR BIN SULTAN, *and* SHARJAH.

SULTAN BIN SAQR AL QASIMI. Remembered as preeminent among the Al Qawasim rulers, Sultan (his name, not a title) ruled over the Qawasim dominions of Sharjah and Ras al-Khaimah as well as Qishm on the Persian side of the Gulf, from 1803 to 1866. He was the principal rival of the Bani Yas rulers in Abu Dhabi but supported the trucial system imposed by the British. Following his death, at an age variously estimated from the late 80s to the advanced 90s, the large Qawasim state soon split, with branches of the Al Qasimi clan ruling in Sharjah and Ras al-Khaimah. *See also* QAWASIM, RAS AL-KHAIMAH, *and* SHARJAH.

SUQ. *Suq* is Arabic for "market" or "bazaar." In the Gulf Arab states the suqs are both open and covered, with the goods offered for sale ranging from camels to computers, and from carpets to CD players.

SUQ AL-MANAKH. The *Suq al-Manakh* was an unofficial and unregulated stock market (named for the building in which it was housed), established in 1976 in Kuwait. Unrestrained speculation made effortless fortunes for many, but when the frenzy ended in August, 1982, as nearly 29,000 postdated checks having a face value of over $90 billion began to be called in, it collapsed. The repercussions were widespread and profound, with financial losses suffered by individuals and institutions in Kuwait and elsewhere in the Gulf. In Kuwait the collapse of the market provoked a sharp political debate over how to deal with the crisis. Those wishing to apply strict financial procedures were overruled by the ruler, Shaikh Jabir, and other members of the Al Sabah who imposed an essentially political solution, still incomplete in 1996, with a bailout of investors (including members of the ruling family) at over $9 billion. The collapse of the Suq al-Manakh dealt a severe economic blow to Kuwait, compounding the effects of the downturn in oil prices. The political attacks on the Al Sabah in the National Assembly, which the crisis engendered, helped lead to the assembly's dissolution in 1986. *See also* KUWAIT.

SUR. Sur is a port located on the coast of Oman just above Ras al-Hadd, at the boundary between the Gulf of Oman to the north and the Arabian Sea to the south. Evidence suggests that it was an important link in commercial networks with other parts of the Middle East as early as 1500 B.C. In more recent times it has been one of the important

Omani ports connecting the country with India and East Africa. Today
it has little commercial significance, but it continues to serve as a
fishing port. A modest industrial project was recently launched in the
Sur area.

SUROOR BIN MUHAMMAD AL NUHAYYAN. Shaikh Suroor is a
key adviser to Shaikh Zayid bin Sultan, ruler of Abu Dhabi and
president of the UAE. His position acknowledges his abilities and
Zayid's sensitivity to the need to share power with members of the Al
Khalifa branch of the Al Nuhayyan, potential rivals to his own Al
Sultan branch.

AL-SUWAIDI, AHMED KHALIFA. A member of one of the leading
families of Abu Dhabi, Ahmed Khalifa al-Suwaidi served as the UAE's
first (and only) foreign minister from its birth in 1971 to his resignation
in 1979. He was the only commoner to have served in that capacity in
any of the Gulf Arab states.

SYRIA (Official name, SYRIAN ARAB REPUBLIC). Relations
between the Gulf Arab states and Syria have been somewhat ambivalent since the former achieved independence. The wealthy Gulf states
have been major donors of financial aid to Syria, both in recognition of
its role as a "confrontation state" and as a form of protection money to
a "radical" Arab state whose position on many Arab issues has been at
odds with that of the conservative Gulf Arab states. Syria's support of
Iran in the Iran-Iraq war and the downturn in oil revenues caused
Kuwait in 1987 and the UAE, perhaps a bit earlier, to cut off financial
aid to Syria. In the longer run, Syria's hostility to Iraq provided a welcome counterweight for the Gulf Arab states to their menacing neighbor at the head of the Gulf. The Gulf crisis of 1990-91 offered Syria an
opportunity to move closer to the West, to the moderate Arabs generally, and to their former Gulf benefactors just when the economic-
political crisis and collapse of the Soviet Union deprived them of their
primary source of military, political, and economic support.

T

TAIMUR BIN FAISAL AL BU SAID (1886-1965). Taimur was sultan of Oman from 1913 to 1931. In 1920 an exchange of letters, often referred to as the "Treaty of Sib," produced an accommodation between the sultanate, controlling the coast from Muscat, and the tribes of the interior under the Ibadi imamate, which had been revived in 1913. Taimur ruled reluctantly, abdicating as soon as the British permitted him to do so in favor of his son Said. *See also* AL BU SAID, OMAN, *and* SAID BIN TAIMUR AL BU SAID.

AL-TAJIR, MAHDI. Al-Tajir, a Bahraini by origin, was the best known and most powerful of the expatriate advisers to Shaikh Rashid bin Said, ruler of Dubai from 1958 to 1990. Al-Tajir served until the mid-1980s as the UAE ambassador in London.

TAMIMAH. In Oman the term *tamimah* refers to the leader of a large and politically important tribe.

TANKER WAR. *See* IRAN-IRAQ WAR.

AL THANI. Although the Al Thani rulers of Qatar claim the same central Arabian origins as do the ruling families of the states of Bahrain and Kuwait, their rule and Qatar's independence came late, going back a century in the de facto sense and only 75 years de jure. Although they are the most recently established, the Al Thani are far and away the largest ruling family in the Gulf Arab states, numbering now by some accounts as many as 20,000. Their size and wealth have firmly established the family's dominant position and, while the quality of the rulers has varied markedly, the family has been able to assure that those whose talents are unequal to the position are replaced before excessive damage is done. Quarrels erupt within the family, but its instinct for collective survival and its wealth keep these contentions from doing irreparable harm. They maintain close control over Qatari affairs by keeping most important government posts in their own hands. Externally, the Al Thani have displayed a pronounced talent for playing threatening outside factors against one another, whether

Ottoman Turks and the British in the past or contemporary Gulf powers.

The Al Thani achieved dominance over a practically independent state in 1868 when the Al Khalifa of Bahrain, then Qatar's rulers, launched a naval attack against dissident Qataris, thereby violating their treaty obligations to the British. The British Political Resident in the Gulf, Lieutenant. Colonel Lewis Pelly, imposed a settlement that implicitly recognized the independence of Qatar and the Al Thani from Bahrain. The first Al Thani ruler, Muhammad bin Thani, was succeeded in 1876 by his son, Qasim, who accepted Ottoman sovereignty, thereby acquiring protection against a reassertion of Bahrain's claim together with the formal position of *qaim maqam*, or "governor," of Qatar. Following the Saudi defeat of the Ottomans in 1913, Qasim established close relations with Abdul Aziz Al Saud. In 1916 an agreement with the British Government of India established essentially the same treaty relations with Great Britain as those of Kuwait, Bahrain, and the Trucial States. A 1935 treaty, signed when Qatar granted an oil concession to the Anglo-Persian Oil Company (subsequently the Anglo-Iranian Oil Company and, later still, British Petroleum), further defined the relationship.

Perhaps in part because of its size, the Al Thani family is less united than most other ruling Gulf Arab state families. It does not observe the rule of primogeniture in succession, and three contending branches, the Bani Hamad, Bani Ali, and Bani Khalid, have sustained family feuds in the 20th century. The Al Thani have, however, managed to cope successfully with intrafamily crises, as in 1972 when Khalifa bin Hamad deposed Ahmed bin Ali, whose avarice and lack of sustained commitment to the challenges of leadership had persuaded leading members of the family that his rule could not be permitted to continue. On June 26, 1995 he was himself deposed by his son, Hamad bin Khalifa, to whom he had entrusted the day-to-day management of the country's affairs three years earlier. Hamad chartered a more independent foreign policy course than his father favored, and increasing friction between them led to Hamad's assumption of formal power. He had secured in advance the support of key Al Thani figures. Thus the change of rulers occurred without violence as had been the case with such transitions previously in Qatar. *See also* HAMAD BIN KHALIFA AL THANI, KHALIFA BIN HAMAD AL THANI, *and* QATAR.

THESIGER, WILFRED (b. 1910). Thesiger is generally regarded as the last of the great British travel writers in Arabia. His book *Arabian Sands* describes two crossings of the Empty Quarter (Arabic, *al-Rub al-Khali*), the second of which took him to the oases at Liwa in Abu Dhabi in 1948, the first time that a European had visited there.

THOMAS, BERTRAM (1892-1950). Thomas served as *wazir* ("adviser") to Sultan Said bin Taimur of Oman and was the first European to cross the Empty Quarter, a feat described in his book *Arabia Felix*.

TREATY OF MARITIME PEACE IN PERPETUITY. *Also* PERPETUAL TREATY OF PEACE. The 1853 Treaty of Maritime Peace in Perpetuity between Britain and the tribal rulers of what at that time were called the Trucial States (or the Trucial Coast or Trucial Oman) and that now comprise the UAE, confirmed and extended the earlier treaties of 1820 and 1835, which aimed at ending attacks on maritime commerce in the Gulf. Britain assumed in the 1853 agreement the obligation of overseeing and enforcing maritime peace and protecting the shaikhdoms from external attack. *See also* PIRACY, TRUCIAL STATES, *and* UNITED KINGDOM.

TRIBES. Traditionally, in the Gulf Arab states tribes were the basic units of society. The tribe is a grouping of families and clans based on patrilineal ties and claiming descent from a common ancestor by whose name, preceded by *bani*, "sons," or *Al*, "house or family," the tribe is identified. The position of leader tends to be hereditary, but lineage must be matched by appropriate leadership qualities for a candidate to become chief of a tribe. Tribes have always existed in both sedentary and nomadic form and, while few are still truly nomadic, tribal identity continues to be socially and politically of great importance, especially in the UAE and Oman. In those two countries, moreover, the ancient division of northern and southern Arabs (Adnanis and Qahtanis, respectively) is still an important source of identity and has been the origin or defining line of division in many disputes up to very recent times in those states. *See also* ADNAN, AHL, A'ILAH, AL, *and* QAHTAN.

TRUCIAL OMAN LEVIES (TOL). The Trucial Oman Levies, created in 1951, were a small, British-officered force drawn largely from the

Trucial States to keep order in the seven shaikhdoms. It marked a significant increase in the level of British involvement in Trucial States affairs. The TOL were called into action in 1952 when Sultan Said bin Taimur of Oman sent them to Buraimi to expel the Saudi force that had occupied that disputed area.

TRUCIAL OMAN SCOUTS (TOS). In the mid-1950s the Trucial Oman Levies were expanded to a force of about 1,000, with most of the recruits coming from Oman, especially Dhofar, and their name was changed to Trucial Oman Scouts. In 1957-59 the scouts helped Sultan Said of Oman to defeat the forces of the Ibadi imam in the interior of Oman, but otherwise their role was confined to the seven Trucial States, maintaining order and performing various civilian tasks.

TRUCIAL STATES. The name "Trucial States" referred (although never in local usage) to the shaikhdoms of the lower Gulf on which a series of treaties with Great Britain, beginning in 1820, imposed a truce that stopped almost constant maritime warfare and allowed commerce and the pearling industry to develop without disruption. In 1971 the Trucial States achieved independence as the United Arab Emirates. *See* ABU DHABI, AJMAN, DUBAI, FUJAIRAH, RAS AL-KHAIMAH, SHARJAH, UMM AL-QAIWAIN, *and* UNITED ARAB EMIRATES.

TRUCIAL STATES COUNCIL. Established in 1952, the Trucial States Council brought together the rulers of the seven states. Although it had only consultative powers, the council was the first forum in which the rulers could meet to discuss issues of common concern. As such, it helped to promote a sense of unity that preceded establishment of the UAE.

TUNBS. The Tunbs are two small but strategically important islands just inside the Strait of Hormuz in the lower Persian/Arab Gulf. Although they had been ruled by the Qawasim of Ras al-Khaimah for about a century, the shah of Iran seized them on the eve of the Trucial States' independence from Britain in 1971, when Shaikh Saqr, ruler of Ras al-Khaimah, refused to make a deal with Iran and resisted the landing of Iranian troops on the islands. They have since remained in Iranian hands. *See also* IRAN, RAS AL-KHAIMAH, *and* UNITED ARAB EMIRATES.

TUNISIA, REPUBLIC OF. There are few important direct ties between Tunisia and the Gulf Arab states, although generally their positions in Arab League councils have been close. Because of strong pro-Iraqi demonstrations in Tunisia, the government did not send a representative to the Arab League summit meeting on August 8, 1990, at which 12 Arab states voted to send troops to Saudi Arabia to defend that country following Iraq's invasion of Kuwait.

TURKEY, REPUBLIC OF. The Ottoman Empire of Turkey was involved in Gulf affairs through its control of the Province of Basra at the head of the Gulf. It exercised authority periodically over Kuwait before its 1899 treaty with Great Britain, and briefly exercised sovereignty over Qatar in the late 19th century. Until very recently, the Turkish Republic had very slight interest in and relations with the Gulf Arab states. This began to change in the 1980s as Turkey moved to strengthen economic and other links with the Gulf Arab states. Turkey firmly supported the alliance against Iraq following the invasion of Kuwait. It has permitted U.S., British, and French flights from its territory to patrol the no-fly zone in northern Iraq, created in 1991 after the Gulf War to protect Iraqi Kurds from Saddam Hussein as part of Operation Provide Comfort. Turkey has, however, grown increasingly concerned over the continuing loss of transit revenues as a result of the closure of the oil pipeline from Iraq and it is worried about the possible impact of developments in Iraq's Kurdish terriories on its own Kurdish population, part of which is rebelling against the Turkish government.

U

UDAID. *See* KHOR AL-UDAID.

ULEMA. *Ulema* (Arabic sing., *alim*) means, literally, those who are "learned" or "scholars" and refers to men in Islamic society who are recognized as authorities in the religious sciences, and hence deemed competent to render judgments in religious matters including the law or *Sharia*. From this group are drawn judges or *qadis* and members of faculties of religion at universities. While generally the ulema do not play as large a role in the Gulf Arab states as in neighboring Saudi

Arabia, in conservative states such as Qatar and Abu Dhabi the rulers regard the ulema as a major pillar of their support and are especially solicitous of their relations with them.

UMM AL-NAR. Umm al-Nar ("mother of fire") is a small island adjacent to the city of Abu Dhabi and the site of an oil refinery. In the 1950s and 1960s archaeological excavations revealed that a settlement had existed there as early as 2700 B.C. Its inhabitants were agriculturalists who had domesticated the camel and traded with their contemporaries in Oman and the Indus Valley.

UMM AL-QAIWAIN. *Also* UMM AL-QAYWAYN *and* UMM AL-GAIWAIN. Umm al-Qaiwain (which spelled with a "g" more closely approximates the local pronunciation) has the second smallest land area of the seven emirates in the UAE, with 300 sq mi (777 sq km), and the smallest population, about 20,000. Most of the population is in the town of Umm al-Qaiwain, built on a sand spit for its defensive advantage. It alone shares Abu Dhabi's advantage of having entirely contiguous territory, simplifying its administration. Exploration for oil and gas has proven largely frustrating and Umm al-Qaiwain is, with Ajman and Fujairah, one of the poorest emirates, heavily dependent on Abu Dhabi's financial largesse for economic development, although it has modest natural gas production. Because of its poverty its population is overwhelmingly indigenous, including very few expatriates, and significant numbers are still engaged in traditional pursuits such as fishing and shipbuilding. The ruling family is the Mu'alla, the dominant family of the Al Ali, the leading tribe of the emirate. Umm al-Qaiwain's society and government remain much more tribal and conservative than those of most of the other Gulf Arab states. The current emir, Shaikh Rashid bin Ahmad, has ruled since 1981 when he succeeded his father, Shaikh Ahmad bin Rashid, who had ruled over half a century, from 1929 to 1981.

UMM SAID. Located on Qatar's east coast about 20 mi south of Doha, Umm Said is a recently established city where the bulk of Qatar's industry is now concentrated; and it is the second port in Qatar after Doha.

UNIFIED ECONOMIC AGREEMENT (EA). The Unified Economic Agreement, or EA, was adopted by the six GCC states six months after the GCC's establishment in 1981. It gave greater specificity to the GCC charter's call for economic integration by setting explicit goals in such areas as coordination of development, technical cooperation, and trade. Although movement toward the EA's goals has been slower than hoped, some progress has been made and the goals remain unchanged.

UNION OF SOVIET SOCIALIST REPUBLICS (USSR). Up to its dissolution in December 1991, the USSR had very limited relations with the Gulf Arab states, partially excepting Kuwait. Its impact on them was mainly indirect, unfriendly, and threatening. The Ribbentrop-Molotov Pact on the eve of World War II had supported the Soviet ambition for a Gulf outlet, and through the 1979 Soviet invasion of Afghanistan, many observers continued to ascribe such a goal to Soviet strategy in the Middle East. However, over the last two decades at least, it appears more probable that neutralization of the Gulf was intended.

Soviet support of allies and surrogates in the region constituted the greatest danger for the Gulf Arab states, especially for Oman, where the Soviets supported the Dhofari Rebellion in the late 1960s and the 1970s, with weapons and by other means through their surrogate Marxist South Yemen, which was the principal external source of aid and encouragement to the rebellion. In the late 1970s, although the Dhofar uprising had been suppressed, Soviet involvement in Afghanistan and the Horn of Africa caused intense Gulf Arab concern, again especially in Oman. Moreover, from 1971 Soviet naval units made conspicuous calls at Iraq's naval base of Umm Qasr. Moscow's support of Iraq and the Arab leftist regimes, which were generally hostile to the Gulf Arab states and frequently engaged in covert actions aimed at destabilizing their governments, caused the USSR to remain suspect and feared, at least until significant shifts in its policy appeared in the 1980s. A partial exception was Kuwait, which until 1985 was the only Gulf Arab state to have diplomatic relations with Moscow. Kuwait purchased weapons from the Soviets (although its primary sources of arms remained the United States and other Western states) and sought to promote superpower neutrality in the Gulf. Kuwait was the only Gulf Arab state to support Brezhnev's December 1980 proposal calling for the banning of all outside military forces and bases from the Gulf.

In the early and mid-1980s, especially after Gorbachev's assumption of Soviet leadership in 1985, there was a significant moderation in Soviet Gulf policy and corresponding lessening of Gulf fears. The

Soviets withdrew what support they had given to leftist, antiregime figures in some of the Gulf Arab states; from 1980 they shared with the Gulf Arabs the policy of supporting Iraq against Iran in the Iran-Iraq war (as well as the desire to see a negotiated settlement), and generally they looked to widened commercial and improved diplomatic relations with the Gulf Arab states. By 1985 both Oman and the UAE had established relations with Moscow, and by 1988 Qatar had done so as well, rather surprisingly not waiting for the lead of Saudi Arabia. The Saudis restored diplomatic relations with the USSR in 1990, while Bahrain established them for the first time only months before the USSR's dissolution. In the aftermath of Iraq's August 1990 invasion of Kuwait, the USSR supported the anti-Iraq coalition, though it attempted to promote mediation efforts rejected by Washington and did not contribute military assistance to the coalition. In part, Moscow's position in the Gulf crisis may be seen as the climax of its evolution away from supporting radical leftist Arab states to supporting moderate Arab regimes that could offer benefits to a Soviet Union undergoing profound political and economic change. This greatly altered policy produced dividends in November 1990 in the form of pledges from the smaller Gulf Arab states and Saudi Arabia for up to $4 billion in financial assistance to Moscow. With the Soviet Union's dissolution in December 1991, the Gulf Arab states faced, along with the United States and other countries, the daunting challenge of constructing relations with the USSR successor states. The fact that much of the population of these states is Muslim and being courted ardently by Iran helps to compel interest on the part of the Gulf Arabs. *See also* RUSSIAN FEDERATION.

UNITED ARAB EMIRATES (UAE). (*Officially* AL-IMARAT AL-ARABIYYA AL-MUTTAHIDA). The UAE is a federal union of seven emirates, each a traditional, patriarchal state under hereditary rule. It was created in December 1971, when the seven shaikhdoms became fully independent with the withdrawal of British protection, and is, along with the Republic of Yemen, one of the two newest states in the Middle East. The UAE and the unified Yemeni state are the only examples of successfully uniting Arab states. With the exploitation of its vast oil wealth, the UAE had, by the late 1970s, the world's highest per capita income, lifting its population dramatically from the poverty that had prevailed before the discovery of oil.

Geography and demography. The UAE has an area of slightly over 32,000 sq mi (82,900 sq km), about the size of the state of Maine. Abu Dhabi has over 87 percent of the total with 28,000 sq mi (72,540 sq km), Dubai and Sharjah follow with 1,500/3,885 and 1,000/2,590, respectively, while the remaining emirates divide the final 5 percent of the territory. The UAE is the only Gulf Arab state to have a coastline on the Gulf of Oman as well as on the Persian/Arab Gulf, with some 60 mi (97 km) on the former and 430 mi (692 km) on the latter, comprising more than 40 percent of the total on the Arab side of the Gulf. Thus it forms a land bridge just south of the strategic Strait of Hormuz. To the south and west it shares a border with Saudi Arabia and to the east, with Oman. Most of the UAE is desert, but it has four distinct areas: the coast and the flat coastal plain, the interior desert into which that plain merges, an elevated plateau, and the rugged Hajar Mountains, which it shares with Oman. On parts of the plateau, especially in the emirate of Ras al-Khaimah, vegetation is sustained by rainfall or the runoff from the mountains, carried by the ancient, underground irrigation channels called *aflaj*. It shares the extreme summer climate of its neighbors with daytime coastal temperatures up to 115°F (46°C) and occasionally even higher, combined with high humidity. Still more extreme temperatures occur in the dry interior. Between October and March pleasant, temperate weather prevails. Scanty rainfall varies from an annual average of less than two inches in Abu Dhabi to over five in Ras al-Khaimah's interior, where most of the UAE's agricultural production occurs.

The population has grown from about 180,000 in 1968 to over two million today. Some three-quarters of the total is found in Abu Dhabi, Dubai, and Sharjah, with the cities of Abu Dhabi and Dubai having in excess of half a million and a quarter million, respectively. This represents one of the most astonishing population explosions anywhere: as late as the mid-1960s Dubai City had no more than 20,000 people, and Abu Dhabi was then little more than a village. Most of this phenomenal growth represents the immigration of foreigners drawn to jobs created by sudden oil wealth. Over 80 percent of the UAE's population is expatriate. Some 50 percent or more are South Asians, the majority of those Indians, about 20 percent are other Arabs, and perhaps as many as 10 percent are East Asians, increasingly looked to as a politically safe source of labor. Emirians of Iranian origin are just under 2 percent of the total and range from taxi drivers to leading merchant families.

About 90 percent of the population is Muslim (including 100 percent of the indigenous population), of which 85 percent is Sunni.

Creation of the union. The United Kingdom's decision, under a Labour government in 1968, to end its security commitments east of Suez by the end of 1971 meant that its protection agreements with the states of the lower Gulf, based on a series of treaties that dated back to 1820, would be terminated. The states affected were the seven Trucial States (or Shaikhdoms): Abu Dhabi, Ajman, Dubai, Fujairah, Ras al-Khaimah, Sharjah, and Umm al-Qaiwain, and Bahrain and Qatar, all of

United Arab Emirates

125 km

Ra's al Khaymah
Umm al Qaywayn
Persian Gulf   Ash Shāriqah
Dubayy   Ajmān
                 Al Fujayrah

ABU DHABI

Ar Ruways

Boundary representation is
not necessarily authoritative.

Source: *The World Factbook 1994*
(Central Intelligence Agency)

which had treaty agreements that provided for U.K. protection against external threats in exchange for allowing London to conduct their foreign relations and pledging themselves not to cede territory to or enter into agreements with other powers except with British assent. These arrangements, which generally left domestic affairs in the lower Gulf states unaffected, suited the local rulers well; the announcement that the British would leave came as an unwelcome surprise. The surprise Conservative victory in June 1970 led to expectations of a policy reversal, given the Conservatives' earlier condemnation of the Labour policy. After a period of vacillation, during which Sir William Luce, former British Political Resident in the Gulf, undertook several missions to consult with Gulf rulers, the Conservatives reaffirmed withdrawal. Kuwait and Saudi Arabia urged a union of all nine Gulf shaikhdoms to create the largest and most viable state possible. Bahrain would have been the dominant element in such a union by virtue of its more advanced economic development and political sophistication and, at that time, larger population. Qatar's traditional hostility vis-à-vis Bahrain (and toward Abu Dhabi as well) and the other states' general unwillingness to be subservient to Bahrain militated against a union of nine. Moreover, until a UN settlement of the issue in 1970, the shah's claim to Bahrain as part of Iran made the other shaikhdoms still less disposed to contemplate a union with Bahrain. Thus in August and September 1971, respectively, Bahrain and Qatar became separate, independent states. The Trucial States became the UAE on December 2, the day after British withdrawal but without Ras al-Khaimah. The latter, smarting from its loss of the Tunbs Islands to Iranian seizure on November 30 and hoping for an oil strike that would enable it to bid for more political weight in the new union, remained outside. With hydrocarbon hopes dashed (at least for the moment) and no viable go-it-alone prospects, Ras al-Khaimah joined the UAE in February 1972.

Ras al-Khaimah and the other poor, small shaikhdoms resented their comparative lack of power, and there were ominous immediate threats from the Dhofari war in neighboring Oman and Saudi Arabia's refusal to accord diplomatic recognition to the UAE because of its territorial dispute with Abu Dhabi. These problems plus the disputes and rivalries among and between the seven emirates led many to predict a short career for the new state. It survived its early trials in large measure because of the leadership of Shaikh Zayid bin Sultan Al Nuhayyan of Abu Dhabi, the union's first and only president, and because each ruler was aware that in a hostile environment of larger and more powerful neighbors, no state could long survive outside the union. Abu Dhabi had the size and wealth but not a full cadre of trained personnel, Dubai had some capable administrators and wealth but insufficient hinterland, Sharjah had some bureaucracy and prospective wealth, and the others lacked all these elements.

The British-established Trucial States Council, although only an advisory body, had created a habit of regular consultation among the seven Trucial States rulers, and, as early as February 1968, Zayid and Shaikh Rashid bin Said Al Maktum, ruler of Dubai, had formed an Abu Dhabi-Dubai federation, meant to be the first step toward a union of nine. While these moves and subsequent meetings of the nine rulers did not bring about the intended result, they did help pave the way to the eventual union of seven. Shaikh Zayid took the initiative in July 1971 to bring the seven Trucial States rulers together and create the State of the United Arab Emirates, pointing toward the independent union. He also launched Abu Dhabi's Fund for Arab Economic Development (ADFAED), looking ahead to the role it would play as aid donor in the Arab world and beyond. It was inevitable that Abu Dhabi and Dubai would dominate the new union. What was surprising was that the much smaller and less powerful Dubai achieved virtual political parity within the union. This was a tribute both to the bargaining capabilities of Shaikh Rashid and to the wisdom and generosity of Shaikh Zayid, who was committed to using Abu Dhabi's wealth to make the union work. It reflected Zayid's determination to promote a strong union government and that of Rashid to preserve as much independence for Dubai as possible. The compromise led to the UAE, but unionists, who favor a strong centralized federal government, still dispute with federalists, who prefer a weak central government and "states' rights" (extensive powers left to the individual emirates).

Structure of the federal government. The UAE federal government is tripartite, with separate executive, legislative, and judicial branches, although the executive dominates and there are no elections. Moreover, much of the actual decisionmaking, especially at the emiral level but also at the federal, is carried out in a traditional, highly personalized way. The Supreme Federal Council (SFC), also referred to as the Supreme Council of the Union, comprises the seven emiral rulers and is the highest political authority in the union. It establishes the UAE's general policy, elects the president and vice president, ratifies federal laws and treaties, and oversees the federal budget. Generally, the SFC meets four times a year. Each ruler has a single vote, with procedural matters settled by a majority and substantive issues requiring five votes, including those of both Abu Dhabi and Dubai. The president, Shaikh Zayid since the UAE's inception, exercises significant but not dominant power. He oversees the country's foreign relations and the implementation of federal legislation and, with the SFC's approval, appoints the prime minister. He links the Supreme Federal Council with the federation's second most important political body, the Council of Ministers, which is the federal cabinet and, presided over by the prime minister, represents the source of legislative authority. The Federal National Council (FNC) is made up of 40 members, eight from both Abu Dhabi and Dubai, six each from Sharjah and Ras al-

Khaimah, and four apiece from the other three emirates. The method of selection is left fairly open, but rulers generally handpick the members, doing so from prominent groups and families. While in appearance closest to a legislative body, the FNC is only advisory, making recommendations on draft laws to the Council of Ministers. It may prove to be, however, a first step toward a more open, representative form of government. The federal judiciary is made up of the Supreme Court and Courts of First Instance, with judges serving indefinite terms and removable only in extraordinary circumstances. The UAE legal system gives great weight to Islamic law (*Sharia*) but is drawn from several sources, including Western ones. The Supreme Court adjudicates interemirate disputes and those between an emirate and the federal government, determines the constitutionality of federal or state laws when challenged, and presides over cases of alleged crimes against the state.

Like the federal bureaucracy, the judiciary has been forced to rely on expatriate expertise because of the paucity of qualified personnel. A concerted effort to staff the courts with Emirians has had some success, while the federal civil service which, within a decade of its establishment in 1973, had expanded tenfold, remains dependent on foreigners, especially Egyptians and Palestinians, although there appear to be efforts to reduce the number of the latter in the wake of the 1990-91 Gulf crisis. Key positions in all ministries are held by UAE citizens.

Economy. The UAE possesses proven oil reserves of close to 100 billion barrels, placing it roughly on a par with Iraq, Kuwait, and Iran with almost 10 percent percent of the world's total. The lion's share of about 90 percent belongs to Abu Dhabi, while Dubai has most of the rest. The UAE has estimated natural gas reserves of some 200 trillion cubic feet, most of it in Abu Dhabi but with large reserves also in Sharjah and significant amounts in Dubai. As in Kuwait and Qatar, oil and oil-derived industries dominate the economy, accounting for about 90 percent of the UAE's national income. The downturn in oil prices in the mid-1980s caused modest austerity measures through budget cuts, but the UAE remains, per capita, one of the wealthiest countries in the world. The estimated GNP per head was $24,000 in 1993.

The collapse of BCCI had a major impact on the UAE in 1991, specifically on the emirate of Abu Dhabi and its ruler, Shaikh Zayid. Abu Dhabi was the 77 percent majority stockholder, and Zayid was reported to have spent up to $6 billion in a vain effort to prevent the bank's collapse, while BCCI stole as much as $2 billion from him. This debacle, following a UAE banking crisis and Kuwait's Suq al-Manakh unofficial stock exchange collapse a decade earlier, indicated the continuing weakness of the banking and financial credit system in the Gulf. By February 1995, with Abu Dhabi's agreement to a $1.8 billion settlement with creditors, the issue appeared resolved and the UAE economy sound.

Foreign and security relations. The UAE maintains close and friendly ties with the other Gulf Arab states and Saudi Arabia and is an active member of the GCC, which it forms with them. The UAE has resisted, however, the formation of a GCC customs union and it has so far also resisted being under the air defense system of Saudi Arabia. Like the others, it has not coordinated arms purchases, so there still is not meaningful interoperability of GCC-member armed forces. While the UAE had earlier emulated Kuwait's neutralist policies, it looked to the United States, as did its Gulf Arab neighbors, as a last resort defender. A week before Iraq's invasion of Kuwait, as tensions were rising, the UAE engaged in joint sea-air exercises with U.S. forces. It joined the other Gulf Arab states in condemning the Iraqi invasion and contributed military forces to the coalition that drove Iraqi forces from Kuwait. The UAE has, in the aftermath of the conflict, reached an agreement with the U.S. for access to military facilities on its soil in the event of future security threats. Generally, the UAE's relations with other moderate Arab states are cordial and those with the more radical regimes strained. Together with Kuwait, the UAE pursued active checkbook diplomacy toward Marxist South Yemen which helped to move it toward a rapprochement with Oman in 1982 and greater moderation. The UAE has been a major donor to the Third World, principally poor Arab states, with all the funding coming from Abu Dhabi.

Political and economic relations with the West have been important and usually friendly. After independence, many British military personnel remained as advisers, and today private British citizens continue in significant civilian advisory positions. The U.K., the U.S., and Japan are the country's major trading partners, each generally supplying between 10 percent and 20 percent of its imports. Japan is far and away the largest UAE customer, mainly for oil. European Union countries account for most of the rest of the UAE's trade, though Dubai and Sharjah maintain a significant trade, largely in reexports, to Iran. As Soviet policies moderated, the UAE developed commercial ties with the Eastern Bloc starting in the early 1980s, and established diplomatic relations with the USSR in 1985. The UAE and the other Gulf Arab states are now challenged with establishing ties with the Soviet Union successor states. Major arms purchases continue to come from the U.S., the U.K., and France, and the U.S. and its European allies continue to compete vigorously for arms sales to the UAE and its neighbors. Relations with the U.S. have been strained by the Arab-Israeli conflict, but the "reflagging" of Kuwaiti tankers in 1987, close cooperation in the 1990-91 Gulf crisis, and the signing of the 1995 Defense Cooperation Agreement, following defense agreements with France, a close UAE security partner, and the U.K., have cemented ties.

Challenges. Two decades of survival as a nation suggest that the union will last. Some of the problems faced at the outset have been overcome. The boundary dispute with Saudi Arabia was settled, clearing the way for close and cordial relations with the UAE's larger neighbor, and resentments among the poorer emirates have been at least partially assuaged by Abu Dhabi's generosity in promoting their economic welfare. (Discovery of modest hydrocarbon wealth in Ras al-Khaimah after independence has also helped to reconcile that disenchanted member to the union.) Moreover, interemirate border disputes have been largely resolved and traditional rivalries are somewhat diminished. Nevertheless, asserting federal over emiral authority in key areas remains a problem, aggravated by the often indistinct distribution of powers in the constitution. Thus a federal military force has proven elusive: there is not yet meaningful integration of the separate forces existing at the time of independence. Although the constitution is reasonably clear in reserving the conduct of foreign relations to the federal government, Dubai's and Sharjah's close commercial ties to Iran caused a significant split with Abu Dhabi during the Iran-Iraq war, as the latter felt obliged to provide significant financial and diplomatic assistance to Iraq. Dubai's jealously independent approach to development of its own wealth led it to remain outside of OPEC and maximize its oil production and leave Abu Dhabi in the position of having to trim production to abide by the UAE's quota. This circumstance helped cause UAE overproduction from the mid-1980s, provoking Saddam Hussein's anger toward the UAE as well as Kuwait. While Shaikh Rashid remained active, he and Shaikh Zayid led the federalist and unionist camps. Political crises were overcome in 1976 and 1979 when Rashid made sufficient concessions to Zayid to induce the latter not to resign as president. There is still a problem of finding a more viable formula for sharing emiral and federal power. It has grown more serious with Rashid's decade-long indisposition and eventual death (1990) and Zayid's advancing age (late '70s or early '80s). It will be difficult to pursue coherent national policies until strong federal institutions are firmly established. The other great challenge is that of leadership when Zayid passes from the scene. Rashid's successor, Maktum, has managed Dubai's affairs capably, ruling with the close cooperation of his three brothers. Zayid's son, Khalifa, has begun a long apprenticeship as his successor. However, none of these will have the same stature as the two figures who dominated the UAE's birth and early years. *See also* ABU DHABI, AJMAN, DUBAI, FUJAIRAH, IRAN-CONTRA SCANDAL, RAS AL-KHAIMAH, RASHID BIN SAID AL-MAKTUM, SHARJAH, UMM AL-QAIWAIN, *and* ZAYID BIN SULTAN AL NUHAYYAN.

UNITED BANK OF THE MIDDLE EAST. *See* BANKING.

UNITED KINGDOM. The British have had a greater political impact on the Gulf Arab states in the modern era than any other outside power, although until the last few decades the Gulf was of derivative and indirect interest to London. The initial interest was commercial, in the form of the British East India Company's desire to develop markets for British goods in Iran. It was attacks on British Indian merchant shipping, extending to the waters just off Bombay, that drew the British militarily and politically into the Gulf. British expeditions were carried out jointly with Oman, with which agreements were made in 1798 and 1799, to defeat the Qawasim fleets of Ras al-Khaimah and Sharjah and impose upon the tribal rulers on the Arab coast of the lower Gulf a General Treaty of Peace in 1820 to end the piracy. Although the British had no interest in the landward concerns of these tribal shaikhs and their followers, provided commerce remained unmolested, the need to establish an enduring maritime peace led to later treaties that drew the British further into Gulf affairs. The key step was taken in 1853 when British-supervised maritime truces were made permanent by lower Gulf rulers' subscribing to the Treaty of Maritime Peace in Perpetuity. This solidified the trucial system that gave the Trucial States (also called Trucial Shaikhdoms and Trucial Oman) their name.

These arrangements immediately benefited the Arabs of the Gulf by expanding trade and pearling, and confirmed tribal power and territorial control as they existed at that moment. When that pattern was frozen, leaders whose authority had been only tribal became rulers of territories that evolved into states. Later, in 1892, the perceived threat of European rivals led the British to draw up "exclusive agreements" with the lower Gulf shaikhdoms, including Bahrain, by which they agreed not to yield territory or sovereignty to any other state without British assent, while Great Britain assumed responsibility for their foreign relations and, by implication, their protection. Similar agreements were made with Kuwait and Qatar in 1899 and 1916, respectively. These agreements capped the process by which solely commercial interests had given way to largely political and strategic concerns and formed the legal-diplomatic basis of British authority in the Gulf. While the Gulf Arab states were protected states, they were not protectorates; they retained, at least in principle, sovereignty in the conduct of their domestic affairs. Oman, although never drawn formally into this system, was in an effectively parallel relationship with Britain. The last step in the evolution of tribal shaikhs to modern chiefs of state and of vague and shifting patterns of tribal writ to territorially defined states with explicitly defined borders began in the 1930s and carried into the 1960s. It was largely the product of oil, its exploration, discovery, and export. When concessions were granted, the fees paid to the rulers were sufficient to elevate them economically above and make them independent of the merchant class. The letting of concessions required that territorial frontiers be defined with European precision, which was done by British officials. The appropriately named Julian Walker literally paced off the borders of the Trucial States with their hodgepodge of enclaves and exclaves. (Walker was called out of retirement in 1991 to assist in demarcating the Kuwait-Iraq border under UN auspices, following the expulsion of Iraqi forces from Kuwaiti in Operation Desert Storm.)

One remarkable feature of the Pax Britannica in the Gulf was the slightness of its institutional structure. Until the late 19th century, Gulf affairs were supervised by the British government of Bombay; thence until Indian independence in 1947, by the British government of India; and finally by the Foreign Office in London. In the Gulf itself a British Political Resident was based in Bushire on the Iranian side until 1946, then in Bahrain. On rare occasions the British used their firepower to keep order. With the exception of Bahrain, where the British played a direct role in the state's administration from 1926, when Charles D. Belgrave was installed as British adviser to the ruler, there was little administrative involvement in the affairs of the Gulf Arab states. This changed in the 1950s, when British-officered forces drove Saudi occupiers from Buraimi in defense of Oman's and Abu Dhabi's territorial claims and helped the sultan of Oman defeat the Ibadi imam in interior Oman, enabling the sultan to reunify Muscat and Oman and opening the way for oil exploration and development in the interior. The Trucial States Council was established to promote consultation among the Trucial States rulers on issues of shared concern, and the Trucial States Development Council undertook useful but very limited projects to promote infrastructure development.

Kuwait became fully independent in 1961, by which time its oil-fueled economic and social development was well advanced and some of the influence of Arab nationalism had been absorbed. Bahrain's level of economic and social sophistication was comparable to Kuwait's (although its wealth was far less), but there, where the Royal Navy's Gulf unit was based, the British retained their control. The lower Gulf remained a somnolent backwater with both the U.K. government and the rulers content with a system which rendered each benefits and had become comfortable for both. Its end came not from any significant Gulf Arab demands for independence, but from the British Labour government's desire to escape the cost of maintaining the last imperial outposts east of Suez. In June 1968 it announced its intention to withdraw all British military forces from the Gulf by the end of 1971, clearly implying the end of the United Kingdom's special relationship with and protection of the lower Gulf Arab states and reversing promises given to the rulers of those states only two months before, when the British withdrawal from Aden was effected. Upon their election in June 1970, the Conservatives faced a dilemma in that they had vigorously opposed the Labour policy of "scuttle," while sober analysis of the decision by Foreign Office specialists in 1970 suggested that, in a practical sense, the decision was not reversible. Not only Iran but Kuwait and Saudi Arabia (and, predictably, the rest of the Arab world) opposed British retention of a military presence in the Gulf, while the rulers of the states affected desired continued British protection. Foreign Secretary Sir Alec Douglas-Home called out of retirement Sir William Luce, former British Political Resident in the Gulf, to consult with the Gulf rulers and determine the best policy toward the Gulf. The Luce Mission confirmed the decision to withdraw.

Saudi Arabia and Kuwait urged that a federation of all nine lower Gulf Arab states (the seven Trucial States plus Bahrain and Qatar) be formed to enable them most effectively to provide for their common defense. Bahrain, the most populous and politically and administratively the most advanced, favored such a federation until Iran's claim to it was dropped in 1970. Subsequently, its preference to go it alone and its long rivalry with Qatar led those two states to declare independence in August and September 1971, respectively. The United Kingdom then faced an embarrassing dilemma as the Trucial States moved toward independence facing Iranian claims to Abu Musa and the Tunbs, islands long claimed by Sharjah and Ras al-Khaimah, respectively. To yield to the shah would incur general Arab anger and undercut British influence in the new federation of seven, but to oppose the shah would undermine the envisaged collaboration of Iran and Saudi Arabia (referred to in the United States as the "twin pillar" Gulf policy). A partial solution came in the form of an agreement between the shah and the ruler of Sharjah to share Abu Musa's sovereignty and suspected oil, an agreement that later proved fatal to Sharjah's Shaikh Khalid. The shah seized the Tunbs, the British suffered denunciation (and Qaddafi's seizure of British oil interests in Libya), but the transition to independence of the Gulf Arab states was successfully completed. Each entered into Treaties of Friendship with the United Kingdom, pledging "consultation" in time of need, but left specific arrangements for security assistance to ancillary documents.

Despite the rather hasty and disjointed nature of the British withdrawal from the Gulf, dire predictions about the survivability of the new small states and the creation of a power vacuum in the Gulf were not borne out. Political radicalism such as Aden experienced had not infected any of the Gulf Arab states, with the partial exception of Bahrain, and judiciously distributed oil-generated wealth served to dampen most political opposition to the rulers. Despite their regional ambitions and historical claims, both the shah's Iran and Saudi Arabia were essentially status quo powers that did not wish to see the Gulf order upset. To some extent, moreover, the United States filled the "vacuum" with its Gulf naval flotilla, the U.S. Middle East Force, at the former British base in Bahrain. Finally, British involvement in the Gulf remained significant after its special, protective relations with the Gulf Arab states were severed. British military advisers played an important part in helping Oman defeat the South Yemen-abetted rebellion in Dhofar, and both seconded and private, contracted military personnel continued to be a key element in the Omani armed forces. To a lesser but significant extent British personnel assisted various emirates in the UAE with internal and external security services. A number of private, civilian British advisers continue to serve Gulf Arab states rulers. Moreover, the United Kingdom's longstanding relations with these states have given British economic and financial interests an advantage of familiarity, that has been exploited to maintain a major share of trade with the Gulf Arab states, including the sale of arms. The United Kingdom's withdrawal from its last remnants of empire in the Middle East was by most accounts a success. *See also* ARMED FORCES, TREATY OF MARITIME PEACE IN PERPETUITY, TRUCIAL STATES, SIR WILLIAM LUCE, *and entries on individual Gulf Arab states.*

UNITED NATIONS. Each Gulf Arab state has, since shortly after its independence, been a member of the United Nations. Through the Food and Agricultural Organization (FAO), expert advice has been tendered on food production. In 1958 the "question of Oman" was inscribed on the UN General Assembly's agenda as part of a diplomatic offensive by nonaligned Afro-Asian states against British support of Sultan Said bin Taimur in his conflict with the Ibadi imam and debated for some time without practical effect. The United Nations has been significantly involved in Gulf Arab affairs on two occasions. In 1970, through a mission of inquiry, it ascertained that Bahrain wished to be independent rather than annexed by Iran, providing a diplomatic cover for the shah's withdrawal of his claim to that nation. By far the most important UN involvement occurred in the Gulf crisis of 1990-91. A series of UN resolutions, from August 2, 1990, to November 29, 1990, progressed from condemnation of the Iraqi invasion of Kuwait to authorization of member states to use "all necessary means" to bring about Iraqi withdrawal and implement other specific adopted measures if Iraqi troops had not withdrawn by January 15, 1991. At the conclusion of Operation Desert Storm the UN became responsible for implementing the cease-fire agreement that ended hostilities with Iraq's defeat. This included the demarcation of the Iraq-Kuwait border.

UNITED STATES. The first Americans to be significantly involved in the Gulf Arab states were medical and educational missionaries in Bahrain, Kuwait, and Muscat (as well as Basra in Iraq), whose devoted work for the betterment of Gulf Arabs' conditions created an enduring legacy of goodwill. American oil companies paved the way to the extraordinary growth of American interest in the Gulf region following World War II. An American company, Standard Oil Company of California (through a Canadian subsidiary), made the first discovery of oil on the Arab side of the Gulf in Bahrain in 1932 and proceeded, in nearby Saudi Arabia, to tap what has proven to be the world's greatest oil reserves. At the same time another American company, Gulf, as partner to the Anglo-Iranian Oil Company (later British Petroleum), was discovering the Kuwaiti oil bonanza. As World War II progressed, there was a growing realization that the world's petroleum center of gravity was shifting to the Gulf. The United States was supplying 80 percent of Allied petroleum needs and beginning to fear imminent exhaustion of U.S. petroleum reserves. American strategic planners focused on the Gulf area increasingly during the war. Because the oil of Saudi Arabia was vast and tapped first and because the small Gulf Arab states remained under British protection, the U.S. fostered an intimate official relationship with the Saudis. Commercial and financial ties were established subsequently and grew rapidly. In Bahrain, from 1949, a small U.S. flotilla, U.S. Middle East Force, was stationed as an earnest of the new American interest in the area. At the same time the British turned aside all requests of their U.S. Ally for establishment of diplomatic posts in the Gulf Arab states, relenting only to the extent of permitting a U.S. consulate in Kuwait in 1950. Full diplomatic relations with Kuwait were established in 1961, when it became fully independent, and the United States became a major source of Kuwait's modest arms requirements in the following decade (although several years passed before the U.S. had a resident ambassador in Kuwait, initially accrediting the ambassador in Jidda, Saudi Arabia, to Kuwait with the same rank).

It was with British withdrawal from its remaining protective relationships and military commitments in the Gulf in 1971 that the United States became intimately involved in Gulf security. As part of President Richard M. Nixon's strategy of reliance on regional proxies, the Nixon Doctrine, U.S. policy took the form of a "twin pillar" strategy. This aimed at building up the military strength of Iran and Saudi Arabia to enable them to repel threats to Gulf security short of

Soviet intervention, in which case the United States would commit its "over-the-horizon" forces. In the absence of a major test, this stratagem appeared to work until near the end of the decade when in 1979 two events made it untenable, Ayatollah Khomeini's Islamic revolution in Iran, which removed one pillar, and the Soviet invasion of Afghanistan, at the end of that fateful year, which raised fears of Soviet designs on the Gulf. From that point to the present, events have impelled more direct U.S. effort to promote Gulf security. Arms sales by the United States and other suppliers to the Gulf Arab states have also continued to spiral upward. The Carter Doctrine, enunciated in President Jimmy Carter's January 1980 State of the Union speech, identified any attempt by an outside power to gain control of the Gulf as "an assault on the vital interests of the United States of America" that would be met "by any means necessary, including military force." The Gulf had effectively become the third most important American strategic interest after U.S. territory and Western Europe.

Only Oman, with its strategic position athwart the Strait of Hormuz, was prepared to make available facilities for prepositioning of supplies and for the use of the Rapid Deployment Joint Task Force (RDJTF) that, under President Ronald Reagan, became the U.S. Central Command (USCENTCOM). Kuwait, following a more neutral stance toward superpower rivalry, was much less enthusiastic than Oman about the new, more forward U.S. policy. The other Gulf Arab states were somewhere in between, and all of them were prevented from adopting a closer relationship with the United States by what they perceived as excessively one-sided American policy toward the Arab-Israeli conflict and the uncertainty of U.S. arms sales because of the frequently exercised congressional veto against them. The Iran-Contra scandal revelations of late 1986-early 1987 shook Gulf Arab confidence as the Iran-Iraq war continued to menace them. In the spring of 1987, however, Iranian attacks on Kuwaiti tankers, designed to force Kuwait to cease providing financial and other assistance to Iraq, prompted Kuwait to request U.S. protection via "reflagging" of its tankers. This meant introducing U.S. naval escorts into the Gulf. Bahrain, where U.S. naval vessels had continued to be homeported in fact, if not by formal definition, under a low-profile arrangement, became the locus of this expanding U.S. strategic presence in the Gulf. This was a prelude to the vast undertaking of Desert Shield/Desert Storm, when all the Gulf Arab states were allied with the U.S. and host to American forces in the military operations that ended the Iraqi occupation of Kuwait. By 1995 all the Gulf Arab states were allied with the United States in varying degrees for prepositioning of military materiel. (Oman updated agreements entered into a decade earlier.) Kuwait, having come full circle from its earlier neutrality, entered into an agreement in September 1991 to conduct periodic joint exercises with U.S. forces (one was held in December, 1991, and a number since). Indeed, Kuwait had earlier called for U.S. troops to be permanently based on its soil. The Gulf Arab states also placed major weapons orders after Desert Storm with the United States and other nations, and Kuwait began receiving F-18 fighters already on order.

Despite the commanding importance of the U.S.-Gulf Arab states security relationship, there are many other significant ties. American technology is generally very highly regarded, represented first in the 1930s by petroleum technology in which the United States has always been preeminent. American engineering and construction firms continue to receive major contracts despite strong European and recently Asian competition. American firms led the effort to extinguish Kuwait's oil field fires and recap its wells, and the Kuwait government asked the U.S. Army Corps of Engineers to oversee the country's reconstruction, in which American firms took the major role, favored not only for obvious political reasons but because of their well-established reputation for the quality of their work. Kuwait and the other super-wealthy Gulf Arab states have invested substantial amounts of their oil incomes in U.S. government securities, industrial enterprises, and real estate. In most years the United States supplies 10 percent-15 percent or more of Gulf Arab state imports. U.S. purchases from the Gulf Arab states are almost exclusively oil and less in value than U.S. exports, yielding a positive trade balance. Political relations between the Gulf Arab states and the United States have been reasonably warm, despite the strains induced by the Arab-Israeli conflict. They have grown closer in the wake of the 1990-91 Gulf crisis, evidence of which was offered in the Gulf Arab states' involvement in the U.S.-brokered Arab-Israeli peace negotiations begun in the fall of 1991 and in their support of the September 13, 1993, Israel-PLO Declaration of Principles calling for limited Palestinian self-rule in Gaza and Jericho. Extensive human ties have been created by the thousands of Gulf Arab students who have pursued their higher education in the United States. More have attended universities in the United States than in any other country. Finally, elements of American popular culture, especially through video-cassettes and audio-cassettes and other means of electronic transmission, have invaded the traditional culture of these states. *See also* ARMED FORCES, CARTER DOCTRINE, IRAN-CONTRA SCANDAL, IRAN-IRAQ WAR, MIDDLE EAST FORCE, OIL, *and entries on individual Gulf Arab states.*

UQAIR. *See* SAUDI ARABIA.

URBANIZATION. *See* CITIES.

UTUB. The Utub were a tribe claiming to be part of the great Anaizah federation of central Arabia, to which the Al Saud belong. The Utub migrated to the Gulf coast in the late 17th century. The Al Sabah rulers of Kuwait, the Al Khalifa of Bahrain, and the Al Thani of Qatar were part of the Utub. *See also* ANAIZAH, BAHRAIN, AL KHALIFA, QATAR, AL SABAH, AL SAUD, *and* AL THANI.

V

VEGETATION. *See* AGRICULTURE *and* FLORA.

VILAYET. The term *vilayet* (from the Arabic *wilaya*) was used by the Ottoman Turks to designate a province. From 1897 to World War I Kuwait was a lesser district in the vilayet of Basra, although the British had in 1899 made a secret agreement with Kuwait obligating its ruler and his successors not to deal with other powers without prior British consent.

W

WADI. *Wadi* (pl., *widyan*) is the Arabic for "valley," referring in the Arabian Peninsula to dry river beds. Wadis are found in all of the Gulf Arab states, but are especially prominent on the Gulf of Oman coast of the UAE and Oman.

WAHHABIS. Wahhabis are members of a reform movement in Islam that arose in mid-18th-century central Arabia as a result of the preaching of Muhammad bin Abd al-Wahhab. He called for a return to the original principles of Islam and a repudiation of subsequent innovations. The movement's founder drew upon the teachings of the theologian Ibn Taymiyyah (13th A.D [4th A.H.] century), a rigorous interpreter of the strict Hanbali school of Islamic jurisprudence. Followers of his teaching reject the term "Wahhabi" as suggesting creation of a sect rather than a reform focused on acknowledgment of God's unqualified oneness (Arabic, *tawhid*) and thus identify themselves as members of a movement described as "the call to the doctrine of the oneness of God." It was the austere zeal of this movement, allied to the martial and political leadership of the Al Saud clan, that led to the creation of the first Saudi state, occupying most of the Arabian Peninsula by the end of the 18th century, and that helped to bring about its reestablishment in the first two and a half decades of the 20th century. This alliance between the Al Saud and the descendants of Abd al-Wahhab remains to this day a central feature of the Saudi polity.

During both phases of Saudi expansion Wahhabism had a significant impact on the Arab tribes and states of the lower Gulf. In the early 19th century the Qawasim allied themselves with the expanding religious-military movement, because of similar religious orthodoxy and as a useful alliance against their Omani rivals. Thus strengthened, the Qawasim increased their maritime attacks, with many directed against British Indian vessels, which prompted the British to form a naval alliance with the Omanis to suppress the Qawasim piracy.

Wahhabi influence grew in Qatar during the 19th century as the Qataris moved toward independence from their Al Khalifa overlords in Bahrain. Following the Saudi defeat of the Ottoman Turks in the Hasa Province of eastern Arabia in 1913, Wahhabi influence spread again. As a result, the Al Thani ruling family and most of Qatar's population are Wahhabis, and the state has generally been closely aligned with Saudi Arabia. *See also* AL-AIN, OMAN, QAWASIM, QATAR, AL SAUD, *and* SAUDI ARABIA.

WAHIBA SANDS. Located in central Oman, between the Arabian Sea and the eastern part of the Hajar Mountains, the Wahiba sands are a large area of dunes that have attracted scientific interest because of fossil sand seas.

WARBAH ISLAND. Together with the larger Bubiyan Island, which also belongs to Kuwait, Warbah Island commands the narrow channel leading from the Gulf to Iraq's port and naval base at Umm Qasr. On several occasions, starting in the early 1970s, Iraq demanded partial cession or lease of the islands, but Kuwait refused each time. The issue remained a major irritant in Kuwaiti-Iraqi relations up to the Iraqi invasion of August 2, 1990.

WOMEN. The position of women in the Gulf Arab states reflects the conservative Islamic culture of these societies. Thus the home remains the woman's domain and relatively few women, expatriates apart, are seen in public in most of these countries. Nevertheless, there is considerable difference in women's mobility, style of dress, and other indexes of social freedom. In the more conservative states women are usually accompanied by male relatives in public and are veiled, while Kuwaiti women are permitted to drive and they and women in Bahrain, Dubai, and Sharjah may frequently be seen unveiled and without male guardians in public. Even in a very conservative setting, women have exercised great power within the family, sometimes with important political consequences. Significant changes in the status of Gulf Arab women are now occurring.

Although, traditionally, women's domestic sphere has been separate from the public sphere in which men operate, forceful women can have a profound impact on public affairs. Thus a recurrence of potentially destabilizing violence in the Al Nuhayyan ruling family of Abu Dhabi was averted when the current ruler's mother, following fratricidal intrigues that killed her husband and three of his brothers, made her sons swear never to harm one another, an oath that has to this day been honored. The grandmother of Dubai's present ruler was the actual political power in the state and on one occasion is reported to have led its defense when her husband, the ruler, failed to act. Such a venture into the public realm of men's affairs was exceedingly rare, however, and it is only in very recent years that women in any numbers have begun to assume nondomestic roles.

The introduction of education for girls has given women new skills and stirred their ambition to use them. Women now generally account for half or more of the Gulf Arab states' university students and usually outperform their male counterparts. In large measure female employment has been restricted to occupations such as teaching in which women can typically work within a purely female environment and preserve the traditional sex segregation. At the same time women have entered other professions, including banking, in a significant way, while still adhering to the pattern of sex segregation by dealing only with other women. Within the same limitations women have served for several years in their own branch of the Royal Omani Police, earning high marks for their performance. Largely within the past decade, however, there has been a significant movement of independent, middle-class women into new and more varied occupations including journalism, engineering, and broadcasting, especially in the socially more liberal states of Kuwait and Bahrain. Even in the generally more conservative UAE and Oman, women have risen to fairly senior positions, not only working with but supervising men. In Oman women have been selected to serve in the National Consultative Council (*majlis al-shura*). In the emirate of Sharjah in the UAE, as well as in Kuwait, women have begun to play a role in the burgeoning arts scene, engaged in literature, painting, and theater. The rector of the University of Kuwait is a woman.

Following the 1990–91 Gulf crisis, many observers speculated that the example of Western women assuming roles traditionally reserved for men, together with the rulers' presumed perception of the need for more open societies to ensure their strength and survival, would have the effect of greatly accelerating the pace at which the public roles of women will expand. Several years after Desert Storm it is not yet certain if this will prove true, but there are straws in the wind. In conservative Abu Dhabi women have been recruited to serve in segregated units in the security forces. Women's suffrage has long been debated in Kuwait, and was discussed 20 years ago in Bahrain on the eve of its brief parliamentary experiment. Shaikh Jabir, the ruler of Kuwait, has intimated on several occasions that women should have the vote, and the 1962 Kuwaiti constitution does not prohibit women from voting. Moreover, in February 1992, a poll showed that 71 percent of Kuwait's men and women favored giving women the vote.

Still, significant numbers of both women and men undoubtedly remain ambivalent on the matter of women's direct participation in the political process, as reflected in prewar Kuwait, when the wife of the heir apparent declared herself opposed to the vote for women and demonstrations by women for the vote engendered larger counter-demonstrations. *See also* AHL, A'ILAH, *and* MARRIAGE.

Y

YA'ARIBAH. Nasir bin Murshid Ya'arabi gained the position of Ibadi imam in Oman in 1624 and laid the basis for a family dynasty by leading the struggle to expel the Portuguese from Oman, a goal almost achieved by the time of his death in 1649. His nephew and successor, Sultan bin Saif, gained the final victory over the Portuguese and created a fleet that carried the conflict to the seas, attacking Dutch, French, and English, as well as Portuguese shipping, and eventually seized Portuguese territory both in India and East Africa, thus creating an overseas Omani empire. Bahrain was taken in 1700 and held briefly. In its first century the Ya'aribah dynasty created great wealth, much of which was spent on a number of major building projects whose creations, including the great fort at Nizwa, represent some of Oman's great architectural monuments. By the 1720s, however, Ya'aribah rule had entered a period of decline, in large part because the religious leaders who elected the imam were not prepared to accept hereditary succession. Conflict over the succession to the imamate resulted in civil war. The damage thus done to the country was greatly compounded when the last Ya'aribah claimants to the imamate invited Persian military intervention to assist their cause, leading to further chaos and destruction. The civil war ended in the victory of Ahmad bin Said Al Bu Said, who established the dynasty that rules to this day. *See also* OMAN *and* PORTUGUESE.

YEMEN ARAB REPUBLIC (YAR). The YAR, which merged with the People's Democratic Republic of Yemen (PDRY or South Yemen) to become the Republic of Yemen in May 1990, was not of central importance to the Gulf Arab states because it was isolated on the other side of the Arabian Peninsula beyond the desert expanse of central and southern Saudi Arabia. Also there were no economic or political ties. The YAR was not an ideological threat to the Gulf Arab states like the Marxist PDRY, which immediately and physically menaced Oman by supporting the Dhofari Rebellion of 1968-75. There was concern over the degree of Soviet influence in the YAR as well as the PDRY. The GCC purposely excluded both the YAR and the PDRY, which they protested. Their view was that the GCC was a restrictive, rich Arabs' club. Kuwaiti and UAE aid to some extent ameliorated their resentment. The Kuwait Fund for Arab Economic Development (KFAED) assisted projects, including the national university at San'a. The UAE aided YAR agriculture, and Shaikh Zayid bin Sultan, ruler of Abu Dhabi and president of the UAE, contributed generously to the construction of the new Ma'rib Dam, near the site of its namesake of antiquity, from which area his ancestors are believed to have migrated eastward *See also* PEOPLE'S DEMOCRATIC REPUBLIC OF YEMEN *and* REPUBLIC OF YEMEN.

YEMEN, REPUBLIC OF. On May 22, 1990 the Yemen Arab Republic (YAR), or North Yemen, and the People's Democratic Republic of Yemen (PDRY), or South Yemen, merged to form the Republic of Yemen. The new nation incorporated a large and populous state of great potential strength but did not represent a threat to the Gulf Arab states. However, the Gulf crisis of 1990–91 left Yemen and the Gulf Arab states on opposite sides. Yemen abstained in the vote at the August 10, 1990, emergency meeting of the Arab League to send Arab troops to Saudi Arabia to help defend it against a possible attack from Iraq. As a member of the UN Security Council it voted with Cuba against Resolution 678, which authorized UN member states to cooperate with the government of Kuwait in using "all necessary means" to uphold the several previous resolutions passed to condemn Iraq's invasion and address related issues, if Iraq did not comply with them by January 15, 1991. This generated a certain degree of tension in Yemen's relations with the Gulf Arab states, resulting in a cutoff of their aid to San'a. By 1993 relations began to warm somewhat. In May 1994 civil war broke out and the south declared its independence but was defeated. *See also* PEOPLE'S DEMOCRATIC REPUBLIC OF YEMEN *and* YEMEN ARAB REPUBLIC.

Z

ZAHIRAH. *See* DHAHIRAH.

ZAKAH. *Zakah*, from the Arabic "to be righteous" or "to thrive," designates an alms tax, one of the Five Pillars of Islam. Assessed on various kinds of property and produce, zakah may be dispensed to the needy directly or paid to the state for disbursement for charitable purposes. In Arabian tribal society payment of zakah was an important criterion in establishing exercise of authority. In the long-running dispute among Abu Dhabi, Oman, and Saudi Arabia over possession of the al-Ain/al-Buraimi area, the Saudis based their claim largely on payment of zakah to them or their representatives by tribes in that area.

ZANZIBAR. Zanzibar, an island off the coast of East Africa, was one of the Portuguese possessions that Oman, under the Ya'aribah dynasty, seized in its period of expansion in the late 17th century. After its loss during Oman's civil war in the mid-18th century, it again became part of the Omani empire as reconstituted by the Al Bu Said rulers. Disputed succession between the sons of Said bin Sultan led, in 1861, to British arbitration in the Canning Award that divided Zanzibar and the rest of Oman into two separate sultanates. In 1890 Great Britain established a protectorate over Zanzibar, ending Al Bu Said rule there. It became independent in December 1963, and in January 1964 its Arab government was overthrown by a Black African movement. Much of the Arab population then emigrated to Oman, where the "Zanzibaris" have formed an important element in Oman's economic life. *See also* AL BU SAID, OMAN, *and* YA'ARIBAH.

ZAYID BIN KHALIFA AL NUHAYYAN. During the long rule (1855-1909) of Shaikh Zayid bin Khalifa, known as the "Great," the power of the Al Nuhayyan family and the Al Bu Falah clan, chiefs of the Bani Yas tribal confederation of Abu Dhabi, reached its apogee. Zayid extended his authority over the tribes of the al-Ain/al-Buraimi Oasis area (in particular the Dhawahir and Na'im), supplanting the influence of the Al Saud. Under Zayid, Abu Dhabi clearly displaced the Qawasim state, based on Sharjah and Ras al-Khaimah, as the preeminent power among the Trucial States. *See also* ABU DHABI, BANI YAS, AL BU FALAH, *and* AL NUHAYYAN.

ZAYID BIN SULTAN AL NUHAYYAN. Grandson of Shaikh Zayid "the Great," Shaikh Zayid bin Sultan has been ruler of Abu Dhabi since 1966 and president of the UAE since its creation in 1971. He was born toward the end of the second decade of this century in Abu Dhabi town on the coast but was raised in the interior, receiving a traditional education with emphasis on Quranic rote learning and absorbing the Bedouin ways and values critical to later successful exercise of authority. In 1946 his older brother Shakhbut, then ruler of Abu Dhabi, appointed Zayid governor of the important al-Ain oasis area in the interior, where he soon exhibited his leadership abilities, reestablishing the loyalty of tribes that had drifted from Al Bu Falah control. In 1966 Zayid's own ambition and the Al Nuhayyan family's concern for maintaining its effective rule led him to act with Abu Dhabi's British protectors to depose Shakhbut, who had proven unable to cope with the challenges that sudden oil wealth had brought.

As ruler of Abu Dhabi, Zayid demonstrated a flexibility that enabled him to preside effectively over the emirate's rapid transformation into a wealthy, oil-exporting welfare state. The success of his rule depended largely on the masterly practice of a patriarchal version of the politics of inclusion. This has meant both sharing wealth and power with the Al Khalifa branch of the ruling family and assuring the support of key groups of commoners, the religious leaders or *ulema*, leading tribal elements, and important emirate families like the al-Otaiba and al-Suwaydi. Together with this solicitude for traditional emiral political relations, Zayid has enthusiastically embraced rapid economic development and social progress, and has expanded the educational system to include all the school-age population, male and female. Zayid practices unostentatious adherence to Islamic values and realizes that an improved life for the population at large is critical to maintaining support for a conservative, hereditary government. Reflecting this philosophy on a wider scale, Abu Dhabi had begun to share its wealth with the poorer Trucial States, well before the UAE was established in 1971.

It was Zayid's role in launching the UAE and ensuring its survival that will remain his principal political legacy. He made effective use of his assets, namely Abu Dhabi's possession of 40 percent of the federation's population, 87 percent of its area, and the bulk of its oil wealth, in placing the new state, the only successful Arab federation, on a secure footing. In large measure it was Zayid's magnanimity in dealing with his principal rival, Shaikh Rashid bin Said Al Maktum, ruler of Dubai, that enabled the UAE to survive against most predictions. Zayid gave Dubai virtual parity in the sharing of political power. He persuaded Rashid to serve as UAE vice president and later as prime minister, while Rashid's son Muhammad became federal minister of defense. The sense of Dubai-Abu Dhabi rivalry remained, however, and Rashid consistently pressed for a loose form of federation, leaving maximum autonomy to the member states, while Zayid continued to urge the unionist (Arabic, *wahdawi*) goal of a strong central government. Rashid's failure to provide Dubai's stipulated share of financial assistance to the poorer emirates left that burden wholly to Abu Dhabi and Zayid. His refusal to permit Dubai's oil production to be affected by OPEC quotas meant that Zayid had either to trim Abu Dhabi's production or suffer the political and other consequences of exceeding the UAE's quota.

In any event, with the UAE having survived a variety of internal and external challenges, Zayid has increasingly turned in his later years to a wider political stage. He has played a key role in the GCC, whose establishment was announced at a meeting of the GCC heads of state in Abu Dhabi in May 1981. In February 1988 he went to Tehran as GCC spokesman to try to negotiate an end to the Iran-Iraq war. In OPEC Zayid has, together with Kuwait and Saudi Arabia, been pressing aggressively to secure a market share commensurate with the UAE's (in effect, Abu Dhabi's) large oil reserves. President Saddam Hussein of Iraq directed special anger at Kuwait and the UAE for overproduction that undercut his efforts to rebuild Iraq's economy after the ravages of the Iran-Iraq war. Finally, Zayid has assumed something of the role of an elder Arab statesman, representing the moderate Arab states on various issues and in various forums, including the 1987 Arab League summit, where he pressed for Egypt's reintegration in the Arab world. Following the summit, he was the first Arab leader to reestablish diplomatic relations with Cairo.

In late 1991 and early 1992 Zayid found himself enmeshed in the disquieting aftermath of the collapse of the BCCI of which he and the government of Abu Dhabi owned 77 percent. Zayid was the largest loser in the collapse resulting from the fraud through which BCCI's Pakistani founder, Agha Hassan Abedi, and other officers of the bank were reported to have stolen billions of dollars. Zayid was taken in by Abedi, a personal friend, and poured large quantities of money into the bank in good faith from the mid-1980s, when its losses began. In December 1991 he had several senior BCCI officers placed in custody in Abu Dhabi to face charges, and in February 1992 he proposed a settlement through which Abu Dhabi stockholders, principally Zayid and his son Khalifa, would compensate creditors. In November 1993 a Luxembourg court approved a settlement whereby the government of Abu Dhabi paid out $1.8 billion, representing 15 cents on the dollar. Zayid appears not to have lost any popularity in his own country as a result of the BCCI scandal. *See also* ABU DHABI, AL BU FALAH, AL NUHAYYAN, *and* UNITED ARAB EMIRATES.

ZUBARAH. Zubarah is a town near the top of the Qatari Peninsula on its west side, opposite Bahrain. The Al Khalifa established Zubarah as their capital in 1766, and it retained that status for a short time after their conquest of Bahrain in 1783. In the later 19th century a series of events in the Qatari Peninsula brought Al Khalifa claims to that territory effectively to an end, but ties to Zubarah remained strong even though it was destroyed in fighting in 1878 between Al Khalifa forces and those of the emerging ruling family of Qatar, the Al Thani. In 1937 the interest of Petroleum Concessions Ltd. in using Zubarah as a port reawakened the issue of ownership, with the Al Khalifa continuing to put forward their claim. Today the ruling family of Bahrain remains unreconciled to the loss of its former capital and this, together with several disputes over ownership of islands and reefs, continues to vex Bahraini-Qatari relations. *See also* BAHRAIN, HAWAR ISLANDS, AL KHALIFA, QATAR, *and* AL THANI.

Bibliography

This bibliography is intended to be useful for both general readers and specialists who have an interest in the smaller Arab states of the Persian/Arab Gulf, Kuwait, Bahrain, Qatar, the United Arab Emirates, and Oman. While most of the works are in English, other European languages and Arabic are represented. Particular emphasis has been given to the inclusion of recently published works.

1. Bibliographies
2. Official Documents
3. Periodicals
4. General References
5. Biographies
6. Country and Regional Surveys
7. History
8. Geography and Demography
9. Society and Culture
10. Economics
11. Politics, Domestic and Regional
12. International Relations and Security Affairs

1. BIBLIOGRAPHIES

Clements, Frank A. *Oman: A Bibliography* Santa Barbara, Calif.: Clio Press, 1984.

————. *United Arab Emirates: A Bibliography*. Santa Barbara, Calif.: Clio Press, 1983.

List, H. "Der Golfkrieg auf dem deutschen Büchermarkt." *Orient* 33, no. 3 (1992).

Newman, David, et al. *The Security of Gulf Oil: An Introductory Bibliography*. Occasional Paper Series, no. 13. Durham, U.K: University of Durham, Center for Middle Eastern and Islamic Studies, 1982.

Ochsenwald, William. "Recent Publications." *Newsletter of the Society for Gulf Arab Studies*, vol. 3 (1993) to present.

Peterson, J. E. *Security in the Arabian Peninsula and Gulf States, 1973-1984*. Washington, D.C.: National Council on U.S.-Arab Relations, 1985.

Selim, George Demitri. *Arab Oil: A Bibliography of Materials in the Library of Congress*. Washington, D.C.: Library of Congress, 1982.

Sharif, Walid I. *Oil and Development in the Arab Gulf States: A Selected Annotated Bibliography*. London: Croom Helm, 1985.

Unwin, P. T. H. *Bahrain: A Bibliography*. Santa Barbara, Calif.: Clio Press, 1984.

————. *Qatar: A Bibliography*. Santa Barbara, Calif.: 1982.

Varisco, Daniel. "The Arab Gulf States Folklore Center: A Resource Center for the Study of Folklore and Traditional Culture." *Middle East Studies Association Bulletin* 23, no. 2 (1989).

2. OFFICIAL DOCUMENTS

Aitchison, C. U., ed. *A Collection of Treaties, Engagements and Sanads Relating to India and Neighboring Countries.* 3rd ed. Calcutta: British Government of India, 1892.

Armstrong, Michael, ed. *Political Diaries of the Persian Gulf, 1904-1958.* 20 vols. London: Archive Editions, 1991. Reports of the British Residents and Agents stationed in the Gulf.

Ashtiany, Julia, ed. *The Arabic Documents in the Archives of the British Political Agency: Kuwait, 1904-1949.* London: British Library, 1982.

Bahrain Central Statistics Organization. *Bahrain Statistical Abstract.* Annual. Manama, Bahrain.

Bahrain Chamber of Commerce. *Bahrain Business Directory.* Annual. Manama, Bahrain.

Bailey, R. W., ed. *Records of Oman, 1867-1947,* 8 vols. Farnham Common, Buckinghamshire, U.K.: Archive Editions, 1988.

Bidwell, Robin. "A Collection of Texts Dealing with the Sultanate of Muscat and Oman and Its International Relations, 1790-1970." *Journal of Oman Studies* 6, no. 1 (1983).

Collins, John, et al. *Petroleum Imports from the Persian Gulf: Use of U.S. Force to Ensure Supplies.* Library of Congress, Congressional Research Service. Washington, D.C.: U.S. Government Printing Office (USGPO), 1981.

Copson, Raymond W. *Persian Gulf Conflict: Post-War Issues for Congress.* Congressional Research Service, Library of Congress. Washington, D.C.: USGPO, 1991.

Great Britain, Central Office of Information, Reference Division. *Arbitration Agreement between the Government of the United Kingdom (Acting on Behalf of the Government of Abu Dhabi and*

His Highness the Sultan Sa'id bin Taimur) and the Government of Saudi Arabia, with Exchange of Notes, Jedda, July 30, 1954. London: Her Majesty's Stationery Office (HMSO), 1954.

Great Britain. Central Office of Information, Reference Division. *Memorial of the Government of Sa'udi Arabia. Arbitration for the Settlement of the Territorial Dispute Between Muscat and Abu Dhabi on One Side and Sa'udi Arabia on the Other.* 3 vols. London: HMSO, 1955.

Great Britain. Central Office of Information, Reference Division. *Memorial of the Government of the United Kingdom of Great Britain and Northern Ireland in Arbitration Concerning Buraimi and the Common Frontier between Abu Dhabi and Saudi Arabia.* 2 vols. London: HMSO, 1955.

Great Britain. Central Office of Information, Reference Division. *Exchange of Notes Concerning the Termination of Special Treaty Relations between the United Kingdom of Great Britain and Northern Ireland and the State of Bahrain and Its Dependencies.* Treaty Series no. 4 (1971), Cmnd. 4827. London: HMSO, 1971.

Great Britain. Central Office of Information, Reference Division. *Treaty of Friendship between the United Kingdom of Great Britain and Northern Ireland and the State of Bahrain and Its Dependencies.* Treaty Series no. 79 (1971), Cmnd. 4828. London: HMSO, 1971.

Great Britain. Central Office of Information, Reference Division. *Exchange of Notes Concerning the Termination of Special Treaty Relations between the United Kingdom of Great Britain and Northern Ireland and the State of Qatar.* Treaty Series no. 4 (1972), Cmnd. 4850. London: HMSO, 1972.

Great Britain. Central Office of Information, Reference Division. *Exchange of Notes Concerning the Termination of Special Treaty Relations between the United Kingdom and the Trucial States.* Treaty Series no. 34 (1972), Cmnd. 4941. London: HMSO, 1972.

Great Britain. Central Office of Information, Reference Division. *Treaty of Friendship between the United Kingdom of Great Britain and Northern Ireland and the State of Qatar*. Treaty Series no. 4 (1972), Cmnd. 4850. London: HMSO, 1972.

Kuwait Ministry of Information. *Annual Statistical Abstract of Kuwait*. Kuwait.

Al-Oteiba, Mana Saeed, ed. *The Petroleum Concession Agreements of the United Arab Emirates: Abu Dhabi 1939-1981*. 2 vols. London: Croom Helm, 1982.

Pearson, J. "Documentation on Oman." *Journal of Oman Studies* 6, no. 1 (1983).

Porter, J. D., ed. *Oman and the Persian Gulf*. Salisbury, N.C.: Documentary Publications, 1982.

Qatar Ministry of Information. *Annual Statistical Abstract of Qatar*. Doha, Qatar.

Rush, A. de L., ed. *Ruling Families of Arabia: Documentary Records of the Dynasties*. 12 vols. London: Archive Editions, 1991. Presents facsimiles of British documents relating to the ruling families of the Gulf states.

Schofield, Richard, ed. *Islands and Maritime Boundaries of the Gulf, 1798-1960*. 20 vols. London: Archive Editions, 1991. A collection of documents including facsimiles of treaties, reports, letters, and other documents from British archives.

United Arab Emirates. "The Provisional Constitution of the United Arab Amirates." *Middle East Journal* 26, no. 3 (1972).

US Congress. Congressional Budget Office. U.S. *Projection Forces: Requirements, Scenarios and Options*. Washington, D.C.: USGPO, 1978.

U.S. Congress. House. Cmte. on Armed Services. Hearings. U.S. *Military Forces to Protect "Reflagged" Kuwaiti Oil Tankers.* Washington, D.C.: USGPO, 1987.

U.S. Congress. House. Cmte. on Armed Services. Report of the Defense Policy Panel and the Investigative Subcommittee. *National Security Policy Implications of United States Operations in the Persian Gulf.* Washington, D.C.: USGPO, 1987.

U.S. Congress. House. Cmte. on Armed Services. Hearings. *Crisis in the Persian Gulf: Sanctions, Diplomacy and War.* December 4-20, 1990. Washington, D.C.: USGPO, 1991.

U.S. Congress. House. Cmte. on Banking, Finance, and Urban Affairs. Hearings. E*conomic Impact of the Persian Gulf Crisis.* November 27-28, 1990. Washington, D.C.: USGPO, 1991.

U.S. Congress. House. Cmte. on the Budget. Hearings. *Military Readiness and the Rapid Deployment Joint Task Force.* Washington, D.C.: USGPO, 1980.

U.S. Congress. House. Cmte. on the Budget. Hearing. *Briefing on Operation Desert Shield: Costs and Contributions.* January 4, 1991. Washington, D.C.: USGPO, 1991.

U.S. Congress. House. Cmte. on the Budget. Hearing. *Update on the Costs of Desert Shield/Desert Storm.* May 15, 1991. Washington, D.C.: USGPO, 1991.

U.S. Congress. House. Cmte. on Foreign Affairs. Hearings. U.S. *Interests in and Policy toward the Persian Gulf.* Washington, D.C.: USGPO, 1972.

U.S. Congress. House. Cmte. on Foreign Affairs. Hearings. *New Perspectives on the Persian Gulf.* Washington, D.C.: USGPO, 1973.

U.S. Congress. House. Cmte. on Foreign Affairs. Hearings. U.S. *Interests in, and Policies Toward, the Persian Gulf.* Washington, D.C.: USGPO, 1980.

U.S. Congress. House. Cmte. on Foreign Affairs. Report of a Staff Study Mission to the Persian Gulf, Middle East, and Horn of Africa. U.S. *Security Interests in the Persian Gulf.* Oct. 21-Nov. 13, 1980. Washington, D.C.: USGPO, 1981.

U.S. Congress. House. Cmte. on Foreign Affairs. Report. *The United States and the Persian Gulf.* Washington, D.C.: USGPO, 1982.

U.S. Congress. House. Cmte. on Foreign Affairs and Joint Economic Committee. Hearings. U.S. *Policy Toward the Persian Gulf.* Washington, D.C.: USGPO, 1983.

U.S. Congress. House. Cmte. on Foreign Affairs. Hearing. *The Middle East in the 1990s.* April 4-July 17, 1990. Washington, D.C.: USGPO, 1991.

U.S. Congress. House. Cmte. on Foreign Affairs. Hearings. *Update on the Situation in the Persian Gulf.* September 2-December 6, 1990. Washington, D.C.: USGPO, 1991.

U.S. Congress. House. Cmte. on Foreign Affairs. Hearing. *Human Rights Abuses in Kuwait and Iraq.* January 8, 1991. Washington, D.C.: USGPO, 1991.

U.S. Congress. House. Cmte. on Foreign Affairs. Hearings. *Post-War Policy Issues in the Persian Gulf.* January 31-April 11, 1991. Washington, D.C.: USGPO, 1991.

U.S. Congress. House. Cmte. on Foreign Affairs. Report. *The Persian Gulf Crisis: Relevant Documents, Correspondence, Reports.* Washington, D.C.: USGPO, 1991.

U.S. Congress. House. Cmte. on International Relations. Report. *Oil Fields as Military Objectives: A Feasibility Study.* Washington, D.C.: USGPO, 1975.

U.S. Congress. House. Cmte. on International Relations. Hearings. *The Persian Gulf 1975: The Continuing Debate on Arms Sales.* Washington, D.C.: USGPO, 1976.

U.S. Congress. House. Cmte. on International Relations. Report of a Staff Survey Mission to Ethiopia, Iran, and the Arabian Peninsula. *United States Arms Policies in the Persian Gulf and Red Sea Areas: Past, Present and Future.* Washington, D.C.: USGPO, 1976.

U.S. Congress. Joint Economic Cmte., with the Congressional Research Service, Library of Congress. *The Persian Gulf: Are We Committed? At What Cost? A Dialogue with the Reagan Administration on U.S. Policy.* Washington, D.C. USGPO, 1981.

U.S. Congress. House. Joint Economic Cmte. and Cmte. on Foreign Affairs. Joint Hearings. *The Persian Gulf Crisis.* August 8-December 11, 1990. Washington, D.C.: USGPO, 1991.

U.S. Congress. Joint Economic Cmte. and Congressional Research Service, Library of Congress. Joint Hearings. *Postwar Economic Recovery in the Persian Gulf.* Proceedings of a workshop, March 28, 1991. Washington, D.C.: USGPO, 1991.

U.S. Congress. Senate. Cmte. on Appropriations. Hearings. *Preparedness for the Persian Gulf.* Washington, D.C.: USGPO, 1991.

U.S. Congress. Senate. Cmte. on Foreign Relations. Report. *United States Arms Sales to the Persian Gulf: Report of a Study Mission to Iran, Kuwait, and Saudi Arabia.* Washington, D.C.: USGPO, 1976.

U.S. Congress. Senate. Cmte. on Foreign Relations. Hearings. *Persian Gulf Situation.* September 17, 1981. Washington, D.C.: USGPO, 1981.

U.S. Congress. Senate. Cmte. on Foreign Relations. Report. *War in the Gulf.* Washington, D.C.: USGPO, 1984.

U.S. Congress. Senate. Cmte. on Foreign Relations. Report. *War in the Persian Gulf, the U.S. Takes Sides.* Washington, D.C.: USGPO, 1987.

U.S. Congress. Senate. Cmte. on Foreign Relations. Hearing. *Persian Gulf: The Question of War Crimes.* April 9, 1991. Washington, D.C.: USGPO, 1991.

U.S. Department of Commerce. *Foreign Economic Trends.* Irregular. Washington, D.C.: USGPO.

U.S. Department of Defense. *Conduct of the Persian Gulf War: Final Report to Congress.* Washington, D.C.: USGPO, 1992.

U.S. Department of State. *Background Notes.* Irregular. Washington, D.C.: USGPO. The most recent *Background Notes* issued on Gulf Arab states are those on Kuwait, November 1994, and Qatar, April 1991.

U.S. Department of State. *Foreign Relations of the United States, 1955-1957*, vol. 13, *Near East: Jordan-Yemen.* Washington, D.C.: USGPO, 1988. Contains documents dealing with Kuwait and Oman.

U.S. Department of State. *Foreign Relations of the United States, 1958-1960*, vol. 12, *Near East Region; Iran; Arabian Peninsula.* Washington, D.C.: USGPO, 1993.

U.S. Library of Congress. Congressional Research Service. *Western Vulnerability to a Disruption of Persian Gulf Oil Supplies: U.S. Interests and Options.* Washington, D.C.: USGPO, 1983.

3. PERIODICALS

Al-Arabi (*The Arab*). Monthly. Kuwait: Ministry of Information.

Asian Affairs (formerly *Journal of the Royal Central Asian Society*). Three times yearly. London: Royal Society for Asian Affairs.

Al-Dara (The Circle). Quarterly. Riyadh, Saudi Arabia: King Abdul Aziz University Research Center.

Foreign Affairs. Five times yearly. New York: Council on Foreign Relations.

Foreign Policy. Quarterly. Washington, D.C.: Carnegie Endowment for International Peace.

International Journal of Islamic and Arabic Studies. Semiannually.: Bloomington, Indiana: International Institute of Islamic and Arabic Studies.

International Journal of Middle East Studies. Quarterly. New York: Cambridge University Press. Covers seventh century to the present.

Al-Majalla (The Journal). Weekly. London: H. H. Saudi Research and Marketing, Ltd. "The International News Magazine of the Arabs."

Majallat Dirasat al-Khalij wa al-Jazira al-Arabiyya (Journal of Gulf and Arabian Peninsula Studies). Quarterly. Kuwait: Academic Publication Council, Kuwait University. With synopses of articles provided in English.

Majallat al-Ulum al-Ijtima'iyya (Journal of the Social Sciences). Quarterly. Kuwait: University of Kuwait. With synopses of articles provided in English.

The Middle East. Monthly. London: IC Publications Ltd. Covering contemporary Middle East events.

Middle East and Africa Economic Outlook. Quarterly. Bala Cynwyd, Pa.: WEFA Group.

Middle East Insight. Bimonthly. Washington, D.C.: International Insight, Inc.

Middle East International. Biweekly (25 issues a year). London and Washington, D.C.: Middle East International Ltd.

The Middle East Journal. Quarterly. Washington, D.C.: Middle East Institute. With chronology, book reviews, review of periodical literature.

Middle East Policy (formerly *American-Arab Affairs*). Quarterly. Washington, D.C.: Middle East Policy Council.

Middle East Studies Association Bulletin. Semiannually. Middle East Studies Association. Tucson: University of Arizona.

Pakistan and Gulf Economist. Karachi, Pakistan.

Revista de Africa y Medio Oriente. Semiannually. Miramar, Spain: Centro de Estudios Sobre Africa y Medio Oriente.

Sourakia. Arabic title conflating the names "Syria" and "Iraq". Weekly. Cardiff, U.K.: Sourakia Limited.

The Washington Report on Middle East Affairs. Monthly. Washington, D.C.: American Educational Trust. U.S. relations with Middle Eastern states.

Al-Watan al-Arabi (The Arab Nation). Weekly. Paris: Societé d'Edition de la Presse Spécialisée. Current issues in the Arab world.

Al Watheekah (The Document). Twice yearly. Manama, Bahrain: The Historical Documents Center. Current and historical issues covered. Some articles are published in English as well as Arabic.

World Today. Quarterly. London: Royal Institute of International Affairs.

4. GENERAL REFERENCES

Adams, Michael, ed. *The Middle East.* Handbooks to the Modern World Series. New York: Facts on File, 1988.

Anthony, John Duke, with J. E. Peterson and Donald Abelson. *Historical and Cultural Dictionary of the Sultanate of Oman and the Emirates of Eastern Arabia.* Metuchen, N.J.: Scarecrow Press, 1976.

The APS Who's Who in Middle East Banking & Trade. 3rd ed. Vol. 1, *The Banks and the Bankers.* Vol. 2, *The Trade Companies and the Traders.* Nicosia, Cyprus: APS (Press and Enterprises) Ltd. , 1985.

Bricault, Giselle C., ed. *Major Companies of the Arab World, 1990-91.* London; Dordrecht; Boston: Graham and Trotman, 1990.

Diller, Daniel, ed. *The Middle East.* 7th ed. Washington, DC: Congressional Quarterly Inc., 1991.

Encyclopedia of Islam. 2nd ed. Leiden: E. J. Brill, from 1960. Entries are now complete through the letter "M."

The Europa World Year Book. Annually. London: Europa Publications Ltd.

Glassé, Cyril. *The Concise Encyclopedia of Islam.* San Francisco: Harper, 1991.

Kalbeel, Soraya. *Source Book on the Arabian Gulf States: Arabian Gulf in General, Kuwait, Bahrain, Qatar, and Oman.* Kuwait: Kuwait University Press, 1975.

Lemarchand, Philippe. *The Arab World, the Gulf, and the Middle East: An Atlas.* Boulder, Colo: Westview Press, 1992.

Lorimer, J. G. *Gazetteer of the Persian Gulf, Oman, and Central Arabia.* 4 vols. Calcutta: Superintendent of Government Printing, 1915. Issued originally as a secret document for official use.

Republished, 9 vols. Neuchâtel, Switzerland: Archive International Group, 1991.

The Middle East and North Africa. Annually. London: Europa Publications.

The Middle East Review, 18th ed. Essex, UK: World of Information, 1991.

Mostyn, Trevor. *Major Political Events in Iran, Iraq and the Arabian Peninsula, 1945-1990.* New York: Facts on File, 1991.

Mostyn, Trevor, and Albert Hourani, eds. *The Cambridge Encyclopedia of the Middle East and North Africa.* New York: Cambridge University Press, 1988.

Paxton, John, ed. *The Statesman's Year-Book.* Annually. New York: St. Martin's Press.

Rabinovich, Itamar and Haim Shaked, eds. *Middle East Contemporary Survey.* Annually. Boulder, Col. and London: Westview Press.

Serjeant, R. B., and R. L. Bidwell. *Arabian Studies.* Cambridge: University of Cambridge Oriental Publications, vol. 42. 1990.

Summers, Harry G. *Persian Gulf War Almanac.* New York: Facts on File, 1995.

Walden, Saffron. *Gulf Guide and Diary, 1984.* London: World of Information, 1983.

Ziring, Lawrence. *The Middle East Political Dictionary.* Santa Barbara, Calif.: ABC-Clio Information Services, 1984.

5. BIOGRAPHIES

Arabian Personalities of the Early Twentieth Century. New York: Oleander Press Ltd., 1986. Reprint of 1917 British Intelligence sourcebook with introduction by Robin Bidwell. Chapter 5, "Gulf Coast."

Belgrave, Charles Dalrymple. *Personal Column.* London: Hutchinson, 1960.

Bidwell, Robin, ed. *Travellers in Arabia.* London: Hamlyn Publishing Group, 1976.

Crystal, Jill. "Abdallah Al-Salim Al Sabah." In *Political Leaders of the Contemporary Middle East and North Africa,* edited by Bernard Reich. New York: Greenwood Press, 1990.

————. "Jabir Al-Ahmad." In *Political Leaders,* Reich.

Dorr, Steven R. "Khalifah ibn Hamad Al Thani." In *Political Leaders,* Reich.

Field, Michael. "Maktoum Family: Anxieties over Succession Ease." *Financial Times* (London), November 30, 1983.

————. "Nahayyan Family: Further United by Marriage." *Financial Times* (London), November 30, 1983.

————. "Al Sabah Family Tree." *Financial Times* (London), February 22, 1984.

Khadduri, Majid. *Arab Personalities in Politics.* Washington, D.C.: Middle East Institute, 1981. (Includes a chapter on Shaikh Zayid, president of the United Arab Emirates.)

Lawson, Fred H. "Isa bin Sulman Al Khalifah." In *Political Leaders,* Reich.

Peck, Malcolm C. "Rashid bin Said Al Maktum." In *Political Leaders,* Reich.

————. "Zayed bin Sultan Al Nuhayyan." In *Political Leaders,* Reich.

Peterson, J.E. "Qabus bin Said." In *Political Leaders,* Reich.

———. "Said bin Taymur." In *Political Leaders,* Reich.

Rush, Alan. *Al Sabah: History and Genealogy of Kuwait's Ruling Family: 1752-1987.* London: Ithaca Press, 1987.

Tammam, Hamdi. *Zayed bin Sultan Al Nahayyan: The Leader and the March.* Abu Dhabi/Tokyo: Dai Nippon Printing Co., 1981.

Wheatcroft, Andrew. *The Life and Times of Shaikh Salman bin Hamad al-Khalifa, Ruler of Bahrain, 1942-1961.* New York: Columbia University Press, 1995.

6. COUNTRY AND REGIONAL SURVEYS

Abu Nab, Ibrahim. *Qatar: A Story of State Building.* Qatar, Doha: 1977.

Akins, James E. "The New Arabia." *Foreign Affairs* 70, no. 3 (1991).

Allen, Calvin H., Jr. "Oman: A Separate Place." *Wilson Quarterly.* Washington, D.C.: Smithsonian Institution, New Year's Edition, 1987.

———. *Oman: The Modernization of the Sultanate.* Boulder, Colo.: Westview Press, 1987.

Anthony, John Duke. *Arab States of the Lower Gulf: People, Politics, Petroleum.* Washington, D.C.: Middle East Institute, 1975.

Ayalon, Ami, ed. *Middle East Contemporary Survey* vol. 9. Boulder, Colo.: Westview Press, 1991. For the Moshe Dayan Center for Middle Eastern and African Studies, Tel Aviv University. Provides extensive coverage of the Iraqi invasion of Kuwait.

"Bahrain: Recent Developments." *Arab Law Quarterly* 9, nos. 1 and 2 (1994).

Bailey, Gerry, ed. *The Economist Business Travellers' Guides: Arabian Peninsula*. New York: Prentice Hall, 1987.

Barger, Thomas C. *Arab States of the Persian Gulf*. Newark, Delaware: University of Delaware Press, 1975.

Bonnenfant, Paul, et al. *L'Arabie: Arabie Saoudite, Emirats du Golfe, Yémen*. Paris: Librairie Larousse, Collection Monde et Voyages, 1986.

Bonnenfant, Paul, et al., eds. *La péninsule Arabique d'aujourd'hui*. 2 vols. Paris: Editions du Centre National de la Recherche Scientifique, 1982.

Bulloch, John. *The Gulf: A Portrait of Kuwait, Qatar, Bahrain and the UAE*. London: Century Publishing, 1984. Published in the U.S. as *The Persian Gulf Unveiled*. New York: Congdon and Weed, 1984.

Clements, F. A. *Oman: The Reborn Land*. London: Longman, 1980.

Cottrell, Alvin J., ed. *The Persian Gulf States: A General Survey*. Baltimore: The Johns Hopkins University Press, 1980.

Crystal, Jill. "Kuwait." In *World Encyclopedia of Political Systems and Parties*, edited by George Delary. New York: Facts on File, 1983.

———. *Kuwait: The Transformation of an Oil State*. Boulder, Colo.: Westview Press, 1992.

Daniels, John. *Abu Dhabi: A Portrait*. London: Longman, 1974.

Deakin, Michael. *Ras Al-Khaimah: Flame in the Desert*. London: Namara, 1976.

Dickson, H. R. P. *Kuwait and Her Neighbors*. London: Allen and Unwin, 1956.

Dickson, Violet. *Forty Years in Kuwait*. London: Allen and Unwin, 1971.

Al-Ebraheem, Hassan Ali. *Kuwait and the Gulf: Small States and the International System.* London: Croom Helm in association with the Center for Contemporary Arab Studies of Georgetown University. Washington, D.C.: Georgetown University, 1984.

Freeth, Zahra, and Victor Winstone. *Kuwait: Prospect and Reality.* London: Allen and Unwin, 1972.

Fullerton, M. "Oman: A Proud Past, Daring Present, and Tentative Future." *International Insight* 1, no. 6 (1981).

Graham, Helga. *Arabian Time Machine: Self-Portrait of an Oil State.* London: Heinemann, 1980.

Graz, Liesl. *The Omanis: Sentinels of the Gulf.* London: Longman, 1982.

————. *The Turbulent Gulf: People, Politics and Power.* New York: I. B. Tauris,1992.

Hawley, Donald. *Oman and Its Renaissance.* 4th rev. ed. Atlantic Heights, N.J.: Humanities Press, 1987.

Heard-Bey, Frauke. *From Trucial States to United Arab Emirates: A Society in Transition.* London: Longman, 1982.

Ishow, Habib. *Le Koweit: Evolution politique, économique, et sociale.* Paris: Editions l'Harmattan, 1989.

Kay, Shirley. *Bahrain: Island Heritage.* Dubai: Motivate Publishing, 1989.

Kaylani, Nabil M. "Politics and Religion in Oman: A Historical Overview." *International Journal of Middle East Studies* [Hereinafter cited as *IJMES*] 10, no. 4 (1979).

Kergan, J. L. "Social and Economic Changes in the Gulf Countries." *Asian Affairs* (London) 62, n.s., no. 6, pt. 3 (1975).

Key, Kerim. *The Arabian Gulf States Today.* Washington, D.C.: Asia Research Center, 1974.

Khalifa, Ali Mohammed. *The United Arab Emirates: Unity in Fragmentation.* Boulder, Colo.: Westview Press, 1979.

Koury, Enver. *The United Arab Emirates: Its Political System and Politics.* Hyattsville, Md.: Institute of Middle Eastern and North African Affairs, 1980.

"Kuwait: An International Perspective." *Arabia: Islamic World Review* 11 (July 1982).

Kuwait Ministry of Information. *Gulf Cooperation Council: Towards New Horizons.* 1984.

Landen, Robert G. "Gulf States." In *The Middle East: Its Governments and Politics,* edited by Abid Al-Marayati, et al. Belmont, Calif.: Duxbury Press, 1972.

————. *Oman since 1856: Disruptive Modernization in a Traditional Arab Society.* Princeton, N.J.: Princeton University Press, 1967.

Lawson, Fred H. *Bahrain: The Modernization of Autocracy.* Boulder, Colo.: Westview Press, 1989.

Mansfield, Peter. *Kuwait: Vanguard of the Gulf.* London: Hutchinson, 1990.

————. *The New Arabians.* Chicago: Ferguson, 1981.

MERI Report: United Arab Emirates. London: Croom Helm for the Middle East Research Institutes, University of Pennsylvania, 1985.

Metz, Helen Chapin, ed. *Persian Gulf States: Country Studies.* Washington, D.C.: Federal Research Division, Library of Congress, 1994.

Moorehead, John. *In Defiance of the Elements.* London: Quartet Books, 1977. (Study of Qatar.)

Morris, James. *Sultan in Oman: Venture into the Middle East.* New York: Pantheon, 1957.

Mostyn, Trevor, ed. *UAE: A MEED Practical Guide.* London: Middle East Economic Digest, 1982.

Nugent, Jeffrey B., and Theodore Thomas, eds. *Bahrain and the Gulf: Past Perspectives and Alternative Futures.* New York: St. Martin's Press, 1985.

"Oman: A New Dawn." *Aramco World Magazine* 34, no. 3 (May 1983).

"Oman: Recent Developments." *Arab Law Quarterly* 9, nos. 1 and 2 (1994).

Oman, Yemen: Country Profile, 1991-92. Annual Survey of Political and Economic Background. London: Business International, 1991.

O'Shea, Raymond. *The Sand Kings of Oman.* London: Methuen, 1947.

Peck, Malcolm C. "Eastern Arabian States: Kuwait, Bahrain, Qatar, United Arab Emirates, and Oman." In *The Government and Politics of the Middle East and North Africa*, edited by Bernard Reich and David E. Long. Boulder, Colo.: Westview Press, 1995.

———. *The United Arab Emirates: A Venture in Unity.* Boulder, Colo.: Westview Press, 1986.

Peterson, Erik R. *The Gulf Cooperation Council: Search for Unity in a Dynamic Region.* Boulder, Colo., and London: Westview Press, 1988.

Peterson, J. E. *Oman in the Twentieth Century: Political Foundations of an Emerging State.* New York: Barnes and Noble, 1978.

Pridham, B. R., ed. *Oman: Economic, Social and Strategic Developments.* London: Croom Helm, 1987.

"Profile: United Arab Emirates." *Arab Perspectives* 3 (January 1983).

Purser, B. H., ed. *The Persian Gulf.* New York: Springer-Verlag, 1973.

Qatina, R. "Kuwait: An Analytical Study." (In Arabic.) *Al-Watheekah* (*The Document*) 1, no. 1 (1982).

Ramazani, R. K., with the assistance of Joseph A. Kechichian. *The Gulf Cooperation Council: Record and Analysis.* Charlottesville, Va.: University Press of Virginia, 1988.

Rentz, George. "A Sultanate Asunder." *Natural History* 83, no. 3 (1974).

Rentz, George, and William E. Mulligan. "Al-Bahrayn." *Encyclopedia of Islam.* 2nd ed. Leiden: E. J. Brill, 1960.

Riemersma, R. "Oman: Arabia Felix Bestat." *International Spectator* 45, no. 4 (1991).

Sadik, Muhammad T., and William P. Snaveley. *Bahrain, Qatar, and the United Arab Emirates: Colonial Past, Present Problems, and Future Prospects.* Lexington, Mass.: Lexington Books, 1972.

Sandwick, John A., ed. *The Gulf Cooperation Council.* Boulder, Colo., and Washington, D.C.: Westview Press and the American-Arab Affairs Council, 1987.

Sapsted, David. *Modern Kuwait.* London: Macmillan, 1980.

Skeet, Ian. *Oman: Politics and Development.* New York: St. Martin's Press, 1992.

Stookey, Robert W. *The Arabian Peninsula: Zone of Ferment.* Stanford, Calif.: Hoover Institution Press, 1984.

Taryam, A. O. *The Establishment of the United Arab Emirates, 1950-85*. London: Croom Helm, 1987.

Tomkinson, Michael. *The United Arab Emirates: An Insight and a Guide*. London: Michael Tomkinson Publishing, 1975.

Townsend, John. *Oman: The Making of a Modern State*. New York: St. Martin's Press, 1977.

"UAE: Recent Developments." *Arab Law Quarterly* 9, no. 2 (1994).

Vine, Peter. *Pearls in Arabian Waters: The Heritage of Bahrain*. London: IMMEL Publishing, 1986.

Vizzi, R. "Emiratos Arabes Unidos: El Pequeño Gigante." *Medio Oriente Informa*, vol. 30 (December 1981 -- January 1982).

Wakefield, M., ed. *UAE: A MEED Practical Guide* 2nd ed. London: Middle East Economic Digest, 1986.

Webman, Esther. "The Gulf States." In *Middle East Contemporary Survey, 1980-81, edited by Colin Legum*. New York: Holmes and Meier, 1982.

Whelan, John, ed. *Bahrain: A MEED Practical Guide*. London: Middle East Economic Digest, 1983.

———. *Kuwait: A MEED Practical Guide*. London: Middle East Economic Digest, 1986.

———. *Oman: A MEED Practical Guide*, 2nd ed. London: Middle East Economic Digest, 1984

——— *Qatar: A MEED Practical Guide*. London: Middle East Economic Digest, 1983..

Whelan, John, and S. Otaqi, eds. "Kuwait and the Middle East." *Middle East Economic Digest*, Special Report, May 1982.

Wilkinson, John. *The Imamate Tradition of Oman.* New York: Cambridge University Press, 1987.

Zahlan, Rosemarie Said. *The Creation of Qatar.* New York: Barnes and Noble, 1979.

―――. *The Making of the Modern Gulf States: Kuwait, Bahrain, Qatar, the United Arab Emirates and Oman.* London: Unwin Hyman, 1989.

7. HISTORY

Abadi, Jacob. *Britain's Withdrawal from the Middle East, 1947-71: The Economic and Strategic Imperatives.* Princeton, N.J.: Kingston Press, 1982.

Abdullah, M. "Muhammad Ali in the Arabian Peninsula and His Relations with the Arabian Gulf." (In Arabic.) *Al-Watheekah*, no. 16 (1990).

Abdullah, Muhammad Morsy. *The United Arab Emirates: A Modern History.* London: Croom Helm; New York: Barnes and Noble, 1978.

Al-Abid, S. "The Omani-Portuguese Conflict During the 17th Century." (In Arabic.) *Al-Watheekah*, no. 13 (1988).

Abu Hakima, Ahmed Mustafa. *History of Eastern Arabia, 1750-1800: The Rise and Development of Bahrain and Kuwait.* Beirut: Catholic Press, 1965.

―――. "Kuwait and the Eastern Arabian Protectorates." In *Governments and Politics of the Contemporary Middle East,* edited by Tareq Y. Ismael, et al. Homewood, Ill.: Dorsey Press, 1970.

―――. *The Modern History of Kuwait.* London: Luzac, 1983.

Abu Husayn, A. "Historical Links between Bahrain and Saudi Arabia during the Reign of King Abd al-Aziz." (In Arabic.) *Al-Watheekah*, no. 16 (1990).

Allen, Calvin, H. "The State of Masqat in the Gulf and East Africa, 1785-1829." *IJMES* 14, no. 2 (May 1982).

Al-Anani, A. "Shaikh Qasim bin Muhammad Al Thani and Problems of Domestic Leadership in the Arab Gulf during the 19th Century." (In Arabic.) *Al-Khalij al-Arabi* (*The Arab Gulf*) 13, no. 2 (1981).

Belgrave, Charles Dalrymple. *The Pirate Coast*. London: Bell and Sons, 1966.

Bhacker, M. Reda. *Trade and Empire in Muscat and Zanzibar*. London: Routledge and Kegan Paul, 1992.

Bibby, Geoffrey. *Looking for Dilmun*. New York: Knopf, 1970.

Boxer, C. "New Light on the Relations between the Portuguese and the Omanis, 1613-1633." *Journal of Oman Studies* 6, no. 1 (1983).

Bulliet, Richard W. *The Camel and the Wheel*. Cambridge: Harvard University Press, 1975.

Clark, A. "Bahrain Through the Ages." *Aramco World* 35, no. 4 (1984).

Cole, D., and S. Al-Torki. "Was Arabia Tribal? A Reinterpretation of the pre-Oil Society." *Journal of South Asian and Middle Eastern Studies (JSAMES)* 15, no. 4 (1992).

D'Enrico, E. "Introduction to Omani Military Architecture of the Sixteenth, Seventeenth, and Eighteenth Centuries." *Journal of Oman Studies* 6, no. 2 (1983).

Dessouki, Assam. "Social and Political Dimensions of the Historiography of the Arab Gulf." In *Statecraft in the Middle East:*

Oil, Historical Memory, and Popular Culture, edited by Eric Davis and Nicolas Gavrielides. Miami: Florida International University Press, 1991.

Fahd, Toufic, ed. *L'Arabie préislamique et son environnement historique et culturel.* Actes du colloque de Strasbourg, 24-27 juin 1987. Leiden: E. J. Brill, 1989.

Al-Hasheimy, R. "A Study of Archeological and Historical Sources in the Arabian Gulf." (In Arabic.) *Majalla Dirasat al-Khalij wa'l Jazira al-Arabiyya (Journal of Gulf and Arabian Peninsula Studies).* [Hereinafter cited as *JGAPS*] 7, no. 28 (1981).

Hassan, A. "The Arabian Commercial Background in Pre-Islamic Times." *Islamic Culture* 71, no. 2 (1987).

Hawley, Donald. "Some Surprising Aspects of Oman's History." *Asian Affairs* (London) 13, n.s., pt. 1 (1982).

Henderson, Edward. *This Strange Eventful History: History of Earlier Days in the UAE and Oman.* London and New York: Quartet Books, 1988.

Hourani, George. *Arab Seafaring.* Beirut: Khayats, 1963.

Hussain, A. "Pages from the History of Bahrain through Ottoman Documents." (In Arabic.) *Al-Watheekah*, no. 15 (1989).

Hussein, R. "The Early Arabian Trade and Marketing." *Islam and the Modern Age* 18, nos. 2-3 (1987).

Joyce, Miriam. "Preserving the Shaikhdom: London, Washington, Iraq and Kuwait, 1958-61." *Middle East Studies* 31, no. 2 (1995).

———. "Washington and Treaty-Making with the Sultan of Muscat and Oman." *Middle East Studies* 30, no. 1 (1994).

Jun-Yan, Z. "Relations between China and the Arabs in Early Times." *Journal of Oman Studies* 6, no. 1 (1983).

Karfan, M., and A. Khaldun. "Qal'at al-Bahrain Excavations Shed New Light on the Country's Heritage." (In Arabic.) *Al-Watheekah*, no. 2 (1983).

Kay, Shirley. *Emirates Archaeological Heritage.* Dubai: Motivate Publishing, 1986.

Kelly, J. B. *Britain and the Persian Gulf, 1795-1880.* Oxford, U.K.: Clarendon Press, 1978.

———. *Eastern Arabian Frontiers.* London: Faber and Faber, 1964.

Al Khalifa, Abdallah bin Khalid, and Abd al-Malik Yusif al-Hamir. *Al-Bahrain abr al-Tarikh (Bahrain through History).* Vol. 1. Bahrain: Ministry of Information, 1982.

Al Khalifa, Abdullah bin Khalid, and Michael Rice, eds. *Bahrain Through the Ages: The History,* 2nd ed. London: KPI, 1993.

Khuri, I. "Expansion of the Ottoman State in the Arabian Gulf." (In Arabic.) *Al-Watheekah*, no. 15 (1989).

Al-Khususi, B. "The USA's Concern with Arabian Gulf Oil between the Two World Wars." (In Arabic.) *JGAPS* 8, no. 31 (July 1982).

Kirkman, J. "The Early History of Oman in East Africa." *Journal of Oman Studies,* 6, no. 1 (1983).

Larsen, Curtis E. *Life and Land Use on the Bahrain Islands: The Geoarchaeology of an Ancient Society.* Chicago: University of Chicago Press, 1983.

Lawless, R. L., ed. *The Gulf in the Early 20th Century: Foreign Institutions and Local Responses.* Durham, U.K.: University of Durham, 1986.

Leemans, W. F. *Foreign Trade in the Old Babylonian Period.* Leiden: E. J. Brill, 1959.

Malone, Joseph J. "America and the Arabian Peninsula: The First Two Hundred Years." *Middle East Journal* 30, no. 3 (1976).

Al-Missiri, H. "Bahrain and Oman in the Rashidun Era." (In Arabic.) *JGAPS*, no. 54 (1988).

Mohammed, D. "Arms in the Muscat of Long Ago." (In Arabic). *Al-Daarah (The Circle)* 2, no. 7 (1981).

Monroe, Elizabeth. *Britain's Moment in the Middle East, 1919-1971.* Rev. ed. Baltimore: The Johns Hopkins University Press, 1981.

Naji, A. "A Comparative Study of the Conditions of the Ports of the Arabian Gulf and Peninsula in the 4th Hijri Century." (In Arabic.) *JGAPS*, no. 56 (1988).

Al-Najjar, M. "Ottoman Administration in the Arabian Gulf." (In Arabic.) *Al-Watheekah*, no. 15 (1989).

Netton, Ian Richard, ed. *Arabia and the Gulf: From Traditional Society to Modern States.* Totowa, N.J.: Barnes and Noble, 1986.

Ozbaran, S. "Bahrain in the 16th Century." (In Arabic.) *Al-Watheekah*, no. 15 (1989).

Phillips, Wendell. *Oman: A History.* New York: Revnal, 1968.

Al Qasimi, Sultan Muhammad (Ruler of Sharjah in the UAE). *The Myth of Arab Piracy in the Gulf.* London: Croom Helm, 1986.

Qatina, R. "Why the British Feared the German Railway Line to Kuwait." (In Arabic.) *Al-Watheekah* 1, no. 2 (1983).

Al-Rashid, Zamil Muhammad. *Saudi Relations with Eastern Arabia and Uman (1800-1871).* London: Luzac and Company, 1981.

Rice, Michael. *The Archaeology of the Arabian Gulf.* London: Routledge and Kegan Paul, 1994.

Rimidh, G. "The Omani-Portuguese Naval Conflict in the Eastern Seas (1650-1720)." (In Arabic.) *Al-Watheekah*, no. 13 (1988).

Al Sabah, Salem al-Jabir. *Les émirats du golfe: Histoire d'un peuple*. Paris: Fayard, 1980.

Salibi, Kamal. *A History of Arabia*. Delmar, N.Y.: Caravan Books, 1980.

Serjeant, R. "Omani Naval Activities off the Southern Arabian Coast in the Late 11th/17th Century from Yemeni Chronicles." *Journal of Oman Studies* 6, no. 1 (1983).

Al-Shatty, S. "The First Published Narrative in the Arabian Gulf." (In Arabic.) *JGAPS* 7, no. 27 (July 1981).

Skeet, Ian. *Muscat and Oman: The End of an Era*. London: Faber and Faber, 1974.

Slot, B. J. *The Origins of Kuwait*. Leiden: E. J. Brill, 1991.

Al-Tadmori, Ahmed. *Idah al-Ma'alim fi Tarikh al-Qawasim: Suqur al-Bahr al-Omani* (*An Explanation of the Landmarks in the History of the Qawasim: Falcons of the Omani Sea*). Damascus: Damascus Cooperative Press, 1976. Distributed by the Information Office of Ras al-Khaimah, UAE.

Al-Tajjar, Mahdi Abdalla. *Bahrain, 1920-1945: Britain, the Shaikh and the Administration*. London and New York: Croom Helm, 1987.

Al-Tibi, A. "Seafaring Terms and Navigational Knowledge in Ibn Jubayr's Voyage, AH 875-88." (In Arabic.) *Majalla al-Dirasat al-Tarikhiyya* (*The Journal of Historical Studies*) 4, no. 2 (1982).

Wilkinson, John C. *Arabia's Frontier: The Story of Britain's Blue and Violet Lines*. New York: St. Martin's Press, 1991.

————. *The Imamate Tradition*. Cambridge: Cambridge University Press, 1987.

————. "The Origins of the *Aflaj* of Oman." *Journal of Oman Studies* 6, no. 1 (1983).

Wilson, Arnold Talbot. *The Persian Gulf: An Historical Sketch from the Earliest Times to the Beginning of the Twentieth Century*. Oxford: Clarendon Press, 1928

Zahlan, Rosemarie Said. *The Origins of the United Arab Emirates: A Political and Social History of the Trucial States*. London: Macmillan, 1978.

8. GEOGRAPHY AND DEMOGRAPHY

Abercrombie, Thomas J. "Oman: Guardian of the Gulf." *National Geographic* 160, no. 3 (1981).

Addleton, Jonathan S. *Undermining the Center: The Gulf Migration and Pakistan*. Karachi: Oxford University Press, 1992.

Al-Athimin, A. "Observations on a Book by European Travelers in the Arabian Gulf." (In Arabic.) *Al-Daarah* (*The Circle*) 15, no. 2 (1989).

Berthoud, T., and S. Cleuziou. "Farming Communities of the Oman Peninsula and the Copper of Makkan." *Journal of Oman Studies* 6, no. 2 (1983).

Blake, G. H. and R. N. Schofield, eds. *Boundaries and State Territory in the Middle East and North Africa*. Cambridgeshire, U.K.: Middle East and North African Studies Press, 1987.

Bourgey, A. "L'Espace social des villes des émirats du Golfe." *Maghreb Machrek*, no. 123 (1989).

Brawer, Moshe, ed. *Atlas of the Middle East.* New York: Macmillan; London: Collier Macmillan, 1988.

Brundsen, Denys, et al. "The Bahrain Surface Materials Resource Survey and Its Applications to Regional Planning." *Geographical Journal* 145, no. 1 (1975).

Burki, Shahid Javed. "International Migration: Implications for Labor Exporting Countries." *Middle East Journal* 38, no. 4 (1984).

Eelens, F., T. Schampers, and J. D. Speckmann, eds. *Labour Migration to the Middle East: From Sri Lanka to the Gulf.* London: Kegan Paul International, 1992.

Eléments sur les centres-villes dans le monde arabe. Tours, France: Centre d'études et de recherches, 1988. Includes paper on Kuwait City.

Grill, N. C. *Urbanisation in the Arabian Peninsula.* Durham, U.K.: Centre for Middle Eastern and Islamic Studies, University of Durham, 1984.

Gross, Christian. *Mammals of the Southern Gulf.* Dubai: Motivate Publishing, 1987.

Al-Hafid, S. "Population Structure and Economic Development and Their Effects on Children in Bahrain." (In Arabic.) *Al-Khalij al-Arabi (The Arab Gulf)* 13, no. 1 (1981).

Harrison, D. "The Mammal Fauna of Oman with Special Reference to Conservation and the Oman Flora and Fauna Surveys." *Journal of Oman Studies* 6, no. 2 (1983).

Harrison, David L. *Mammals of the Arabian Gulf.* Winchester, Mass.: Allen and Unwin, 1981.

Hassan bin Talal (Crown Prince of Jordan). "Manpower Migration in the Middle East: An Overview." *Middle East Journal* 38, no. 4 (1984).

Held, Colbert C. *Middle East Patterns: Places, Peoples, and Politics.* 2nd ed. Boulder, Colo.: Westview Press, 1994.

Holes, C. "Towards a Dialect Geography of Oman." *Bulletin of the School of Oriental and African Studies (BSOAS)* 52, no. 3 (1989).

Al-Jaaly, A. "The Legal Framework for the Protection of the Gulf Marine Environment: Kuwait Regional Convention for Its Protection against Pollution (1978)." (In Arabic.) *JGAPS.* 7, no. 27 (1981).

Mandaville, James P., Jr. "Studies in the Flora of Arabia. XI: Some Historical and Geographical Aspects of a Principal Floristic Frontier." *Notes from the Royal Botanic Garden, Edinburgh* 42, no. 1 (1984).

Marin, M. "References to Oman in the Literature on Arabian Geography." *Journal of Oman Studies* 6, no. 1 (1983).

Miles, Samuel Barrett. *The Countries and Tribes of the Persian Gulf.* London: Cass, 1966.

Al-Musa, A. "Development and Population Distribution in Kuwait." (In Arabic.) *Al-Majalla al-Ulum al-Ijtima'iyya (Journal of the Social Sciences)* 10, no. 3 (September 1982).

Pledge, Tom. "War within a War: Fighting the Gulf Oil Spill." *Aramco World* 42, no. 3 (1991).

Rahman, Mushtaqur, ed. *Muslim World: Geography and Development.* Lanham, Md.: University Press of America, 1987. Includes a study focused on Kuwait.

Russell, Sharon Stanton, and Muhammad Ali al-Ramadhan. "Kuwait's Migration Policy since the Gulf Crisis." *IJMES* 26, no. 1 (1994).

The Scientific Results of the Royal Geographic Society's Oman Wahiba Sands Projects, 1985-1987. Muscat, Oman: Office of the Adviser for Conservation of the Environment, Diwan of the Royal Court, 1988. *Journal of Oman Studies*, Special Report no. 3.

Scoville, Sheila A., ed. *Gazetteer of Arabia: A Geographical and Tribal History of the Arabian Peninsula* Vol. 1, A-E. Graz, Austria: Akademische Druck u. Verlaganstalt, 1979.

Serageldin, Ismail, et al. *Manpower and International Labor Migration in the Middle East and North Africa.* New York: Oxford University Press, 1983.

————. "Some Issues Related to Labor Migration in the Middle East and North Africa." *The Middle East Journal* 38, no. 4 (1984).

Severin, Tim. *The Sindbad Voyage.* New York: G. P. Putnam's Sons, 1983.

Shah, N., et al. "Asian Women Workers in Kuwait." *International Migration Review* 25, no. 3 (1991).

Shah, N., and S. al-Qudsi. "The Changing Characteristics of Migrant Workers in Kuwait." *IJMES* 21, no. 1 (1989).

Al-Sharnouby, M. "Demographic Characteristics of the Labor Force in the Arab Gulf States (the Kuwaiti Model)." (In Arabic). *Nashra al-Buhuth wa'l-Dirasat al-Arabiyya (Bulletin of Arab Research and Studies)* 13-14 (1987).

Sherbiny, Naiem A. "Expatriate Labor Flows to the Arab Oil Countries in the 1980s." *Middle East Journal* 38, no. 4 (1984).

Smythe, Kathleen. *Seashells of the Arabian Gulf.* Winchester, Mass.: Allen and Unwin, 1982.

Valdani, A. "Unstable Borders in the Persian Gulf." *Iranian Journal of International Affairs (IJIA)* 5, nos. 3-4 (1993-94).

Winser, Nigel. *The Sea of Sands and Mists: Desertification— Seeking Solutions in the Wahiba Sands.* London: Century Hutchinson, 1989. Distributed by David and Charles, North Pomfret, Vt.

9. SOCIETY AND CULTURE

Allen, M. "Falconry in Arabia." *Bulletin of the School of Oriental and African Studies* 44, no. 3 (1989).

"Bank Ltd. v. Galadari and Others." *Arab Law Quarterly* 9, no. 4 (1994).

Bill, James A. "Resurgent Islam in the Persian Gulf." *Foreign Affairs* 63, no. 1 (1984).

Birks, J. S., and J. A. Rimmer. *Developing Education Systems in the Oil States of Arabia: Conflicts of Purpose and Focus.* Durham, U.K.: Centre for Middle East and Islamic Studies, University of Durham, 1984.

"Case Reports from the UAE." *Arab Law Quarterly* 9, no. 3 (1994).

Chatty, D. "The Bedouin of Central Oman: Adaptation or Fossilization?" *Journal of Oman Studies* 6, no. 1 (1983).

Codrai, Ronald. *The Seven Shaikhdoms: Life in the Trucial States before the Federation of the United Arab Emirates.* London: Stacey, 1990.

"Constitution: State of Bahrain." *Arab Law Quarterly* 10, no. 1 (1995).

Costa, P. "Notes on Settlement Patterns in Traditional Oman." *Journal of Oman Studies* 6, no. 2 (1983).

Cottrell, Alvin J. "Islam." *National Defense* 68, no. 389 (1983).

Davis, Eric, and Nicolas Gavrielides. "Statecraft, Historical Memory, and Popular Culture in Iraq and Kuwait." In *Statecraft in the*

Middle East: Oil, Historical Memory, and Popular Culture, edited by Eric Davis and Nicolas Gavrielides. Miami: Florida International University Press, 1991.

Al-Dhib, A. "The Revival of Cultural Heritage after the Reunification of the Gulf." (In Arabic.) *Al-Daarah (The Circle)* 15, no. 2 (1989).

Dickey, Christopher. *Expats: Travels in Arabia, from Tripoli to Tehran.* New York: Atlantic Monthly Press, 1990.

Dostal, Walter. "The Shihuh of Northern Oman: A Contribution to Cultural Ecology." *Geographical Journal* (London) 138, no. 1 (1972).

Al-Easa, J. "Changing Family Functions in Qatar." *JSAMES* 7, no. 1 (1983).

Eickelman, Dale P. "Omani Village: The Meaning of Oil." In *The Politics of Middle Eastern Oil,* edited by J. E Peterson. Washington, D.C.: The Middle East Institute, 1983.

———. "Religious Knowledge in Inner Oman." *Journal of Oman Studies* 6, no. 1 (1983).

Fakhru, Ali. "Gulf Interests: Man and Education." (In Arabic.) *Al-Arab (The Arab),* no. 286 (September 1982).

Al-Falah, Noura. "Power and Representation: Social Change, Gender Relations, and the Education of Women in Kuwait." In *Statecraft in the Middle East: Oil, Historical Memory, and Popular Culture,* edited by Eric Davis and Nicolas Gavrielides. Miami: Florida International University Press, 1991.

Farah, Tawfic E. "Alienation and Expatriate Labor in Kuwait." *JSAMES* 4, no. 1 (1980).

———. "Political Socialization in Kuwait: Survey Findings." *JSAMES* 6, no. 2 (1982).

Ghabra, Shafeeq N. *Palestinians in Kuwait: The Family and the Politics of Survival.* Boulder, Colo.: Westview Press, 1987.

Al-Hajri, A. "A Study in the Major Teaching Problems and Difficulties Faced by Social Studies Teachers." (In Arabic.) *JGAPS*, no. 58 (1989).

Hall, M. J., trans. *Business Laws of the United Arab Emirates*, 2 vols. London: Graham and Trotman, 1982. International Law Series.

Hamada, A. "Fundamentals of Child Education in the Arabian Gulf." (In Arabic.) *JGAPS* 7, no. 28 (1981).

Hamzeh, A. Nizar. "Qatar: The Duality of the Legal System." *Middle East Studies*, no. 30 (1994).

Hengst, H., and M. Rasheed. "The Arab Bureau of Education for the Gulf States: A Descriptive Analysis." *American Arab Affairs*, no. 29 (1989).

Hijab, Nadia. *Womanpower: The Arab Debate on Women at Work.* Cambridge and New York: Cambridge University Press, 1988.

Hijazi, Ahmad. "Kuwait: Development from a Semi-Tribal, Semi-Colonial Society to Democracy and Sovereignty." *American Journal of Comparative Law* 13, no. 3 (1964).

Hillenbrand, R. "Traditional Architecture in the Arabian Peninsula." *British Society for Middle Eastern Studies Bulletin* 16, no. 2 (1989).

Holden, David. *Farewell to Arabia.* New York: Walker and Company, 1966.

Holes, Clive. *Colloquial Arabic of the Gulf and Saudi Arabia.* New York: Routledge and Kegan Paul, 1984.

Hopwood, Derek, ed. *The Arabian Peninsula: Society and Politics.* Totowa, N.J.: Rowman and Littlefield, 1972.

Hussain, A. "Pages from the History of the Education of Girls in Bahrain between 1905 and 1961." (In Arabic). *Al-Watheekah,* no. 14 (1989).

Ibrahim, Saad Eddin. *The New Arab Social Order: A Study of the Social Impact of Oil Wealth.* Boulder, Colo.: Westview Press, 1982.

Insall, D. "The Code Languages of Oman." *Journal of Oman Studies* 6, no. 1 (1983).

Al-Isa, Shamlan Yusif, and K. al-Manufi. *Trends in Public Opinion Regarding the Gulf Cooperation Council* (In Arabic.) Kuwait: University of Kuwait, 1985.

Ismael, Jacqueline S. *Kuwait: Social Change in Historical Perspective.* Syracuse, N.Y.: Syracuse University Press, 1982.

Al-Jassani, A. "Indications of the Importance of Linking Education Curricula with Development Programs in Arab Gulf Society." (In Arabic.) *Al-Khalij al-Arabi (The Arab Gulf)* 13, no. 3 (1981).

Jayyusi, Salma Khadra, ed. *The Literature of Modern Arabia.* New York: Kegan Paul International, 1988.

Jenkins, Marilyn, ed. *Islamic Art in the Kuwait National Museum: The al-Sabah Collection.* Totowa, N.J.: Sotheby Publications, 1983.

Johnstone, T. "Folk-Tales and Folklore of Dhofar." *Journal of Oman Studies* 6, no. 1 (1983).

Khalek, N. "Development and Development Administration in the UAE." (In Arabic). *JGAPS,* no. 57 (1989).

Khuri, Fuad Ishaq. *Tribe and State in Bahrain: The Transformation of Social and Political Authority in an Arab State.* Chicago: University of Chicago Press, 1980.

Lesch, A. "Kuwait Diary: A Scarred Society." *MERIP (Middle East Research and Information Project) Middle East Report* 21, no. 5 (1991).

―――. "Palestinians in Kuwait." *Journal of Palestine Studies* 20, no. 4 (1991).

Lewicki, T. "Ibadiyya." In *The Encyclopedia of Islam* 3, edited by Bernard Lewis, et al. Leiden: E. J. Brill, 1968.

Longva, Anh Nga. "Kuwaiti Women at a Crossroads: Privileged Development and the Constraints of Ethnic Stratification." *IJMES* 25, no. 3 (1993).

Malik, Hafeez. "Islam and Women: Some Experiments in Qatar." *JSAMES* 4, no. 2 (winter 1980).

Melikian, Levon H. *Jassim: A Study in the Psychological Development of a Young Man in Qatar.* London and New York: Longman, 1981.

Melikian, L., and J. al-Easa. "The Motivation for Work among Qatari and Bahraini University Students." *Arab Gulf Journal* 1, no. 1 (1981).

―――. "Oil and Social Change in the Gulf." *Journal of Arab Affairs* 1, no. 1 (1981).

Menoufi, K. "Formation politique et organisations des valeurs dans le monde Arabe: Etude d'un cas de formation scolaire (enseignement primaire) en Egypte et au Koweit." *Bulletin du CEDEJ*, no. 23 (1988).

Mertz, Robert A. *Education and Manpower in the Arabian Gulf.* Washington, D.C.: American Friends of the Middle East, September 1972.

Al-Mughni, Haya. *Women in Kuwait: The Politics of Gender.* London: Saqi Books, 1993.

Musaiqir, A. "Folk Beliefs and Medical Treatment in Bahrain." (In Arabic.) *Al-Ma'thurat al-Sha'biyya (Folk Traditions)*, no. 9 (1988).

Musaiqir, A., and M. Sajwani. "Folk Medicine in the United Arab Emirates." (In Arabic.) *Al-Ma'thurat al-Sha'biyya* no. 14 (1989).

Al-Najjar, Muhammad Rajab. "Contemporary Trends in the Study of Folklore in the Arab States." In *Statecraft in the Middle East: Oil, Historical Memory, and Popular* Culture, edited by Eric Davis and Nicolas Gavrielides. Miami: Florida International University Press, 1991.

Al-Naqeeb, Khaldoun Hassan,. *Society and State in the Gulf and the Arab Peninsula: A Different Perspective,* translated by L. M. Kenny. London and New York: Routledge and Kegan Paul; Beirut: Center for Arab Unity Studies, 1990.

Nath, Kamla. "Education and Employment among Kuwaiti Women." In *Women in the Muslim World,* edited by Lois Beck and Nikki Keddie. Cambridge: Harvard University Press, 1978.

"Oman: The Patent Law." *Arab Law Quarterly* 9, no. 2 (1994).

Omar, F. "The Islamization of the Gulf." In *The Islamic World from Classical to Modern Times: Essays in Honor of Bernard Lewis,* edited by C. E. Bosworth, et al. Princeton, N.J.: Darwin Press, 1988.

Powell, T. "The Expanding Role of Social Work in Kuwait." *Journal of Social Sciences* 2 (1982).

Qayed, H. "Press and Authorities in the Arab World: The Case of Kuwait." *Arab Affairs*, no. 9 (1989).

Raban, Jonathan. *Arabia: A Journey through the Labyrinth.* New York: Simon and Schuster, 1979.

Ramadan, K. "Child Education through Journalism in Kuwait." (In Arabic.) *JGAPS*, no. 56 (1988).

Rubinacci, Roberto. "The Ibadis." In *Religion in the Middle East: Three Religions in Concord and Conflict.* II: *Islam,* edited by A. J. Arberry. Cambridge: Cambridge University Press, 1969.

Al-Rumahi, S. "Tribalism and Modernization in the Arabian Peninsula." (In Arabic.) *Al-Khalij al-Arabi* (*The Arab Gulf* 1, no. 1 (1981).

Sabagh, Georges. "Immigrants in the Arab Gulf Countries: 'Sojourners or Settlers'?" In *The Arab States,* edited by Giacomo Luciani. Berkeley, Calif.: University of California Press, 1990.

Safwat, K. "Approaching the Source of Folklore in the Arabian Gulf." (In Arabic.) *Al-Ma'thurat al-Sha'biyya*, no. 10 (1988).

St. Albans, Suzanne. *Green Grows the Oil: Desert Oil and Modern Society.* London: Quartet Books Limited, 1978.

Al-Sarraf, Q. "The Effect of Nationality and the Educational Level of Mothers on the Child-Mother Relationship in the Gulf Region." (In Arabic.) *JGAPS*, no. 60 (1989).

Seccombe, Ian, and Richard Lawless. *Work Camps and Company Towns: Settlement Patterns and the Gulf Oil Industry.* Durham, U.K.: Centre for Middle Eastern and Islamic Studies, University of Durham, 1987.

Seikaly, May. "Women and Social Change in Bahrain." *IJMES* 26, no. 3 (1994).

Shami, S. "The Social Implications of Population Displacement and Resettlement: An Overview with a Focus on the Arab Middle East." *International Migration Review* 27, no. 1 (1993).

Al-Suri, M. "The Use of Folklore in Kuwaiti Theatrical Works." (In Arabic.) *Al-Ma'thurat al-Sha'biyya*, no. 21 (1991).

Tétreault, Mary Ann. "Civil Society in Kuwait: Protected Spaces and Women's Rights." *Middle East Journal* 47, no. 2 (1993).

Tétreault, Mary Ann, and Haya al-Mughni. "Modernization and Its Discontents: State and Gender in Kuwait." *Middle East Journal* 49, no. 3 (1995).

Thesiger, Wilfred. *Arabian Sands.* New York: Viking Press, 1984.

Townsend, John. "Le sultanat d'Oman: Vers la fin d'un particularisme séculaire." *Maghreb Machrek*, no. 94 (October-December 1981).

"UAE Federal Law No. 18 of 1993: Law of Commercial Procedure." *Arab Law Quarterly* 10, no. 1 (1995).

Varisco, Daniel Martin. "Pearls of the Gulf." *World & I* 6, no. 1 (May 1991).

Weiss, Julian. "Arabian Gateway: In Dubai, Business Is Culture." *World &I* 10, no. 9 (1995).

Wheatcroft, Andrew. *Arabia and the Gulf in Original Photographs.* London: Routledge and Kegan Paul, 1982.

Wikan, Unni. *Behind the Veil in Arabia: Women in Oman.* Baltimore: The Johns Hopkins University Press, 1982.

Wilkinson, John. *The Imamate Tradition.* Cambridge: Cambridge University Press, 1987.

————. *Water and Tribal Settlement in Southeast Arabia, A Study of the Falaj of Oman.* Oxford: Clarendon Press, 1977.

Zayid bin Sultan Al Nuhayyan (Abu Dhabi ruler and UAE president). *Falconry as a Sport: Our Arab Heritage.* Abu Dhabi: n. p., 1976.

10. ECONOMICS

Aarts, Paul, and Gep Eisenloeffel. *Kuwait Petroleum Corporation as New Seventh Sister?* Occasional Paper no. 2. Amsterdam: Middle East Research Associates, 1989.

Aarts, P. and M. Renner. "Oil and the Gulf War."*MERIP Middle East Report* 21, no. 4 (1991).

Abed, George T. "The Lean Years: The Political Economy of Arab Oil in the Coming Decade." In *The Next Arab Decade: Alternative Futures,* edited by Hisham Sharabi. Boulder, Colo.: Westview; London: Mansell, 1988.

AbiNader, Jean R. "The U.S. Role in Gulf Industrialization." *American-Arab Affairs,* no. 32 (1990).

Abdul Hadi, Ayman S. *Stock Markets of the Arab World: Trends, Problems, and Prospects.* New York: Routledge and Kegan Paul, 1988. (Includes evaluations of stock markets in Kuwait and Bahrain.)

Aburdene, Odeh. "U.S. Economic and Financial Relations with Saudi Arabia, Kuwait and the United Arab Emirates." *American-Arab Affairs,* no. 7 (1983-84).

Ahmed, A. A. "Kuwait Public Commercial Investments in Arab Countries." *Middle Eastern Studies* 31, no. 2 (1995).

Alessa, Shamlan Y. *The Manpower Problem in Kuwait.* Boston: Kegan Paul, 1981.

Anckonie, Alex, III. "The Banking Sector as an Agent of Economic Diversification in the Arab Gulf Countries." *American-Arab Affairs,* no. 11 (1984-85).

Askari, Hossein. "Management of External Surpluses in the Gulf Countries." *American-Arab Affairs,* no. 7 (1983-84).

Assiri, A. "Kuwait's Dinar Diplomacy: The Role of Donor-Mediator." *JSAMES* 14, no. 3 (1991).

Atiqah, Ali Ahmad, and Rafat Shafiq Bisada. *Al-Naft wa'l-Tanmiya al-Sina'iyya fi'l-Watan al-Arabi (Petroleum and Industrial Development in the Arab World)*. Safat, Kuwait: Kadhma Company Publishers, 1985.

El-Azhary, M. S., ed. *The Impact of Oil Revenues on Arab Gulf Development*. Boulder, Colo.: Westview Press, 1984.

Badawi, A. "Collective Labor Relations in Work Legislation in the Gulf Arab States." (In Arabic.) *Majalla al-Dirasat al-Khalij wa'l-Jazira al-Arabiyya (Journal of Gulf and Arabian Peninsula Studies)* [Hereinafter cited as *JGAPS*] no. 34 (April 1983).

Bailey, Robert, and John Whelan. *The Reconstruction and Re-Equipment of Kuwait: New Business Opportunities* 1, no. 1. London, Dordrecht, and Boston: Graham and Trotman, 1991.

Basha, Z. "The Role of the Private Sector in Sustaining Economic Cooperation among the Gulf Countries." (In Arabic.) *JGAPS*, no. 33 (January 1983).

———. "Toward a Unified Gulf Policy for the Development of Manufacturing Enterprises upon the Japanese Experience." (In Arabic.) *JGAPS*, no. 30 (April 1982).

Beblawi, Hazem. *The Arab Gulf Economy in a Turbulent Age*. New York: St. Martin's Press, 1984.

———. "The Arab Oil Era (1973-1983): A Story of Lost Opportunity." *Journal of Arab Affairs* 5, no. 1 (1986).

———. "The Rentier State in the Arab World." In *The Arab State*, edited by Giacomo Luciani. Berkeley, Calif.: University of California Press, 1990.

Burney, N. "Workers' Remittances from the Middle East and Their Effect on Pakistan's Economy." *Pakistan Development Review* 26, no. 4 (1987).

Cain, M., and K. al-Badri. "An Assessment of the Trade and Restructuring Effects of the Gulf Cooperation Council." *IJMES* 21, no. 1 (1989).

Carlin, P. "Sustaining the Arab Oil Markets." *Arab Affairs* 1, no. 8 (1988-89).

Coeck, M. "Olie en Economische Ontwikkeling in Arabische-Golfstaten." *International Spectator* 43, no. 1 (1989).

Conant, Melvin. "Recognizing U.S.-Arab Interdependence. The U.S. Stake in Gulf Oil." *American-Arab Affairs*, no. 20 (1987).

Cooper, Mary H. "Persian Gulf Oil." Editorial Research Reports (October 1987).

Cunningham, Andrew. *Gulf Banking and Finance: Facing up to Change: MEED Industry Perspective*, no. 1. London: Middle East Economic Digest, November 1989.

Dickman, François M. "Economic Realities in the Gulf." *American-Arab Affairs*, no. 7 (1983-84).

Dunn, Roderic W. "A Rural Development Project in Oman." In *Change and Development in the Middle East*, edited by John I. Clarke and Howard Bowen-Jones. London: Methuen, 1981.

Dutton, R. "Interdependence, Independence, and Rural Development in Oman: The Experience of the 'Khabura Development Project." *Journal of Oman Studies* 6, no. 2 (1983).

Economic and Social Infrastructure in Qatar. Doha, Qatar: Al Noor Publishing, 1984.

Eltony, M. N., and Y. H. Mohammad. "The Structure of Demand for Electricity in the Gulf Cooperation Council Countries." *Journal of Energy and Development* 18, no. 2 (1993).

Al-Fayez, Khaled. "The Gulf Investment Corporation." *American-Arab Affairs*, no. 11 (winter 1984-85).

———. "International Developments and Their Impact on Gulf Banks." *Middle East Policy* 3, no. 4 (1995).

Fesharaki, Fereidun, and David T. Isaak. *OPEC, the Gulf, and the World Petroleum Market: A Study in Government Policy and Downstream Operations.* Boulder, Colo.: Westview Press, 1983.

Field, Michael. *The Merchants: The Big Business Families of Saudi Arabia and the Gulf States.* Woodstock, N.Y.: Overlook Press, 1985.

Ghorban, N. and M. Sarir. "Oil and Gas: An Outlook for Future Cooperation among the Persian Gulf States." *IJIA* 5, nos. 3-4 (1994).

Gnichtel, William Van Orden. "The Arab States' Gulf Cooperation Council: Unified Rules for Trade and Industry." *International Lawyer* 20, no. 1 (1986).

Guecioueur, A. "Problems and Prospects of Economic Integration among the Members of the Arab Gulf Cooperation Council." *Arab Gulf Journal* 2, no. 2 (October 1982).

"Gulf Cooperation— Theory or Practice?" *Middle East Economic Digest* 27, no. 43 (1983).

Hamauzu, Tetsuo. "Arab Oil and Japan." *Arab Gulf Journal* 6 (1986).

Hassan bin Talal. "Manpower Migration in the Middle East: An Overview." *Middle East Journal* 38, no. 4 (1984).

Hay, Rupert. "The Impact of the Oil Industry on the Persian Gulf Sheikhdoms." *Middle East Journal* 9, no. 4 (1955).

Hindi, A. "A Strategy for Agricultural Development in the Sultanate of Oman: An Environmental Perspective." (In Arabic.) *JGAPS*, no. 29 (1982).

Humaidan, Ali. *Les Princes de l'Or Noir*. Paris: Hachette, 1968.

Al-Imadi, M. "The Role of Oil Revenues Channeled through Arab Funds in the Development of the Third World." (In Arabic). *Naft wa'l-Ta'awun al-Arabi* (*Oil and Arab Cooperation*) 9, no. 1 (1983).

Imady, M. "Arab Aid to Developing Countries." *Arab Gulf Journal* 4, Supp. 2 (1984).

Isa, A. "Industrial Integration of Arab Gulf Countries and Its Relation to the Aim of Arab Economic Integration." *Arab Gulf* 13, no. 1 (1981).

Kassem, M. Sami, et al. *Strategic Management of Services in the Arab Gulf States: Company and Industry Cases*. New York and Berlin: Walter de Gruyter, 1989.

Kassem, O. "The Manakh Bubble and Its Impact on the Economy of Kuwait." *Arab Gulf Journal* 3, Supp. 1 (1983).

Al-Kawari, A., and H. al-Kawari. "Toward a New Economic Policy of the Arab Gulf States." (In Arabic.) *JGAPS*, no. 52 (1987).

Kawkali, N. "The Impact of the Gulf Crisis on the Palestinian Economy." (In Arabic.) *Shu'un Filastiniyya* (*Palestinian Affairs*), nos. 213-14 (1990-91).

Keely, Charles B., and Bassam Saket. "Jordanian Migrant Workers in the Arab Region: A Case Study of Consequences for Labor-Supplying Countries." *Middle East Journal* 38, no. 4 (1984).

Kennedy, C. "Multinational Corporations and Political Risk in the Persian Gulf." *IJMES* 16, no. 3 (1984).

Khalaf, A. "Structural Development of Basic Industries in the Arab Gulf Countries." (In Arabic.) *JGAPS*, no. 32 (1982).

Kubursi, Atif. *Oil, Industrialisation and Development in the Arab Gulf States*. London: Croom Helm, 1984.

"Kuwaiti Securities Market Needs Better Organization." *Arab Economist* 12, no. 147 (1981).

El-Kuwaize, Abdulla. "Dynamics of Trade in Refined Petroleum Products Between the Gulf Cooperation Council and Western Europe." *Journal of Energy and Development* 11, no. 1 (1986).

Al-Kuwari, A. K. *Oil Revenues in the Gulf Emirates: Patterns of Allocation and Impact on Economic Development*. Boulder, Colo.: Westview Press, 1978.

LaPorte, Robert, Jr. "The Ability of South and East Asia to Meet the Labor Demands of the Middle East and North Africa." *Middle East Journal* 38, no. 4 (1984).

Licklider, Roy. "Arab Oil and Japanese Foreign Policy." *Middle East Review* 18, no. (1985).

Longuenesse, E. "Rente petrolière et structure de classe dans les pays du Golfe." *Peuples Méditerranéens* 26 (1984).

Looney, Robert. "An Assessment of the Benefits of Economic Integration for the Arabian Gulf States: The Effects of Increased Size." *Journal of Economic Cooperation among Islamic Countries* 10, no. 2 (1989).

————. "Employment Creation in an Oil-Based Economy: Kuwait." *Middle Eastern Studies* 28, no. 3 (1992).

————. "The Impact of Defense Expenditure on Industrial Development in the Arab Gulf." *Middle Eastern Studies* 30, no. 2 (1994).

————. "Manpower Dilemmas in Kuwait: Scope for Indigenous Job Creation through Attrition of the Foreign Workforce." *Orient* 31, no. 3 (1990).

————. *Manpower Policies and Development in the Persian Gulf Region*. Westport, Conn: Praeger, 1994.

————. "Structural and Economic Changes in the Arab Gulf after 1973." *Middle Eastern Studies* 26, no. 4 (1990).

————. "World Oil Market Outlook: Implications for Stability in the Gulf States." *Middle East Review* 22, no. 2 (1989-90).

Looney, Robert, and D. Winterford. "Patterns of Arab Gulf Exports: Implications for Industrial Diversification of Increased Inter-Arab Trade." *Orient* 33, no. 4 (1992).

Maachou, Abdelkader. *OAPEC: The Organization of Arab Petroleum Exporting Countries*. New York: St. Martin's Press, 1983.

Mabro, R. "Oil Market Developments and the Role of OPEC." *Arab Gulf Journal* 2, no. 2 (1982).

Al-Mahmid, M., and R. Amir. Money Supply in Kuwait." (In Arabic.) *Al-Mal wa'l-Sina'a (Money and Business)*, no. 10 (1989).

El-Mallakh, Dorothea H., ed. *Energy Watchers*. I: *Shadow OPEC: New Element for Stability?* and *A "Reintegrated" Oil Industry: Implications for Supply, Marketing, Pricing, and Investment*. Boulder, Colo.: International Research Center for Energy and Economic Development, 1990.

————. *Energy Watchers*. II: *Changing Structures, Markets, and Future Stability and the Oil-Gas Relationship*. Boulder, Colo.:

International Research Center for Energy and Economic Development, 1991.

El-Mallakh, Ragaei. *The Economic Development of the United Arab Emirates*. New York: St. Martin's Press, 1981.

El-Mallakh, Ragaei, and Jacob K. Atta. *The Absorptive Capacity of Kuwait: Domestic and International Perspectives*. Lexington, Mass.: D. C. Heath, 1981.

Maylah, M. "Measuring the Role of Discrimination in Kuwait's Labor Market." (In Arabic.) *Al-Mal wa'l-Sina'a (Money and Business)*, no. 10 (1989).

Meyer-Reumann, R. "The Jebel Ali Free Zone in the Emirate of Dubai: A Commercial Alternative after the Gulf Crisis." *Arab Law Quarterly* 6, no. 1 (1991).

Mofid, Kamran. *The Economic Consequences of the Gulf War*. London: Routledge and Kegan Paul, 1990.

Mohyuddin, B. "Policy Structure for Promoting Manufacturing Industry: A Framework for the States of the Arabian Peninsula." *Arab Gulf Journal* 4, no. 2 (1984).

Al-Moosa, A. A., and K. S. McLachlan. *Immigrant Labor in Kuwait*. London: Croom Helm, 1985.

———. "Wage Patterns among the Foreign Labor Forces in Kuwait." *Arab Gulf Journal* 2, no. 2 (1982).

Morse, Edward L. "The Coming Oil Revolution." *Foreign Affairs* 69, no. 5 (1990-91).

Moubarak, Walid E. "The Kuwait Fund in the Context of Arab and Third World Politics." *Middle East Journal* 41, no. 4 (1987).

Al-Mubarek, Abdel Raoof. "Economic Development and Industrialization in the UAE." *American-Arab Affairs*, no. 32 (1990).

Nakhjavani, Mehran. "After the Persian Gulf War: The Potential for Economic Reconstruction and Development in the Persian Gulf Region." *Working Papers*, no. 34. Ottawa: Canadian Institute for International Peace and Security, 1991.

―――. "Resources, Wealth, and Security: The Case of Kuwait." In *The Many Faces of National Security in the Arab World*, edited by Bahgat Korany, Paul Noble, and Rex Brynen. New York: St. Martin's Press, 1993.

Nashashibi, H. "The Development of Capital Markets in the Gulf." *Journal of Arab Affairs* 1, no. 1 (1981).

Niblock, Tim. *Dilemmas of Non-Oil Economic Development in the Arab Gulf.* London: Arab Research Centre, 1980.

Osama, Abdul Rahman. *The Dilemma of Development in the Arabian Peninsula.* London: Croom Helm, 1986.

"Progress Report of OAPEC Joint Venture Companies." *Arab Economist* 24, no. 148 (1982).

Al-Qudsi, S. , and N. Shah. "The Relative Economic Progress of Male Foreign Workers in Kuwait." *International Migration Review* 25, no. 1 (1991).

Rahim, A., and H. Jummah. "Accounting Policy in Light of the Manakh Crisis." (In Arabic.) *JGAPS*, no. 60 (1989).

Rihan, M. "An Analytical Economic Study on the Effect of Bedouin Settlement upon Agricultural Development in the UAE." (In Arabic.) *Al-Khalij al-Arabi* 13, no. 3 (1981).

Road, S. "Prospects for Trade between Britain and the Arab Gulf." *Arab Gulf Journal* 4, no. 2 (1984).

Robins, Philip. *The Future of the Gulf: Politics and Oil in the 1990s.* Brookfield, Vt: Gower Publishing Company (for the Royal Institute of International Affairs, 1989).

Al Sabah, S. A. "Gulf Banking during the 'Nineties: Reality and Ambitions," *Middle East Policy* 3, no. (1995).

Al-Sabah, Youssif S.F. *The Oil Economy of Kuwait*. London: Kegan Paul International, 1980.

Sadowski, Yahya. "Power, Poverty, and Petrodollars: Arab Economies after the Gulf War." *MERIP Middle East Report* 21, no. 3 (1991).

Saif, M. "Fish Resources in the Arabian Gulf and Their Importance as a Source of Food and National Income." (In Arabic.) *JGAPS*, no. 54 (1988).

Sakr, Naomi. *The United Arab Emirates to the 1990s: One Market or Seven?* London: Economist Intelligence Unit, Special Report no. 238, 1986.

Saleh, Nabil. *The General Principles of Saudi Arabian and Omani Company Laws*. Plymouth, U.K.: MacDonald and Evans, 1981.

Sambar, David. "Arab Investment Strategies." *Arab Gulf Journal* vol. 1, no. 1 (1981).

Schliephake, K. "Wasser am Arabisch/Persichen Golf: Natürliches Potential und Krisenfaktor." *Orient* 33, no. 2 (1992).

Serageldin, Ismail, et al. "Some Issues Related to Labor Migration in the Middle East and North Africa." *Middle East Journal* 38, no. 4 (1984).

Al-Shar'a, A. "Economic Integration in the Gulf." (In Arabic.) *Al-Khalij al-Arabi* 13, no. 3 (1981).

Sherbiny, Naiem A. "Expatriate Labor Flows to the Arab Oil Countries in the 1980s." *The Middle East Journal* 38, no. 4 (1984).

———. *Trends in Alternative Energies: Their Implications for Arab Members of OPEC*. Safat, Kuwait: Industrial Bank of Kuwait, 1989.

Shirawi, Yousuf A. GCC Diversification and Industrialization: The Bahrain Example." *American-Arab Affairs*, no. 32 (1990).

Simmons, André. *Arab Foreign Aid*. East Brunswick, N.J.: Fairleigh Dickinson University Press, 1981.

Tétreault, Mary Ann. *The Organization of Arab Oil Exporting Countries: History, Policies, and Prospects*. Westport, Conn.: Greenwood Press, 1981.

Unwin, Tim. "Agriculture and Water Resources in the United Arab Emirates." *Arab Gulf Journal* 3, no. 1 (1983).

Utaybah, Mani Said. *Essays on Petroleum*. London: Croom Helm, 1982.

Uthman, Nasir Muhammad. *With Their Bare Hands: The Story of the Oil Industry in Qatar*. New York: Longman, 1984.

Vernon, Raymond. *Two Hungry Giants: The U.S. and Japan in the Quest for Oil and Ores*. Cambridge, Mass.: Harvard University Press, 1983.

Whelan, John, ed. *Oman: A MEED Guide*. London and Boston: Routledge and Kegan Paul, 1981.

Wilson, R. "The Determinants of Commercial Bank Deposits and Lending in the Arab Gulf: The Cases of Kuwait, Qatar, and the United Arab Emirates." *Arab Gulf Journal* 2, no. 2 (1982).

Wilson, Rodney J. A. "Japan's Exports to the Middle East: Directional and Commodity Trends and Price Behavior." *The Middle East Journal* 38, no. 3 (1984).

Wirth, Eugen. *Dubai: Ein Modernes städtisches Handels und Dienstleistungszentrum am Arabisch-Persischen Golf*. Erkangen, F.R.G.: Frankischen Geographischen Gesellschaft, 1988.

———. "Irak am Vorabend des Überfalls auf Kuwait: Zur Wirtschaftlichen und Sozialen Dynamik im Jahrzehnt des Golfkriegs, 1980-1990." *Orient* 31, no. 3 (1990).

Yorke, Valerie, and Louis Turner. *European Interests and Gulf Oil.* Brookfield, Vt.: Gower Publishing, 1986.

Al-Yousuf, Ala'a. *Kuwait and Saudi Arabia: From Prosperity to Retrenchment.* Oxford, U.K.: Oxford Institute for Energy Studies, 1990.

11. POLITICS, DOMESTIC AND REGIONAL

Aarts, P. "Democracy, Oil and the Gulf War." *Third World Quarterly* 13, no. 3 (1992).

Abed, G. "The Palestinians and the Gulf Crisis." *Journal of Palestine Studies* 20, no. 2 (1991).

Ahsani, H. "Pakistan's Persian Gulf Policy." *Pakistan Horizon* 45, no.2 (1992).

Ajami, Fouad. "The Summer of Arab Discontent." *Foreign Affairs*, vol. 69, no. 5 (1990-91).

Akbar, M. "Regional Integration under the Arab Cooperation Council." *Strategic Studies* 13, no. 1 (1989).

Alashaal, A. "Some Reflections on the Voting Practices in the UN of Members of the Gulf Cooperation Council." *Revue Egyptienne de Droit International* 41 (1988).

Albaharna, Husain M. *The Arabian Gulf States: Their Legal and Political Status and Their International Problems.* 2nd rev. ed. Beirut, Lebanon: Librairie du Liban, 1975.

———. "The Enforcement of Foreign Judgments and Arbitral Awards in the GCC Countries with Particular Reference to Bahrain." *Arab Law Quarterly* 4, no. 4 (1989).

Ali, Sheikh R. *Oil and Power: Political Dynamics in the Middle East.* New York: St. Martin's Press, 1987.

Amir, Hassan Sayed. *International and Legal Problems of the Gulf.* Cambridgeshire, U.K.: Menas Press, 1981.

Amirahmadi, Hooshang, and Nader Entessar, eds. *Reconstruction and Regional Diplomacy in the Persian Gulf.* London and New York: Routledge and Kegan Paul, 1992.

Anthony, John Duke. "The Gulf Cooperation Council." *JSAMES* 5, no. 4 (1982).

Assiri, Abdul-Reda. "Kuwait's Political Survival in the 1980s and Beyond: Small-Nation Response to Regional Pressure." *American-Arab Affairs*, no. 30 (1989).

Baaklini, Abdo. "Legislatures in the Gulf Area: The Experience of Kuwait, 1961-1976." *IJMES* 14, no. 3 (1982).

Bahaijoub, A. "The Impact of the Gulf War on the Maghreb." *Journal of the Society for Moroccan Studies*, no. 2 (1992).

Al-Baz, A. "Forms of Parliamentary Systems between Traditionalism and Modernization: An Applied Contrastive Study of the Constitutions of Kuwait, the GCC States and Egypt." (In Arabic.) *JGAPS*, no. 58 (1989).

Bhutani, Surendra. "The Organizational Elite: Abu Dhabi, a Case Study." In *Contemporary Gulf,* edited by Surendra Bhutani. New Delhi: Academic Press, 1980.

Bill, James A. "Resurgent Islam in the Persian Gulf." *Foreign Affairs* 63, no. 1 (1984).

Bishara, Abdulla Y. "Gulf Cooperation: Its Nature and Outlook." Gulf Cooperation Council Reports Series, no. 1. Washington, D.C.: National Council on U.S.-Arab Relations, 1986.

Bishku, Michael B. "Iraq's Claim to Kuwait: A Historical Overview." *American-Arab Affairs*, no. 37 (1991).

Brahimi, R. "L'Impact de la crise du Golfe sur la Ligue des Etats arabes." *Les Cahiers de l'Orient*, nos. 25-26 (1992).

Brynen, R., and P. Noble. "The Gulf Conflict and the Arab State System: A New Regional Order?" *Arab Studies Quarterly* 13, nos. 1-2 (1991).

Carré, O. "Après-guerres du Golfe: cohésion arabe affermie, dangers 'ethniques.' " *Peuples Méditerranéens*, nos. 58-59 (1992).

Crystal, Jill. *Oil and Politics in the Gulf: Rulers and Merchants in Kuwait and Qatar*. Cambridge, U.K. and New York: Cambridge University Press, 1990.

Daher, A., and F. al-Salem. "Kuwait's Parliamentary Elections." *Journal of Arab Affairs* 3, no. 1 (1984).

Ebert, Barbara Gregory. "The War and Its Aftermath: Arab Responses." *Middle East Policy*, vol. 1, no. 4 (1992).

Ehteshami, Anoushiravan, et al. *War and Peace in the Gulf: Domestic Politics and Regional Relations into the 1990s*. Reading, U.K.: Ithaca Press, 1991.

Eickelman, Dale F. "Kings and People: Oman's State Consultative Council." *Middle East Journal* 38, no. 1 (1984).

Evans, E. "Arab Nationalism and the Persian Gulf War." *Harvard Middle Eastern and Islamic Review* 1, no. 1 (1994).

Faour, Muhammad. *The Arab World after Desert Storm*. Washington, D.C.: United States Institute of Peace, 1993.

Farah, Talal Toufic. *Protection and Politics in Bahrain, 1869-1915.* Syracuse, N.Y.: Syracuse University Press, 1986.

"The Federal Code of Procedure of the United Arab Emirates." *Arab Law Quarterly* 7, no. 4 (1992).

Freedman, Robert O., ed. *The Middle East after Iraq's Invasion of Kuwait.* Gainesville, Fla.: University Press of Florida, 1993.

Fuller, Graham E. "Respecting Regional Realities." *Foreign Policy,* no. 83 (summer 1991).

Garnham, D. "Explaining Middle Eastern Alignments during the Gulf War." *Jerusalem Journal of International Relations,* vol. 13, no. 3 (1991).

Gavlak, D. "The Kuwait 1992 Elections: 'Rainbow Coalition after a Desert Storm.'" *JIME Review (Japanese Institute of Middle East Economics),* no. 19 (1992-93).

Goodhind, Gilliam. "Iraq-Kuwait." In *Border and Territorial Disputes,* edited by Alan J. Day. Harlow, Essex, U.K.: Longman, 1982.

———. "Kuwait-Saudi Arabia." In *Border and Territorial Disputes,* edited by Alan J. Day. Harlow, Essex, U.K.: Longman, 1982.

Hallaj, Muhammad. "The Palestinians after the Gulf War." *American-Arab Affairs,* no. 35 (1990-91).

———. "Taking Sides: Palestinians and the Gulf Crisis." *Journal of Palestine Studies* 20, no. 3 (1991).

Halliday, Fred. *Arabia Without Sultans: A Survey of Political Instability in the Arab World.* New York: Vintage Books, 1975.

Hardy, Roger. *Arabia after the Storm: Internal Stability of the Gulf Arab States.* London: Royal Institute of International Affairs, 1992.

Hosni, S. "Commercial and Civil Companies in UAE Law." *Arab Law Quarterly* 7, no. 3 (1992).

Hottinger, Arnold. "Notes from the Gulf." *Swiss Review of World Affairs* 30 (1984).

Howeidy, F. "The Arab-Iranian Crisis over the Three Gulf Islands." *JIME Review*, no. 19 (1992-93).

Human Rights Watch World Report, 1993: Events of 1992. Washington, D.C. and New York: Human Rights Watch, 1993. (Includes chapter on Kuwait.)

Ismael, Tareq and Jacqueline Ismael. "Arab Politics and the Gulf War: Political Opinion and Political Culture." *Arab Studies Quarterly*, vol. 15, no. 1 (1993).

Ismael, Tareq. "Comparative Governments: The Arabian Peninsula." In *Politics and Government in the Middle East,* by Tareq Ismael and Jacqueline Ismael, with contributions from others. Miami: Florida International University Press, 1991.

Joffe, G. "The GCC Comes of Age." *Arab Affairs*, no. 9 (1989).

Kapeliouk, A. "The USSR and the Gulf Crisis." *Journal of Palestine Studies* 20, no. 3 (1991).

Kappeler, D. "Le Golfe et le droit international." *Etudes Internationales*, no. 44 (1992).

Katzman, K. "How Stable Are Saudi Arabia and Kuwait?" *Middle East Quarterly* 1, no. 3 (1994).

Kechichian, Joseph. "Oman and the World." *American-Arab Affairs Journal*, no. 35 (1990-91).

———. *Political Dynamics and Security in the Arabian Peninsula through the 1990s.* Santa Monica, Calif.: RAND Corporation, 1993.

Al-Khatib, M. "Territorial Waters According to Legal Theoretical Analysis." (In Arabic.) A*l-Khalij al-Arabi* 13, no. 2 (1981).

Al-Kobeisi, A. "Two Decades of Public Administration and Development in the State of Qatar." (In Arabic). *JGAPS* 7, no. 28 (1981).

Kostiner, Joseph. "Kuwait and Bahrain." In *The Politics of Islamic Revivalism: Diversity and Unity,* edited by Shireen Hunter. Bloomington, Ind.: Indiana University Press, in association with the Center for Strategic and International Studies, Washington, D.C. 1988.

Koury, Enver. "The Impact of the Geopolitical Situation of Iraq upon the Gulf Cooperation Council." *Middle East Insight* 2, no. 5 (1982).

Kumarasamy, P. "The Gulf and the Palestinians: Crisis from Within." *Strategic Analysis* 13, no. 9 (1990).

Laurens, H. "Le contentieux territorial entre l'Irak et le Koweit." *Maghreb-Machrek*, no. 130 (1990).

Laying the Foundations: Human Rights in Kuwait— Obstacles and Opportunities. New York: Lawyers Committee for Human Rights, 1993.

Levins, J. M. "The Kuwaiti Response." *Middle East Quarterly* 2, no. 1 (1995).

Long, David E. "The Impact of the Iranian Revolution on the Arabian Peninsula and the Gulf States." In *The Iranian Revolution: Its Global Impact,* edited by John L. Esposito, Miami: Florida International University Press, 1990.

MacDonald, Charles. "Regionalism and the Law of the Sea: The Persian Gulf Perspective." U.S. *Naval War College Review*, vol. 33, no. 5 (1980).

Al-Majid, Majeed. *The Gulf Cooperation Council: Crisis of Politics and Legality*. London: Taha Publishers, 1986.

Martin, Leonore G. "Policy Implications of Boundary Disputes in the Persian Gulf." *Middle East Review* 15, nos. 1-2 (fall-winter 1982-83).

Mattar, Philip. "The PLO and the Gulf Crisis." *Middle East Journal* 48, no. 1 (1994).

Al-Nafisi, Abd Allah Fahd. *Majlis al-Ta'awun al-Khaliji: Al-Itar al-Siyasi wa'l-Istaratiji (The Gulf Cooperation Council: Its Political and Strategic Framework)*. London: Taha Publishers, 1982.

Nakhleh, Emile A. *The Gulf Cooperation Council: Policies, Problems, and Prospects*. Westport, Conn.: Praeger, 1986.

Al-Naqeeb, Khaldoun Hasan. *Society and State in the Gulf and Arab Peninsula*. New York: Routledge and Kegan Paul, 1991.

Al-Nihari, Abdullah. "An Independent View of the Gulf Cooperation Council." *Dinar: The Business and Financial Review* 1, no. 4 (1983).

Nufal, A. "The Gulf States and the Crisis over Kuwait." *Arab Studies Quarterly* 13, nos. 1-2 (1991).

Pelletiere, Stephen C. *The Kurds: An Unstable Element in the Gulf*. Boulder, Colo.: Westview Press, 1984.

Peterson, J. E. "The Arab Gulf States: Steps toward Political Participation." *Washington Papers*, no. 131. New York: Praeger, for the Center for Strategic and International Studies, Washington, D. C. , 1988.

―――. "The GCC States after the Iran-Iraq War." *American-Arab Affairs*, no. 26 (1988).

————. "Legitimacy and Political Change in Yemen and Oman." *Orbis* 27, no. 4 (winter 1984).

Pipes, Daniel. *The Long Shadow: Culture and Politics in the Middle East.* New Brunswick, N.J. and Oxford, U.K.: Transaction Publishers, 1988. Includes a section titled "The Persian Gulf."

Pipes, Daniel, and Patrick Clawson. "Ambitious Iran, Troubled Neighbors." *Foreign Affairs: America and the World, 1992/93* 72, no. 1 (1993).

"Political Participation and Constitutional Democracy in Kuwait." Edited transcript of a conference held on April 29, 1991. Washington, D.C.: National Republican Institute for International Affairs, 1991.

Pridham, B. R., ed. *The Arab Gulf and the Arab World.* London: Croom Helm, 1988.

Rahman, H. "Kuwaiti Ownership of Warba and Bubiyan Islands." *Middle Eastern Studies* 29, no. 2 (1993).

Reed, Stanley. "Jordan and the Gulf Crisis." *Foreign Affairs* 69, no. 5 (1990-91).

Robins, P. "Can Gulf Oil Monarchies Survive the Oil Bust?" *Middle East Quarterly* 1, no. 4 (1994).

Saghafi-Ameri, N. "Kuwait: Political Consequences of Modernization, 1950-1986." *Middle Eastern Studies* 27, no. 1 (1991).

————. "A Solution to the Persian Gulf Crisis." *IJIA* 2, no. 4 (1990-91).

Salih, K. "Kuwait's Parliamentary Elections, 1963-1985: An Appraisal." *JSAMES* 16, no. 2 (1992).

Schofield, Richard. *Kuwait and Iraq: Historical Claims and Territorial Disputes.* London: Royal Institute of International Affairs, 1991.

——, ed. *Territorial Foundations of the Gulf States.* The SOAS/GRC Geopolitics Series. New York: St. Martin's Press, 1994.

Sen, K. "Nationalism in the Gulf." *Review of Middle Eastern Studies* 4 (1988).

Sfeir, A. "La contestation au Koweit." *Les Cahiers de l'Orient*, nos. 25-26 (1992).

Slymovics, S. "Cartoon Commentary: Algerian and Moroccan Caricatures from the Gulf War." *MERIP Middle East Report* 23, no. 1 (1993).

Soliman, S. Regional Cooperation for Marine Pollution in the Arabian Gulf." *Revue Egyptienne de Droit International* 41 (1985).

Stookey, Robert W. *The Arabian Peninsula: Zone of Ferment.* Oxford: Clio Press, 1984.

Al-Tamimi, A. "Some Issues of the Nationalist Movement in the Arab Gulf." (In Arabic.) *Al-Mustaqbal al-Arabi* (*The Arab Future*), 61 (1984).

Troxler, Nancy C. "The Gulf Cooperation Council: The Emergence of an Institution." *Millennium* (1987).

Tschirgi, Dan, ed. *The Arab World Today.* Boulder, Colo.: Lynne Rienner Publishers, 1994. Deals with aftermath of Gulf crisis of 1990-91.

Twinam, Joseph Wright. *The Gulf, Cooperation and the Council.* Washington, D.C.: Middle East Policy Council, 1993.

——. "The Gulf Cooperation Council since the Gulf War: The State of the States." *Middle East Policy* 1, no. 4 (1992).

——, et al. "Political Implication of the Gulf Crisis. "*American-Arab Affairs*, no. 35 (1991).

"United Arab Emirates, Federal Law No. 10, 1992, Issuing the Law of
Proof in Civil and Commercial Transactions." *Arab Law Quarterly*
8, no. 1 (1993).

A Victory Turned Sour: Human Rights in Kuwait since Liberation. New
York: Middle East Watch, 1991.

Viorst, Milton. "After the Liberation." *New Yorker.* September 30,
1991.

"What Now for the Middle East? Arabs Weigh the Gulf War, part III."
World & I 6, no. 5 (1991).

Wingerter, Rex B. "The GCC and Gulf Unity." *Middle East
International*, no. 276 (May 30, 1986).

Al Yahya, Mohammed. *Kuwait: Fall and Rebirth.* London: Kegan Paul
International, 1993.

12. INTERNATIONAL RELATIONS AND SECURITY AFFAIRS

Acharya, Amitav. *The Gulf War and "Irangate:" American Dilemmas.*
Canberra, Australia: Strategic and Defence Studies Centre,
Australian National University, 1987.

Ackerman, Julia, and Michael Collins Dunn. "The United States,
Japan and the Gulf: Common Interests, Potential Competition."
American-Arab Affairs, no. 32 (1990).

After the Storm: Challenges for America's Middle East Policy. Report.
Washington, D.C.: Strategic Study Group, Washington Institute
for Near East Policy, 1991.

Al-Ahnaf, M. "L'Opposition Maghrebine face à la crise du Golfe."
Maghreb-Machrek, no. 130 (1990).

Ahrari, M. E., ed. *The Gulf and International Security: The 1980s and Beyond.* New York: St. Martin's Press, 1989.

Akehurst, John. *We Won a War: The Campaign in Oman, 1965-1975.* Guildford, Surrey, U.K.: Michael Russell, 1982.

Akhtar, S. "Spoils of the Gulf War." *Pakistan Horizon* 44, no. 3 (1991).

Akins, James E., et al. *Oil and Security in the Arabian Gulf.* New York: St. Martin's Press, 1981.

Alaolmolki, Nozar. *Struggle for Dominance in the Persian Gulf: Past, Present and Future Prospects. Political Science*, ser. 10, vol. 31. New York: Peter Lang, 1991.

Alnasrawi, Abbas, and Cheryl Rubenberg, eds. *Consistency of U.S. Foreign Policy: The Gulf War and the Iran-Contra Affair.* Belmont, Mass.: Association of Arab-American University Graduates, 1989.

Alpher, Joseph. *War in the Gulf: Implications for Israel.* Boulder, Colo.: Westview Press, 1992.

Alpher, Joseph, et al. *The Middle East Military Balance, 1989-1990.* Boulder, Colo.: Westview Press, for the Jaffe Center for Strategic Studies, Tel Aviv University, 1990.

Ameri, N. S. "The Persian Gulf, Iran and the West." *India Quarterly* 49, no. 4 (1993).

Amin, Sayad Hassan. *International and Legal Problems of the Gulf.* Cambridgeshire, U.K.: Menas Press; Boulder, Colo.: Westview Press, 1981.

Amin, Sayed Hassan. *Political and Strategic Issues in the Gulf.* Glasgow: Royston, 1984.

Anthony, John Duke. "Oman: Stable and Strategic." *Journal of Defense and Diplomacy* 1, no. 11 (1983).

Aspin, Les. "The Aspin Papers: Sanctions, Diplomacy, and War in the Persian Gulf." *Significant Issues Series*, vol 13, no. 2. Washington, D.C.: Center for Strategic and International Studies, 1991.

Asri, A. "The Gulf and American Foreign Policy." (In Arabic.) *Al-Majalla al-Arabiyya li'l-Dirasat al-Dawliyya (Arab Journal of International Studies)* 2, no. 1 (1989).

Assiri, Abdul-Reda. *Kuwait's Foreign Policy: City-State in World Politics*. Boulder, Colo.: Westview Press, 1989.

Atkinson, Rick. *Crusade: The Untold Story of the Persian Gulf War*. New York: Houghton Mifflin, 1993.

Attyah, Khalil. "La seconde guerre du Golfe." *Le Nouvel Afrique Asie*, no. 25 (1991).

Axelgard, Frederick. "The Gulf States Gird Themselves against an Iran-Iraq Spillover." *Journal of Defense and Foreign Affairs* 12, no. 3 (1984).

Azhary, M. "The Attitudes of the Superpowers towards the Gulf War." *International Affairs* (London) 59, no. 4 (1983).

Balaj, B. "France and the Gulf War." *Mediterranean Quarterly* 4, no. 3 (1993).

Barnaby, Frank. *Arms Control after the Gulf War*. London: Research Institute for the Study of Conflict and Terrorism, 1991.

Barzilai, Gad, Aharon Klieman, and Gil Shidlo, eds. *The Gulf Crisis and Its Global Aftermath*. London: Routledge and Kegan Paul, 1993.

Barzilai, G., and E. Inbar. "Do Wars Have an Impact? Israeli Public Opinion after the Gulf War." *Jerusalem Journal of International Relations* 14, no. 1 (1992).

Beker, A. "The Arms-Oil Connection: Fueling the Arms Race." *Armed Forces and Society* 8, no. 3 (1982).

Bengio, Ofra, ed. *Saddam Speaks on the Gulf Crisis: A Collection of Documents.* Tel Aviv: Dayan Center for Middle Eastern and African Studies, Tel Aviv University, 1992. Distributed by Syracuse University Press, Syracuse, N.Y.

Bennis, Phyllis, and Michel Moushabeck. *Beyond the Storm: A Gulf Crisis Reader.* New York: Olive Branch Press, 1991.

Bill, James. "Regional Security and Domestic Stability in the Persian Gulf." *IJIA* 5, nos. 3-4 (1994).

Billiere, Peter de la. *A Personal Account of the Gulf War.* New York: HarperCollins, 1992.

El-Bizri, D. "Mouvement islamiste et guerre du Golfe." *Peuples Méditerranéens*, nos. 58-59 (1992).

Blackwell, James. *Thunder in the Desert: The Strategy and Tactics of the Persian Gulf War.* New York: Bantam Books, 1991.

Blackwell, James, et al. *The Gulf War: Military Lessons Learned.* Washington, D.C.: Center for Strategic and International Studies, 1991.

Blank, S. "Russia, the Gulf and Central Asia in a New Middle East." *Central Asian Survey* 13, no. 2 (1994).

Bradley, C. Paul. *Recent United States Policy in the Persian Gulf.* Hamden, Conn.: Shoe String Press, 1982.

Bresheeth, Haim, and Nira Yuval-Davis, eds. *The Gulf War and the New World Order.* Atlantic Highlands, N.J.: Zed Books, 1991.

Brittain, Victoria, ed. *The Gulf between Us: The Gulf War and Beyond.* London: Virago, 1991.

Brown, J. "Turkey and the Persian Crisis." *Mediterranean Quarterly* 2, no. 2 (1991).

Bulloch, John, and Harvey Morris. *The Gulf War: Its Origins, History and Consequences.* London: Methuen, 1989.

Bundy, McGeorge. "Nuclear Weapons and the Gulf." *Foreign Affairs* 70, no. 4 (1991).

Campbell, David. *Politics Without Principle: Sovereignty, Ethics, and the Narratives of the Gulf War.* Boulder, Colo.: Lynne Rienner Publishers, 1993.

Campbell, W., and D. Darvich. "Global Implications of the Islamic Revolution for the Persian Gulf." *JSEMAS* 5, no. 1 (1981).

Chaalan, Fahd. "A la recherche de la sécurité perdue." *Le Nouvel Afrique Asie*, no. 25 (1991).

Childers, Erskine. "The Use and Abuse of the UN in the Gulf Crisis." *MERIP Middle East Report* 21, no. 2 (1991). Issued by Middle East Research and Information Project, Washington, D.C.

Chubin, Shahram. "The Iran-Iraq War and Persian Gulf Security." *International Defense Review* (Geneva) 17, no. 5 (1984).

———, ed. *Security in the Persian Gulf 1: Domestic Political Factors.* Totowa, NJ: Allanheld, Osmun, for the International Institute for Strategic Studies (London), 1982.

———. *Security in the Persian Gulf 4: The Role of Outside Powers.* Totowa, NJ: Allanheld, Osmun, for the International Institute for Strategic Studies, 1982.

Cigar, Norman. "Chemical Weapons and the Gulf War: The Dog That Did not Bark." *Studies in Conflict and Terrorism* 15, no. 2 (1992).

———. "The Soviet Navy in the Persian Gulf: Naval Diplomacy in a Combat Zone. "*Naval War College Review*, vol. 42, no. 2 (1989).

Cordesman, Anthony M. *After the Storm: The Changing Military Balance in the Middle East.* Boulder, Colo.: Westview Press, 1993.

———. *The Gulf and the Search for Strategic Stability: Saudi Arabia, the Military Balance in the Gulf, and Trends in the Arab-Israeli Military Balance.* London: Mansell, and Boulder, Colo.: Westview Press, 1984.

———. *The Gulf and the West: Strategic Relations and Military Realities.* Boulder, Colo.: Westview Press, 1988.

———. *The Iran-Iraq War and Western Security, 1984-87: Strategic Implications and Policy Options.* London: Jane's, for the Royal United Services Institute, 1987.

Cordesman, Anthony M., and Abraham R. Wagner. *The Lessons of War. Vol. 2. The Iran-Iraq War.* Boulder, Colo.: Westview Press, 1990.

Cottrell, Alvin J., and Michael L. Moodie. "The United States and the Persian Gulf, Past Mistakes and Present Needs." *Agenda Paper no. 13.* New York: National Strategy Information Center, 1984.

Cover, M. "FMF for the RDF." (Fleet Marine Force for the Rapid Deployment Force). *U.S. Naval Institute Proceedings (USNIP)* 108, no. 6 (1982).

Cromwell, W. "Europe, the United States, and the Pre-War Gulf Crisis." *International* 48, no. 1 (1992-93).

Cunningham, Michael. *Hostages to Fortune: The Future of Western Interests in the Arabian Gulf.* London: Pergamon; Washington, D.C. (McLean, Va.): Brassey's, 1988.

Dabiri, M. "Abu Musa Island: A Binding Understanding or a Misunderstanding?" *IJIA* 5, nos. 3-4 (1994).

Danchev, Alex, and Dan Keohane, eds. *International Perspectives on the Gulf Conflict.* New York: St. Martin's Press, 1994.

Danspeckgruber, Wolfgang, and Charles H. R. Tripp, eds. *Iraq's Aggression: Regional and International Implications.* Boulder, Colo.: Westview Press, 1993.

Danziger, Raphael. "The Naval Race in the Persian Gulf." *U.S. Naval Institute Proceedings* 108, no. 3 (1982).

Davies, Charles. E., ed. *After the War: Iraq and the Arab Gulf.* Chichester, UK: Carden, 1990.

———, ed. *Global Interests in the Arab Gulf.* New York: St. Martin's Press, 1992.

Decosse, David E., ed. *But Was It Just? Reflections on the Morality of the Gulf War.* New York: Doubleday, 1992.

Demack, G. "Perception and Misperception in the Persian Gulf: The Iran-Iraq War." *Parameters: Journal of the U.S. Army War College* 13, no. 6 (1983).

Doran, Charles F., and Stephen W. Buck, eds. *The Gulf, Energy, and Global Security: Political and Economic Issues.* Boulder, Colo.: Lynne Rienner Publishers, 1991.

Ederington, L. Benjamin, and Michael J. Mazarr. *Turning Point: The Gulf War and U.S. Military Strategy.* Boulder, Colo.: Westview Press, 1995.

Ehteshami, Anoushiravan. "Arms Transfers and the Search for Security in the Persian Gulf." *Strategic Studies* 14, nos. 1-2 (1990-91).

———. *From the Gulf to Central Asia: Players in the New Great Game.* Exeter, U.K.: University of Exeter Press, 1994.

Eilts, Hermann F. "Security Considerations in the Persian Gulf." *International Security* 5, no. 2 (1980).

————. "U.S. Perception of Persian/Arabian Gulf Security." *Asian Affairs* 25, no. 3 (1994).

Emami, M. "Perspectives on the Security of the Persian Gulf." *IJIA* 5, nos. 3-4 (1994).

Engelhardt, Joseph P. *Gulf Crisis*. Carlisle Barracks, Pa.: Department of National Security and Strategy, U.S. Army War College, 1991.

Epstein, Joshua M. *Strategy and Force Planning: The Case of the Persian Gulf*. Washington, D.C.: Brookings Institution, 1987.

Fadil, S. "The GCC States and Possible Alternatives for the Endangered Strait of Hormuz." (In Arabic.) *JGAPS*, no. 56 (1988).

Farid, Abdel Majid, ed. *Oil and Security in the Arabian Gulf*. New York: St. Martin's Press, 1981.

Farley, J. "The Gulf War and the Littoral States." *World Today* 40, no. 7 (July 1984).

Al-Fayez, Khaled M. "Rationale for Promoting Joint U.S.-GCC Projects." *Middle East Policy* 2, no. 3 (1993).

Frank, A. "Third World War: A Political Economy of the Gulf War and the New World Order." *Third World Quarterly* 13, no. 2 (1992).

Freedman, Lawrence, and Efraim Karsh. *The Gulf Conflict, 1990-1991: Diplomacy and War in the New World Order*. Princeton, N.J.: Princeton University Press, 1993.

Freedman, Robert O. "Moscow and the Gulf War." *Problems of Communism* 40, no. 4 (1991).

Fried, Edward R., and Nanette M. Blandin, eds. *Oil and America's Security*. Washington, D.C.: Brookings Institution, 1988.

Friedman, Norman. *Desert Victory: The War for Kuwait*. Annapolis, Md.: Naval Institute Press, 1991.

Fuller, Graham E. Moscow and the Gulf War." *Foreign Affairs* 70, no. 3 (summer 1991).

Garfinkle, Adam. "The Gulf War: Was It Worth It?" *World & I* 6, no. 10 (October 1991).

Gause, F. Gregory, III. *Oil Monarchies: Domestic and Security Challenges in the Arab Gulf States.* New York: Council on Foreign Relations Press, 1994.

————. "The Post-Gulf Crisis Crisis: The Middle East after the War for Kuwait." *Beirut Review*, no. 1 (1991).

Georgiou, G. "The Persian Gulf Crisis and the Future of OPEC." *Mediterranean Quarterly* 3, no. 1 (1991).

Gerges, F. "Regional Security after the Gulf Crisis: The American Role." *Journal of Palestine Studies* 20, no. 4 (1991).

Ghabra, Shafeeq. "The Iraqi Occupation of Kuwait: An Eyewitness Account." *Journal of Palestine Studies* 20, no. 2 (1991).

Gittings, John. *Beyond the Gulf War: The Middle East and the New World Order.* London: Catholic Institute for International Relations, 1991.

Gold, Dore. *America, the Gulf and Israel: CENTCOM (Central Command) and Emerging U.S. Regional Security Policies in the Mideast.* Tel Aviv: Jaffee Center for Strategic Studies, Tel Aviv University; Boulder, Colo.: Westview Press, 1988.

Goodman, M., and C. Ekedahl. "Trends in Soviet Policy in the Middle East and the Gulf." *International Journal* 45, no. 3 (1990).

Gordon, Murray. *Conflict in the Persian Gulf.* New York: Facts on File, 1981.

Graubard, Stephen R. *Mr. Bush's War: Adventures in the Politics of Illusion.* New York: Hill and Wang, 1992.

Guazzone, L. "Italy and the Gulf Crisis: European and Domestic Dimensions." *International Spectator* 26, no. 4 (1991).

———. "Kuwait's National Security Policy and Its Influence on the Gulf Region." *International Spectator* 24, no. 2 (1989).

"The Gulf Crisis— An Israeli View: An Interview with Mattityahu Peled." *Journal of Palestine Studies* 20, no. 2 (1991).

"The Gulf Crisis— A Kuwaiti Perspective: An Interview With Hassan al-Ebraheem." *Journal of Palestine Studies* 20, no. 2 (1991).

"The Gulf Crisis: Political and Economic Implications." Special issue, *Middle East Insight* 7, no. 4 (1990).

"The Gulf Crisis— Regional Aspects: An Interview With George Crom." *Journal of Palestine Studies*, vol. 20, no. 2 (1991).

Al-Hakim, Hassan Hamdan. *The Foreign Policy of the United Arab Emirates*. London: Saqi Books, 1989.

Hallaj, M. "U.S. Gulf Policy: Going the Extra Mile for War." *Arab Studies Quarterly* 13, nos. 1-10 (1991).

Halliday, Fred. "The Gulf War and Its Aftermath: First Reflections." *International Affairs* 67, no. 2 (1991).

Hameed, Mazher A. *Arabia Imperilled: The Security Imperatives of the Arab Gulf States*. Washington, D.C.: Middle East Assessments Group, 1986.

———. *Saudi Arabia, the West and the Security of the Arab Gulf*. London: Croom Helm, 1986.

Hammond, Thomas T. "Afghanistan and the Persian Gulf." *Survey* (London) 26, no. 2 (spring 1982).

Hanat, S. "Configuration of the Security Dimensions of Developing Countries: Special Reference to the Persian Gulf Region, 1971-1978." *IJIA* 2, no. 4 (1990-91).

————. "Iran-Iraq and the Regional Security System of the Persian Gulf." *Strategic Studies*. 11, no. 4 (1988).

Harb, U. "The Security of the Gulf and Arab Security." (In Arabic.) *Al-Shu'un al-Arabiyya (Arab Affairs)* 35 (1984).

Hart, J. "Current Issues in Persian Gulf Security." *IJIA* 5, nos. 3-4 (1994).

Heidenrich, John G. "The Gulf War: How Many Iraqis Died?" *Foreign Policy*, no. 90 (1993).

Heisbourg, F. "Quelles leçons stratégiques de la guerre du Golfe?" *Politique Etrangère* 56, no. 2 (1991).

Heller, Mark A. *The Iran-Iraq War: Implications for Third Parties*. Tel Aviv: Jaffee Center for Strategic Studies, Tel Aviv University; Cambridge, Mass.: Center for International Affairs, Harvard University, 1984.

Hensel, Howard M. "Soviet Policy toward the Rebellion in Dhofar." *Asian Affairs* (London) 13, New Series, Pt. 2 (1982).

Hooglund, Eric. "U.S. Perspectives on Persian Gulf Security." *IJIA* 5, nos. 3-4 (1994).

Hopp, G. "Kriege am Golf: Krise in Islam?" *Orient*. 32, no. 3 (1991).

Hudson, Michael C. "After the Gulf War: Prospects for Democratization in the Arab World." *Middle East Journal* 45, no. 3 (1991).

Hunter, Shireen. "Persian Gulf Security: Lessons of the Past and the Need for New Thinking." *SAIS Review* 12, no. 1 (1992).

Hussain, M. "Gulf War: Impact on Pakistan." *Strategic Perspectives* 1, no. 1 (1991).

———. "The Persian Gulf Crisis: Impact on the Muslim World." *Strategic Studies* 14, nos. 1-2 (1990-91).

Ignotus, Miles (pseud.). "Seizing Arab Oil: A Blueprint for Fast and Effective Action." *Harper's.* March 1975.

"The Intellectuals and the War: An Interview with Edward W. Said." *MERIP Middle East Report* 21, no. 4 (1991).

Isenberg, David. "Desert Storm Redux?" *The Middle East Journal* 47, no. 3 (1993).

Ismael, Tareq Y., and Jacqueline S. Ismael, eds. *The Gulf War and the New World Order: International Relations of the Middle East.* Gainesville, Fla.: University Press of Florida, 1994.

Ispahani, M. "Alone Together: Regional Security Arrangements in Southern Africa and the Arabian Gulf." *International Security* 8, no. 4 (1984).

Iungerich, Raphael. "How Real Is the Soviet Threat to the Gulf?" *Armed Forces Journal International (AFSI)* (October 1984).

———. "US Rapid Deployment Forces— USCENTCOM— What Is It? Can It Do the Job?" *AFJI* 122 (1984).

Jabber, Paul, et al. Eds. *Great Power Interests in the Persian Gulf.* New York: Council on Foreign Relations, 1989.

Jampoler, A. "America's Vital Interests: Is the New Rapid Deployment Force Old Wine in a New Bottle?" *USNIP* 107, no. 1 (1981).

Johnson, Maxwell Orme. *The Military as an Instrument of U.S. Policy in Southwest Asia: The Rapid Deployment Joint Task Force, 1979-1982.* Boulder, Colo.: Westview Press, 1983.

Johnson, T., and R. Barrett. "Mining the Strait of Hormuz." *USNIP* 107, no. 12 (1981).

————. "Omani Navy: Operating in Troubled Waters." *USNIP* 108, no. 3 (1982).

Johnstone, Ian. *Aftermath of the Gulf War: An Assessment of UN Action.* International Peace Academy Occasional Paper Series. Boulder, Colo.: Lynne Rienner Publishers, 1993.

Jordan, K. "Naval Diplomacy in the Persian Gulf." *USNIP* 107, no. 11 (1981).

El-Kareh, R. "Les médias français et la crise du Golfe." *Revue d'Etudes Palestiniennes*, no. 38 (1991).

Karsh, Efraim, ed. *The Iran-Iraq War: Impact and Implications.* New York: St. Martin's Press, 1989.

Katz, Mark N. *Russia and Arabia: Soviet Foreign Policy toward the Arabian Peninsula.* Baltimore: The Johns Hopkins University Press, 1986.

Kaur, K. "United Nations and Gulf Crisis." *India Quarterly* 48, nos. 1-2 (1992).

Kechichian, Joseph A. "The GCC and the West." *American-Arab Affairs*, no. 29 (1989).

————. "The Gulf Cooperation Council: Search for Security." *Third World Quarterly* 7, no. 4 (1985).

————. *Oman and the World: The Emergence of an Independent Foreign Policy.* Santa Monica, Calif.: RAND, 1995.

Kellner, Douglas. *The Persian Gulf TV War.* Boulder, Colo.: Westview Press, 1992.

Kelly, J. B. *Arabia, the Gulf and the West*. New York: Basic Books, 1980.

———. "Hadramaut, Oman, Dhufar: The Experience of Revolution." *Middle Eastern Studies* 12, no. 2 (1976).

Kelly, J. B., and Hermann F. Eilts. "Point/Counterpoint: Security in the Persian Gulf." *International Security*, vol. 5, no. 4 (1981).

Kelly, Michael. *Martyrs' Day: Chronicle of a Small War*. New York: Random House, 1993.

Kemp, Geoffrey, and Janice Gross Stein, eds. *Powder Keg in the Middle East*. Lanham, Md.: Rowman & Littlefield Publishers, Inc., 1995. Includes several chapters by the editors and other authors on Gulf security issues.

Khadduri, Majid. *The Gulf War: The Origins and Implications of the Iraq-Iran Conflict*. New York: Oxford University Press, 1988.

Khadir, Bichara. *The EEC and the Gulf: Relations and Stakes and the Gulf, Palestine and the West*. Louvain-la-Neuve, Belgium: Centre d'Etudes et de Recherche sur le Monde Arabe Contemporain, 1987.

Khaled bin Sultan, HRH General, with Patrick Seale. *Desert Warrior: A Personal View of the Gulf War by the Joint Forces Commander*. New York: HarperCollins, 1995.

Khalid, Zulfikar A. "Straits of Hormuz, the Fulcrum of Persian Gulf Oil Security." *Asian Defence Journal* (Kuala Lumpur), February 1982.

Khalidi, Rashid, and Camille Mansour, eds. *Palestine and the Gulf*. Beirut: Institute for Palestine Studies, 1982.

Khalidi, Walid. "The Gulf Crisis: Origins and Consequences." *Journal of Palestine Studies* 20, no. 2 (1991).

Khorassani, R. "War in the Persian Gulf." *Strategic Studies* 14, no. 3 (1991).

Al-Kilani, H. "U.S. Strategy in the Arabian Peninsula: The Position of Israel and Its Constant Integral Role." (In Arabic.) *Shu'un Filastiniyya*, no. 185 (1988).

Kodmani-Darwish, Bassma, and May Chartouni-Dubarry. *Golfe et Moyen-Orient: les conflits*. Paris: Editions Dunod, 1991.

Kohler, W. "German Approaches to the Arabian Gulf: A Provisional Survey." (In Arabic.) *Al-Watheekah* , no. 16 (1990).

Korany, Bahgat, and Ali E. Hilal Dessouki, eds. *The Foreign Policies of Arab States: The Challenge of Change*. Rev. ed. Boulder, Colo.: Westview Press, 1991.

Kreisler, Harry, ed. "Confrontation in the Gulf: University of California Professors Talk about the War." *Insights in International Affairs*, no. 1. Berkeley, Calif.: International and Area Studies, University of California, 1992.

Kumarasmy, P. "The U.S. Responses to the Gulf Crisis." *Strategic Analysis* 3, no. 7 (1990).

Kuniholm, Bruce R. "A Political/Military Strategy for the Persian Gulf and Southwest Asia." In *Security in the Middle East: Regional Change and Great Power Strategies*, edited by Samuel F. Wells, Jr., and Mark A. Bruzonsky. Boulder, Colo.: Westview Press, 1987.

Laidi, Z. "Berlin-Koweit: les rapports après la double secousse." *Politique Etrangère* 56, no. 2 (1991).

Lee, David. *Flight from the Middle East: A History of the Royal Air Force in the Arabian Peninsula and Adjacent Territories, 1945-72*. London: HMSO, 1980.

"Lessons of the Gulf War." *Israel and Palestine*, no. 162 (1991).

Lewis, Tim, with Josie Brooks. *The Human Shield*. Lichfield, Staffordshire, U.K.: Leomansley Press, 1992.

Litwak, Robert. *Security in the Persian Gulf 2: Sources of Inter-State Conflict*. Totowa, N.J.: Allanheld, Osmun, for the International Institute for Strategic Studies (London), 1982.

Long, David E. "Prospects for Armed Conflict in the Gulf in the 1990s: The Impact of the Gulf War." *Middle East Policy* 2, no. 1 (1993).

MacArthur, John R. *Second Front: Censorship and Propaganda in the Gulf War*. Berkeley, Calif.: University of California Press, 1993.

McNaugher, Thomas L. *Arms and Oil: U.S. Military Strategy and the Persian Gulf*. Washington, DC: Brookings Institution, 1985.

———. "The Superpowers in the Persian Gulf." *Current*, no. 256 (1983).

Malone, Joseph J. "Security: A Priority for Gulf Council." *Journal of Defense and Diplomacy* 1, no. 6 (1983).

Al-Mani, S. "The Politics of the GCC Dialogue with the European Community." *JSAMES* 7, no. 4 (1989).

Mansur, Abdul Kasim (pseud.). "The Military Balance in the Persian Gulf: Who Will Guard the Gulf States from Their Guardians?" *AFJI* 118, no. 4 (1980).

Matthews, Ken. *The Gulf Conflict and International Relations*. London: Routledge and Kegan Paul, 1993.

Mazarr, Michael J., Don M. Snider, and James A. Blackwell, Jr. *Desert Storm: The Gulf War and What We Learned*. Boulder, Colo.: Westview Press, 1993.

Al-Mazidi, Feisal. *The Future of the Gulf: The Legacy of the 1990s*. London: I. B. Tauris, 1993.

Menos, Dennis. *Arms over Diplomacy: Reflections on the Persian Gulf War*. New York: Praeger, 1992.

Merfakhraie, H. "Miscalculation and Strategic Naiveté in the Iraq-Kuwait Crisis." *IJIA* 2, no. 4 (1990-91).

Milan, S. "Innocent Passage Through the Strait of Hormuz." *IJIA* 1, nos. 2-3 (1989).

The Military Balance, 1991-1992. Oxford, U.K.: Brassey's, for the International Institute for Strategic Studies, 1991.

Miller, Ronnie. *Following the Americans to the Persian Gulf: Canada, Australia, and the Development of a New World Order*. Rutherford, N.J.: Fairleigh Dickinson University Press, 1994.

Mirsky, Yehudah, ed. "The Soref Symposium: American Strategy after the Gulf War." Proceedings, April 28-29, 1991. Washington, D.C.: Washington Institute for Near East Policy, 1991.

Mohammed, S. "U.S. Presence in the Gulf." *Pakistan Horizon* 41 (1988).

Mojtahed-Zadeh, P. "Crisis in the Northwest of the Persian Gulf." *IJIA* 2, no. 4 (1990-91).

Mottale, Morris Mehrdad. *The Arms Buildup in the Persian Gulf*. New York: University Press of America, 1986.

Mowlana, Hamid, George Gerbner, and Herbert I. Schillar, eds. *Triumph of the Image: The Media's War in the Persian Gulf— A Global Perspective*. Boulder, Colo.: Westview Press, 1992.

Naff, Thomas, ed. *Gulf Security and the Iran-Iraq War*. Washington, D.C.: National Defense University Press, 1985.

Nakhleh, Emile. "The Palestine Conflict and U.S. Strategic Interests in the Persian Gulf." *Parameters: Journal of the U.S. Army War College* 11, no. 1 (March 1981).

Nardulli, Bruce, et al. *Future Gulf Dynamics and U.S. Security: Documented Briefing*. Santa Monica, Calif.: RAND Corporation, 1994.

Al-Nashif, T. "Conclusions Drawn from the Gulf War." (In Arabic.) *Shu'un Filastiniyya*, nos. 223-4 (1991).

Neimark, M. "American Jews and Palestine: The Impact of the Gulf War." *MERIP Middle East Report* 22, no. 2 (1992).

Newsom, David. "America enGulfed." *Foreign Policy*, no. 43 (1981).

Nonneman, Gerd. *Iraq, the Gulf States and the War: A Changing Relationship, 1980-1986 and Beyond*. London: Ithaca Press, 1986.

Noyes, James H. *The Clouded Lens: Persian Gulf Security and U.S. Policy*. 2nd ed. Stanford, Calif.: Hoover Institution Press, Stanford University, 1982.

———. "Through the Gulf Labyrinth: Naval Escort and U.S. Policy." *American-Arab Affairs*, no. 29 (1989).

Olson, William J. "The Iran-Iraq War and the Future of the Persian Gulf." *Military Review* 64, no. 23 (March 1984).

———. U.S. *Strategic Interests in the Gulf Region*. Boulder, Colo.: Westview Press, 1987.

Otsuka, S. "The Gulf War and Japan's Efforts to Restore Peace." *JIME Review*, no. 13 (1991).

Pagonis, William G., and Jeffrey L. Cruikshank. *Moving Mountains: Lessons in Leadership and Logistics from the Gulf War*. Boston: Harvard Business School Press, 1992.

Palmer, Michael A. *Guardians of the Gulf: The Growth of American Involvement in the Persian Gulf, 1833-1991*. New York: Free Press, 1992.

————. *On Course to Desert Storm.* Washington, DC: Naval Historical Center, Department of the Navy, 1992.

Pamir, P. "Peace-Building Scenarios after the Gulf War." *Third World Quarterly* 13, no. 2 (1992).

Panda, R. "Japan and the Gulf Crisis: An Appraisal." *India Quarterly* 47, no. 3 (1991).

Pasha, A. K. "Kuwait's Quest for Security." *India Quarterly* 49, no. 4 (1993).

Perry, William J. Desert Storm and Deterence." *Foreign Affairs* 70, no. 4 (fall 1991).

Peterson, J. E. "American Policy in the Gulf and the Sultanate of Oman." *American-Arab Affairs*, no. 8 (1984).

————. *Defending Arabia.* New York: St. Martin's Press, 1986.

————. "Guerrilla Warfare and Ideological Confrontation in the Arabian Peninsula: The Rebellion in Dhufar." *World Affair* 139, no. 4 (1977).

Piscatori, James, ed. *Islamic Fundamentalism and the Gulf Crisis.* Chicago: University of Chicago Press, 1992.

Plascov, Avi. *Security in the Persian Gulf 3: Modernization, Political Development and Stability.* Totowa, N.J.: Allanheld, Osmun, for the International Institute for Strategic Studies (London) 1982.

Pollock, David. "Reporting the Middle East: An Overview." *The Media and the Gulf: A Closer Look.* Proceedings of a conference, Graduate School of Journalism, May 3-4, 1991. Berkeley, Calif.: University of California Press, 1991.

Prater, F. "La France et la crise du Golfe." *Politique Etrangère* 56, no. 2 (1991).

Quandt, William B. "After the Gulf Crisis: Challenges for American Policy." *American-Arab Affairs*, no. 35 (1990-91).

Quinlan, D. "Naval Forces Are Rapid Deployment Forces." U.S. *Naval Institute Proceedings* 107, no. 11 (1981).

Ramazani, Rouhollah K. *The Persian Gulf and the Strait of Hormuz. International Straits of the World.* Vol. 3. Alphen aan den Rijn, Netherlands: Sitjhoff and Noordhoff, 1979.

Renshon, Stanley A., ed. *The Political Psychology of the Gulf War: Leaders, Publics, and the Process of Conflict.* Pittsburgh: University of Pittsburgh Press, 1993.

Rezun, Miron. *Saddam Hussein's Gulf Wars: Ambivalent Stakes in the Middle East.* New York: Praeger, 1992.

Rochlin, Gene I., and Chris Demchak. "Lessons of the Gulf War: Ascendant Technology and Declining Capability." *Policy Papers in International Affairs*, no. 39. Berkeley, Calif.: International and Area Studies, University of California Press, 1992.

Rodman, Peter W. "Middle East Diplomacy after the Gulf War." *Foreign Affairs* 70, no. 2 (1991).

Rogers, P. "Oil and Security in the Persian Gulf." *IJIA* 5, nos. 3-4 (1994).

Rondot, Pierre. "L'Etat de Koweit: a-t-il le droit d'exister?" *L'Afrique et l'Asie Moderne*, no. 167 (1990-91).

Ross, Dennis. "Considering Soviet Threats to the Persian Gulf." *International Security* 6, no. 2 (1981).

Rousillon, A. "L'Opposition Egyptienne et la crise du Golfe." *Maghreb-Machrek*, no. 130 (1990).

Rowe, Peter, ed. *The Gulf War, 1990-91, in International and English Law.* London: Routledge and Kegan Paul, 1993.

Rubin, Barry. "Drowning in the Gulf." *Foreign Policy*, no. 69 (winter 1987–88).

Rubinstein, Alvin Z. "The Gulf War and East Asian Security." *Korea and World Affairs* 15, no. 4 (1991).

———. "After the Gulf War." *Foreign Affairs* 70, no. 4 (fall 1991).

———. ed. *The Great Game: Rivalry in the Persian Gulf and South Asia*. New York: Praeger, 1983.

Al-Rumaihi, Mohammed. "Kuwaiti-American Relations: A Case of Mismanagement." *American-Arab Affairs*, no. 9 (1984).

Saaf, A. "Réflections sur la guerre." *Peuples Méditerranéens*, nos. 58-59 (1992).

Saikal, A. "The U.S. Approach to the Security of the Persian Gulf." *IJIA* 5, nos. 3-4 (1994).

———. "The United States and Persian Gulf Security." *World Policy Journal* 9, no. 3 (1992).

Saivetz, Carol R. *The Soviet Union and the Gulf in the 1980s*. Boulder, Colo.: Westview Press, 1989.

Salameh, G. "Le Golfe: nuages après la tempête." *Politique Etrangère* 56, no. 2 (1991).

Al-Salem, F. "The U.S. and the Gulf: What Do the Arabs Want?" *JSAMES* 6, no. 1 (1982).

Salinger, Pierre, and Eric Laurent. *Secret Dossier: The Hidden Agenda behind the Gulf War*. New York: Viking Penguin, 1991.

Sanad, Jamal S. "Iraqi Invasion of Kuwait and UAE's Political Orientations." *JSAMES* 18, no. 2 (1994).

Saunders, Harold. "Political Settlement and the Gulf Crisis." *Mediterranean Quarterly* 2, no. 2 (1991).

Savinkova, E., and I. Chirokikh. "Les Répercussions de la Crise du Golfe sur l'Economie Mondiale." *L'Afrique et l'Asie Moderne*, no. 168 (1991).

Sayari, S. "Turkey: The Changing European Security Environment and the Gulf Crisis." *Middle East Journal* 46, no. 1 (1992).

Schiff, Ze'ev. "Israel after the War." *Foreign Affairs* 70, no. 2 (1991).

Schwarzkopf, H. Norman. *It Doesn't Take a Hero*. New York: Bantam Books, 1992.

Segal, Jerome. "The Gulf War and the Israeli-Palestinian Conflict." *World Policy Journal* 8, no. 2 (1991).

Serfaty, Simon, ed. *The Media and Foreign Policy*. New York: St. Martin's Press, 1991. Includes a chapter on news media coverage of Operation Desert Storm.

Shahi, A., et al. "Flashpoint in the Gulf." *Pakistan Horizon* 43, no. 4 (1990).

Shahin, A. "The Gulf Crisis: Toward a New World Order." (In Arabic.) *Shu'un Filastiniyya*, nos. 213-14 (1990-91).

Sharif, Walid, ed. *The Arab Gulf States and Japan: Prospects for Cooperation*. London: Croom Helm, 1986.

Sharpe, Kenneth E. "The Real Cause of Irangate." *Foreign Policy*, no. 68 (1987).

Shwadran, Benjamin. "The Kuwait Incident." *Middle Eastern Affairs* 8, no. 2 (1962).

Sifry, Micah L., and Christopher Cerf, eds. *The Gulf Reader: History, Documents, Opinions*. New York: Random House, 1991.

Sil, N. "Caesaropopulism in Action: U.S. Military Intervention in Panama and the Persian Gulf." *India Quarterly* 47, nos. 1-2 (1991).

Simpson, J. "The Aftermath of the Gulf War." *Arab Affairs* 23, no. 2 (1992).

Sindelar, Richard H., III, and J. E. Peterson, eds. *Crosscurrents in the Gulf: Arab, Regional and Global Interests.* London: Routledge for the Middle East Institute, Washington, D.C., 1988.

Sirriyeh, Hussein. U.S. *Policy in the Gulf 1968-1977: Aftermath of British Withdrawal.* London: Ithaca Press, 1984.

Smallwood, William L. *Strike Eagle: Flying the F-15E in the Gulf War.* Washington, D.C. and London: Brassey's, 1994.

Smith, Jean Edward. *George Bush's War.* New York: Holt, 1992.

Smock, David R. *Religious Perspectives on War: Christian, Muslim, and Jewish Attitudes toward Force after the Gulf War.* Washington, D.C.: United States Institute of Peace Press, 1992.

Snyder, Jed C. *Defending the Fringe: NATO, the Mediterranean and the Persian Gulf.* Boulder, Colo.: Westview Press, and London: The Johns Hopkins Foreign Policy Institute, 1987.

Sowell, Lewis C., Jr. "Base Development and the Rapid Deployment Force: A Window to the Future." National Security Affairs Monograph Series, no. 82-5. Washington, DC: National Defense University Press, 1982.

Stanley, B. "Drawing from the Well: Syria in the Persian Gulf." *Journal of South Asian and Middle Eastern Studies* 14, no. 2 (1990).

Sterner, Michael. "The Iran-Iraq War." *Foreign Affairs* 63, no. 1 (fall 1984).

————. "Navigating the Gulf." *Foreign Policy*, no. 81 (winter 1990-91).

Stojanovic, R. "Geostrategic Interests of the Two Blocs in the Arabian Gulf." *Review of International Affairs* 32, no. 758 (1981).

Subraman, Belinda, ed. *The Gulf War: Many Perspectives*. El Paso: Vergin Press, 1992.

Sullivan, D. "The Gulf Cooperation Council: Regional Security or Collective Defense?" *JSAMES* 7, no. 4 (1989).

Swearingen, Will D. "Sources of Conflict over Oil in the Persian/Arabian Gulf." *The Middle East Journal* 35, no. 3 (1985).

Tahir-Kheli, Shirin, ed. U.S. *Strategic Interests in Southwest Asia*. New York: Praeger, 1982.

Talbott, Strobe. "Post-Victory Blues." *Foreign Affairs* 71, no. 1 (1992).

Tamamoto, M. "Trial of an Ideal: Japan's Debate over the Gulf Crisis." *World Policy Journal* 8, no. 1 (1990-91).

Taylor, Phillip M. *War and the Media: Propaganda and Persuasion in the Gulf War*. New York: St. Martin's Press, 1992.

Teicher, Howard, and Gayle Radley Teicher. *Twin Pillars to Desert Storm: America's Flawed Vision in the Middle East from Nixon to Bush*. New York: William Morrow, 1993.

Terrill, A. "Chemical Warfare and 'Desert Storm:' The Disaster That Never Came." *Small Wars and Insurgencies* 4, no. 2 (1993).

Terrill, W. "The Gulf War and Ballistic Missile Proliferation." *Comparative Strategy* 11, no. 2 (1992).

Thompson, W. Scott. "The Persian Gulf and the Correlation of Forces." *International Security* 7, no. 1 (1982).

Twinam, Joseph W. "America and the Gulf Arabs," Pts. 1 and 2. *American-Arab Affairs*, nos. 25 and 26 (1988).

————. *The Gulf, Cooperation and the Council: An American Perspective*. Washington, D.C.: Middle East Policy Council, 1992.

The United States and the New Middle East: Strategic Perspectives after the Persian Gulf War. Report of the CSIS Aftermath Policy Council. Washington, D.C.: Center for Strategic and International Studies, 1992.

U.S. News & World Report staff. *Triumph Without Victory: The Unreported History of the Persian Gulf War*. New York: Times Books, 1992.

Van Hollen, Christopher. "Don't Engulf the Gulf." *Foreign Affairs* 59, no. 3 (1981).

Vaux, Kenneth L. *Ethics and the Gulf War: Religion, Rhetoric, and Righteousness*. Boulder, Colo.: Westview Press, 1992.

Võ Xuân, Hân. *Oil, the Persian Gulf States, and the United States*. Westport, Conn.: and London: Praeger, 1994.

Vuono, Carl E. "Desert Storm and the Future of Conventional Forces." *Foreign Affairs* 70, no. 2 (1991).

Wakeman, Carolyn, ed. *The Media and the Gulf: A Closer Look*. Berkeley, Calif.: University of California Press, 1991.

Waltz, Kenneth. "A Strategy for the Rapid Deployment Force." *International Security* 5, no. 4 (1981).

Welch, D. "The Politics and Psychology of Restraint: Israeli Decision-Making in the Gulf War." *International Journal* 47, no. 2 (1992).

West, F., Jr. "NATO II Common Boundaries for Common Interests." (On Gulf-NATO links.) *U.S. Naval War College Review* 34, no. 1 (1981).

Wiley, Marshall W. "American Security Concerns in the Gulf." *Orbis* 28, no. 3 (1984).

Wizarat, Talat. "The Role of the Gulf Cooperation Council in Regional Security." *Strategic Studies* 10, no 1. (1987).

Wolfe, Ronald G., ed. *The United States, Arabia, and the Gulf.* Washington, D.C.: Center for Contemporary Arab Studies, Georgetown University, 1980.

Wolfowitz, Paul. "Remarks on the Conclusion of the Gulf War." *American-Arab Affairs*, no. 35 (1990-91).

Woodward, Bob. *The Commanders.* New York: Simon and Schuster, 1991.

Yodat, Aryeh Y. *The Soviet Union and the Arabian Peninsula: Soviet Policy Towards the Persian Gulf and Arabia.* New York: St. Martin's Press, 1983.

Zahlan, Rosemarie Said. "The Gulf and the Palestine Question, 1936-1948." (In Arabic.) *Al-Mustaqbal al-Arabi (The Arab Future)* 3, no. 26 (1981).

Zunes, Stephen. "The U.S.-GCC Relationship: Its Rise and Potential Fall." *Middle East Policy* 2, no. 1 (1993).

Appendix A

Principal Government Officials of the Gulf Arab States

BAHRAIN

Emir: Shaikh Isa bin Salman Al Khalifa

Heir Apparent: Shaikh Hamad bin Isa Al Khalifa

Prime Minister: Shaikh Khalifa bin Salman Al Khalifa

Minister of Cabinet Affairs and Information: Muhammad Ibrahim al-Mutawa

Minister of Commerce: Ali Saleh Abdullah al-Saleh

Minister of Defense: Maj.-Gen. Shaikh Khalifa bin Ahmad Al Khalifa

Minister of Education: Abdel-Aziz Muhammad al-Fadhil

Minister of Electricity and Water: Abdullah Muhammad al-Jumaa

Minister of Finance and National Economy: Ibrahim Abd al-Karim Muhammad

Minister of Foreign Affairs: Shaikh Muhammad bin Mubarak bin Hamad Al Khalifa

Minister of Health: Faisal Radhi al-Musawi

Minister of Housing, Municipalities, and Environment: Khalid bin Abdullah Al Khalifa

Minister of the Interior: Shaikh Muhammad bin Khalifa bin Hamad Al Khalifa

Minister of Justice and Islamic Affairs: Shaikh Abdullah bin Khalid Al Khalifa

Minister of Labor and Social Affairs: Abdel-Nabi al-Shuala

Minister of Oil and Industry: Shaikh Isa bin Ali Al Khalifa

Minister of Public Works and Agriculture: Majid Jawad al-Jishi

Minister of Transport and Communications: Shaikh Ali bin Khalifa bin Salman Al Khalifa.

Minister of State: Jawad Salem al-Arayed

Minister of State in charge of the Emiri Court: Yusif Rahamah al-Dousari

Source: CIA List of Heads of State, Government, and Cabinet Ministers, October 1996.

KUWAIT

Emir: Shaikh Jabir al-Ahmed Al Sabah

Heir Apparent and Prime Minister: Shaikh Sa'ad Abdullah al-Salem Al Sabah

First Deputy Prime Minister and Minister of Foreign Affairs: Shaikh Sabah al-Ahmed al-Jabir Al Sabah

Deputy Prime Minister and Minister of Defense: Nasser Abdullah al-Roudhan

Deputy Prime Minister and Minister of Finance: Shaikh Salem Al Sabah

Minister of State for Cabinet Affairs: Abd al-Aziz Dakhil al-Abdullah al-Dakhil

Minister of Commerce and Industry: Jassem Abdullah al-Mudhaf

Minister of Communications, Electricity, and Water: Jasim Muhammad al-Oun

Minister of Education and Higher Education: Abdullah Yousef al-Ghunaim

Minister of Information and Acting Minister of Health: Shaikh Saud Nasir Al Sabah

Minister of Interior: Shaikh Muhammad Khalid Al Sabah

Minister of Justice, Awqaf, and Islamic Affairs: Muhammad Dhaifallah Sharar

Minister of Justice and Legal Affairs: Mishari Jasem al-Anjari

Minister of Petroleum: Issa Muhammad al-Mazidi

Minister of Public Works and Minister of State for Housing Affairs: Abdullah Rashid al-Hajiri

Minister of Social Affairs and Labor: Ahmed Khalid al-Kulaid

Source: Embassy of the State of Kuwait, Press Office, Washington, D.C. (October 1996).

OMAN

Sultan: Qabus bin Said Al Bu Said

Prime Minister and Minister of Defense, Finance, and Foreign Affairs: Sultan Qabus bin Said

Deputy Prime Minister for Cabinet Affairs: Sayid Fahd bin Mahmoud Al Bu Said

Deputy Prime Minister for Security and Defense: Sayid Fahar bin Taimur Al Bu Said

Minister of Agriculture and Fisheries: Shaikh Muhammad bin Abdullah bin Zahir al-Hinai

Minister of the Civil Service: Abdul-Aziz bin Matar al-Azizi

Minister of Commerce and Industry: Maqbul bin Ali bin Sultan

Minister of Communications: Col. Salem bin Abdullah al-Ghazali

Minister of Economy: Ahmed bin Abd al-Nabi al-Makki

Minister of Education: Saud bin Ibrahim Al Bu Saidi

Minister of Electricity and Water: Muhammad bin Ali al-Qutaibi

Minister of Health: Dr. Ali bin Muhammad al-Mousa

Minister of Information: Abd al-Aziz bin Muhammad al-Ruwas

Minister of the Interior: Sayid Badr bin Saud bin Hareb Al Bu Saidi

Minister of Justice and Awqaf (Religious Endowments) and Islamic Affairs: Hamoud bin Abdullah al-Harthi

Minister of National Heritage and Culture: Sayed Faisal bin Ali al-Said

Minister of Palace Affairs: Gen. Ali bin Majid al-Mu'amari

Minister of Petroleum and Minerals: Said bin Ahmad bin Said al-Shanfari

Minister of Posts, Telegraphs and Telephones: Ahmad bin Suwaidan al-Baluchi

Minister of Regional Municipalities and the Environment: Shaikh Amir bin Shuwain al-Hosni

Minister of the Royal Court: Sayed Saif bin Hamad Al Busaidi

Minister of Social Affairs and Labor: Ahmad bin Salim al-Isa'i

Minister of Water Resources: Lt. Gen. Hamed Said al-Aufi

Minister of State for Development: Muhammad bin Musa al-Yusif

Minister of State for Foreign Affairs: Yusif bin al-Alawi bin Abdullah

Governor of the Capital and Minister of State: Sayed al-Mutassim bin Hamud Al Busaidi

President of the Majlis: Abdullah bin Ali al-Qatabi

Source: CIA List of Heads of State, Government, and Cabinet Ministers, October 1996.

QATAR

Emir and Minister of Defense: Shaikh Hamad bin Khalifa Al Thani

Prime Minister and Minister of Interior: Shaikh Abdullah bin Khalifa Al Thani

Minister of State for Interior Affairs: Shaikh Abdullal bin Khalid Al Thani

Minister of Civil Service and Housing: Shaikh Falah bin Jassim bin Jabir Al Thani

Minister of Communication and Transport: Shaikh Ahmed bin Nasser Al Thani

Minister of Economy, Finance and Trade: Shaikh Muhammad bin Khalifa Al Thani

Minister of Education: Dr. Muhammad Kafoud

Minister of Electricity and Water: Ahmad Muhammad Ali al-Subai

Minister of Energy and Industry: Abdullah bin Hamad al-Attiya

Minister of Foreign Affairs: Shaikh Hamad bin Jaber Al Thani

Minister of Health: Dr. Abdulrahman al-Kuwari

Minister of Justice: Dr. Najib Muhammad al-Nuaimi

Minister of Labor, Social Affairs, and Housing: Abdul-Rahman Saad al-Dirham

Minister of Municipal Affairs and Agriculture: Ali bin Said al-Khayyarin

Minister for Cabinet Affairs: Muhammad bin Khalid Al Thani

Minister of State for Foreign Affairs: Ahmad Abdullah al-Mahmoud

Source: U.S. Department of State, report of Qatar Emiri Decrees nos. 3, 4, and 5, October 30, 1996).

UNITED ARAB EMIRATES

President: Shaikh Zayid bin Sultan Al Nuhayyan

Vice President: Shaikh Maktum bin Rashid Al Maktum

Supreme Council of Rulers
(With dates of accession)

Ruler of Abu Dhabi: Shaikh Zayid bin Sultan Al Nuhayyan (1966)

Ruler of Dubai: Shaikh Maktum bin Rashid Al Maktum (1990)

Ruler of Ajman: Shaikh Humaid bin Rashid Al-Nuaimi (1981)

Ruler of Fujairah: Shaikh Hamad bin Muhammad Al-Sharqi (1974)

Ruler of Ras al-Khaimah: Shaikh Saqr bin Muhammad Al-Qasimi (1948)

Ruler of Sharjah: Shaikh Sultan bin Muhammad Al-Qasimi (1972)

Ruler of Umm al-Qaiwain: Shaikh Rashid bin Ahmad Al-Mualla (1981)

Council of Ministers

Prime Minister: Shaikh Maktum bin Rashid Al Maktum

Deputy Prime Minister: Shaikh Sultan bin Zayid Al Nuhayyan

Minister of Agriculture and Fisheries: Said Muhammad al-Ragabani

Minister of Communications: Muhammad Said Al-Mu'alla

Minister of Defense: Shaikh Muhammad bin Rashid Al Maktum

Minister of Economy and Commerce: Said Ghobash

Minister of Education: Hamad Abd al-Rahman al-Madfa

Minister of Electricity and Water: Humaid Nasser al-Owais

Minister of Finance and Industry: Shaikh Hamdan bin Rashid Al Maktum

Minister of Foreign Affairs: Shaikh Rashid Abdullah Al Nuaimi

Minister of Health: Ahmed Said al-Badi

Minister of Higher Education: Shaikh Nuhayyan bin Mubarak Al Nuhayyan

Minister of Information and Culture: Khalfan al-Roumi

Minister of the Interior: Lt.-Gen. Muhammad Said al-Badi

Minister of Islamic Affairs and Awqaf (Religious Endowments): Shaikh Muhammad bin Hassan al-Khazraji

Minister of Justice: Abdullah bin Omran Taryam

Minister of Labor and Social Affairs: Saif al-Jarwan

Minister of Petroleum and Mineral Resources (acting): Ahmed Said al-Badi

Minister of Planning: Shaikh Humaid bin Ahmad Al Mu'alla

Minister of Public Works and Housing: Rakad bin Salem bin Rakadh

Minister of Youth and Sports: Shaikh Faisal bin Khalid bin Muhammad Al Qasimi

Minister of State for Cabinet Affairs: Said Khalfan al-Ghaith

Minister of State for Finance and Industrial Affairs: Ahmad al-Humaid al-Tayer

Minister of State for Foreign Affairs: Shaikh Hamdan bin Zayid Al Nuhayyan

Minister of State for Supreme Council Affairs: Shaikh Muhammad bin Saqr bin Muhammad Al Qasimi

Source: Embassy of the United Arab Emirates, Washington, D.C. (October 31, 1996).

Appendix B

UN Security Council Resolutions on Iraq, August–November 1990

August 2, Resolution 660. Condemns Iraq's invasion of Kuwait and demands unconditional and immediate withdrawal. Vote: 14-0 in favor, 1 abstention (Yemen).

August 6, Resolution 661. Imposes mandatory economic sanctions against Iraq, including a total trade embargo, with only food and medicine exempted. Vote: 13-2 in favor, 2 abstentions (Yemen and Cuba).

August 9, Resolution 662. Declares Iraq's invasion of Kuwait null and void. Vote 15-0 in favor.

August 18, Resolution 664. Condemns Iraq's holding of foreign hostages and demands their immediate release. Vote: 15-0 in favor.

August 25, Resolution 665. Authorizes coalition warships to use force if necessary to prevent evasion of trade embargo against Iraq. Vote: 13-0 in favor, 2 abstentions (Yemen and Cuba).

September 13, Resolution 666. Establishes guidelines for humanitarian food aid to Iraq and occupied Kuwait, reaffirming exemption of medical supplies from embargo. Vote: 13-0 in favor, 2 abstentions (Yemen and Cuba).

September 16, Resolution 667. Condemns Iraq for violence against foreign embassies and diplomats in Kuwait and demands protection for them. Vote 15-0 in favor.

September 24, Resolution 669. Agrees to consider exceptions to Resolution 661 for shipment of humanitarian supplies to Iraq. Vote: 15-0 in favor.

September 25, Resolution 670. Tightens embargo on air traffic to and from Iraq and authorizes detention of Iraq's merchant fleet. Vote: 15-0 in favor.

October 29, Resolution 674. Holds Iraq responsible for all financial losses caused by its invasion of Kuwait, calls on UN members to gather evidence of Iraqi human rights abuses in Kuwait, and demands release of third country nationals. Vote: 13-0, 2 abstentions (Yemen and Cuba).

November 28, Resolution 677. Condemns Iraqi attempts to alter demographic composition of Kuwait and destroy civil records of its legitimate government. Vote: 15-0 in favor.

November 29, Resolution 678. Authorizes "member states cooperating with the government of Kuwait" to use "all necessary means" to carry out above resolutions if Iraq has not complied with them by January 15, 1991. Vote: 12 in favor, 2 against (Yemen and Cuba), 1 abstention (China).

Source: *The Middle East*, 7th ed. Washington, DC: Congressional Quarterly, 1991.

Appendix C

Text of the "Kuwait Declaration" issued by the Gulf
Cooperation Council (GCC) at the conclusion of its summit
meeting in Kuwait, December 1991

The six nations seek, in international dealings, good neigh-
borliness, respect for the sovereignty of other nations, noninterference
in their internal affairs and peaceful settlement of all conflicts;

They adopt a united stand in confronting the Iraqi regime and
those states that supported its invasion of Kuwait. They will continue
this policy until the Iraqi regime implements all UN Security Council
resolutions relating to its aggression against Kuwait;

They support Arab action within the framework of the Arab
League and consider the Damascus Declaration a starting point for a
new Arab order. They consider the GCC's economic development
fund for Arab countries as a tool for promoting development in Arab
states;

They support the peace efforts aimed at a just and permanent
resolution of the Palestinian problem and resolving the Arab-Israeli
conflict on the basis of international resolutions, particularly UN
Security Council Resolutions 242 and 338, and Resolution 425
regarding the unconditional Israeli withdrawal from southern Lebanon;

They welcome the positive steps taken by the Lebanese
government in its effort to maintain the security, stability and
prosperity of its people, and express readiness to promote these efforts;

They welcome changes at the international level and the emergence of a new world order, particularly since the liberation of Kuwait was one of the products of this order, which gives each country the right to control its national and economic resources.

About the Author

MALCOLM C. PECK (A.B. and A.M., Harvard University; M.A., M.A.L.D., and Ph.D., The Fletcher School of law and Diplomacy) is a program officer at Meridian International Center in Washington, D.C. He has taught at the University of Tennessee, Chattanooga; was a post doctoral fellow at the Harvard University Center for Middle Eastern Studies; and, from 1970 to 1981, was director of programs at the Middle East Institute in Washington, D.C. In 1981-1983 he served as the Arabian Peninsula analyst at the U.S. Department of State. Dr. Peck has written on Gulf-Arabian Peninsula issues in chapters contributed to several books and in a number of articles. He is the author of *The United Arab Emirates: A Venture in Unity* (1986), and is a contributor to *The World Book Encyclopedia* and the *Encyclopedia of the Modern Middle East.*